W9-CFJ-056

Other Kaplan Books for College-Bound Students

College Admissions and Financial Aid

Conquer the Cost of College
Parent's Guide to College Admissions
Scholarships
The Unofficial, Unbiased Insider's Guide to the 320 Most Interesting Colleges
The *Yale Daily News* Guide to Succeeding in College

Test Preparation

ACT
AP Biology
AP Calculus AB
AP Chemistry
AP English Literature and Composition
AP Macroeconomics/Microeconomics
AP Physics B
AP Statistics
AP U.S. Government & Politics
AP U.S. History
SAT & PSAT
SAT Math Mania
SAT Math Workbook
SAT Verbal Velocity
SAT Verbal Workbook
SAT II: Biology
SAT II: Chemistry
SAT II: Literature
SAT II: Mathematics Levels IC and IIC
SAT II: Physics
SAT II: Spanish
SAT II: U.S. History
SAT II: World History
SAT II: Writing

AP* ENGLISH LANGUAGE & COMPOSITION

By Stephen P. Burby

Simon & Schuster

SYDNEY · LONDON · SINGAPORE · NEW YORK

* AP is a registered trademark of the College Entrance Examination Board, which neither sponsors nor endorses this book.

Kaplan Publishing
Published by Simon & Schuster
1230 Avenue of the Americas
New York, New York 10020

Copyright © 2003 by Apex Learning Inc.

All rights reserved. No part of this book may be reproduced or transmitted in any form or by any means, electronic or mechanical, including photocopying, recording, or by any information storage and retrieval system, without the written permission of the Publisher, except where permitted by law.

Kaplan® is a registered trademark of Kaplan, Inc.

For all references in this book, AP is a registered trademark of the College Entrance Examination Board, which is not affiliated with this book.

For bulk sales to schools, colleges, and universities, please contact: Order Department, Simon and Schuster, 100 Front Street, Riverside, NJ 08075. Phone: (800) 223-2336. Fax: (800) 943-9831.

Contributing Editors: Trent Anderson, Seppy Basili, and Chad Schaedler
Special Contributor: Denise Pivarnik-Nova
Project Editor: Megan Duffy
Interior Page Layout: Martha P. Torres and Jan Gladish
Cover Design: Cheung Tai
Production Editor: Maude Spekes
Production Manager: Michael Shevlin
Editorial Coordinator: Déa Alessandro
Executive Editor: Del Franz

Special Thanks to Ruth Baygell and Eileen Mager

Manufactured in the United States of America.
Published simultaneously in Canada.

March 2003
10 9 8 7 6 5 4 3 2 1

ISBN: 0-7432-2587-2

Table of Contents

SECTION V: TYPES OF READING ON THE EXAM

SECTION VI: PRACTICE TESTS

ABOUT THE AUTHOR

Stephen P. Burby, M.A., received his Bachelor of Arts in English Literature from the State University of New York at Stony Brook and his Master of Arts in English Literature at Long Island University. Burby has been teaching high school English for nine years; he is currently in Brentwood, New York. He has taught grades 9 through 12 as well as AP English. In addition, as an adjunct faculty member of Suffolk Community College, he taught Basic Writing Skills and Freshman Composition. While teaching, Burby has advised drama and poetry clubs, as well as run many activities for students and the community. He is an active participant in the National Writing Program, which encourages teachers to model writing skills for their students. Prior to his career as a teacher, Burby worked as an editor for several different corporations. He is currently studying English Literature as a Doctoral Fellow at St. John's University.

The author is greatly indebted to Apex, Inc. for the extensive use of copyrighted materials, which formed the basis of and contributed greatly to the structure of this book; to Denise Pivarnik-Nova, for invaluable assistance with exam essays and questions; to Wendy Sleppin for editorial guidance; and to project editor Megan Duffy and Liza Burby for editorial advice and limitless patience.

Kaptest.com/publishing

The material in this book is up-to-date at the time of publication. However, the College Entrance Examination Board may have instituted changes in the test after this book was published. Be sure to carefully read the materials you receive when you register for the test.

If there are any important late-breaking developments—or any changes or corrections to the Kaplan test preparation materials in this book—we will post that information online at **kaptest.com/publishing**. Check to see if there is any information posted there regarding this book.

GETTING STARTED

Inside the AP English Language & Composition Exam

So you've decided to take the Advanced Placement English Language & Composition exam. What exactly is the test, and why should you be interested in taking it? If you have taken AP English Language & Composition in high school or have a good foundation in the subject, taking the AP exam could help you earn college credit and/or placement into advanced coursework.

This book is designed to help you prepare for the AP exam. We've included information about the format of the exam, test-taking strategies, and an extensive review of essential topics. Also included are three practice tests with answers and explanations. With Kaplan's proven test-taking strategies, dozens of practice questions, reviews of literary terms, and guidelines for writing your essay responses, you'll be able to take the test with confidence.

ABOUT THE EXAM

The AP English Language & Composition examination has two parts: a multiple-choice section, which accounts for 45 percent of your grade, and a free-response section, which counts toward 55 percent of your final score.

- Section I contains approximately 50–55 multiple-choice questions that you must answer in 60 minutes. Each question has five possible answers. The multiple-choice questions are scored and standardized to national norms. (There's a 25 percent penalty for wrong answers, so guess only if you can eliminate a few possible answers.) These questions are based on five different reading selections provided with the test, with approximately 10 multiple-choice questions per selection. The selections represent a range of literary time periods, with at least one selection dating from before 1900 and at least one more modern selection. The selections are always prose, and usually nonfiction (they are never poetry). Thus your reading in this book will consist of essays, speeches, letters, diaries, biographies, autobiographies, writings on history, social and cultural criticism, science and nature writing, and some short fiction.

• Section II of the AP English Language test is the free-response section. In the free-response section you'll have to write three essays in 120 minutes. For two of these essays, you'll be asked to analyze a selection for style, diction, syntax, imagery, tone, and purpose. The third essay gives you a brief quotation containing a philosophical statement and asks you to write a persuasive essay stating and supporting a position regarding that statement. Each essay is scored on a 9-point evaluation scale (9 being the highest).

Scoring

The exam is given in May, and the multiple-choice section is scored electronically soon after they are submitted. But the free-response section is evaluated by human readers, who will read and score your essays in June.

As stated above, 45 percent of your grade is based on how well you did on the multiple-choice questions, and the rest depends on your performance on the essays. All AP exams are rated on a scale of 1 to 5, with 5 being the highest. The scores are defined as follows:

5	Extremely well qualified
4	Well qualified
3	Qualified
2	Possibly qualified
1	No recommendation

AP Grade Reports are sent in July to each student's home, high school, and any colleges designated by the student. Students may designate the colleges they would like to receive their grade on the answer sheet at the time of the test. Students may also contact AP Services to forward their grade to other colleges after the exam, or to cancel or withhold a grade.

AP Grades by Phone

AP Grades by Phone are available for $15 a call beginning July 1. A touch-tone phone is needed. The toll-free number is (888) 308-0013.

Registration

To register for the AP English Language & Composition exam, contact your school guidance counselor or AP Coordinator. If your school does not administer the exam, contact AP Services for a listing of schools in your area that do.

KAPLAN

Fees

At press time, the fee for each AP exam is $80. The College Board offers a $22 credit to qualified students with acute financial need. A portion of the exam fee may be refunded if a student does not take the test. There is a $20 late fee for late exam orders. Check with AP Services for application deadlines.

Additional Resources

The College Board offers a number of publications about the Advanced Placement Program, including *AP Course Description—English*, *AP Program Guide*, and *AP Bulletin for Students and Parents*. You can order these and other publications online at store.collegeboard.com and at www.collegeboard.com/ap/library/; or you can call AP Order Services at (609) 771-7243.

For More Information

For more information about the AP Program and/or the AP English Language examination, contact your school's AP Coordinator or guidance counselor, or contact AP Services at:

AP Services
P.O. Box 6671
Princeton, NJ 08541-6671
Phone: (609) 771-7300; (888) CALL-4-AP
TTY: (609) 882-4118
Fax: (609) 530-0482
Email: apexams@ets.org
Website: www.collegeboard.com/ap/students/

Terminology Review

The actual AP English Language & Composition exam changes every year, of course, but the same skills are tested time and time again. This book will help you hone and strengthen these skills.

This chapter contains terms that could appear on the AP exam. You may have to use these terms to answer a question, or you may need to know what they mean to understand a question. There's no guarantee that these terms will be on the exam, of course, but any of them very well *could be*.

You may find other words that you feel should be included on this list. That's great! Feel free to add more. Your grammar or composition handbook and other class materials are terrific sources of AP terminology.

Term	Definition
Abstract	Not related to the concrete properties of an object; pertaining to ideas, concepts, or qualities, as opposed to physical attributes.
Aesthetic	Pertaining to the value of art for its own sake or for form.
Allegory	Narrative form in which characters and actions have meanings outside themselves; characters are usually personifications of abstract qualities.
Alliteration	The repetition of initial consonant sounds or any vowel sounds within a formal grouping, such as a poetic line or stanza, or in close proximity in prose.
Allusion	A figure of speech which makes brief, even casual reference to a historical or literary figure, event, or object to create a resonance in the reader or to apply a symbolic meaning to the character or object of which the allusion consists. For example, in John Steinbeck's *Of Mice and Men*, the surname of the protagonist, George Milton, is an allusion to John Milton, author of *Paradise Lost*, since by the end of the novel, George has lost the dream of having a little ranch of his own to share with his friend Lennie.
Ambiguity	Use of language in which multiple meanings are possible. Ambiguity can be unintentional through insufficient focus on the part of the writer; in good writing, ambiguity is frequently intentional in the form of multiple connotative meanings, or situations in which either the connotative or the denotative meaning can be valid in a reading.
Anachronism	Use of historically inaccurate details in a text; for example, depicting a 19th-century character using a computer. Some authors employ anachronisms for humorous effect, and some genres, such as science fiction or fantasy, make extensive use of anachronism.
Anadiplosis	Repetition of the last word of one clause at the beginning of the next clause. For example, "The crime was common, common be the pain." (Alexander Pope)
Analogy	Comparison of two things that are alike in some respects. **Metaphors** and **similes** are both types of analogy.
Analytical writing	A style of writing in which the subject is broken into its components and the components are subjected to detailed scrutiny.

KAPLAN

Term	Definition
Anaphora	The regular repetition of the same word or phrase at the beginning of successive phrases or clauses. For example, "We shall fight in the trenches. We shall fight on the oceans. We shall fight in the sky."
Antagonist	Character or force in a literary work that opposes the main character, or **protagonist**.
Antihero	Protagonist of a literary work who does not embody the traditional qualities of a hero (e.g., honor, bravery, kindness, intelligence); for example, the protagonists created by Byron in *Don Juan* and *Childe Harold*, and the characters of Rosencrantz and Guildenstern in Tom Stoppard's *Rosencrantz and Guildenstern Are Dead*.
Anaphora	Literary device of repetition, in which a word or phrase is repeated at the beginning of a series of lines.
Aphorism	A concise statement designed to make a point or illustrate a commonly held belief. The writings of Benjamin Franklin contain many aphorisms, such as "Early to bed and early to rise/Make a man healthy, wealthy, and wise."
Apology	Most commonly used as a synonym of the word *defense*, as in Sidney's *Apology for Poetry*.
Apostrophe	A figure of speech in which a person, thing, or abstract quality is addressed as if present; for example, the invocation to the muses usually found in epic poetry.
Appeals to: • authority • emotion • logic	Rhetorical arguments in which the speaker: either claims to be an expert or relies on information provided by experts (appeal to authority), attempts to affect the listener's personal feelings (appeal to emotion), or attempts to persuade the listener through use of deductive reasoning (appeal to logic).
Anecdote	A brief story or tale told by a character in a piece of literature.
Assonance	The repetition of identical or similar vowel sounds, usually in successive or proximate words.
Asyndeton	The practice of omitting conjunctions between words, phrases, or clauses. In a list, it gives a more extemporaneous effect and suggests the list may be incomplete. For example, "He was brave, fearless, afraid of nothing."
Antithesis	The juxtaposition of sharply contrasting ideas in balanced or parallel words or phrases.
Audience	The person(s) reached by a piece of writing.

Term	Definition
Begging the question	To sidestep or evade the real problem.
Bildungsroman	A novel or story whose theme is the moral or psychological growth of the main character.
Canon (canonical)	The works of an author that have been accepted as authentic.
Carpe diem	"Seize the day"; the philosophy that one should enjoy life to the fullest.
Catharsis	Purification or cleansing of the spirit through the emotions of pity and terror as a witness to a tragedy.
Chiasmus	Figure of speech by which the order of the terms in the first of parallel clauses is reversed in the second.
Claim	An assertion of something as fact; to demand as a right or as due.
Closure	Bringing to an end or conclusion.
Colloquial/ colloquialism	Ordinary language; the vernacular. For example, depending on where in the United States you live, a sandwich is called a sub, a grinder, or a hero.
Connotation	What is implied by a word. For example, the words *sweet*, *gay*, and *awesome* have connotations that are quite different from their actual definitions.
Consonance	The repetition of two or more consonants with a change in the intervening vowels, such as *pitter-patter*, *splish-splash*, and *click-clack*.
Contradiction	A direct opposition between things compared; inconsistency.
Convention	An accepted manner, model, or tradition.
Deductive	The reasoning process by which a conclusion is drawn from set of premises and contains no more facts than these premises.
Delayed sentence	A sentence that withholds its main idea until the end. For example: Just as he bent to tie his shoe, a car hit him.
Denotation	The dictionary definition of a word; the direct and specific meaning.
Deus ex machina	As in Greek theater, use of an artificial device or contrived solution to solve a difficult situation, usually introduced suddenly and unexpectedly.
Devices	A particular word pattern or combination of words used in a literary work to evoke a desired effect or arouse a desired reaction in the reader.

KAPLAN

Term	Definition
Diction	An author's choice of words to convey a tone or effect.
Didactic	Intended for teaching or to teach a moral lesson.
Digression	Movement away from the main story or theme of a piece of writing. An author digresses by temporarily focusing attention on subplot or minor character.
Discourse	A formal discussion of a subject.
Doppelganger	Ghostly counterpart of a living person or an alter ego.
Dystopia	An imaginary place where people live dehumanized, often fearful lives. The opposite of a **utopia**.
Elegy	Poem or prose lamenting the death of a particular person. Perhaps the most famous elegy is Thomas Grey's poem, "Elegy Written in a Country Churchyard."
Epigraph	Quote set at the beginning of a literary work or at its divisions to set the tone or suggest a theme.
Epiphany	A sudden or intuitive insight or perception into the reality or essential meaning of something usually brought on by a simple or common occurrence or experience.
Epistrophe	The repetition of a word or words as the end of two or more successive verses, clauses, or sentences.
Epistolary	A piece of literature contained in or carried on by letters.
Epitaph	A piece of writing in praise of a deceased person.
Ethos	In dramatic literature, the moral element that determines a character's actions, rather than thought or emotion.
Euphemism	Substitution of a milder or less direct expression for one that is harsh or blunt. For example, using "passed away" for "dead."
Evidence	An indication or a sign.
Expletive	A single word or short phrase intended to emphasize surrounding words. Commonly, expletives are set off by commas. Examples: *in fact, of course, after all, certainly*.
Explication	The interpretation or analysis of a text.
Exposition	The explanation or analysis of a subject; presenting the meaning or purpose of an issue.
Eulogy	A speech or writing in praise of a person or thing; an oration in honor of a deceased person.
Flashback	**Retrospection**, where an earlier event is inserted into the normal chronology of a narrative.

Term	Definition
Foil	A person or thing that makes another seem better by contrast.
Formal/ informal/ colloquial	Language that is lofty, dignified, or impersonal; informal or colloquial language is similar to everyday speech.
Foreshadow	To hint at or present things to come in a story or play.
Genre	Term used to describe literary forms, such as tragedy, comedy, novel, or essay.
Hamartia	Aristotle's term for the main character's tragic flaw or error in judgment.
Hyperbole	An **overstatement** characterized by exaggerated language.
Imagery	Sensory details in a work; the use of figurative language to evoke a feeling, call to mind an idea, or describe an object. Imagery involves any or all of the five senses.
Inductive	Conclusion or type of reasoning whereby observation or information about a part of a class is applied to the class as a whole. Contrast with **deductive**.
Inference	The process of arriving at a conclusion from a hint, implication, or suggestion.
Invective	The use of angry and insulting language in satirical writing.
In medias res	Refers to opening a story in the middle of the action, requiring filling in past details by exposition or flashback.
Irony: verbal, dramatic, and situational	A situation or statement characterized by significant difference between what is expected or understood and what actually happens or is meant. Irony is frequently humorous, and can be sarcastic when using words to imply the opposite of what they normally mean.
Isocolon	Parallel structure in which the parallel elements are similar not only in grammatical structure, but also in length. For example, "An envious heart makes a treacherous ear" (*Their Eyes Were Watching God*, Zora Neale Hurston).
Juxtaposition	Placing of two items side by side to create a certain effect, reveal an attitude, or accomplish some other purpose.
Literal	The strict meaning of a word or words: not figurative or exaggerated.
Litote	Form of **understatement** in which the negative of the contrary is used to achieve emphasis and intensity. For example, "She is not a bad cook."

KAPLAN

Term	Definition
Metaphor	The implicit comparison or identification of one thing with another unlike itself without the use of a verbal signal such as *like* or *as*. One thing is pictured as if it were something else, suggesting a likeness or analogy between them.
Metonymy	A figure of speech that uses the name of one thing to name or designate something, as in, "The White House announced today . . ."
Mood	The feeling or ambience resulting from the tone of a piece as well as the writer/narrator's attitude and point of view. The effect is created through descriptions of feelings or objects that establish a particular feeling such as gloom, fear, or hope.
Motif	Recurrent device, formula, or situation that often serves as a signal for the appearance of a character or event.
Narrative	A form of writing that tells a story.
Narrative device	Use of techniques such as flashbacks and/or digression in the telling of a story.
Narrator	The "character" who "tells" the story.
Nostalgia	Desire to return in thought or fact to a former time.
Onomatopoeia	A word capturing or approximating the sound of what it describes, such as *buzz* or *hiss*.
Opening	The first part or beginning of a piece of writing.
Overstatement	Exaggerated language; see also, **hyperbole**.
Oxymoron	A figure of speech that combines two apparently contradictory elements, as in "jumbo shrimp" or "deafening silence."
Paradox	A statement that seems contradictory, but is actually true.
Parallelism	Recurrent syntactical similarity where several parts of a sentence or several sentences are expressed alike to show that the ideas in the parts or sentences equal in importance. It also adds balance, rhythm, and clarity to the sentence. For example, "I have always searched for, but never found the perfect painting for that wall."
Parody	A satirical imitation of a work of art for purpose of ridiculing its style or subject.
Persona	The voice or figure of the author who tells and structures the story and who may or may not share of the values of the actual author.

Term	Definition
Personification	Treating an abstraction or nonhuman object as if it were a person by giving it human qualities.
Perspective	A character's view of the situation or events in the story.
Point of view	The view the reader gets of the action and characters in a story.
Propaganda	Information or rumor deliberately spread to help or harm a person, group, or institution.
Prose	The ordinary of form of written language without metrical structure, as distinguished from poetry or verse.
Protagonist	The chief character in a work of literature.
Realism	The literary practice of attempting to describe life and nature without idealization and with attention to detail.
Reflective	A piece of writing that gives considered thought to something.
Repetition	Repeating or repeated action.
Retrospection	Looking back on things past.
Rhetoric	The language of a work and its style.
Rhetorical device	Particular use of word patterns and styles used to clarify, make associations, and focus the writing in a piece of literature. Some rhetorical devices are **expletives**, **parallelism**, **metaphor**, **analogy**, **assonance**, etc.
Sarcasm	A sharp caustic remark. A form of **verbal irony** in which apparent praise is actually bitterly or harshly critical. For example, a coach saying to a player who misses the ball, "Nice catch."
Satire	A literary style used to make fun of or ridicule an idea or human vice or weakness.
Setting	The time and place of the action in a story, poem, or play.
Simile	A direct comparison of one thing to another, usually using the words *like* or *as* to draw the connection.
Speaker	The person—not necessarily the author—who is the voice of the poem or story.
Syllogism	A form of deduction. An extremely subtle, sophisticated, or deceptive argument.
Symbolism	A person, place, thing, event, or pattern in a literary work that designates itself and at the same time figuratively represents something else. The use of one object to suggest another hidden, object or idea.

Term	Definition
Synecdoche	A figure of speech in which a part signifies the whole, such as "head of cattle" or "hands on deck."
Syntax	The way words are put together to form phrases, clauses, and sentences. It is sentence structure and how it influences the way a reader perceives a piece of writing.
Theme	The central or dominant idea or concern of a work; the main idea or meaning.
Thesis statement	Focus statement of an essay; premise statement upon which the point of view or discussion in the essay is based.
Tone	The attitude a literary work takes towards its subject and theme. It reflects the narrator's attitude.
Transition words	Words and devices that bring unity and coherence to a piece of writing. Examples: *however*, *in addition*, and *on the other hand*.
Trope	The use of a word in a figurative sense with a decided change or extension in its literal meaning.
Understatement	Deliberate expression of an idea or event as less important than it actually is or was.
Utopia	An imaginary place of ideal perfection. The opposite of a **dystopia**.
Voice	The acknowledged or unacknowledged source of words of the story; the speaker, a "person" telling the story or poem.
Wit	Quickness of intellect and talent for saying brilliant things that surprise and delight by their unexpectedness.
Zeugma	Grammatically correct linkage of one subject with two or more verbs or a verb with two or more direct objects. The linking shows a relationship between ideas more clearly. For example: Bob exceeded at sports; Jim at academics; Mark at eating.

Fundamental Skills

CHAPTER 3

> **KEY TERMS**
> - audience
> - convention
> - formal/informal/colloquial (See also: diction, tone)

READING NONFICTION

To read nonfiction writing effectively, you need to engage in a dialogue with the text. This means that you have to take notes while you're reading. You should keep a notebook in which you jot down ideas as you read. These ideas might include passages from the text that you find especially interesting or confusing, questions that you have about a particular concept or idea in the text, or points you want to make about the text either in discussion or in writing assignments. If you take notes when you're reading or rereading, your ideas will be more immediate. You'll also be able to use the notes later, when you might have forgotten your original thoughts.

Another way to engage in dialogue with the text is by answering questions about it. This independent study includes a set of questions that you should answer each time you have a reading assignment. Whenever you read a piece of writing, you should think about how you'd respond to these questions. The habit you develop, one in which you look for set items in the reading, will help you become a quicker and more insightful reader. This, in turn, will help you produce clearer writing.

Don't panic if you think your answers are a little simplistic the first time through. Just try your best with the knowledge and experience you have. You may find that your answers to these questions will become more sophisticated and insightful as you use them more.

These aren't the only questions you can answer about nonfiction, but they are standard questions from which you can build your own analysis. These questions may be supplemented by questions more specific to a particular piece of writing, but they'll give you a good foundation for reading actively.

Review this list of study questions and answer them, in order, each time you read a text. After the list of questions, you will find some hints or strategies to help you develop detailed answers. The answers to these questions will take some thinking about. They may not be obvious the first time you read the text, which means that you may need to reread part or all of the text to be able to answer a question fully. Give complete answers to the questions; if you give short answers, you short-change yourself.

Study Questions

1. What is this text about?
2. How is the text structured?
3. How would you describe the language of the text?
4. To whom is the text addressed? How do you know this?
5. What effect does the text have on the reader?
6. What is the text arguing?
7. Is the text effective at its goal? Why?

Below you'll find a set of hints or strategies for answering each question.

1.   What is this text about?
To answer this question you need to:
  • Take notes
  • For each paragraph, list a word or phrase that identifies the point of the paragraph
  • Collect your notes and phrases to create a summary of the piece

2.   How is the text structured?
To answer this question you need to:
  • Identify which of the statements function as claims, premises or reasons, evidence, and conclusions
  • Be able to describe the structure or composition of the essay
  • Read for relationships between sentences and paragraphs

3. *How would you describe the language of the text?*

To answer this question you need to:

- Examine the syntax, diction, tone, and figures of speech used by the author
- Be able to describe the effect of each of these elements

4. *To whom is the text addressed? How do you know this?*

To answer this question you need to:

- Use historical or contextual evidence to speculate about the intended audience
- Identify the speaker's tone

5. *What effect does the text have on the reader?*

To answer this question you need to:

- Identify rhetorical strategies used by the author
- Examine your emotional and intellectual responses to the text
- Figure out how the rhetorical strategies create the intellectual and emotional effects

6. *What is the text arguing?*

To answer this question you need to:

- Put the main points of all the paragraphs together to see what argument emerges
- Read for implied meaning
- Read for the relationships between sentences and paragraphs
- Look at the structure, language, and subject to see how these elements work together to produce an argument

7. *Is the text effective at its goal? Why?*

To answer this question you need to:

- Identify the point or argument of the text
- Consider the rhetorical strategies at work in the text
- Determine whether the strategies work to supplement the point or argument

NOTICING TRENDS

When you read texts from an earlier historic period, you will immediately notice that they sound different from contemporary writing. In the exercise below, you'll have an opportunity to compare a contemporary text with one that is more than one hundred years old. Pay attention to the characteristics of writing from different periods of time.

PRACTICE READING

For this exercise, read "Abraham Lincoln" by Nathaniel Hawthorne and "The Way to Rainy Mountain" by N. Scott Momaday. Then answer both sets of study questions below and compare your answers with the sample answers provided after the texts.

Study Questions Set I

Answer these questions for each text:

1. What is the piece of writing about?

2. How is the piece structured?

3. How would you describe the language of the piece?

4. To whom is the piece addressed? How do you know this?

5. What effect does the piece have on the reader?

6. What is the piece arguing?

7. Is the text effective at its goal? Why?

Study Questions Set II

Compare the two texts to answer these questions:

1. Aside from the publication date, how can you tell that the texts were written more than 100 years apart?

2. What are some historical and political implications of each text?

3. How is the narrator's persona different in each text? What might these differences have to do with the time periods of the texts?

Abraham Lincoln
Nathaniel Hawthorne

Of course, there was one other personage, in the class of statesmen, whom I should have been truly mortified to leave Washington without seeing; since (temporarily, at least, and by force of circumstances) he was the man of men. But a private grief had built up a barrier about him, impeding the customary free intercourse of Americans with their chief magistrate; so that I might have come away without a glimpse of his very remarkable physiognomy, save for a semi-official opportunity of which I was glad to take advantage. The fact is, we were invited to annex ourselves, as supernumeraries, to a deputation that was about to wait upon the President, from a Massachusetts whip factory, with a present of a splendid whip.

Our immediate party consisted only of four or five (including Major Ben Perley Poore, with his note-book and pencil), but we were joined by several other persons, who seemed to have been lounging about the precincts of the White House, under the spacious porch, or within the hall, and who swarmed in with us to take the chances of a presentation. Nine o'clock had been appointed as the time for receiving the deputation, and we were punctual to the moment; but not so the President, who sent us word that he was eating his breakfast, and would come as soon as he could. His appetite, we were glad to think, must have been a pretty fair one; for we waited about half an hour in one of the antechambers, and then were ushered into a reception-room, in one corner of which sat the Secretaries of War and of the Treasury, expecting, like ourselves, the termination of the Presidential breakfast. During this interval there were several new additions to our group, one or two of whom were in a working-garb, so that we formed a very miscellaneous collection of people, mostly unknown to each other, and without any common sponsor, but all with an equal right to look our head servant in the face.

By and by there was a little stir on the staircase and in the passageway, and in lounged a tall, loose-jointed figure, of an exaggerated Yankee port and demeanor, whom (as being about the homeliest man I ever saw, yet by no means repulsive or disagreeable) it was impossible not to recognize as Uncle Abe.

Unquestionably, Western man though he be, and Kentuckian by birth, President Lincoln is the essential representative of all Yankees, and the veritable specimen, physically, of what the world seems determined to regard as our characteristic qualities. It is the strangest and yet the fittest thing in the jumble of human vicissitudes, that he, out of so many millions, unlooked for, unselected by any intelligible process that could be based upon his genuine qualities, unknown to those who chose him, and unsuspected of what endowments may adapt him for his tremendous responsibility, should have found the way open for him to fling his lank personality into the chair of state—where, I presume, it was his first impulse to throw his legs on the council-table, and tell the Cabinet Ministers a story. There is no describing his lengthy awkwardness, nor the uncouthness of his movement; and yet it seemed as if I had been in the habit of seeing him daily, and had shaken hands with him a thousand times in some village street; so true was he to the aspect of the pattern American, though with a certain extravagance which, possibly, I exaggerated still further by the delighted eagerness with which I took it in. If put to guess his calling and livelihood, I should have taken him for a country school-master as soon as anything else. He was dressed in a rusty black frock coat and pantaloons, unbrushed, and worn so faithfully that the suit had adapted itself to the curves and angularities of his figure, and had grown to be an oûter skin of the man. His hair was black, still unmixed with gray, stiff, somewhat bushy, and had apparently been acquainted with neither brush nor comb that morning, after the disarrangement of the pillow; and as to a nightcap, Uncle Abe probably knows nothing of such effeminacies. His complexion is dark and sallow, betokening, I fear, a insalubrious atmosphere around the White House; he has thick black eyebrows and an impending brow; his nose is large, and the lines about his mouth are very strongly defined.

The whole physiognomy is as coarse a one as you would meet anywhere in the length and breadth of the States; but, withal, it is redeemed, illuminated, softened, and brightened by a kindly though serious look out of his eyes, and an expression of homely sagacity, that seems weighted with rich results of village experience. A great deal of native sense; no bookish cultivation, no refinement; honest at heart, and thoroughly so, and yet, in some sort, sly—at least, endowed with a sort of tact and wisdom that are akin to craft, and would impel him, I think, to take an antagonist in flank, rather than to make a bull-run at him right in front. But, on the whole, I like this sallow, queer, sagacious visage, with the homely human sympathies that warmed it; and, for my small share in the matter, would as lief have Uncle Abe for a ruler as any man whom it would have been practicable to put in his place.

Immediately on his entrance the President accosted our member of Congress, who had us in charge, and, with a comical twist of his face, made some jocular remark about the length of his breakfast. He then greeted us all round, not waiting for an introduction, but shaking and squeezing everybody's hand with the utmost cordiality, whether the individual's name was announced to him or not. His manner towards us was wholly without pretence, but yet had a kind of natural dignity, quite sufficient to keep the forwardest of us from clapping him on the shoulder and asking him for a story. A mutual acquaintance being established, our leader took the whip out of its case, and began to read the address of presentation. The whip was an exceedingly long one, its handle wrought in ivory (by some artist in the Massachusetts State Prison, I believe), and ornamented with a medallion of the President, and other equally beautiful devices; and along its whole length there was a succession of golden bands and ferrules. The address was shorter than the whip, but equally well made, consisting chiefly of an explanatory description of these artistic designs, and closing with a hint that the gift was a suggestive and emblematic one, and that the President would recognize the use to which such an instrument should be put.

This suggestion gave Uncle Abe rather a delicate task in his reply, because, slight as the matter seemed, it apparently called for some declaration, or intimation, or faint foreshadowing of policy in reference to the conduct of the war, and the final treatment of the Rebels. But the President's Yankee aptness and not-to-be-caughtness stood him in good stead, and he jerked or wiggled himself out of the dilemma with an uncouth dexterity that was entirely in character; although, without his gesticulation of eye and mouth—and especially the flourish of the whip, with which he imagined himself touching up a pair of fat horses—I doubt whether his words would be worth recording, even if I could remember them. The gist of the reply was, that he accepted the whip as an emblem of peace, not punishment; and, this great affair over, we retired out of the presence in high good humor, only regretting that we could not have seen the President sit down and fold up his legs (which is said to be a most extraordinary spectacle), or have heard him tell one of those delectable stories for which he is so celebrated. A good many of them are afloat upon the common talk of Washington, and are certainly the aptest, pithiest, and funniest little things imaginable; though, to be sure, they smack of the frontier freedom, and would not always bear repetition in a drawing-room, or on the immaculate page of the Atlantic.

Good Heavens! what liberties have I been taking with one of the potentates of the earth, and the man on whose conduct more important consequences depend than on that of any other historical personage of the century! But with whom is an American citizen entitled to take a liberty, if not with his own chief magistrate? However, lest the above allusions to President Lincoln's little peculiarities (already well known to the country and to the world) should be misinterpreted, I deem it proper to say a word or two in regard to him, of unfeigned respect and measurable confidence. He is evidently a man of keen faculties, and, what is still more to the purpose, of powerful character. As to his integrity, the people have that intuition of it which is never deceived. Before he actually entered upon his great office, and for a considerable time afterwards, there is no reason to suppose that he adequately estimated the gigantic task about to be imposed on him, or, at least, had any distinct idea how it was to be managed; and I presume there may have been more than one veteran politician who proposed to himself to take the power out of President Lincoln's bands into his own, leaving our honest friend only the public responsibility for the good or ill success of the career. The extremely imperfect development of his statesmanly qualities, at that period, may have justified such designs. But the President is teachable by events, and has now spent a year in a very arduous course of education; he has a flexible mind, capable of much expansion, and convertible towards far loftier studies and activities than those of his early life; and if he came to Washington a backwoods humorist, he has already transformed himself into as good a statesman (to speak moderately) as his prime minister.

KAPLAN

The Way to Rainy Mountain
N. Scott Momaday

A single knoll rises out of the plain in Oklahoma, north and west of the Wichita Range. For my people, the Kiowas, it is an old landmark, and they gave it the name Rainy Mountain. The hardest weather in the world is there. Winter brings blizzards, hot tornadic winds arise in the spring, and in summer the prairie is all anvil's edge. The grass turns brittle and brown, and it cracks beneath your feet. There are green belts along the rivers and creeks, linear groves of hickory and pecan, willow and witch hazel. At a distance in July or August the steaming foliage seems almost to writhe in fire. Great green and yellow grasshoppers are everywhere in the tall grass, popping up like corn to sting the flesh, and tortoises crawl about on the red earth, going nowhere in the plenty of time. Loneliness is an aspect of the land. All things in the plain are isolate; there is no confusion of objects in the eye, but *one* hill or *one* tree or *one* man. To look upon that landscape in the early morning, with the sun at your back, is to lose the sense of proportion. Your imagination comes to life, and this, you think, is where Creation was begun.

I returned to Rainy Mountain in July. My grandmother had died ill the spring, and I wanted to be at her grave. She had lived to be very old and at last infirm. Her only living daughter was with her when she died, and I was told that in death her face was that of a child.

I like to think of her as a child. When she was born, the Kiowas were living the last great moment of their history. For more than a hundred years they had controlled the open range from the Smoky Hill River to the Red, from the headwaters of the Canadian to the fork of the Arkansas and Cimarron. In alliance with the Comanches, they had ruled the whole of the southern Plains. War was their sacred business, and they were among the finest horsemen the world has ever known. But warfare for the Kiowas was preeminently a matter of disposition rather than of survival, and they never understood the grim, unrelenting advance of the U.S. Cavalry. When at last, divided and ill-provisioned, they were driven onto the Staked Plains in the cold rains of autumn, they fell into panic. In Palo Duro Canyon they abandoned their crucial stores to pillage and had nothing then but their lives. In order to save themselves, they surrendered to the soldiers at Fort Sill and were imprisoned in the old stone corral that now stands as a military museum. My grandmother was spared the humiliation of those high gray walls by eight or ten years, but she must have known from birth the affliction of defeat, the dark brooding of old warriors.

Her name was Aho, and she belonged to the last culture to evolve in North America. Her forebears came down from the high country in western Montana nearly three centuries ago. They were a mountain people, a mysterious tribe of hunters whose language has never been positively classified in any major group. In the late seventeenth century they began a long migration to the south and east. It was a journey toward the dawn, and it led to a golden age. Along the way the Kiowas were befriended by the Crows, who gave them the culture and religion of the Plains. They acquired horses, and their ancient nomadic spirit was suddenly free of the ground. They acquired Tai-me, the sacred Sun Dance doll, from that moment the object and symbol of their worship, and so shared in the divinity of the sun. Not least, they acquired the sense of destiny, therefore courage and pride. When they entered upon the southern Plains they had been transformed. No longer were they slaves to the simple necessity of survival; they were a lordly and dangerous society of fighters and thieves, hunters and priests of the sun. According to their origin myth, they entered the world through a hollow log. From one point of view, their migration was the fruit of an old prophecy, for indeed they emerged from a sunless world.

Although my grandmother lived out her long life in the shadow of Rainy Mountain, the immense landscape of the continental interior lay like memory in her blood. She could tell of the Crows, whom she had never seen, and of the Black Hills, where she had never been. I wanted to see in reality what she had seen more perfectly in the mind's eye, and traveled fifteen hundred miles to begin my pilgrimage.

Yellowstone, it seemed to me, was the top of the world, a region of deep lakes and dark timber, canyons and waterfalls. But, beautiful as it is, one might have the sense of confinement there. The skyline in all directions is close at hand, the high wall of the woods and deep cleavages of shade. There is a perfect freedom in the mountains, but it belongs to the eagle and the elk, the badger and the bear. The Kiowas reckoned their stature by the distance they could see, and they were bent and blind in the wilderness.

Descending eastward, the highland meadows are a stairway to the plain. In July the inland slope of the Rockies is luxuriant with flax and buckwheat, stonecrop and larkspur. The earth unfolds and the limit of the land recedes. Clusters of trees, and animals grazing far in the distance, cause the vision to reach away and wonder to build upon the mind. The sun follows a longer course in the day, and the sky is immense beyond all comparison. The great billowing clouds that sail upon it are the shadows that move upon the grain like water, dividing light. Farther down, in the land of the Crows and Blackfeet, the plain is yellow. Sweet clover takes hold of the hills and bends upon itself to cover and seal the soil. There the Kiowas paused on their ways they had come to the place where they must change their lives. The Sun is at home on the plains. Precisely there does it have the certain character of a god. When the Kiowas came to the land of the Crows, they could see the dark lees of the hills at dawn across the Bighorn River, the profusion of light on the grain shelves, the oldest deity ranging after the solstices. Not yet would they veer southward to the caldron of the land that lay below; they must wean their blood from the northern winter and hold the mountains a while longer in their view. They bore Tai-me in procession to the east.

A dark mist lay over the Black Hills, and the land was like iron. At the top of a ridge I caught sight of Devil's Tower upthrust against the gray sky as if in the birth of time the core of the earth had broken through its crust and the motion of the world was begun. There are things in nature that engender an awful quiet in the heart of man; Devil's Tower is one of them. Two centuries ago, because they could not do otherwise, the Kiowas made a legend at the base of the rock. My grandmother said:

Eight children were there at play, seven sisters and their brother. Suddenly the boy was struck dumb; he trembled and began to run upon his hands and feet. His fingers became claws, and his body was covered with fur. Directly there was a bear where the boy had been. The sisters were terrified; they ran, and the bear after them. They came to the stump of a great tree, and the tree spoke to them. It bade them climb upon it, and as they did so it began to rise into the air. The bear came to kill them, but they were just beyond its reach. It reared against the tree and scored the bark all around with its claws. The seven sisters were borne into the sky, and they became the stars of the Big Dipper.

From that moment, and so long as the legend lives, the Kiowas have kinsmen in the night sky. Whatever they were in the mountains, they could be no more. However tenuous their well-being, however much they had suffered and would suffer again, they had found a way out of the wilderness.

My grandmother had a reverence for the sun, a holy regard that now is all but gone out of mankind. There was a wariness in her, and an ancient awe. She was a Christian in her later years, but she had come a long way about, and she never forgot her birthright. As a child she had been to the Sun Dances; she had taken part in those annual rites, and by them she had learned the restoration of her people in the presence of Tai-me. She was about seven when the last Kiowa Sun Dance was held in 1887 on the Washita River above Rainy Mountain Creek. The buffalo were gone. In order to consummate the ancient sacrifice—to impale the head of a buffalo bull upon the medicine tree—a delegation of old men journeyed into Texas, there to beg and barter for an animal from the Goodnight herd. She was ten when the Kiowas came together for the last time as a living Sun Dance culture. They could find no buffalo; they had to hang an old hide from the sacred tree. Before the dance could begin, a company of soldiers rode out from Fort Sill under orders to disperse the tribe. Forbidden without cause the essential act of their faith, having seen the wild herds slaughtered and left to rot upon the ground, the Kiowas backed away forever from the medicine tree. That was July 20, 1890, at the great bend of the Washita. My grandmother was there. Without bitterness, and for as long as she lived, she bore a vision of deicide.

Now that I can have her only in memory, I see my grandmother in the several postures that were peculiar to her: standing at the wood stove on a winter morning and turning meat in a great iron skillet; sitting at the south window, bent above her beadwork, and afterwards, when her vision failed, looking down for a long time into the fold of her hands; going out upon a cane, very slowly as she did when the weight of age came upon her; praying. I remember her most often at prayer. She made long rambling prayers out of suffering and hope, having seen many things. I was never sure that I had the right to hear, so exclusive were they of all mere custom and company. The last time I saw her she prayed standing by the side of her bed at night, naked to the waist, the light of a kerosene lamp moving upon her dark skin. Her long, black hair, always drawn and braided in the day, lay upon her shoulders and against her breasts like a shawl. I do not speak Kiowa, and I never understood her prayers, but there was something inherently sad in the sound, some merest hesitation upon the syllables of sorrow. She began in a high and descending pitch, exhausting her breath to silence; then again and again—and always the same intensity of effort, of something that is, and is not, like urgency in the human voice. Transported so in the dancing light among the shadows of her room, she seemed beyond the reach of time. But that was illusion; I think I knew then that I should not see her again.

Houses are like sentinels in the plain, old keepers of the weather watch. There, in a very little while, wood takes on the appearance of great age. All colors wear soon away in the wind and rain, and then the wood is burned gray and the grain appears and the nails turn red with rust. The windowpanes are black and opaque; you imagine there is nothing within, and indeed there are many ghosts, bones given up to the land. They stand here and there against the sky, and you approach them for a longer time than you expect. They belong in the distance; it is their domain.

Once there was a lot of sound in my grandmother's house, a lot of coming and going, feasting and talk. The summers there were full of excitement and reunion. The Kiowas are a summer people; they abide the cold and keep to themselves, but when the season turns and the land becomes warm and vital they cannot hold still; an old love of going returns upon them. The aged visitors who came to my grandmother's house when I was a child were made of lean and leather, and they bore themselves upright. They wore great black hats and bright ample shirts that shook in the wind. They rubbed fat upon their hair and wound their braids with strips of colored cloth. Some of them painted their faces and carried the scars of old and cherished enmities They were an old council of warlords, come to remind and be reminded of who they were. Their wives and daughters served them well. The women might indulge themselves; gossip was at once the mark and compensation of their servitude. They made loud and elaborate talk among themselves, full of jest and gesture, fright and false alarm. They went abroad in fringed and flowered shawls bright beadwork and German silver. They were at home in the kitchen, and they prepared meals that were banquets.

There were frequent prayer meetings, and great nocturnal feasts. When I was a child I played with my cousins outside, where the lamplight fell upon the ground and the singing of the old people rose up around us and carried away into the darkness. There were a lot of good things to eat, a lot of laughter and surprise. And afterwards, when the quiet returned, I lay down with my grandmother and could hear the frogs away by the river and feel the motion of the air.

Now there is a funeral silence in the rooms, the endless wake of some final word. The walls have closed in upon my grandmother's house. When I returned to it in mourning, I saw for the first time in my life how small it was. It was late at night, and there was a white moon, nearly full. I sat for a long time on the stone steps by the kitchen door. From there I could see out across the land; I could see the long row of trees by the creek, the low light upon the rolling plains, and the stars of the Big Dipper. Once I looked at the moon and caught sight of a strange thing. A cricket had perched upon the handrail, only a few inches away from me. My line of vision was such that the creature filled the moon like a fossil. It had gone there, I thought, to live and die, for there, of all places, was its small definition made whole and eternal. A warm wind rose tip and purled like the longing within me.

The next morning I awoke at dawn and went out on the dirt road to Rainy Mountain. It was already hot, and the grasshoppers began to fill the air. Still, it was early in the morning, and the birds sang out of the shadows. The long yellow grass on the mountain shone in the bright light, and a scissortail hied above the land. There, where it ought to be, at the end of a long and legendary way, was my grandmother's grave. Here and there on the dark stones were ancestral names. Looking back once, I saw the mountain and came away.

Sample Answers for "Abraham Lincoln" by Nathaniel Hawthorne

1.   What is the piece of writing about?

The piece is about the narrator's experience of meeting Abraham Lincoln at the White House; Lincoln's common appearance and coarseness; Lincoln's "uncouth dexterity" and his capacity to learn from experience in the position of the president.

2.   How is "Abraham Lincoln" structured?

It's structured as a short, journalistic sketch of the president that first sets the scene of the narrator's encounter with Lincoln, then describes Lincoln's appearance and manner, and finally, evaluates his character and competence.

3.   How would you describe the language of "Abraham Lincoln"?

The language is formal, with complex sentences and sophisticated diction, including words like "insalubrious" and "physiognomy." The tone is arch (slightly sarcastic). The combination of the sentence structure and diction indicates 19th century language.

4.   To whom is "Abraham Lincoln" addressed? How do you know this?

It's addressed to an educated, politically interested readership of a 19th century magazine. Only educated readers would understand the language, and the topic is political. The description of Lincoln as a "veritable specimen" indicates that respect for the president among the audience is not taken for granted by the writer. However, the fact that several pages, including this descriptive phrase, were omitted from publication may indicate that the *Atlantic Monthly* editor's assessment of the sensibilities of the audience was different from the author's.

5.   What effect does "Abraham Lincoln" have on the reader?

It leaves the reader with the impression that Abraham Lincoln was mocked and looked down on by many of the educated elite of the time because of his coarse manner. At the same time, it reinforces the honesty, integrity, and down-to-earth personality of the president.

6.   What is "Abraham Lincoln" arguing?

Although the piece doesn't explicitly make any arguments, it does implicitly suggest that Abraham Lincoln was not prepared for the office of the president before he took the position. It also suggests that the election process is haphazard and uninformed, and that Lincoln's success as the president is due to his quick learning abilities rather than prior experience or talent.

7.   Is the text effective at its goal? Why?

If the goal of the text is to make fun of Lincoln's appearance and dress, it's effective because of descriptions like that of his hair, which had "apparently been acquainted with neither comb nor brush that morning." If the goal is to seriously question Lincoln's appropriateness for the position of the presidency, it's not effective because of too many complimentary descriptions, such as those about Lincoln's "keen faculties" and "powerful character." If the goal is to flatter the readers of the *Atlantic Monthly* because they are more socially graceful than Lincoln, the piece is effective in its combination of mockery and self-conscious statements such as, "But with whom is an American citizen entitled to take a liberty, if not with his own chief magistrate?"

Sample Answers for "The Way to Rainy Mountain" by N. Scott Momaday

1.   What is the topic of "The Way to Rainy Mountain"?

The topic is the narrator's pilgrimage to his grandmother's burial place following the route the Kiowas had taken from western Montana to Oklahoma; the importance of the sun to the history, beliefs, and rituals of the Kiowas; the narrator's memories of his grandmother.

2.   How is "The Way to Rainy Mountain" structured?

It's structured as a narrative following the order of the places of the narrator's pilgrimage interwoven with details from his grandmother's life and the history of the Kiowas.

3.   How would you describe the language of "The Way to Rainy Mountain"?

The narrator's language is descriptive and full of imagery. The tone is nostalgic. The sentences are relatively short and simple, but illustrative.

4. *To whom is "The Way to Rainy Mountain" addressed? How can you tell?*

The story is addressed to a contemporary audience who are not Kiowas. The simple sentences mark the piece as written in the 20th century, and the narrator's words "my people, the Kiowas" indicate that he is speaking to an audience outside his tribe.

5. *What effect does "The Way to Rainy Mountain" have on the reader?*

The imagery makes the reader feel that he or she can see the land the narrator describes, from Yellowstone to Rainy Mountain. The introduction of the death of the narrator's grandmother gives an immediate seriousness to the piece, and the description shows the narrator's respect and love for his grandmother. The strong connection between the grandmother's history and the history of the Kiowas impresses the importance of the narrator's culture on the reader.

6. *What is the text arguing?*

The story makes no explicit arguments, but implicitly argues for the importance of family and place in the culture of the Kiowas. It also implicitly argues that the unrelenting advance of the U.S. cavalry caused deicide in the culture of the Kiowas when they were prevented from performing the Sun Dance rites and so were "forbidden without cause the essential act of their faith."

7. *Is the text effective at its goal? Why?*

If the goal of the text is to create respect for and knowledge of the history of the Kiowas, it is effective because it engages the reader through a nostalgic description of the life of a grandmother. The warm, respectful, reminiscent tone conveys a respect for the history of the people as well as the woman. If the goal is to convey a sense of how important the land is to the Kiowas, the imagery and illustrative descriptions of the narrator's pilgrimage do so.

Sample Answers for Comparing the Texts

1. *Aside from the publication date, how can you tell that the texts were written more than 100 years apart?*

Although the tone of "Abraham Lincoln" is not completely serious, the sentences are complex, and the diction includes many words not used in everyday conversation today. In contrast, the sentences in "The Way to Rainy Mountain" are relatively simple and concise despite the more serious tone. Additionally, Abraham Lincoln was a 19th century president, and in "The Way to Rainy Mountain," the narrator's grandmother was born after Lincoln's death.

2. *What are some historical and political implications of each text?*

"Abraham Lincoln" was written to affect an elite, educated audience's perception of the current United States president. The text implicitly critiques the popular election process and positions a powerful politician as an apt pupil. In this manner, it comments on the electoral political system of the time and a powerful political figure. "The Way to Rainy Mountain" was written immediately following an upsurge in the political awareness of American Indians of the 1960s. The Civil Rights Act and activism of the 1960s set the stage for more people of diverse racial backgrounds to assert the legitimacy of their cultural heritage and to critique the oppressive actions of the white mainstream in their histories.

3. *How is the narrator's persona different in each text? What might these differences have to do with the time periods of the texts?*

In "Abraham Lincoln," the narrator provides a strong commentary in addition to his descriptions. For example, his interjection "Good Heavens!" asserts his personality as a key aspect of the text. In addition, he puts himself in the position of judge by saying "I deem it proper to say a word or two." This type of self-conscious narration contrasts with the narrator's relative transparency in "The Way to Rainy Mountain." In the latter text, we know more about the narrator's journey than his personality or individual interpretation of the details presented in the text. These differences in narrative style could result from differences between a magazine commentary and a novel. Conventions of narration also differ in different time periods.

MORE PRACTICE: ADOPTING A WRITING STYLE

Choose either Nathaniel Hawthorne's "Abraham Lincoln" or N. Scott Momaday's "The Way to Rainy Mountain" and rewrite it in the style of the other text.

When you change the style while keeping the content constant, you should particularly pay attention to details like sentence length and complexity, the formality of the language, what the language "sounds like," and the structure.

Examples

Here are two examples of sentences that have been changed from one style to another.

> These statements seem so absurd on their face, especially when I add that I am a young man apparently of about thirty years of age, that no person can be blamed for refusing to read another word of what promises to be a mere imposition on his credulity.
>
> —Edward Bellamy, *Looking Backward*

Rewritten: "What I'm going to say sounds like a lie, especially because I'm only thirty. I don't blame you if you don't even want to go on reading."

> A year in the mill was all Mama could take after they buried Lyle; the dust in the air got to her too fast.
>
> —Dorothy Allison, *Bastard Out of Carolina*

Rewritten: "One year exhausted dear Mother's tolerance for the working conditions of her place of employment, the mill, after the demise and interment of Lyle. The airborne particles carried by the draughts through the cavernous chambers of the establishment proved to irritate her sensitive membranes beyond what could be borne."

PREPARING FOR THE EXAM

Strategies to Test Your Best

This chapter gives you tips and strategies to prepare for both the practice exams in this book and the actual AP exam. Once you are familiar with how the test is set up and how we suggest you tackle each section, turn to chapters 5 and 6 for a chance to practice answering some sample questions.

Before we get into specific strategies for each section of the exam, though, let's discuss ways to tackle that all-important obstacle to any test: stress.

THE BASICS OF STRESS MANAGEMENT

The countdown has begun. Your date with the test is looming on the horizon. Anxiety is on the rise. The butterflies in your stomach have gone ballistic. Your thinking is getting cloudy. Maybe you think you won't be ready. Maybe you already know your stuff, but you're going into panic mode anyway. Don't freak! It's possible to tame that anxiety and stress—before and during the test.

Remember, a little stress is good. Anxiety is a motivation to study. The adrenaline that gets pumped into your bloodstream when you're stressed helps you stay alert and think more clearly. But if you feel that the tension is so great that it's preventing you from using your study time effectively, here are some things you can do to get it under control.

Take Control

Lack of control is a prime cause of stress. Research shows that if you don't have a sense of control over what's happening in your life, you can easily end up feeling helpless and hopeless. Try to identify the sources of the stress you feel. Which ones can you do something about? Can you find ways to reduce the stress you're feeling about any of these sources?

Focus on Your Strengths

Make a list of areas of strength you have that will help you do well on the test. We all have strengths, and recognizing your own is like having reserves of solid gold at Fort Knox. You'll be able to draw on your reserves as you need them, helping you solve difficult questions, maintain confidence, and keep test stress and anxiety at a distance. And every time you recognize a new area of strength, solve a challenging problem, or score well on a practice test, you'll increase your reserves.

Imagine Yourself Succeeding

Close your eyes and imagine yourself in a relaxing situation. Breathe easily and naturally. Now, think of a real-life situation in which you scored well on a test or did well on an assignment. Focus on this success. Now turn your thoughts to the test, and keep your thoughts and feelings in line with that successful experience. Don't make comparisons between them; just imagine yourself taking the upcoming test with the same feelings of confidence and relaxed control.

Set Realistic Goals

Facing your problem areas gives you some distinct advantages. What do you want to accomplish in the time remaining? Make a list of realistic goals. You can't help feeling more confident when you know you're actively improving your chances of earning a higher test score.

Exercise Your Frustrations Away

Whether it's jogging, biking, pushups, or a pickup basketball game, physical exercise will stimulate your mind and body, and improve your ability to think and concentrate. A surprising number of students fall out of the habit of regular exercise, ironically because they're spending so much time prepping for exams. A little physical exertion will help to keep your mind and body in sync and sleep better at night.

Avoid Drugs

Using drugs (prescription or recreational) specifically to prepare for and take a big test is definitely self-defeating. (If they are illegal drugs, you may end up with a bigger problem on your hands than the AP English examination!) Mild stimulants, such as coffee or cola can sometimes help as you study, since they keep you alert. On the down side, too much of these can also lead to agitation, restlessness, and insomnia. It all depends on your tolerance for caffeine.

Eat Well

Good nutrition will help you focus and think clearly. Eat plenty of fruits and vegetables, low-fat protein such as fish, skinless poultry, beans, and legumes, and whole grains such as brown rice, whole wheat bread, and pastas. Don't eat a lot of sugar and high-fat snacks, or salty foods.

Work at Your Own Pace

Don't be thrown if other test takers seem to be working more furiously than you during the exam. Continue to spend your time patiently thinking through your answers; it will lead to better results. Don't mistake the other people's sheer activity as signs of progress and higher scores.

Keep Breathing

Conscious attention to breathing is an excellent way to manage stress while you're taking the test. Most of the people who get into trouble during tests take shallow breaths: They breathe using only their upper chests and shoulder muscles, and may even hold their breath for long periods of time. Conversely, those test takers who breathe deeply in a slow, relaxed manner are likely to be in better control during the session.

Stretch

If you find yourself getting spaced out or burned out as you're taking the test, stop for a brief moment and stretch. Even though you'll be pausing on the test for a moment, it's a moment well spent. Stretching will help to refresh you and refocus your thoughts.

Whew! Feeling better? Let's move on to section-specific strategies.

THE STRUCTURE OF THE EXAM

The three practice exams in this book are based on the AP English Language exam. They each take three hours to complete and consist of two sections. They're good practice for test day.

The first section of each practice test has approximately 50 multiple-choice questions, and takes an hour to complete. On the AP exam, there may be up to 55 questions. The number of questions on the AP exam varies from year to year.

In the multiple-choice section, you'll read a number of short passages then answer questions about them that analyze their rhetorical elements. This section counts toward 45% of your total exam grade on each practice exam, as on the AP exam.

The second section of the AP test (and each practice test) has three essay questions, and takes two hours to complete. The section counts toward 55% of your grade.

THE MULTIPLE-CHOICE QUESTIONS

The multiple-choice questions test the following skills:

- The ability to understand the literal and deeper meanings of the excerpt
- The ability to see how elements like sentence structure, word choice, and rhetorical devices contribute to the meaning
- The ability to describe how these features function rhetorically. In other words, how do they help the author achieve his or her purpose?

How to Approach the Multiple-Choice Questions

Follow our tried-and-true suggestions for tackling Section I of the test:

- First, read the passage once, quickly, for general understanding. Then go directly to the questions and begin to answer them. Start with the first question, then move on to the second, the third, and so on.

- Read the questions carefully: keep an eye out for words such as *not* or *except* (as in "All of the following statements except one are true," for example).

- Answer the questions you're most certain about first and the ones you have difficulty with last. If you still find that you're spending too much time on a question, make a note of it and come back to it once you've answered all the questions you're confident about. However, it's better to go back to it before continuing to the next section because it's hard to go back once you've moved into a new section.

- If you're having difficulty with a question, try to eliminate wrong answers. The AP test deducts one-fourth of a point from your total score for each question you answer incorrectly. If you don't have any idea which answer is the best one, it's better to leave the question unanswered. However, *if you can eliminate even one wrong answer, the odds are in your favor to guess.*

- Budget your time. Count the number of passages on the test and divide the hour up between them. If there are four passages, you have 15 minutes to answer the questions about each. You won't have time to reread the passage multiple times and take notes. However, do go back and reread the passage to find the answer to a difficult question.

- When a question directs you to a specific word or line, go directly to that line to find the answer to the question.

Types of Multiple-Choice Questions

The multiple-choice section of the AP exam usually includes four or five passages and 10–15 questions about each passage. The questions aren't ordered by level of difficulty: harder questions are mixed in with easier questions. The multiple-choice questions fall into several categories: main idea, rhetorical effects, authorial purpose, rhetorical modes, and passage organization.

- *Main Idea:* Main idea questions test whether you've understood the meaning of the passage. One way to prepare for these questions is to summarize the main point of each passage you read, silently or on paper, before answering the questions.

- *Rhetorical Effects:* Questions about rhetorical effects test your knowledge of rhetorical devices and types of figurative language. They also test your ability to interpret their function in a passage. To prepare for these questions, review section 3 of this book, which covers rhetorical devices and figurative language. As you read the test passages, underline or mark these devices and figurative language, especially when they seem to affect the meaning of the passage.

- *Authorial Purpose:* Authorial purpose questions test your ability to see why authors make the rhetorical choices they do. Usually these questions focus on specific words and phrases from the passage. To prepare for these questions, assess the persona of the author as you read—what do you learn about the author from the tone, diction, perspective, and style of the passage?

- *Rhetorical Modes:* These questions ask you to say what the rhetorical mode of the passage is and think about the effects of rhetorical modes. To prepare for these questions, review section 3 of this book.

- *Passage Organization:* Questions about organization ask you to identify the structure of the passage. They also ask you to evaluate the effects of the author's organizational choices. These questions may ask you to think about organization in terms of sentences and paragraphs or in terms of evidence, definitions, and arguments. As you read the test passage, try to understand how each paragraph functions and evaluate the way in which the author develops his or her point.

Reading Strategies

You need to be an active reader to work through the multiple-choice questions effectively. This means reading carefully and marking important words and points. You should also closely read the multiple-choice questions and their answer choices. As you read each question, think about what kind of question it is and where you might look in the passage to find the answer. Underline key words and phrases in the question. As you choose your answer, be sure you've read all the choices before you make your final decision.

Another reading strategy is to skim the questions before you read the passage. Then you'll be able to read with the questions in mind. If you do choose to skim, be sure to reread the questions carefully as you answer them.

Time Management

Working through the passages and questions efficiently is very important in the multiple-choice section of the exam. If you get behind on one passage, you'll need to rush through the later ones. Divide up your time equally between passages, and finish the questions for each passage before you move on to the next. Answer the easy questions first, and leave the difficult ones for last. Cross out the answers you know are incorrect so you can narrow your choices.

THE FREE-RESPONSE QUESTIONS

The free-response section tests your ability to write analytically.

There are two different types of free-response questions: style analysis and personal essay. For the style (or rhetorical) analysis question, you'll closely analyze a passage. In the personal essay question, you'll draw on evidence from your personal experience, observations, and/or reading.

How to Approach the Free-Response Questions

Here are our suggestions for successfully preparing for Section II of the test:

- Read the prompt. It's important to read the prompt carefully and understand everything it's asking you to do. If the prompt is lengthy, you may want to mark the most important parts so you can refer to them as you're working on your response without having to re-read the entire prompt.

- Remember to address all aspects of the question—test reviewers check that you at least attempted to do this. (Depending on the question, of course, you may be able to talk more about certain elements, and less about others, but it's always a good idea to address everything that you think the question is asking.) However, if the prompt asks you to write about *x* and you write a beautiful essay about *y*, you can only get a low score.

- Read the passage. Read the passage—with the prompt in mind—as many times as you need in order to get a detailed understanding of it. Your first reading should be to get a general understanding of the passage. In your second read-through, make notes about what you think the writer's purpose in the passage is. Mark any words, phrases, or sentences that contribute to the effect or meaning the author is trying to communicate. Use these notes as the groundwork for an outline of your essay.

- Brainstorm your thesis and evidence. Because of time limits, you won't have time to substantially revise your essay. This makes preparing for the essay crucial. By the time you begin writing, you should have written your thesis and made notes about evidence you can use to support it. However, keep in mind you have only 40 minutes to write the essay. Don't spend more than 10–12 minutes preparing.

- In your preparation, spend time making notes about why the passages you marked are important—that is, how they contribute to what the author is trying to achieve in the passage. Brainstorm other evidence and reasoning that support your thesis.

- Next, organize your evidence. Sketch out what will go in the first paragraph, the second, and so on.

- Write the essay. Once you have your thesis and evidence laid out the way you want them, begin writing. *Remember that you're being evaluated not only on **what** you say, but also **how** you say it.* Be sure that you know the meaning of all the words you use. Keep your audience in mind—you're writing for teachers, not peers.

- Don't worry too much about perfecting your style during the exam—if you have to choose between style and substance, focus on substance. A beautiful-sounding essay that says nothing can only earn a low grade. A substantial essay that has style errors here and there may not earn the highest grade, but it will still score high. The readers know that this is a first, not a final, draft.

- Always support your thesis with evidence from the text. If you make a statement about the passage, you should cite an example or quote from the passage to illustrate your point. Don't make unsupported claims about the passage or the writer.

- If you have time left over, read your essay and make minor adjustments as necessary. Keep in mind as you work that you must budget your time. You have two hours to write three essays; this means you have about 40 minutes per essay. Write down your start time, and check your watch often to stay on track. If you still haven't finished after 40 minutes, you know you either have to finish quickly, or risk losing time on your other essays.

Free-Response Strategies

The essay section of the AP exam asks you to respond to three questions in two hours. The suggested time for each essay is 40 minutes. Stay aware of time, but don't let it make you nervous. Although you want to be aware of the time you have for each question, don't rush through your answer. Each free-response essay should be substantial. That is, it should have a main point and evidence that supports that point. Being aware of the time you have to script each part of your answer will help you write a coherent essay. Place your watch on your desk, so you don't have to stop writing to check time. Before you begin answering the test question, calculate the time you have, the stop time, and the halfway point. Write these times down! At the halfway point, stop and assess how far you've gotten. If you're less than halfway through writing your essay, speed up your pace. If you're more than halfway through writing your essay, you might slow down your pace a bit. Make sure you budget time to proofread your completed essay—plan for about five minutes to read and proofread your writing.

Remember to read the essay prompt before you read the textual excerpt. Doing this will help you focus your reading. Take notes if you need to or underline sections of the prompt that are most important. During the AP exam, scratch paper will be provided. Use it to take notes on as you prepare for writing your essay.

Underline important sections in the textual excerpt that you may want to use as supporting evidence and take quick notes as you read. Think of your note-taking as creating an outline as you go. This way when you get to the end of the excerpt you'll already have some direction for your essay. You won't have time to write a rough draft and a second draft, so planning as you're reading and after you've finished reading the excerpt is very important.

Make sure before you begin writing that you understand the textual excerpt and the essay prompt. Also make sure that the evidence you've gathered from the text helps you construct a strong answer to the prompt. After you've completed your reading, underlining, and note-taking go back to the prompt and verify that you clearly understand what you're asked to write about. Next, check the supporting data that you underlined and the notes you took on scratch paper. Can you see the connections? Do you see a direction your essay should go? Now, begin drafting a clear and well-constructed answer, using the ideas and evidence you gathered while reading the prompt and the text.

Common Types of Essay Questions

Essay questions usually fall into one of the following categories.

- *Agree or Disagree:* These questions ask you to agree or disagree with an idea and to support your opinion. You can base your argument on evidence from your own experience or on a passage. This type of question requires that you be adept at persuasive writing.

- *Rhetorical Effects:* This type of essay question asks you to analyze the rhetorical devices in a passage. You'll need to be familiar with rhetorical devices and able to interpret their effects. Usually you'll need to discuss at least two devices.

- *Authorial Attitude or Purpose:* These questions ask you to discuss the author's attitude in a passage or his or her purpose in writing the passage. The type of essay required here is literary analysis. Your evidence will come from the passage, and you'll need to understand and describe elements such as tone, perspective, persona, and point of view.

- *Society and Human Nature:* These questions ask you to use your own experience to make a general statement about society or human nature. They may be introduced by a quotation, but are usually not based on a reading passage.

- *Comparison/Contrast:* Comparison/contrast questions ask you to analyze the similarities and differences between two passages. When answering these questions, it's important to write a thesis statement that goes beyond the obvious similarities and differences and shows the significance of putting the passages side by side.

Multiple-Choice Practice

The best way to get a sense of what the multiple-choice questions will be like is to go to the College Board's website and look at questions used on previous exams.

Go to www.collegeboard.com/ap/students/english/ and click on the links for "Sample Multiple-Choice Question Set #1" and "Sample Multiple-Choice Question Set #2." When you're finished reading the passage and answering the questions, click on the link at the bottom of the page that will bring you to the answers and rationales for the questions. How many questions did you answer correctly? Did your rationales match theirs?

On the following pages we've put together a practice set for you as well. Be sure to answer the questions on your own before turning to the sample answers.

SAMPLE MULTIPLE-CHOICE EXAM QUESTIONS

Directions: Read the passage below and answer the multiple-choice questions that follow. Then review our answers and read the rationales behind them.

Novels are excluded from "serious reading," so that the man who, bent on self-improvement, has been deciding to devote
Line ninety minutes three times a week to a
(5) complete study of the works of Charles Dickens will be well advised to alter his plans. The reason is not that novels are not serious—some of the great literature of the world is in the form of prose fiction—the reason is that
(10) bad novels ought not to be read, and that good novels never demand any appreciable mental application on the part of the reader. It is only the bad parts of Meredith's novels that are difficult. A good novel rushes you forward like
(15) a skiff down a stream, and you arrive at the end, perhaps breathless, but unexhausted. The best novels involve the least strain. Now in the cultivation of the mind one of the most important factors is precisely the feeling of
(20) strain, of difficulty, of a task which one part of you is anxious to achieve and another part of you is anxious to shirk; and that feeling cannot be got in facing a novel. You do not set your teeth in order to read *Anna Karenina*.
(25) Therefore, though you should read novels, you should not read them in those ninety minutes.

Imaginative poetry produces a far greater mental strain than novels. It produces probably the severest strain of any form of
(30) literature. It is the highest form of literature. It yields the highest form of pleasure, and teaches the highest form of wisdom. In a word, there is nothing to compare with it. I say this with sad consciousness of the fact that
(35) the majority of people do not read poetry.

I am persuaded that many excellent persons, if they were confronted with the alternatives of reading *Paradise Lost* and going round Trafalgar Square at noonday on
(40) their knees in sack-cloth, would choose the

ordeal of public ridicule. Still, I will never cease advising my friends and enemies to read poetry before anything.

If poetry is what is called "a sealed book"
(45) to you, begin by reading Hazlitt's famous essay on the nature of "poetry in general." It is the best thing of its kind in English, and no one who has read it can possibly be under the misapprehension that poetry is a mediaeval
(50) torture, or a mad elephant, or a gun that will go off by itself and kill at forty paces. Indeed, it is difficult to imagine the mental state of the man who, after reading Hazlitt's essay, is not urgently desirous of reading some poetry
(55) before his next meal. If the essay so inspires you I would suggest that you make a commencement with purely narrative poetry.

There is an infinitely finer English novel, written by a woman, than anything by George
(60) Eliot or the Brontes, or even Jane Austen, which perhaps you have not read. Its title is *Aurora Leigh*, and its author E.B. Browning. It happens to be written in verse, and to contain a considerable amount of genuinely fine
(65) poetry. Decide to read that book through, even if you die for it. Forget that it is fine poetry. Read it simply for the story and the social ideas. And when you have done, ask yourself honestly whether you still dislike poetry. I
(70) have known more than one person to whom *Aurora Leigh* has been the means of proving that in assuming they hated poetry they were entirely mistaken.

Of course, if, after Hazlitt, and such an
(75) experiment made in the light of Hazlitt, you are finally assured that there is something in you which is antagonistic to poetry, you must be content with history or philosophy. I shall regret it, yet not inconsolably. *The Decline*
(80) *and Fall* is not to be named in the same day

with *Paradise Lost*, but it is a vastly pretty thing; and Herbert Spencer's *First Principles* simply laughs at the claims of poetry and refuses to be accepted as aught but the most (85) majestic product of any human mind. I do not suggest that either of these works is suitable for a tyro in mental strains. But I see no reason why any man of average intelligence should not, after a year of continuous reading, (90) be fit to assault the supreme masterpieces of history or philosophy. The great convenience of masterpieces is that they are so astonishingly lucid.

I suggest no particular work as a start. The (95) attempt would be futile in the space of my command. But I have two general suggestions of a certain importance. The first is to define the direction and scope of your efforts. Choose a limited period, or a limited subject, (100) or a single author. Say to yourself: "I will know something about the French Revolution, or the rise of railways, or the works of John Keats." And during a given period, to be settled beforehand, confine yourself to your (105) choice. There is much pleasure to be derived from being a specialist.

The second suggestion is to think as well as to read. I know people who read and read, and for all the good it does them they might (110) just as well cut bread-and-butter. They take to reading as better men take to drink. They fly through the shires of literature on a motor-car, their sole object being motion. They will tell you how many books they have read in a year.

(115) Unless you give at least forty-five minutes to careful, fatiguing reflection (it is an awful bore at first) upon what you are reading, your ninety minutes of reading a night are chiefly wasted. This means that your pace will be slow. (120) Never mind.

Forget the goal; think only of the surrounding country; and after a period, perhaps when you least expect it, you will suddenly find yourself in a lovely town on a hill.

1. In the first paragraph, the author uses all of the following EXCEPT

    (A) evidence to prove his thesis
    (B) concrete examples to illustrate an argument
    (C) figurative language to explain an idea
    (D) a counterargument to further an argument
    (E) tone to establish ethos

2. The author's use of metaphor in this passage is intended to do what?

    (A) Help him establish an authoritative tone
    (B) Lend humor to the essay
    (C) Reinforce the evidence he presents to support his ideas
    (D) Demonstrate that figurative language is intellectually challenging
    (E) Demonstrate that poetry can be a pleasure to read

3. From the first paragraph of this passage we can infer that

   (A) the piece will show little respect for English writers such as Dickens
   (B) the author thinks that Dickens's work is illustrative of "serious reading"
   (C) the piece is intended for those interested in American literature
   (D) the piece is intended for those interested in self-improvement
   (E) the piece is intended for people looking for an easy read

4. The author's attitude toward people who read as many books as they can is best characterized as

   (A) admiring
   (B) disdainful
   (C) obsequious
   (D) envious
   (E) angry

5. In lines 79–85, *The Decline and Fall* is presented by the author as

   (A) "pretty," and therefore not serious
   (B) inferior to *Paradise Lost,* and therefore not worth reading
   (C) meritorious in its own way
   (D) much more challenging than *Paradise Lost*
   (E) much less challenging than *First Principles*

7. The tone of the piece as a whole is best described as

   (A) academic and formal
   (B) authoritative and empirical
   (C) dry and objective
   (D) cordial and advisory
   (E) condescending

8. From the context of lines 120–124, we can infer that "Never mind" means

   (A) "Never mind that you should reflect on the piece"
   (B) "Never mind that your 90 minutes will be wasted"
   (C) "Never mind that your pace is slow"
   (D) "Never mind that it is an awful bore at first"
   (E) "Never mind the surrounding country"

9. We can infer from lines 27–35 that the author thinks that
    - (A) difficulty is no more beneficial than ease
    - (B) difficulty causes emotional pain
    - (C) difficulty is beneficial
    - (D) pleasure brings wisdom
    - (E) most people are lazy and ignorant

10. The author of this passage uses the second-person point of view to
    - (A) describe his thoughts about serious reading
    - (B) deride those who read only for leisure
    - (C) give specific instructions about what kinds of poetry are considered serious reading
    - (D) encourage the reader to record their feelings about the poetry they read
    - (E) adopt the tone of a friend or adviser

11. *The Decline and Fall* and *First Principles* are mostly likely what kinds of works?
    - (A) *The Decline and Fall* is a work of imaginative poetry; *First Principles* is a work of narrative poetry
    - (B) *The Decline and Fall is* not serious reading; *First Principles* is a work of serious reading
    - (C) *The Decline and Fall* is a work of history; *First Principles* is a work of philosophy
    - (D) *The Decline and Fall* and *First Principles* are both about writing and reading poetry
    - (E) *The Decline and Fall* is not a masterpiece; *First Principles* is a masterpiece

Answers to Sample Multiple-Choice Exam Questions

1. (A)

The author of this piece doesn't give evidence to prove his thesis that novels aren't serious reading, although he does use the examples of Dickens and Meredith to illustrate his idea (B). He uses figurative language, specifically simile (see chapter 8), to explain his ideas: "A good novel rushes you forward like a skiff down a stream" (C). He also mentions a counterargument to further his own argument (D): saying that "some of the great literature of the world is in the form of prose fiction" strengthens his argument because it shows he's taken the opposite side into account. He uses tone (E) to create a persona of someone authoritative giving friendly advice (note the use of the second person, "you.")

2. (B)

Metaphors comparing reading poetry to "a mediaeval torture, or a mad elephant, or a gun that will go off by itself and kill at forty paces" serve to give the essay a lighthearted tone, even while discussing the value and rigor of "serious reading."

Answer (E) is incorrect because the metaphors illustrate the misconception that poetry is difficult to read. They don't try to show that poetry can be a pleasure to read (as the sentence "reading poetry is like eating candy" would, for example). The humor implied in these metaphors does little or nothing to establish authority (A), and has little to do with the evidence he presents to illustrate his ideas (C). And though the essay as a whole does demonstrate that figurative language is intellectually challenging (D), this is unrelated to the use of metaphor in this passage.

3. (D)

The paragraph argues that novels aren't serious reading, and that those interested in self-improvement shouldn't read them. The author ends the paragraph by telling the reader that he or she shouldn't read novels during the time set aside for serious reading. From this we can infer that his audience is interested in self-improvement through reading.

The author doesn't disrespect Dickens or novel writers; he admits that "some of the great literature of the world is in the form of prose fiction" (A). However, novels require too little from the reader to be of use in improving the mind, and are therefore not "serious reading" (B). His mention of Charles Dickens, an English writer, makes choice (C) an unlikely inference. Finally, his advice isn't aimed at people looking for an easy read (E).

4. (B)

In lines 106–114, the author derides these people by saying that "they take to reading as better men take to drink," and suggests that their goal in reading isn't to improve their thinking, but to impress others.

This attitude is in direct conflict with answers (A), (C), and (D), all of which suggest that he respects this kind of behavior. And though answer (E) is one possible interpretation of the author's attitude, it's somewhat overstated considering the subtlety with which this author makes his points throughout the rest of the essay.

5. (C)

The author says that *The Decline and Fall* [*of the Roman Empire*] may be inferior to *Paradise Lost*, but also that it is "a vastly pretty thing." In other words, Bennett is saying that it's an aesthetically rich piece, and thus meritorious in its own way. He says that if you can't read poetry, then read history or philosophy instead.

The author doesn't use "pretty" as the opposite of serious (A), nor does he imply that *The Decline and Fall* is more challenging than *Paradise Lost* (D), or less challenging than *First Principles* (E). Finally, though he does think *The Decline and Fall* is inferior to *Paradise Lost*, he still thinks it's worth reading (B).

6. (D)

The tone of the piece is friendly and warm—note the use of humorous metaphors (lines 23–27) and asides. For example, the author tells the reader that if they study history instead of poetry, "[he] shall regret it, though not inconsolably." The author has incorporated humor in this piece to make the advice he gives to the reader more palatable.

Though the author uses some polysyllabic words, the tone of this piece is more conversational than academic. He's not trying to prove a thesis, as academic writing does, only explain one (A). He does take a somewhat authoritative tone, but it's not empirical—it doesn't restrict itself to the material or the scientific (B). The tone isn't particularly dry. It's also not strictly objective: the author makes clear that this is his opinion (C). Finally, although the tone is "teacherly," it's going too far to say that it's condescending (E).

7. (C)

The sentence immediately preceding "Never mind" ("This means that your pace will be slow") and the one that follows it ("Forget the goal; think only of the surrounding country. . . .") imply that readers shouldn't worry that their pace is slow, and that they should enjoy the process of reading rather than worrying too much about the goal. It doesn't imply any of the other statements.

8. (C)

Here, the author says that poetry is the most difficult form of literature, producing the greatest "mental strain." He also says that it teaches "the highest form of wisdom." This means that he thinks the mental strain of reading poetry is beneficial to readers. Conversely, it can be implied that easy reading gives no such benefit, so we can eliminate choices (A) and (D). It isn't implied that difficulty causes emotional pain (B), and though the author suggests that most people don't read poetry, it's going too far to say he thinks that most people are lazy and ignorant (E).

9. (E)

The tone of the piece becomes more conversational and "teacherly" when the author switches to the second-person point of view. This is especially evident in lines 94–106.

Answer (A) would be more relevant to a question about first-person point of view, and (D) would be more relevant to the third-person point of view. The author doesn't go into much detail about what kinds of poetry are considered serious reading (C), and he never openly derides those who read only for pleasure, though he may gently criticize them (B).

10. (C)

The author alludes to both of these works as alternatives to poetry, not poetry itself (A), and he clearly intends both to be thought of as serious works (B) and masterpieces (E). The author says nothing to suggest that either book is about poetry (D).

Free-Response Practice

Your answer to the free-response questions will be evaluated according to a rubric, or a set of guidelines for evaluating student work. Each question has its own specific rubric.

The best way to get an idea of how answers are scored is to visit the College Board's website, which has questions, student answers, and scorer's comments from previous exams:

- Go to the following address and click on the links for free-response questions from earlier AP exams: www.collegeboard.com/ap/students/english/.

- Read the passages and the prompts. For each question, mark phrases and sections in the passage that could be used as evidence in an essay. Brainstorm a thesis, and sketch out evidence.

- From the same web page, link to the scoring guidelines, sample essays, and reader's comments.

- (On this page there are links to sample answers for both AP English Language and AP English Literature. Remember that the test you'll be taking is AP English Language.) Take notes as you read the sample answers and their evaluation, and answer our questions on the following page.

What do the papers that scored nines and eights have in common?

_____

_____

_____

_____

_____

Make a list of the criteria by which the papers were judged. Use the rubrics and the scorer's comments. For example, all papers must address the prompt in a detailed way. They must also have a clear thesis that analyzes rather than summarizes the text. What else?

_____

_____

_____

_____

_____

Based on your notes, what score might your own essays have received? How could you improve them to earn a higher score?

_____

_____

_____

_____

SAMPLE FREE-RESPONSE QUESTION

Directions: Review the free-response question below. Spend 40 minutes writing an essay in response to the prompt. You have only 40 minutes to read the passage, make notes, organize your thesis and evidence, and write your essay—just as you would if you were taking the real test.

When you've finished writing, compare your answer to the sample answer, then read about what makes the sample answer successful.

Free-Response Prompt

Read the passage below, from Emily Post's 1922 book *Etiquette*. Then write a carefully reasoned essay that analyzes how Post uses rhetorical and stylistic devices to achieve her purpose in the piece.

Etiquette
Emily Post

IDEAL conversation should be a matter of equal give and take, but too often it is all "take." The voluble talker—or chatterer—rides his own hobby straight through the hours without giving anyone else, who might also like to say something, a chance to do other than exhaustedly await the turn that never comes. Once in a while—a very long while—one meets a brilliant person whose talk is a delight; or still more rarely a wit who manipulates every ordinary topic with the agility of a sleight-of-hand performer, to the ever increasing rapture of his listeners.

But as a rule the man who has been led to believe that he is a brilliant and interesting talker has been led to make himself a rapacious pest. No conversation is possible between others whose ears are within reach of his ponderous voice; anecdotes, long-winded stories, dramatic and pathetic, stock his repertoire; but worst of all are his humorous yarns at which he laughs uproariously though every one else grows solemn and more solemn.

There is a simple rule, by which if one is a voluble chatterer (to be a good talker necessitates a good mind) one can at least refrain from being a pest or a bore. And the rule is merely, to stop and think.

"THINK BEFORE YOU SPEAK"

Nearly all the faults or mistakes in conversation are caused by not thinking. For instance, a first rule for behavior in society is: "Try to do and say those things only which will be agreeable to others." Yet how many people, who really know better, people who are perfectly capable of intelligent understanding if they didn't let their brains remain asleep or locked tight, go night after night to dinner parties, day after day to other social gatherings, and absent-mindedly prate about this or that without ever taking the trouble to think what they are saying and to whom they are saying it! Would a young mother describe twenty or thirty cunning tricks and sayings of the baby to a bachelor who has been helplessly put beside her at dinner if she thought? She would know very well, alas! that not even a very dear friend would really care for more than a hors d'oeuvre of the subject, at the board of general conversation.

The older woman is even worse, unless something occurs (often when it is too late) to make her wake up and realize that she not only bores her hearers but prejudices everyone against her children by the unrestraint of her own praise. The daughter who is continually lauded as the most captivating and beautiful girl in the world, seems to the wearied perceptions of enforced listeners annoying and plain. In the same way the "magnificent" son is handicapped by his mother's—or his father's—overweening pride and love in exact proportion to its displayed intensity. On the other hand, the neglected wife, the unappreciated husband, the misunderstood child, takes on a glamour in the eyes of others equally out of proportion. That great love has seldom perfect wisdom is one of the great tragedies in the drama of life. In the case of the overloving wife or mother, some one should love her enough to make her stop and think that her loving praise is not merely a question of boring her hearers but of handicapping unfairly those for whom she would gladly lay down her life—and yet few would have the courage to point out to her that she would far better lay down her tongue.

The cynics say that those who take part in social conversation are bound to be either the bores or the bored; and that which you choose to be, is a mere matter of selection. And there must be occasions in the life of everyone when the cynics seem to be right; the man of affairs who, sitting next to an attractive looking young woman, is regaled throughout dinner with the detailed accomplishments of the young woman's husband; the woman of intellect who must listen with interest to the droolings of an especially prosy man who holds forth on the super-everything of his own possessions, can not very well consider that the evening was worth dressing, sitting up, and going out for.

Answer to Sample Free-Response Prompt

In a passage from her 1922 book *Etiquette*, Emily Post uses tone and anecdotal examples to persuade her readers that they should not be too verbose at social occasions, and should "think before [they] speak."

To begin, Post uses a direct, disdainful, sophisticated, and witty tone to persuade her readers. First, Post's tone is direct and disdainful: she says openly that verbose talkers are bores, and makes no effort to hide her distaste for them. For example, she describes one hypothetical "pest" whose "anecdotes, long-winded stories, stock his repertoire; but worst of all are his humorous yarns at which he laughs uproariously though everyone else grows solemn and more solemn." In some places, this distaste intensifies into exasperation, such as in the sketch Post gives us of the mothers talking about their children. Post uses this tone to show how others will react to the reader if he or she talks too much. It reflects and reinforces her argument that talkers are disapproved of and disliked.

Second, Post's tone is sophisticated, which helps establish her ethos, or authority. Her persona is that of an expert and advice-giver; she is not a novice. Nor is she simply reflecting on a topic. She uses rhetorical devices to give her writing force and emphasis and to show off her control of language. For example, Post uses parallelism in the following sentence for emphasis: "the man who has been led to believe that he is a brilliant and interesting talker has been led to make himself a rapacious pest." Phrases such as "a wit who manipulates every . . . topic with the agility of a sleight-of-hand performer" uses metaphor for effect.

Third, Post's tone is witty. This makes her essay more entertaining. More importantly, however, it reinforces the sophisticated, "expert" persona she has created. Post is giving advice on how to socialize, and her wit proves that she is an expert at the kind of parlance and wordplay that was a part of socializing in her time. Consider the following example: "Ideal conversation should be a matter of equal give and take, but too often it is all 'take.'" For a more scathing example, consider the last half of paragraph five, where Post says of the loving, talkative mother that "some one should love her enough to make her stop."

In addition to tone, Post uses anecdotal examples to illustrate her argument and persuade her reader. She draws five detailed pictures of verbose talkers, all of which are scathingly critical. These give the reader a vivid negative image, not only of the talkers but also of the disdain they arouse in other people. For example, it's not enough that the verbose talker in paragraph two is pathetic; Post also tells us that no one laughs at his jokes. This is a subtle appeal to the reader's fear of committing social blunders. It is also a veiled threat: if you act like this, you will be disliked by others. This fear sets the stage for her solution, which is to "think before you speak."

In sum, Post uses tone and anecdotal examples to persuade her readers to refrain from talking too much, and to think before they speak.

Analysis of Sample Response

What makes this essay successful?

- It doesn't just sum up what stylistic and rhetorical elements Post uses. It analyzes *how* she uses tone and evidence to achieve her purpose.

- The thesis clearly states the purpose Post is trying to achieve. It also clearly states which elements will be discussed (tone and anecdotal examples).

- The paragraphs are clearly organized, with the first three paragraphs given to tone and the last to use of anecdotal examples. Each paragraph is headed by a topic sentence that sums up the main idea.

- Each idea in the body is supported by a specific quote or reference to the text.

- The essay refers to specific examples of rhetorical devices like parallelism and metaphor.

- The conclusion sums up the essay and restates the thesis.

- The essay is well-written and clear, with no distracting grammatical or stylistic errors.

- This essay serves as a model; it is more polished than a first draft essay. Keep in mind that you won't have time to rewrite your essay to a final-draft level of quality.

FREE-RESPONSE EXERCISE

In this activity you'll practice answering two free-response questions. The standard length of time for a free-response question is 40 minutes. However, in this activity, allow yourself a bit more time for the questions, since their readings are substantially longer than those on the exam. Be aware of your time as you answer each question. Your essays should be approximately the same length, the equivalent of no more than one single-spaced, typed page.

Question 1 (Suggested time—40 minutes)

Read Chief Seattle's Treaty Oration (as it was originally published in the *Seattle Sunday Star* on October 29, 1887). Chief Seattle purportedly gave this speech in 1854.

Prompt: Write an essay in which you identify two rhetorical devices in the speech that would make it especially powerful to the listener. In your essay, address how these rhetorical devices synchronize with the content of Chief Seattle's speech and its purpose. Use textual evidence from the speech to support your ideas.

Treaty Oration
Chief Seattle

Yonder sky that has wept tears of compassion upon my people for centuries untold, and which to us appears changeless and eternal, may change. Today is fair. Tomorrow it may be overcast with clouds. My words are like the stars that never change. Whatever Seattle says the great chief at Washington can rely upon with as much certainty as he can upon the return of the sun or the seasons. The White Chief says that Big Chief at Washington sends us greetings of friendship and goodwill. This is kind of him for we know he has little need of our friendship in return. His people are many. They are like the grass that covers vast prairies. My people are few. They resemble the scattering trees of a storm-swept plain. The great—and I presume—good White Chief sends us word that he wishes to buy our lands but is willing to allow us enough to live comfortably. This indeed appears just, even generous, for the Red Man no longer has rights that he need respect, and the offer may be wise also, as we are no longer in need of an extensive country.

There was a time when our people covered the land as the waves of a wind-ruffled sea cover its shell paved floor, but that time long since passed away with the greatness of tribes that are now but a mournful memory. I will not dwell on, nor mourn over, our untimely decay, nor reproach my paleface brothers with hastening it, as we too may have been somewhat to blame.

Youth is impulsive. When our young men grow angry at some real or imaginary wrong, and disfigure their faces with black paint, it denotes that their hearts are black, and that they are often cruel and relentless, and our old men and old women are unable to restrain them. Thus it has ever been. Thus it was when the white man first began to push our forefathers westward. But let us hope that the hostilities between us may never return. We would have everything to lose and nothing to gain. Revenge by young men is considered gain, even at the cost of their own lives, but old men who stay at home in times of war, and mothers who have sons to lose, know better.

Our good father at Washington—for I presume he is now our father as well as yours, since King George has moved his boundaries further north—our great and good father, I say, sends us word that if we do as he desires he will protect us. His brave warriors will be to us a bristling wall of strength, and his wonderful ships of war will fill our harbors so that our ancient enemies far to the northward—the Hydas and Tsimpsians—will cease to frighten our women, children and old men. Then in reality will he be our father and we his children, but can that ever be? Your God is not our God! Your God loves your people and hates mine. He folds his strong protecting arms lovingly about the pale face and leads him by the hand as a father leads his infant son—but He has forsaken His red children—if they really are His. Our God, the Great Spirit, seems also to have forsaken us. Your God makes your people wax strong every day. Soon they will fill all the land. Our people are ebbing away like a rapidly receding tide that will never return. The white man's God cannot love our people or He would protect them. They seem to be orphans who can look nowhere for help. How then can we be brothers? How can your God become our God and renew our prosperity and awaken in us dreams of returning greatness. If we have a common heavenly father He must be partial—for He came to His paleface children. We never saw Him. He gave you laws but had no word for his red children whose teeming multitudes once filled this vast continent as stars fill the firmament. No; we are two distinct races with separate origins and separate destinies. There is little in common between us.

To us the ashes of our ancestors are sacred and their resting-place is hallowed ground. You wander far from the graves of your ancestors and seemingly without regret. Your religion was written upon tables of stone by the iron finger of your God so that you could not forget. The Red Man could never comprehend nor remember it. Our religion is the traditions of our ancestors—the dreams of our old men, given them in the solemn hours of night by the Great Spirit; and the visions of our sachems, and is written in the hearts of our people.

Your dead cease to love you and the land of their nativity as soon as they pass the portals of the tomb and wander way beyond the stars. They are soon forgotten and never return. Our dead never forget the beautiful world that gave them being. They still love its verdant valleys, its murmuring rivers, its magnificent mountains, sequestered vales and verdant lined lakes and bays, and ever yearn in tender, fond affection over the lonely hearted living, and often return from the Happy Hunting Ground to visit, guide, console and comfort them.

Day and night cannot dwell together. The Red Man has ever fled the approach of the White Man, as the morning mist flees before the morning sun.

However, your proposition seems fair and I think that my people will accept it and will retire to the reservation you offer them. Then we will dwell in peace, for the words of the Great White Chief seem to be the words of nature speaking to my people out of dense darkness.

It matters little where we pass the remnant of our days. They will not be many. The Indians' night promises to be dark. Not a single star of hope hovers above his horizon. Sad-voiced winds moan in the distance. Grim fate seems to be on the Red Man's trail, and wherever he goes he will hear the approaching footsteps of his fell destroyer and prepare stolidly to meet his doom, as does the wounded doe that hears the approaching footsteps of the hunter.

A few more moons, a few more winters, and not one of the descendants of the mighty hosts that once moved over this broad land or lived in happy homes, protected by the Great Spirit, will remain to mourn over the graves of a people-once more powerful and hopeful than yours. But why should I mourn at the untimely fate of my people? Tribe follows tribe, and nation follows nation like the waves of the sea. It is the order of nature, and regret is useless.

Your time of decay may be distant, but it will surely come, for even the White Man whose God walked and talked with him as friend with friend, cannot be exempt from the common destiny. We may be brothers after all. We will see.

We will ponder your proposition and when we decide we will let you know. But should we accept it, I here and now make this condition that we will not be denied the privilege without molestation of visiting at any time the tombs of our ancestors, friends and children. Every part of this soil is sacred in the estimation of my people. Every hillside, every valley, every plain and grove, has been hallowed by some sad or happy event in days long vanished. Even the rocks, which seem to be dumb and dead as they swelter in the sun along the silent shore, thrill with memories of stirring events connected with the lives of my people, and the very dust upon which you now stand responds more lovingly to their footsteps than to yours, because it is rich with the blood of our ancestors and our bare feet are conscious of the sympathetic touch. Our departed braves, fond mothers, glad, happy-hearted maidens, and even our little children who lived here and rejoiced here for a brief season, will love these somber solitude's and at eventide they greet shadowy returning spirits. And when the last Red Man shall have perished, and the memory of my tribe shall have become a myth among the White Men, these shores will swarm with the invisible dead of my tribe, and when your children's children think themselves alone in the field, the store, the shop, upon the highway, or in the silence of the pathless woods, they will not be alone. In all the earth there is no place dedicated to solitude. At night when the streets of your cities and villages are silent and you think them deserted, they will throng with the returning hosts that once filled them and still love this beautiful land. The White Man will never be alone.

Let him be just and deal kindly with my people, for the dead are not powerless. Dead, did I say? There is no death, only a change of worlds.

FREE-RESPONSE PRACTICE

Question 2 (Suggested time—50 minutes)

Read Frederick Douglass's essay "Learning to Read" and respond to the essay prompt below. This essay comes from Douglass's longer work, *Narrative of the Life of Frederick Douglass, An American Slave, Written by Himself*, published in 1845.

Prompt: In this piece Douglass discusses how he learned to read and write. He talks about how the ability to read empowers him and how it ensnares him. Write an essay in which you analyze why Douglass would "at times feel that learning to read had been a curse rather than a blessing." Use textual evidence from Douglass's essay to discuss the tension between the empowering and the ensnaring aspects of literacy.

Learning to Read
Frederick Douglass

I lived in Master Hugh's family about seven years. During this time, I succeeded in learning to read and write. In accomplishing this, I was compelled to resort to various stratagems. I had no regular teacher. My mistress, who had kindly commenced to instruct me, had, in compliance with the advice and direction of her husband, not only ceased to instruct, but had set her face against my being instructed by any one else. It is due, however, to my mistress to say of her, that she did not adopt this course of treatment immediately. She at first lacked the depravity indispensable to shutting me up in mental darkness. It was at least necessary for her to have some training in the exercise of irresponsible power, to make her equal to the task of treating me as though I were a brute.

My mistress was, as I have said, a kind and tender-hearted woman; and in the simplicity of her soul she commenced, when I first went to live with her, to treat me as she supposed one human being ought to treat another. In entering upon the duties of a slaveholder, she did not seem to perceive that I sustained to her the relation of a mere chattel, and that for her to treat me as a human being was not only wrong, but dangerously so. Slavery proved as injurious to her as it did to me. When I went there, she was a pious, warm, and tender-hearted woman. There was no sorrow or suffering for which she had not a tear. She had bread for the hungry, clothes for the naked, and comfort for every mourner that came within her reach. Slavery soon proved its ability to divest her of these heavenly qualities. Under its influence, the tender heart became stone, and the lamblike disposition gave way to one of tiger-like fierceness. The first step in her downward course was in her ceasing to instruct me. She now commenced to practise her husband's precepts. She finally became even more violent in her opposition than her husband himself. She was not satisfied with simply doing as well as he had commanded: she seemed anxious to do better. Nothing seemed to make her more angry than to see me with a newspaper. She seemed to think that here lay the danger. I have had her rush at me with a face made all up of fury, and snatch from me a newspaper, in a manner that fully, revealed her apprehension. She was an apt woman; and a little experience soon demonstrated, to her satisfaction, that education and slavery were incompatible with each other.

From this time I was most narrowly watched. If I was in a separate room any considerable length of time, I was sure to be suspected of having a book, and was at once called to give an account of myself. All this, however, was too late. The first step had been taken. Mistress, in teaching me the alphabet, had given me the inch, and no precaution could prevent me from taking the ell.

The plan which I adopted, and the one by which I was most successful, was that of making friends of all the little white boys whom I met in the street. As many of these as I could, I converted into teachers. With their kindly aid, obtained at different times and in different places, I finally succeeded in learning to read. When I was sent of errands, I always took my book with me, and by going one part of my errand quickly, I found time to get a lesson before my return. I used also to carry bread with me, enough of which was always in the house, and to which I was always welcome; for I was much better off in this regard than many of the poor white children in our neighborhood. This bread I used to bestow upon the hungry little urchins, who, in return, would give me that more valuable bread of knowledge. I am strongly tempted to give the names of two or three of those little boys, as a testimonial of the gratitude and affection I bear them; but prudence forbids;—not that it would injure me, but it might embarrass them; for it is almost an unpardonable offence to teach slaves to read in this Christian country. It is enough to say of the dear little fellows, that they lived on Philpot Street, very near Durgin and Bailey's ship-yard. I used to talk this matter of slavery over with them. I would sometimes say to them, I wished I could be as free as they would be when they got to be men. "You will be free as soon as you are twenty-one, *but I am a slave for life!* Have not I as good a right to be free as you have?" These words used to trouble them; they would express for me the liveliest sympathy, and console me with the hope that something would occur by which I might be free.

I was now about twelve years old, and the thought of being *a slave for life* began to bear heavily upon my heart. Just about this time, I got hold of a book entitled "The Columbian Orator." Every opportunity I got, I used to read this book. Among much of other interesting matter, I found in it a dialogue between a master and his slave. The slave was represented as having run away from his master three times. The dialogue represented the conversation which took place between them, when the slave was retaken the third time. In this dialogue, the whole argument in behalf of slavery was brought forward by the master, all of which was disposed of by the slave. The slave was made to say some very smart as well as impressive things in reply to his master— things which had the desired though unexpected effect; for the conversation resulted in the voluntary emancipation of the slave on the part of the master.

In the same book, I met with one of Sheridan's mighty speeches on and in behalf of Catholic emancipation. These were choice documents to me. I read them over and over again with unabated interest. They gave tongue to interesting thoughts of my own soul, which had frequently flashed through my mind, and died away for want of utterance. The moral which I gained from the dialogue was the power of truth over the conscience of even a slaveholder. What I got from Sheridan was a bold denunciation of slavery, and a powerful vindication of human rights. The reading of these documents enabled me to utter my thoughts, and to meet the arguments brought forward to sustain slavery; but while they relieved me of one difficulty, they brought on another even more painful than the one of which I was relieved. The more I read, the more I was led to abhor and detest my enslavers. I could regard them in no other light than a band of successful robbers, who had left their homes, and gone to Africa, and stolen us from our homes, and in a strange land reduced us to slavery. I loathed them as being the meanest as well as the most wicked of men. As I read and contemplated the subject, behold! that very discontentment which Master Hugh had predicted would follow my learning to read had already come, to torment and sting my soul to unutterable anguish. As I writhed under it, I would at times feel that learning to read had been a curse rather than a blessing. It had given me a view of my wretched condition, without the remedy. It opened my eyes to the horrible pit, but to no ladder upon which to get out. In moments of agony, I envied my fellow-slaves for their stupidity. I have often wished myself a beast. I preferred the condition of the meanest reptile to my own. Anything, no matter what, to get rid of thinking! It was this everlasting thinking of my condition that tormented me. There was no getting rid of it. It was pressed upon me by every object within sight or hearing, animate or inanimate. The silver trump of freedom had roused my soil to eternal wakefulness. Freedom now appeared, to disappear no more forever. It was heard in every sound, and seen in every thing. It was ever present to torment me with a sense of my wretched condition. I saw nothing without seeing it, I heard nothing without hearing it, and felt nothing without feeling it. It looked from every star, it smiled in every calm, breathed in every wind, and moved in every storm.

I often found myself regretting my own existence, and wishing myself dead; and but for the hope of being free, I have no doubt but that I should have killed myself, or done something for which I should have been killed. While in this state of mind, I was eager to hear any one speak of slavery. I was a ready listener. Every little while, I could hear something about the abolitionists. It was some time before I found what the word meant. It was always used in such connections as to make it an interesting word to me. If a slave ran away and succeeded in getting clear, or if a slave killed his master, set fire to a barn, or did any thing very wrong in the mind of a slaveholder, it was spoken of as the fruit of *abolition*. Hearing the word in this connection very often, I set about learning what it meant. The dictionary afforded me little or no help. I found it was "the act of abolishing"; but then I did not know what was to be abolished. Here I was perplexed. I did not dare to ask any one about its meaning, for I was satisfied that it was something they wanted me to know very little about. After a patient waiting, I got one of our city papers, containing an account of the number of petitions from the north, praying for the abolition of slavery in the District of Columbia, and of the slave trade between the States. From this time I understood the words *abolition* and *abolitionist*, and always drew near when that word was spoken, expecting to hear something of importance to myself and fellow-slaves. The light broke in upon me by degrees. I went one day down on the wharf of Mr. Waters; and seeing two Irishmen unloading a scow of stone, I went, unasked, and helped them. When we had finished, one of them came to me and asked me if I were a slave. I told him I was. He asked, "Are ye a slave for life?" I told him that I was. The good Irishman seemed to be deeply affected by the statement. He said to the other that it was a pity so fine a little fellow as myself should be a slave for life. He said it was a shame to hold me. They both advised me to run away to the north; that I should find friends there, and that I should be free. I pretended not to be interested in what they said, and treated them as if I did not understand them; for I feared they might be treacherous. White men have been known to encourage slaves to escape, and then, to get the reward, catch them and return them to their masters. I was afraid that these seemingly good men might use me so; but I nevertheless remembered their advice, and from that time I resolved to run away. I looked forward to a time at which it would be safe for me to escape. I was too young to think of doing so immediately; besides, I wished to learn how to write, as I might have occasion to write my own pass. I consoled myself with the hope that I should one day find a good chance. Meanwhile, I would learn to write.

The idea as to how I might learn to write was suggested to me by being in Durgin and Bailey's ship-yard, and frequently seeing the ship carpenters, after hewing, and getting a piece of timber ready for use, write on the timber the name of that part of the ship for which it was intended. When a piece of timber was intended for the larboard side, it would be marked thus—"L." When a piece was for the starboard side, it would be marked thus—"S." A piece for the larboard side forward, would be marked thus—"L. F." When a piece was for starboard side forward, it would be marked thus—"S.F." For larboard aft, it would be marked thus—"L. A." For starboard aft, it would be marked thus—"S. A." I soon learned the names of these letters, and for what they were intended when placed upon a piece of timber in the shipyard. I immediately commenced copying them, and in a short time was able to make the four letters named. After that when I met with any boy who I knew could write, I would tell him I could write as well as he. The next word would be, "I don't believe you. Let me see you try it." I would then make the letters which I had been so fortunate as to learn, and ask him to beat that. In this way I got a good many lessons in writing, which it is quite possible I should never have gotten in any other way. During this time, my copy-book was the board fence, brick wall, and pavement; my pen and ink was a lump of chalk. With these, I learned mainly how to write. I then commenced and continued copying the Italics in Webster's Spelling Book, until I could make them all without looking on the book. By this time, my little Master Thomas had gone to school, and learned how to write, and had written over a number of copy-books. These had been brought home, and shown to some of our near neighbors, and then laid aside. My mistress used to go to class meeting at the Wilk Street meetinghouse every Monday afternoon, and leave me to take care of the house. When left thus, I used to spend the time in writing in the spaces left in Master Thomas's copy-book, copying what he had written. I continued to do this until I could write a hand very similar to that of Master Thomas. Thus, after a long, tedious effort for years, I finally succeeded in learning how to write.

Self-Assessment

One way to improve your writing is to look at it with a critical eye. If you can answer questions about what your writing does well and where it needs improvement, you'll become a stronger and more careful writer.

In this activity you'll study your writing, answer questions about it, and generate ideas for revision. Even though you won't actually rewrite, thinking about ways to revise your writing will help you see different ways to communicate your ideas.

You should complete the self-assessment workshop below for each essay. Answer all the questions for one essay before you move on to the next essay. Make sure your answers are complete. Each answer should be at least two or three sentences long. Reading the two essays and answering the questions for each one should take you about 45 minutes.

Self-Assessment Workshop

1. Read through your essay, and then write a five-sentence summary of it.

2. Each free-response question contains a specific prompt. To what extent does your response stays on topic and fully answer the question at hand? Does your essay respond to the essay question adequately? If so, write two sentences that explain why you feel you've done a good job answering the question. If not, write two sentences that explain why you feel you haven't done a good job.

3. What textual or observational evidence did you use to develop your main point? Identify your strongest piece of evidence and write two sentences that explain what it helps you communicate. Identify your weakest piece of evidence and write two sentences that explain how it could better help you develop your point.

4. Describe the way you've organized your essay. Do you have different sections that are distinguishable from each other (an introduction, a body, a conclusion)? Is your essay organized in a logical fashion? Do the ideas follow each other such that your reader can understand your point? Make an outline of your essay to help answer these questions.

5. As you look at your organization, also think back to your time management. Does your essay show the results of hurried writing toward the end? Is the first essay response stronger and more complete than the second essay response? Either of these tendencies in your writing may indicate a need for more awareness of time as you write.

6. Both of the free-response preparation questions asked you to write about a different aspect or topic. In the first question you were asked to identify two rhetorical devices in Chief Seattle's speech and to discuss the effect they might have on a listener. In the second question you needed to analyze a tension in Frederick Douglass's writing. When you think back to writing these essays, which of them did you find easiest, and which, most difficult? Figure out why this was the case. Were certain of the questions easier to understand than others? Is there a particular style of question you like to write about? Is it easier for you to respond to a concrete quotation than to a longer selection or an entire essay? Determining where your response comforts and discomforts lie will help you prepare for the exam. You can begin to develop strategies about responding to the free-response questions as you discover the kinds of questions you like and dislike.

READING TECHNIQUES

Section III

Modeling Inquiry

Becoming a more engaged critical reader involves asking questions that probe more deeply into texts. You'll always want to ask a set of basic study questions of each text. But after that, you can ask more penetrating questions. The questions in this activity move from your observations about details of the text "Stranger in the Village" by James Baldwin, to the significance, or meaning, of those observations.

PRACTICE READING

To complete this activity, read James Baldwin's "Stranger in the Village," from his 1955 work *Notes of a Native Son*. Then answer the critical reading questions below. Our answers follow the text.

Critical Reading Questions

1. What is this piece about?

2. How is the piece structured?

3. How does the structure affect the topic of the piece?

4. How would you describe the language of the piece?

5. What might the changes in language in the text have to do with the topic of racial difference in the text?

6. To whom is the piece addressed?

7. How does the text construct the narrator's relationship with the reader?

8. What effect does the piece have on the reader?

9. Near the end of the essay, the narrator writes, "The cathedral at Chartres, I have said, says something to the people of this village which it cannot say to me; but it is important to understand that this cathedral says something to me which it cannot say to them." Why is it important for the narrator to relate what the cathedral says to him?

10. What is the purpose, or goal, of the piece?

11. Is the piece effective at its goal? Why?

Stranger in the Village
James Baldwin

From ALL available evidence no black man had ever set foot in this tiny Swiss village before I came. I was told before arriving that I would probably be a "sight" for the village; I took this to mean that people of my complexion were rarely seen in Switzerland, and also that city people are always something of a "sight" outside of the city. It did not occur to me—possibly because I am an American—that there could be people anywhere who had never seen a Negro.

It is a fact that cannot be explained on the basis of the inaccessibility of the village. The village is very high, but it is only four hours from Milan and three hours from Lausanne. It is true that it is virtually unknown. Few people making plans for a holiday would elect to come here. On the other hand, the villagers are able, presumably, to come and go as they please—which they do: to another town at the foot of the mountain, with a population of approximately five thousand, the nearest place to see a movie or go to the bank. In the village there is no movie house, no bank, no library, no theater; very few radios, one jeep, one station wagon; and, at the moment, one typewriter, mine, an invention which the woman next door to me here had never seen. There are about six hundred people living here, all Catholic—I conclude this from the fact that the Catholic church is open all year round, whereas the Protestant chapel, set off on a hill a little removed from the village, is open only in the summertime when the tourists arrive. There are four or five hotels, all closed now, and four or five *bistros*, of which, however, only two do any business during the winter. These two do not do a great deal, for life in the village seems to end around nine or ten o'clock. There are a few stores, butcher, baker, *épicerie*, a hardware store, and a money-changer—who cannot change travelers' checks, but must send them down to the bank, an operation which takes two or three days. There is something called the *Ballet Haus,* closed in the winter and used for God knows what, certainly not ballet, during the summer. There seems to be only one schoolhouse in the village, and this for the quite young children; I suppose this to mean that their older brother and sisters at some point descend from these mountains in order to complete their education—possibly, again, to the town just below. The landscape is absolutely forbidding, mountains towering on all four sides, ice and snow as far as the eye can reach. In this white wilderness, men and women and children move all day, carrying washing, wood, buckets of milk or water, sometimes skiing on Sunday afternoons. All week long boys and young men are to be seen shoveling snow off the rooftops, or dragging wood clown from the forest in sleds.

The village's only real attraction, which explains the tourist season, is the hot spring water. A disquietingly high proportion of these tourists are cripples, or semi-cripples, who come year after year—from other parts of Switzerland, usually—to take the waters. This lends the village, at the height of the season, a rather terrifying air of sanctity, as though it were a lesser Lourdes. There is often something beautiful, there is always something awful, in the spectacle of a person who has lost one of his faculties, a faculty he never questioned until it was gone, and who struggles to recover it. Yet people remain people, on crutches or indeed on deathbeds;

KAPLAN

and wherever I passed, the first summer I was here, among the native villagers or among the lame, a wind passed with me—of astonishment, curiosity, amusement, and outrage. That first summer I stayed two weeks and never intended to return. But I did return in the winter, to work; the village offers, obviously, no distractions whatever and has the further advantage of being extremely cheap. Now it is winter again, a year later, and I am here again. Everyone in the village knows my name, though they scarcely ever use it, knows that I come from America—though, this, apparently, they will never really believe: black men come from Africa—and everyone knows that I am the friend of the son of a woman who was born here, and that I am staying in their chalet. But I remain as much a stranger today as I was the first day I arrived, and the children shout *Neger!* *Neger!* as I walk along the streets.

It must be admitted that in the beginning I was far too shocked to have any real reaction. In so far as I reacted at all, I reacted by trying to be pleasant—it being a great part of the American Negro's education (long before he goes to school) that he must make people "like" him. This smiles-and-the-world-smiles-with-you routine worked about as well in this situation as it had in the situation for which it was designed, which is to say that it did not work at all. No one, after all, can be liked whose human weight and complexity cannot be, or has not been, admitted. My smile was simply another unheard-of phenomenon which allowed them to see my teeth—they did not, really, see my smile and I began to think that, should I take to snarling, no one would notice any difference. All of the physical characteristics of the Negro which had caused me, in America, a very different and almost forgotten pain were nothing less than miraculous—or infernal—in the eyes of the village people. Some thought my hair was the color of tar, that it had the texture of wire, or the texture of cotton. It was jocularly suggested that I might let it all grow long and make myself a winter coat. If I sat in the sun for more than five minutes some daring creature was certain to come along and gingerly put his fingers on my hair, as though he were afraid of an electric shock, or put his hand on my hand, astonished that the color did not rub off. In all of this, in which it must be conceded there was the charm of genuine wonder and in which there was certainly no element of intentional unkindness, there was yet no suggestion that I was human: I was simply a living wonder.

I knew that they did not mean to be unkind, and I know it now; it is necessary, nevertheless, for me to repeat this to myself each time that I walk out of the chalet. The children who shout *Neger!* have no way of knowing the echoes this sound raises in me. They are brimming with good humor and the more daring swell with pride when I stop to speak with them. Just the same, there are days when I cannot pause and smile, when I have no heart to play with them; when indeed, I mutter sourly to myself, exactly as I muttered on the streets of a city these children have never seen, when I was no bigger than these children are now: *Your* mother *was a nigger.* Joyce is right about history being a nightmare—but it may be the nightmare from which no one *can* awaken. People are trapped in history and history is trapped in them.

There is a custom in the village—I am told it is repeated in many villages—of "buying" African natives for the purpose of converting them to Christianity. There stands in the church all year round a small box with a slot for money, decorated with a black figurine, and into this box the villagers drop their francs. During the *carnaval* which precedes Lent, two village children have their faces blackened—out of which bloodless darkness their blue eyes shine like ice—and fantastic horsehair wigs are placed on their blond heads; thus disguised, they solicit among the villagers for money for the missionaries in Africa. Between the box in the church and the blackened children the village "bought" last year six or eight African natives.

This was reported to me with pride by the wife of one of the *bistro* owners and I was careful to express astonishment and pleasure at the solicitude shown by the village for the souls of black folk. The *bistro* owner's wife beamed with a pleasure far more genuine than my own and seemed to feel that I might now breathe more easily concerning the souls of at least six of my kinsmen.

I tried not to think of these so lately baptized kinsmen, of the price paid for them, or the peculiar price they themselves would pay, and said nothing about my father, who having taken his own conversion too literally never, at bottom, forgave the white world (which he described as heathen) for having saddled him with a Christ in whom, to judge at least from their treatment of him, they themselves no longer believed. I thought of white men arriving for the first time in an African village, strangers there, as I am a stranger here, and tried to imagine the astounded populace touching their hair and marveling at the color of their skin. But there is a great difference between being the first white man to be seen by Africans and being the first black man to be seen by whites. The white man takes the astonishment as tribute, for he arrives to conquer and to convert the natives, whose inferiority in relation to himself is not even to be questioned; whereas I, without a thought of conquest, find myself among a people whose culture controls me, has even, in a sense, created me, people who have cost me more in anguish and rage than they will ever know, who yet do not even know of my existence. The astonishment with which I might have greeted them, should they have stumbled into my African village a few hundred years ago, might have rejoiced their hearts. But the astonishment with which they greet me today can only poison mine.

And this is so despite everything I may do to feel differently, despite my friendly conversations with the *bistro* owner's wife, despite their three-year-old son who has at least become my friend, despite the *saluts* and *bonsoirs* which I exchange with people as I walk, despite the fact that I know that no individual can be taken to task for what history is doing, or has done. I say that the culture of these people controls me—but they can scarcely be held responsible for European culture. America comes out of Europe, but these people have never seen America, nor have most of them seen more of Europe than the hamlet at the foot of their mountain. Yet they move with an authority which I shall never have; and they regard me, quite rightly, not only as a stranger in their village but as a suspect latecomer, bearing no credentials, to everything they have—however unconsciously—inherited.

For this village, even were it incomparably more remote and incredibly more primitive, is the West, the West onto which I have been so strangely grafted. These people cannot be, from the point of view of power, strangers anywhere in the world; they have made the modern world, in effect, even if they do not know it. The most illiterate among them is related, in a way that I am not, to Dante, Shakespeare, Michelangelo, Aeschylus, Da Vinci, Rembrandt, and Racine; the cathedral at Chartres says something to them which it cannot say to me, as indeed would New York's Empire State Building, should anyone here ever see it. Out of their hymns and dances come Beethoven and Bach. Go back a few centuries and they are in their full glory—but I am in Africa, watching the conquerors arrive.

The range of the disesteemed is personally fruitless, but it is is also absolutely inevitable; this rage, so generally discounted, so little understood even among the people whose daily bread it is, is one of the things that makes history. Rage can only with difficulty, and never entirely, be brought under the domination of the intelligence and is therefore not susceptible to any arguments whatever. This is a fact which ordinary representatives of the *Herrenvolk*, having never felt this rage and being unable to imagine it, quite fail to understand, Also, rage cannot be hidden, it can only be dissembled. This dissembling deludes the thoughtless, and strengthens rage and adds, to rage, contempt. There are, no doubt, as many ways of coping with the resulting complex of tensions as there arc black men in the world, but no black man can hope ever to be entirely liberated from this internal warfare—rage, dissembling, and contempt having inevitably accompanied his first realization of the power of white men. What is crucial here is that, since white men represent in the black man's world so heavy a weight, white men have for black men a reality which is far from being reciprocal; and hence all black men have toward all white men an attitude which is designed, really, either to rob the white man of the jewel of his naïveté, or else to make it cost him dear.

The black man insists, by whatever means he finds at his disposal, that the white man cease to regard him as an exotic rarity and recognize him as a human being. This is a very charged and difficult moment, for there is a great deal of will power involved in the white man's naïveté. Most people are not naturally reflective any, more than they are naturally malicious, and the white man prefers to keep the black man at a certain human remove because it is easier for him thus to preserve his simplicity and avoid being called to account for crimes committed by his forefathers, or his neighbors. He is inescapably aware, nevertheless, that he is in a better position in the world than black men are, nor can he quite put to death the suspicion that he is hated by black men therefore. He does not wish to be hated, neither does he wish to change places, and at this point in his uneasiness he can scarcely avoid having recourse to those legends which white men have created about black men, the most usual effect of which is that the white man finds himself enmeshed, so to speak, in his own language which describes hell, as well as the attributes which lead one to hell, as being as black as night.

Every legend, moreover, contains its residuum of truth, and the root function of language is to control the universe by describing it. It is of quite considerable significance that black men remain, in the imagination, and in overwhelming numbers in fact, beyond the disciplines of salvation; and this despite the fact that the West has been "buying" African natives for centuries. There is, I should hazard, an instantaneous necessity to be divorced from this so visibly unsaved stranger, in whose heart, moreover, one cannot guess what dreams of vengeance are being nourished; and, at the same time, there are few things on earth more attractive than the idea of the unspeakable liberty which is allowed the unredeemed. When, beneath black mask, a human being begins to make himself felt one cannot escape a certain awful wonder as to what kind of human being it is. What one's imagination makes of other people is dictated, of course, by the laws of one's own personality and it is one of the ironies of black-white relations that, by means of what the white man imagines the black man to be, the black man is enabled to know who the white man is.

I have said, for example, that I am as much a stranger in this village today as I was the first summer I arrived, but this is not quite true. The villagers wonder less about the texture of my hair than they did then, and wonder rather more about me. And the fact that their wonder now exists on another level is reflected in their attitudes and in their eyes. There are the children who make those delightful, hilarious, sometimes astonishingly grave overtures of friendship in the unpredictable fashion of children; other children, having been taught that the devil is a black man, scream in genuine anguish as I approach. Some of the older women never pass without a friendly greeting, never pass, indeed, if it seems that they will be able to engage me in conversation; other women look down or look away or rather contemptuously smirk. Some of the men drink with me and suggest that I learn how to ski—partly, I gather, because they cannot imagine what I would look like on skis—and want to know if I am married, and ask questions about my *métier*. But some of the men have accused *le sale nègre*—behind my back—of stealing wood and there is already in the eyes of some of them that peculiar, intent, paranoiac malevolence which one sometimes surprises in the eyes of American white men when, out walking with their Sunday girl, they see a Negro male approach.

There is a dreadful abyss between the streets of this village and the streets of the city in which I was born, between the children who shout *Neger!* today and those who shouted *Nigger!* yesterday—the abyss is experience, the American experience. The syllable hurled behind me today expresses, above all, wonder: I am a stranger here. But I am not a stranger in America and the same syllable riding on the American air expresses the war my presence has occasioned in the American soul.

For this village brings home to me this fact: that there was a day, and not really a very distant day, when Americans were scarcely Americans at all but discontented Europeans, facing a great unconquered continent and strolling, say, into a market place and seeing black men for the first time. The shock this spectacle afforded is suggested, surely, by the promptness with which they decided that these black men were not really men but cattle. It is true that the necessity on the part of the settlers of the New World of reconciling their moral assumptions with the fact—and the necessity—of slavery enhanced immensely the charm of this idea, and it is also true that this idea expresses, with a truly American bluntness, the attitude which to varying extents all masters have had toward all slaves.

But between all former slaves and slave-owners and the drama which begins for Americans over three hundred years ago at Jamestown, there are at least two differences to be observed. The American Negro slave could not suppose, for one thing, as slaves in past epochs had supposed and often done, that he would ever be able to wrest the power from his master's hands. This was a supposition which the modern era, which was to bring about such vast changes in the aims and dimensions of power, put to death, it only begins, in unprecedented fashion, and with dreadful implications, to be resurrected today. But even had this supposition persisted with undiminished force, the American Negro slave could not have used it to lend his condition dignity, for the reason that this supposition rests on another: that the slave in exile yet remains related to his past, has some means—if only in memory—of revering and sustaining the forms of his former life, is able, in short, to maintain his identity.

This was not the case with the American Negro slave. He is unique among the black men of the world in that his past was taken from him, almost literally, at one blow. One wonders what on earth the first slave found to say to the first dark child he bore. I am told that there are Haitians able to trace their ancestry back to African kings, but any American Negro wishing to go back so far will find his journey through time abruptly arrested by the signature on the bill of sale which served as the entrance paper for his ancestor. At the time—to say nothing of the circumstances—of the enslavement of the captive black man who was to become the American Negro, there was not the remotest possibility that he would ever take power from his master's hands. There was no reason to suppose that his situation would ever change, nor was there, shortly, anything to indicate that his situation had ever been different. It was his necessity, in the words of E. Franklin Frazier, to find a "motive for living under American culture or die." The identity of the American Negro comes out of this extreme situation, and the evolution of this identity was a source of the most intolerable anxiety in the minds and the lives of his masters.

For the history of the American Negro is unique also in this: that the question of his humanity, and of his rights therefore as a human being, became a burning one for several generations of Americans, so burning a question that it ultimately became one of those used to divide the nation. It is out of this argument that the venom of the epithet *Nigger!* is derived. It is an argument which Europe has never had, and hence Europe quite sincerely fails to understand how or why the argument arose in the first place, why its effects are so frequently disastrous and always so unpredictable, why it refuses until today to be entirely settled. Europe's black possessions remained—and do remain—in Europe's colonies, at which remove they represented no threat whatever to European identity. If they posed any problem at all for the European conscience, it was a problem which remained comfortingly abstract: in effect, the black man, *as a man*, did not exist for Europe. But in America, even as a slave, he was an inescapable part of the general social fabric and no American could escape having an attitude toward him. Americans attempt until today to make an abstraction of the Negro, but the very nature of these abstractions reveals the tremendous effects the presence of the Negro has had on the American character.

When one considers the history of the Negro in America it is of the greatest importance to recognize that the moral beliefs of a person, or a people, are never really as tenuous as life—which is not moral—very often causes them to appear; these create for them a frame of reference and a necessary hope, the hope being, that when life has done its worst they will be enabled to rise above themselves and to triumph over life. Life would scarcely be bearable if this hope did not exist. Again, even when the worst has been said, to betray a belief is not by any means to have put oneself beyond its power; the betrayal of a belief is not the same thing as ceasing to believe. If this were not so there would be no moral standards in the world at all. Yet one must also recognize that morality is based on ideas and that all ideas are dangerous—dangerous because ideas can only lead to action and where the action leads no man can say. And dangerous in this respect: that confronted with the impossibility of remaining faithful to one's beliefs, and the equal impossibility of becoming free of them, one can be driven to the most inhuman excesses. The ideas on which American beliefs are based are not, though Americans often seem to think so, ideas which originated in America. They came out of Europe. And the establishment of democracy on the American continent was scarcely as radical a break with the past as was the necessity, which Americans faced, of broadening this concept to include black men.

This was, literally, a hard necessity. It was impossible, for one thing, for Americans to abandon their beliefs, not only because these beliefs alone seemed able to justify the sacrifices they had endured and the blood that they had spilled, but also because these beliefs afforded them their only bulwark against a moral chaos as absolute as the physical chaos of the continent it was their destiny to conquer. But in the situation in which Americans found themselves, these beliefs threatened an idea which, whether or not one likes to think so, is the very warp and woof of the heritage of the West, the idea of white supremacy.

Americans have made themselves notorious by the shrillness and the brutality with which they have insisted on this idea, but they did not invent it; and it has escaped the world's notice that those very excesses of which Americans have been guilty imply a certain, unprecedented uneasiness over the idea's life and power, if not, indeed, the idea's validity. The idea of white supremacy rests simply on the fact that white men are the creators of civilization (the present civilization, which is the only one that matters; all previous civilizations are simply "contributions" to our own) and are therefore civilization's guardians and defenders. Thus it was impossible for Americans to accept the black man as one of themselves, for to do so was to jeopardize their status as white men. But not so to accept him was to deny his human reality, his human weight and complexity, and the strain of denying the overwhelmingly undeniable forced Americans into rationalizations so fantastic that they approached the pathological.

At the root of the American Negro problem is the necessity of the American white man to find a way of living with the Negro in order to be able to live with himself. And the history of this problem can be reduced to the means used by Americans law and segregation and legal acceptance, terrorization and concession—either to come to terms with this necessity, or to find a way around it, or (most usually) to find a way of doing both these things at once. The resulting spectacle, at once foolish and dreadful, led someone to make the quite accurate observation that "the Negro-in-America is a form of insanity which overtakes white men."

In this long battle, a battle by no means finished, the unforeseeable effects of which will be felt by many future generations, the white man's motive was the protection of his identity; the black man was motivated by the need to establish an identity. And despite the terrorization which the Negro in America endured and endures sporadically until today, despite the cruel and totally inescapable ambivalence of his status in his country, the battle for his identity has long ago been won. He is not a visitor to the West, but a citizen there, an American; as American as the Americans who despise him, the Americans who fear him, the Americans who love him—the Americans who became less than themselves, or rose to be greater than themselves by virtue of the fact that the challenge he represented was inescapable. He is perhaps the only black man in the world whose relationship to white men is more terrible, more subtle, and more meaningful than the relationship of bitter possessed to uncertain possessor. His survival depended, and his development depends, on his ability to turn his peculiar status in the Western world to his own advantage and, it may be, to the very great advantage of that world. It remains for him to fashion out of his experience that which will give him sustenance, and a voice.

The cathedral at Chartres, I have said, says something to the people of this village which it cannot say to me; but it is important to understand that this cathedral says something to me which it cannot say to them. Perhaps they are struck by the power of the spires, the glory of the windows; but they have known God, after all, longer than I have known him, and in a different way, and I am terrified by the slippery bottomless well to be found in the crypt, down which heretics were hurled to death, and by the obscene, inescapable gargoyles jutting out of the stone and seeming to say that God and the devil can never be divorced. I doubt that the villagers think of the devil when they face a cathedral because they have never been identified with the devil. But I must accept the status which myth, if nothing else, gives me in the West before I can hope to change the myth.

Yet, if the American Negro has arrived at his identity by virtue of the absoluteness of his estrangement from his past, American white men still nourish the illusion that there is some means of recovering the European innocence of returning a state in which black men do not exist. This is one of the greatest errors Americans can make. The identity they fought so hard to protect has, by virtue of that battle, undergone a change: Americans are as unlike any other white people in the world as it is possible to be. I do not think, for example, that it is too much to suggest that the American vision of the world—which allows so little reality, generally speaking, for any of the darker forces in human life, which tends until today to paint moral issues in glaring black and white—owes a great deal to the battle waged by Americans to maintain between themselves and black men a human separation which could not be bridged. It is only now beginning to be borne in on us—very faintly, it must be admitted, very slowly, and very much against our will—that this vision of the world is dangerously inaccurate, and perfectly useless. For it protects our moral high-mindedness at the terrible expense of weakening our grasp of reality. People who shut their eyes to reality simply invite their own destruction, and anyone who insists on remaining in a state of innocence long after that innocence is dead turns himself into a monster.

The time has come to realize that the interracial drama acted out on the American continent has not only created a new black man, it has created a new white man, too. No road whatever will lead Americans back to the simplicity of this European village where white men still have the luxury of looking on me as a stranger. I am not, really, a stranger any longer for any American alive. One of the things that distinguishes Americans from other people is that no other people has ever been so deeply involved in the lives of black men, and vice versa. This fact faced, with all its implications, it can be seen that the history of the American Negro problem is not merely shameful, it is also something of an achievement. For even when the worst has been said, it must also be added that the perpetual challenge posed by this problem was always, somehow, perpetually met. It is precisely, this black-white experience which may prove of indispensable value to us in the world we face today. This world is white no longer, and it will never be white again.

Answers to Critical Reading Questions

1. What is this piece about?

The piece is about the narrator's experiences as the only black man in a small, isolated, Swiss village. It's also about the relationship between blacks and whites in the United States, including white supremacy and the effects of slavery on white Americans and American identity.

2. How is the piece structured?

The first half of the piece anecdotally describes the narrator's experiences with the Swiss villagers and his reactions to them. The second half of the piece makes broader observations about the different place of blacks in the United States and in Europe, the idea of civilization, and the relationship of race to American identity.

3. How does the structure affect the topic of the piece?

By locating the initial half of the text in a remote Swiss village, Baldwin displaces the issue of race somewhat from its American context. The second half of the piece reconnects this remote location to broader concerns about race in the United States, and so puts the American experience of race in a different light.

4. How would you describe the language of the piece?

The descriptive passages of the Swiss village are characterized by relatively short sentences. The tone is thoughtful, but somewhat tentative, and includes phrases like "God knows what" and many qualifying words like "seems" and "I suppose." When it moves to an analysis of the villagers' reactions to his race, the tone becomes more certain, and the sentences become more complex. This tendency continues as the ideas become more abstract and philosophical at the end of the essay. The use of the word "Negro" throughout positions the text in the middle of the 20th century (before the 1960s).

5. What might the changes in language in the text have to do with the topic of racial difference in the text?

Because the narrator's tone is so tentative when describing the daily life of the villagers, it indicates the differences in their experiences (including race, nationality, and environment). Here he is modeling a respect for racial difference and marking his inability to fully know the Swiss villagers' experiences. As his tone becomes more confident when he addresses the effects their comments have on him, it demonstrates the significance of his own experiences and interpretations of them to his broader understanding of racial difference.

6. To whom is the piece addressed?

The piece is addressed to a relatively educated audience who is interested in the topic of race. That the audience is primarily American is indicated by the text's use of "our" to describe American beliefs.

7. How does the text construct the narrator's relationship with the reader?

The narrator never overtly addresses his readers, most of whom are probably white Americans. Instead, by beginning with a tale of a "curiosity"—a black stranger in a remote

European village, he avoids confronting white readers head on with their own responsibility for the legacies of racial discrimination. However, by the end, when he claims that "the interracial drama acted out on the American continent . . . has created a new white man, too," he's making a directly challenging, controversial point that puts him in a potentially more adversarial position in relationship to readers.

8. *What effect does the piece have on the reader?*

By moving between describing "Americans" and "us," the narrator moves the reader to a position of responsibility for the situation of the "American Negro" and racial issues in the United States. With the statement, "For it protects our moral high-mindedness at the terrible expense of weakening our grasp of reality," the narrator lessens the accusatory tone of the criticism by including himself in the group of Americans, and so makes it easier to accept. The primary effect is that the reader will consider his or her own racial position and relationship to Baldwin and to the contemporary racial situation in the United States.

9. *Near the end of the essay, the narrator writes, "The cathedral at Chartres, I have said, says something to the people of this village which it cannot say to me; but it is important to understand that this cathedral says something to me which it cannot say to them." Why is it important for the narrator to relate what the cathedral says to him?*

It validates the fact that there is more than one interpretation of a particular historical object or event, and relates these interpretations to the social position, including the racial position, of the person interpreting the event.

10. *What is the purpose, or goal, of the piece?*

The purpose of the piece is to convince white Americans that white American identity is fully connected with black American identity and the history of racial problems in the United States. It also criticizes illusions of racial innocence that white Americans have.

11. *Is the piece effective at its goal? Why?*

It's effective in its critique of illusions of racial innocence because it represents the narrator's painful reactions to what even he perceives as the racial innocence of the Swiss villagers. Whether the piece is effective at convincing white Americans that their identity is more connected to black Americans than they may be willing to admit depends on their willingness to accept the criticism that Americans deny reality and are invested in maintaining an artificial racial separation.

SELF-ASSESSMENT

1. Read through your essay. When you've finished reading it, write a five-sentence summary of your essay.

2. Underline your thesis. Now paraphrase it. That is, rewrite your claim using different words. Then compare the two versions of the claim. Which version does a better job of conveying your main idea? Give a specific explanation about why the better version is better.

3. Does your essay adequately respond to the essay question? If so, write two sentences that explain why you feel you did a good job answering the question. If not, write two sentences that explain why you feel you didn't do a good job answering the question.

4. Describe the way you organized your essay. Do you have different sections that are distinguishable from each other (an introduction, a body, a conclusion)? Is your essay organized in a logical fashion? Do the ideas follow each other such that your reader can understand your point? Make an outline of your essay to help answer these questions.

5. Have you chosen evidence that responds to the question and helps you develop your main point? Identify your strongest piece of evidence and write two sentences that explain how it supports your argument. Identify your weakest piece of evidence and write two sentences that explain how you could make it better support your argument.

6. Do you have transitions between sections of your essay? Do these transitions help guide the reader through your essay? Pick one transition section and write two sentences in which you explain how the transition connects your paragraphs or ideas.

7. Look at the style of your writing. In three sentences describe your writing style. Do you write lengthy sentences or short sentences? Are the sentences complex or simple? Do you use strong and vivid verbs? What kind of vocabulary do you use in your essay? In one phrase identify the stylistic element you'd most like to improve.

8. Does this essay represent your best effort to answer the essay question? If so, identify your favorite part of the essay and explain why you picked this part. If not, identify your least favorite part and explain why you don't like this part.

Reading Journal

Now that you've answered all the self-assessment questions, it's time to learn about keeping a reading journal. Each time you read a text you should take notes. Since you always have study questions to answer, you know that taking notes as you read can help you with the study questions. The notes you take can also help you construct stronger answers to writing questions. You can keep these notes in a reading journal so you can refer to them again when you need to.

When you do your self-assessment, make sure your writing journal is open. As you look at your writing, also look at your reading journal to see what other ideas you had while you were reading. Certainly not all of these ideas made it into your writing. However, as you assess the ideas you did include, you can look to see whether they were your best ideas or if they were the best ideas for the assignment. Make notes in your reading journal about your writing assignments. Are there particular kinds of questions you like to answer or questions that you find more difficult? What steps do you take when you encounter a writing assignment? If you note these things in your reading journal after each writing assignment, the next time you have to do a piece of writing, you'll have a record of your thoughts about the process. This record could help you troubleshoot a future assignment or remind you that you've had success with writing in the past.

READING ON YOUR OWN

Directions: Select a reading of your choice, and answer the study questions below. Next, do a critical reading, posing and answering more sophisticated questions about the text.

Study Questions

1. What is the piece of writing about?

2. How is the piece structured?

3. How would you describe the language of the piece?

4. To whom is the piece addressed? How do you know this?

5. What effect does the piece have on the reader?

6. What is the piece arguing?

7. Is the text effective at its goal? Why?

Recognizing Rhetoric

CHAPTER 8

KEY TERMS

- allegory (See also: metaphor, symbolism)
- analogy
- deductive
- ethos
- euphemism
- hyperbole (See also: overstatement, understatement)
- inductive
- irony: verbal, dramatic, situational (See also: satire, rhetorical device)
- metaphor (See also: rhetorical device, simile)
- metonymy (See also: metaphor, synecdoche)
- paradox (See also: juxtaposition, contradiction, oxymoron)
- parallelism (See also: anaphora, rhetorical device)
- parody
- personification (See also: metaphor, simile)
- repetition (See also: rhetorical device)
- rhetoric
- rhetorical device (See also: repetition, parallelism, metaphor, irony: verbal, dramatic, situational)
- satire (See also: irony: verbal, dramatic, situational)
- simile (See also: metaphor, rhetorical device)
- symbolism
- synecdoche (See also: metaphor, metonymy)
- understatement (See also: overstatement, rhetorical device)

RHETORICAL TECHNIQUES THAT DEPEND ON WORD MEANINGS

The rhetorical devices in this section refer to effects created by the use of a word to suggest two or more different types of meanings. A rhetorical device of this sort is called a "play on words." These devices can be used repeatedly and in combination with other devices within the same sentence or paragraph, and they can extend even beyond a paragraph and be used repeatedly throughout long passages. Below are examples of each rhetorical device and explanations of how each creates different effects. The type of effects produced by each device depends on the rhetorical context of the actual message—who is speaking, when, and where, as well as for what purpose.

ANALYZING PUNS, DOUBLE ENTENDRES, AND ONOMATOPOEIA: PLAYING WITH WORDS

A *pun* is the most commonly recognized use of language as a "play on words." Puns are created by using one word to suggest two different meanings, both of which in some way seem appropriate in the context of a sentence or paragraph, even though the meanings they suggest may be very different or even opposite. Although a pun often entertains the audience because of its humorous effects, it can also create a serious emotional tone, as in the case of the religious poem "Hymn to God the Father," by John Donne, in which he puns and plays on his name and the verb "done."

A *double entendre* is a kind of pun that suggests two meanings, one of which is risqué, or highly suggestive in a sexual sense. For example, many commonplace words are used to express both sexual activities as well as nonsexual ones, such as "to come." In the Renaissance, the verb "to die" was used to indicate both the loss of one's life through death as well as to consummate the sexual act. Consequently, in many love poems of the period, you'll find double entendres such as "I can't stand to be away from you, my love—I wish to die upon your breast," meaning that the speaker misses his lover so much that only death would put an end to his misery as well as that only sexual union will save him.

Onomatopoeia is a variation on the pun. It refers not to a play on meanings so much as a play on the sound of words. This rhetorical device is the use of words whose sound somehow echoes, imitates, or indicates its meaning. Consider, for example, the word "buzz," as in, "The bee buzzed in front of my nose." The quick movement of the bee is imitated by the sound of the word referring to that movement, since the noise the bee makes as it moves sounds like buzz.

Example

Benjamin Franklin used a familiar pun when he urged the independent colonies to band together to fight the revolutionary war against England: "We must, indeed, all hang together or, most assuredly, we shall all hang separately." The pun here is created by the two different meanings of the word "hang." In the first clause, the implied meaning of *hang* is to "band together" as one nation; in the second clause, *hang* means being hanged by the neck.

KAPLAN

The play on words here isn't exactly humorous, considering the morbid nature of the last meaning of *hang*. So how else might the pun function? What does it accomplish for Franklin? One clue lies in the nature of Franklin's character—his personality or ethos. Here the pun on *hang* conveys an impression of Franklin as a witty, knowledgeable user of the language—a literate and educated man in the classic sense of a "man of letters," schooled in the language arts. Given that education was at a premium in the American colonies, the skilled use of rhetoric by Franklin sets him apart from the average citizen and portrays him as a wise statesman and therefore worthy of the public's trust. In other words, his use of a pun here contributes to the social prestige of his character. In this way, his rhetoric contributes to the ethical effects of what he has to say.

In addition, the literal image of individuals being hanged evokes the image of death and therefore adds emotional impact. The pun appeals, therefore, to "the people"—both through informal commonsense and emotions—as much as it appeals to individuals with a fine appreciation for the play of meanings suggested by words.

Take a Shot at Analyzing Puns

Shakespeare's dramas are often filled with witty puns, which often add an element of humor even to his tragedies. Consider the character Mercutio's final words, as he is dying, in the play *Romeo and Juliet*.

See if you can recognize the pun in the following line from the play and how it might function in the context, given what has been revealed about Mercutio's character up to this point in the play. Throughout the play, Mercutio is portrayed as a skilled user of the language, never at a loss for words (perhaps less skilled with the sword, given the fatal wound he receives). On stage he frequently engages in entertaining banter with Romeo, which gives the audience the impression that Mercutio has a playful (nonserious) character.

Identify the pun and describe how it contributes to the audience's impression of Mercutio's character or type of personality.

> [As he lies dying, Mercutio says to Romeo, his close friend]
> "Ask for me tomorrow and you shall find me a grave man."

Analysis

The pun is created by the two meanings of "grave" that are suggested by the context.

The phrase "a grave man" conveys the literal sense of a dead man being placed in a grave; it also conveys the more abstract sense of a "serious" man—in a sense this meaning is ironically appropriate. Given that Mercutio has been portrayed in Shakespeare's drama as a playful character, less serious than Romeo in many ways, for Mercutio to suddenly become a "grave man" would mean that he is not himself. Since in death a man is no longer a man, then for Mercutio to be a "grave" man rather than his usual self would mean that he is (literally) no longer the man he was. In addition, having suffered a grievous sword wound on one day, the character, on the next day, would no longer be happy and carefree but no doubt "seriously" wounded.

That Mercutio should create a pun in his last few moments of life contributes to the notion of his character as "never at a loss for words." In this context, the use of a pun at the moment of death shows what some critics have noted is a typical trait of Shakespeare's plays—the mixture of bittersweet emotions, which move audiences to complex responses.

ANALYZING SIMILES, METAPHORS, AND ANALOGIES:RHETORICAL DEVICES THAT COMPARE

A *simile* is the use of *like* or *as* to compare two different ideas or things and to express some way that they're similar or share a certain quality: "My love is like a fever, burning me up," for example. A *metaphor* is an implied comparison; it doesn't use the words *like* or *as*: "My love is a fever burning me up." An *analogy* is an implicit comparison that sets up a proportional relationship between two sets of ideas, with each set consisting of at least two different qualities or elements, so that the different qualities of each set of ideas can be compared or equated to each other. For example, "If knowledge is a tree, the different fields of knowledge are its branches." Because it's easy to recognize similes (they always use *like* or *as*), we'll focus primarily on metaphors and analogies.

Example

The speech purportedly given by Chief Seattle in 1854—its origins, its verbiage, and even its very existence have long been debated—is filled with rhetorical devices that make comparisons. As history has it, Chief Seattle, patriarch of the Duwamish and Suquamish Indians of Puget Sound, gave this oration when the then-governor of the Washington Territory was in town attending a treaty council and negotiating land cessations from various Indian tribes.

The speech is reprinted in this book in chapter 6. Go back and read the first paragraph, looking for any comparative rhetorical devices.

It is easy to find examples of simile in the speech. In the first paragraph, for example, Chief Seattle states, "My words are like the stars that never change." The comparison to stars suggests that his words are immutable, and continues his extended analogy of the sky as having features that change and some that do not.

Take a Shot at Analyzing Similes, Metaphors, and Analogies

See if you can recognize by yourself the use of similes, metaphors, and analogies in this piece of writing, before consulting the provided answer.

Go back to Chief Seattle's speech and read paragraphs two through five, beginning with "There was a time when . . . " and ending with " . . . and is written in the hearts of our people." Stop reading after that sentence.

Next, identify the rhetorical devices in the selection that make comparisons (similes, metaphors, and analogies) and analyze their effects. How do these devices contribute to the logical, emotional, and ethical effects of the speech?

Answer

This selected excerpt opens with a simile: "There was a time when our people covered the land as the waves of a wind-ruffled sea cover its shell paved floor . . . ." This simile suggests that once there were many more Native Americans than in Chief Seattle's time. The next paragraph opens with a general statement that "youth is impulsive." He describes how the young men "disfigure their faces with black paint," and goes on to establish an analogy between the black faces and the anger the young men feel, using the metaphor "their hearts are black" to describe their state of anger. He later uses a series of similes to suggest the declining numbers of his people as opposed to their former ubiquity: "Our people are ebbing away like a rapidly receding tide that will never return"; "He gave you laws but had no word for his red children whose teeming multitudes once filled this vast continent as stars fill the firmament." In the fifth paragraph, he uses analogy, contrasting the religion of the red man with that of the white man, closing with the metaphor of hearts as surfaces upon which the religion can be written: "Our religion is the traditions of our ancestors, the dreams of our old men, given them in the solemn hours of night by the Great Spirit; and the visions of our sachems, and is written in the hearts of our people."

The use by Chief Seattle of these devices contributes to his use of pathos, or the appeal to emotion, to describe the plight of his people. The appeal to emotion is the primary rhetorical approach used in this speech.

ANALYZING PERSONIFICATION, ALLEGORY, AND FABLES:PLAYING WITH HUMAN QUALITIES

When we use human qualities to describe abstract ideas, animals, or inanimate objects, we're using the rhetorical device of *personification*. Personification is a specific kind of implicit comparison, like metaphor, where the inanimate or nonhuman object is characterized by some quality or action we normally associate with human behavior—either physical or mental actions as well as emotional reactions.

Allegories are extended comparisons (beyond a sentence): a set of abstract ideas (or some philosophical statement or argument) is personified through human characters and specific events in which they engage. *Fables* are short allegorical stories that point out a lesson or moral. The characters in fables are usually animals with human qualities (in other words, the animals are personified).

We'll focus on analyzing personification, since by definition both allegories and fables are created using this rhetorical device.

Example

In this excerpt from *Civil Disobedience*, the author, Henry David Thoreau, uses personification to describe his thoughts or meditations. The essay was written to encourage American citizens to stand up for individual rights and liberties and to resist the government if its policies and actions compromised those liberties. Thoreau was well known for promoting and engaging in what today is known as peaceful demonstration or passive resistance.

> I have paid no poll-tax for six years.
>
> I was put into a jail once on this account, for one night; and, as I stood considering the walls of solid stone, two or three feet thick.
>
> I could not help being struck with the foolishness of that institution which treated me as if I were mere flesh and blood and bones, to be locked up.
>
> They thought that my chief desire was to stand on the other side of that stone wall.
>
> I could not but smile to see how industriously they locked the door on my meditations, which followed them out again without let or hindrance, and they were really all that was dangerous.
>
> As they could not reach me, they had resolved to punish my body.

The fifth sentence expresses the personification. His meditations, or thoughts, are portrayed as the real criminal here, and they're represented as being free to come and go "without let or hindrance," as a free man would. The implication is that one's mind is always free, and its thoughts know no bounds, unlike the limits of the physical body.

By personifying his thinking as the real criminal, which at the same time is the only thing that's really free, Thoreau creates a logical paradox. He indicates that meditations are free to move beyond the material limits of the prison cell because they themselves are immaterial; at the same time he compares them to a free man who can walk about. The effect of the personification is to say that the real definition of a man who is alive is not the state of his body, but of his mind. And the product of the human mind—its meditations—can never be bounded, even though the human body is limited by flesh and blood as well as physical (material) circumstances. Personification is a way to make abstract entities or ideas take concrete, material form, as here the abstract notion of a thought takes the form of a man who is free to come and go as he pleases.

Take a Shot at Analyzing Personification

The example is Psalm 23, from the Old Testament of the Bible. A psalm is a short religious poem or song. What abstract quality or idea is being personified and what is the effect of the personification? To help answer this question, it's helpful to consider the context of the psalm. It was written thousands of years ago at a time when civilization was far less industrialized than today. The Psalms of the Old Testament were addressed to people whose way of life was typically limited to farming, grazing sheep, and other unmechanized occupations.

The Lord is my shepherd,
I shall not want.
He makes me lie down in green pastures;
He leads me beside quiet waters.
Even though I walk through the valley of the shadow of death,
I fear no evil, for Thou are with me;
Thy rod and Thy staff, they comfort me.

Analysis

Because some people think of God in the concrete terms of Jesus Christ—a man who was sent to live amongst humankind—it might be difficult for them to see the rhetorical device of personification operating here. It may seem almost "natural" for those that believe this to think of the Lord as a shepherd, for the Bible frequently, refers to Christ in these terms. However, if the reader considers that the idea of a god may be a philosophical concept, an idea that refers to an all-powerful, perfect spiritual essence (rather than a mere material thing that exists on the earth only in imperfect form), then the reader can see how here the implicit comparison of God to a human shepherd tending his flock is an attempt to personify an otherwise abstract concept of a possible unseen force in the universe. In Psalm 23, God, as a shepherd, is responsible for creating and nurturing all living creatures.

Notice also how here personification is combined with analogy, so that the "rod" and "staff" of the shepherd corresponds to the laws God set forth, such as in the Ten Commandments, to guide human beings and in so doing provide us with the security, or "comfort," of knowing right from wrong.

The overall effect of the personification is to portray God in terms familiar to those who were being addressed at the time, since the occupation of shepherd would have been well known to them. God, therefore, is made to seem accessible to the average human being. The personification, in other words, creates a certain ethos, or personality, for God that encourages us to feel at home with what otherwise is a powerful, untouchable force and potentially one to be feared. The individual is encouraged to literally walk with God, to follow this nurturing and positive force, rather than to stray from the "fold." Emotionally the personification also has the effect of offering a comforting image, which might increase the likelihood the audience will be persuaded by the argument of the psalm.

ANALYZING METONYMY AND SYNECDOCHE

Both of these rhetorical devices are ways of playing with opposite meanings. In the case of *metonymy*, abstract and complex processes are referred to by means of a single concrete part typically associated with the more complex processes. In the case of *synecdoche*, a concrete, complex entity is represented by a single part. In other words, metonymy is a rhetorical device that reduces abstractions to concrete particulars, and synecdoche is a device that uses one part to refer to a more complex concrete whole.

Examples

To see the differences between these very similar devices, consider the following examples. The commonplace saying "The pen is mightier than the sword" is an example of metonymy because the word "pen" reduces the abstract, complex process of attacking others or defending oneself with written words to the single, concrete object needed to write those words. On the other hand, the phrase "All hands on deck" is an example of synecdoche. "Hands" refer to concrete objects that are part of a whole person, which is a relatively definite and concrete entity, in contrast to the abstract process of composition referred to in the example of metonymy. In both cases, the effect is to use simpler concrete terms to reference more complex wholes—whether concrete or abstract entities.

Synecdoche also includes an opposite technique—using a word that refers to a whole or complex entity when only a specific entity is meant (a whole is substituted for a part).

This last point alerts us to the fact that we need to pay attention to the whole context of a sentence or paragraph—and even to use our background knowledge of a subject—to recognize which device is being used as well as what sort of rhetorical effects its achieving.

Consider one additional example, from "The Lord's Prayer" from the New Testament Gospel of Matthew. The prayer refers to God as "father" (a personification), who is being asked for daily assistance while at the same time being praised:

> Our father, who art in heaven, hallowed be thy name. . . . Give us this day our daily bread, and forgive us our trespasses as we forgive those who trespass against us.

The reference to "daily bread" here actually combines both metonymy and synecdoche. Bread is something we eat to sustain ourselves on a daily basis; it's a concrete, material object often eaten with other things in order to create a whole meal. Bread, therefore, is a synecdoche, referring to the more complex meal. On the other hand, because bread and meals also satisfy our hunger, bread is also used metonymically to refer to the more general idea of any human desire that needs to be satisfied.

The effect of these rhetorical devices is to define God in everyday terms and to show that God satisfies not merely physical hunger, but spiritual hunger as well. The prayer therefore relies on the logic of familiar, everyday practices, such as eating, to assert in very concrete terms the value of a spiritual life. In other words, the rhetorical devices create the impression that praying is a logical thing to do to meet one's daily needs. The devices also construct religion in familiar terms, so that God is personified as a source of comforting sustenance, which contributes to the ethical appeal of the prayer.

Take a Shot at Analyzing Metonymy and Synecdoche

Does this statement contain an example of metonymy, synecdoche, or both, and what's the effect?

Recently the women's soccer team sponsored by the United States won the world championship for the first time in the nation's history. It wasn't uncommon to hear sports announcers say that, "The U.S. won the women's soccer championship."

Analysis

At the literal level of meaning, the United States did not win the championship—the individual players on the U.S. soccer team were the ones who played the game and won it. It is important to realize that the soccer players do make up part of the more complex nation we refer to as "the United States"—therefore, although this example refers to the whole nation, really it means to refer to only a part (a small group) representing the whole. This is one way that synecdoche functions. The nation as a whole has been substituted for a reference to the more concrete and specific players who actually won the championship, but who indeed do represent on an abstract level the nation that supports them.

One effect of the synecdoche here is that it credits the nation with the accomplishment of its individual members, adding to the prestige or social status of the United States relative to the other nations who participated in the championship and lost. In other words, the synecdoche creates a powerful ethos for the United States as a nation.

ANALYZING APPOSITION AND EPITHETS: REDEFINING A NOUN IN OTHER TERMS

The rhetorical device of *apposition* refers to the placing a word or phrase immediately following another word or phrase to add more detailed information about the idea suggested by the first word or to limit or modify the meaning of the first word. In effect, the appositive word or phrase renames a noun in more specific or concrete terms. Apposition is commonly seen whenever we give someone's name and their title, which defines who he or she is relative to some social organization or structure, such as "Franklin Delano Roosevelt, the thirty-second President of the Unted States, served four terms." We say that the title "President of the United States" is apposed, or stands in apposition, to "Franklin Delano Roosevelt" in this example.

An *epithet* is the use of a single-word adjective linked to a person or thing to describe a specific quality associated with it, such as the well-known reference to the ancient king of Greece as "Alexander the Great," with "great" functioning as the epithet. Other examples include: "world-renowned chef," "championship soccer team," and "fleet-footed Achilles." An important distinguishing feature of an epithet, which sets it apart from mere use of an adjective, is that it expresses some distinctive quality associated with the noun it modifies, some quality that sets the thing apart from others like it. For example, "championship soccer team" distinguishes the team from other teams that may play soccer but haven't earned the distinction of being champions.

Since the forms of apposition are often more complex than the single-word adjective forms used in epithets, we'll focus on recognizing the former.

Example

The Declaration of Independence relies on a series of clauses functioning as appositives, creating, in effect, a whole series or list of statements that defines the initial noun, "these truths." The paragraph develops by repetition of clauses in apposition, one on top of another:

> We hold these truths to be self-evident, that all men are created equal, that they are endowed by their Creator with certain unalienable Rights, that among these are Life, Liberty, and the pursuit of Happiness, that to secure these rights, Governments are instituted among Men, deriving their just powers from the consent of the governed, that whenever any Form of Government becomes destructive of these ends, it is the right of the People to alter or to abolish it.

The noun "these truths" is restated by each of the phrases following it and beginning with "that." In effect, the appositive clauses provide very specific definitions for what the framers of the Declaration believed to be the self-evident "truths," or basic premises on which to found the new government of the United States. By expressing these premises explicitly, the appositive clauses establish what is known as a syllogistic, deductive argument: universally held truths or premises are set forth so that a logical conclusion can be derived from them. This is exactly what happens in the remaining text of the Declaration.

In sections not presented in the quoted passage above, the writers set forth specific evidence that shows how the British government violated these basic truths, and therefore the logical conclusion is to abolish ties with that government, based on the premises outlined here by the appositive clauses. In other words, the clauses contribute to the logical structure of the argument—they create logical rhetorical effects. Based on the logic of the deductive argument being set out here, the new colonies seem logically justified in making a break with Britain.

Take a Shot at Analyzing Apposition and Epithets

Apposition can function in other ways than contributing to the logic of a passage. Consider the following example, taken from American writer Washington Irving's famous story *The Legend of Sleepy Hollow*.

Identify the use of apposition and epithets and describe their effects. The context is what many consider to be a highly entertaining American "horror" story, which takes as its subject a supernatural, ghostly phenomenon.

> The dominant spirit, however, that haunts this enchanted region and seems to be commander-in-chief of all powers of the air, is the apparition of a figure on horseback without a head.
> It is said by some to be the ghost of a Hessian trooper, whose head had been carried away by a cannon-ball, in some nameless battle during the revolutionary war; and who is ever and anon seen by the country folk, hurrying along in the gloom of night, as if on the wings of the wind.

Analysis

First consider the possible use of epithets. Although there are a number of different uses of adjectives here, few could really be considered epithets in the sense that they are being used to define a distinctive quality of a person or thing, given what we know from the context of the whole passage, in the way that a title such as "Alexander the Great" sets him apart as a ruler whom we know distinguished himself by conquering the better part of the ancient world. In the passage here, "enchanted region" comes close to being an epithet. The point of the passage is to suggest that, indeed, it is haunted by the ghost of a headless horseman, so that being "enchanted" is what gives the region its "distinctive quality."

Compared to identifying epithets, it may be easier to see how many clauses and phrases are functioning in apposition to preceding nouns, so as to add more descriptive and specific information. For example, the clause "that haunts this enchanted region" provides more information about "the dominant spirit," the preceding noun that begins the passage. Added to this appositive clause is another, "seems to be commander-in-chief," which provides additional descriptive information to help visualize the image of the ghostly creature. The second sentence consists of several appositive clauses and phrases, one on top of the other in succession, that add detailed and realistic information about the "Hessian trooper," who is apparently the headless horseman.

One effect of all of these appositive phrases and clauses is to create an "artful" impression—we are dealing with a well-told, entertaining story. The passage is highly descriptive and filled with detail, which creates an impression that the horseman being referred to exists in some reality, for the details are so vivid and so much seems to be known about him. Overall, the rhetorical effect is to make the fantastic seem believable. The wealth of vivid details added by the apposition enables the reader to visualize the scene; the details about how the horseman may have lost his head creates an element of horror, encouraging the reader to enter into an emotional state where one is willing to suspend disbelief for the sake of an entertaining and imaginative story.

ANALYZING HYPERBOLE, UNDERSTATEMENT, AND EUPHEMISM

Each of these rhetorical devices defines an idea in terms of some sort of extreme. *Hyperbole* is the use of language to overstate or exaggerate an idea to its furthest extreme. At the other end of the extreme, *understatement* and *euphemism* tend to play down the magnitude of an idea. What we mean by "extreme" depends on the context, but often these rhetorical devices are easiest to spot when they exaggerate or understate something in terms of size or quantity—such as "He was as tiny as a mouse," or "A billion people were at the concert last night."

Euphemism is a special form of understatement used in contexts where a more graphic or direct reference to an idea might be offensive to the audience. For example, often we say, "I need to use the restroom," rather than the more graphic (but perhaps more descriptively accurate), "I need to urinate." Euphemism tends to be a roundabout way of expressing an idea compared to other forms of expression.

Example

In *The Right Stuff*, well-known writer Tom Wolfe captured some of the characteristic effects of euphemism and the art of understatement in his observations on what the wife of a U.S. astronaut is typically told when her husband has been killed in a spacecraft accident. The following passage gets at the heart of the difference between understatement, euphemism, and hyperbole:

> When the final news came [and she was informed that] her husband's body ... [was] "burned beyond recognition," [Judy] realized [the phrase] was quite an artful euphemism to describe a human body that now looked like an enormous fowl that has burned up in a stove, [and turned] a blackish brown all over, greasy and blistered, fried, in a word.

Wolfe points out that the phrase "burned beyond recognition" is a euphemism for *killed*. But notice the way the descriptive details that follow—"enormous fowl," "blackish brown all over," and "greasy and blistered"—heighten the disturbing quality of the image of a dead man's body having been badly burned. By launching the passage with the understatement of euphemism, his ending description is all that much more graphic and has the feel of overstatement by comparison. The combination of devices creates, therefore, a highly dramatic statement, shifting quickly from one extreme to another.

Take a Shot at Analyzing Hyperbole, Understatement, and Euphemism

President Lincoln's "Gettysburg Address" was delivered in November of 1863 on the field of one of the bloodiest battles of the United States Civil War, on the occasion of dedicating the battlefield as a national cemetery for the fallen soldiers. The battles at Gettysburg, Pennsylvania, marked the turning point in the war, with huge loses on both the Confederate and Union sides. Soldiers continued to fight for both sides for the next two years, leaving the Union (and the principles of government it fought to uphold) intact and victorious over the Confederacy.

Read the following excerpt from the Gettysburg Address and identify whether Lincoln uses understatement, euphemism, or hyperbole in this passage and analyze the rhetorical effects. How do the rhetorical devices function in this context? What do they say about Lincoln's purposes?

> Four score and seven years ago, our fathers brought forth upon this continent a new nation: conceived in liberty, and dedicated to the proposition that all men are created equal.
> Now we are engaged in a great civil war, testing whether [the nation] . . . can long endure.
> We are met on a great battlefield of that war.
> We have come to dedicate a portion of that field as a final resting place for those who here gave their lives that this nation might live.

Analysis

Note in the first sentence that the nation is presented as emerging from a birth rather than death, by using the word *conceived* instead of, for example, discussing the blood shed during the American Revolutionary War. In other words, one could say that the country was born of bloodshed, rather than of the ideas of liberty and equality, but Lincoln instead chose to focus on the positive ideas that helped to define America. "Conceived" could therefore be considered a euphemism.

Lincoln repeats the adjective "great"—first in sentence 2 in connection with the Civil War as a whole, and then in the third sentence in connection with the specific battle at Gettysburg. In many ways, it is no hyperbole to call the war "great," in that it affected the lives and property of thousands of people. The effect of the war also was great enough to tear the nation apart. You could say, however, that there is something hyperbolic about the adjective "great," for the implication is that no matter what the cost, the war was worth fighting.

On the other hand, there is also something vaguely euphemistic about the adjective "great" because it seems to downplay the horrible fact that the war killed thousands of people, which is anything but great. Indeed, the occasion for this address is defined by this bittersweet, or mixed, set of emotions about the need to fight a war to free the slaves, while at the same time great losses have to be suffered. The adjective "great" tends to elevate war to something beyond ordinary experience. In this regard, you could consider its use to be somewhat of a hyperbole. Calling a war "great" helps to heighten our emotional commitment to its cause.

In sentence 3, notice how rather than refer to the field as a cemetery, Lincoln refers to the field as what will be a "final resting place" for "those who gave their lives," two euphemisms that minimize any graphic connotations of bodies strewn across a field, lying dead, bloodied, and maimed, or of decayed bodies having to be put into a grave six feet below ground. Lincoln refers to the dead soldiers as not ones who were killed or even who died but "who gave their lives," avoiding having to say that indeed these men were killed and that some were compelled to join an army to fight a war the government believed necessary. By saying that they "gave their lives," the implication is that these men willingly sacrificed themselves for the sake of the nation. The ethical effect is to see these men as deserving honor for fighting for an honorable, or "great," cause. The rhetorical devices therefore contribute to the delicate emotional situation created by the loss of lives in an unfortunate but ultimately necessary war.

ANALYZING PARADOX AND OXYMORON: THE RHETORIC OF CONTRADICTIONS

A *paradox* is the expression of an apparent contradiction, where opposing ideas are nevertheless on some level true. A paradox therefore is a way to make an illogical statement seem logical. Paradox tends to challenge the traditional notion of logical consistency, which assumes that for a statement to be logical, either one idea or its opposite must be true, but not both simultaneously. For example, arithmetic depends on the law of logical consistency: if $2 + 2 = 4$, then $2 + 2$ can't also equal 5 or 3 or any other number except 4. So, too, does algebra rely on the logic of consistency: if A is equal to B, then it can't be the case that A is not equal to B—one statement must be true, and the other false. In the language of words rather than numbers, paradox can be expressed in a single sentence or longer passages of text.

A typical example is the commonplace belief that the more quickly you try to get a job or task accomplished, the more you'll find yourself behind schedule, expressed by the maxim, "The hurrier I go, the behinder I get." The paradox is that logically, if you do things more quickly, you should get ahead of your schedule. However, the truth of the opposite becomes apparent when we realize that as we hurry, we often aren't careful with what we're doing and break things and create problems that require more time to fix than the original task would have taken if we'd approached the work more carefully. Often a paradox occurs whenever there is an apparent violation of the laws of time and space, such as the logical impossibility of being in two different places at the same time.

An *oxymoron* is a paradox created by linking together two apparently contradictory words in a single phrase or clause. Common examples include "bittersweet emotions," "cheerful pessimist," and "cruel kindness."

Example

The gospels of the New Testament are filled with paradoxical statements. Take, for example, this pronouncement of Christ to his disciples:

> Truly I say to you, unless you are converted and become like children, you shall not enter the kingdom of heaven. Whoever humbles himself as this child, he is the greatest in the kingdom of heaven. [Matthew 18: 3–4]

The paradox here is that typically we think of those who are humble as the *opposite* of great. To understand the significance of the paradox in this context, it's necessary to know something of Christian philosophy. In contrast to the strict laws of the Jewish religion, which were codified in the books of the Old Testament, the message of Christ in the New Testament reverses many of those old laws and substitutes a philosophy of love and forgiveness. The effect of the paradox here is to challenge the logic of hierarchy and social rank on earth, promoting humility rather than greatness as a basis for one's place in heaven. This paradox constructs a different logic from the one governing social order on earth.

Take a Shot at Analyzing Paradoxical Statements

Ralph Waldo Emerson, the well-known American author and philosopher who wrote during the mid-19th century, relies on the use of paradox in this passage from *Self-Reliance*.

Identify the nature of the paradox and analyze how this rhetorical device contributes to the meaning of Emerson's message. To help you analyze the rhetorical effects, you'll want to consider that Emerson promoted a philosophy known as *transcendentalism*. This view emphasizes individualism and self-reliance, challenges the traditional view that God is merely some external force, and asserts that God is located in man and nature. The true spirit of God must be recognized as internal and not limited to the external forms visible to the eye. In other words, the spirit transcends the material world.

God will not have his work made manifest by cowards.

A man is relieved and gay when he has put his heart into his work and done his best; but what he has said or done otherwise will give him no peace—it is a deliverance which does not deliver.

Trust thyself: every heart vibrates to that iron string.

Accept the place the divine providence has found for you.

Great men have always done so, and confided themselves childlike to the genius of their age.

Analysis

There are two obvious paradoxes in this passage: the first is in the second sentence, "a deliverance which does not deliver." Emerson here is referring to a man who does not put his heart into his work and do his best. Such passionless efforts might seem on the one hand to deliver or produce a result, but paradoxically, according to Emerson, such a result "does not deliver" the higher satisfaction felt within one's heart, which transcends whatever might be delivered or produced materially by one's efforts or work. The paradox here has the effect of reversing the logic of a materialism, which judges results solely according to the actual thing produced without regard for the spirit in which it was produced.

The second paradox occurs in the fifth sentence: "Great men have . . . confided themselves childlike to the genius of their age." Emerson, as in the example of Christ, reverses the usual meaning of "great" by associating it with that which is considered "small"—a child. The effect here is to evoke the humility we often associate with Christ, which conveys the impression that Emerson does support similar principles, even if his philosophy challenges traditional Christianity in many respects. In other words, the rhetorical device creates positive ethical effects.

RHETORICAL TECHNIQUES THAT DEPEND ON THE ORDER OF PARTS WITHIN A SENTENCE

Many different rhetorical techniques order the words making up a sentence. The three most common techniques are repetition, subordination, and questions. In this section we'll focus in particular on parallelism—a rhetorical device of repetition—and the different forms associated with this rhetorical technique, since the other two techniques (subordination and questions) are easily understood in terms of basic grammatical knowledge.

ANALYZING THE RHETORIC OF PARALLELISM AND ELLIPSIS

Parallelism is the repetition within a sentence (or several sentences within the same paragraph) of the same type of grammatical forms—either the same part of speech, such as a noun, adjective, or verb, or the same type of grammatical unit, such as a phrase or clause. Often parallelism—the repetition of grammatical form—is combined with repetition of one or more of the same words. (Note: If you're unfamiliar with the parts of speech as well as types of phrases and clauses, it's useful to review them so you can recognize parallelism.)

To see what we mean by parallelism, consider the following sentence from Lincoln's "Gettysburg Address":

> Government of the people, by the people, for the people shall not perish from the earth.

The grammatical form repeated here is the prepositional phrase, which in general consists of a preposition plus a noun. Three prepositional phrases are repeated here: "of the people," "by the people," and "for the people." Notice also the repetition of the word "people," combined with the repetition of prepositional phrases.

Ellipsis is the omission of a word or phrase that is implied by the context. Usually the missing word or phrase is easy to recognize because the wording of the context relies on parallelism of grammatical form to indicate which of the words or phrases is meant to be repeated. For example, "Some like their hamburgers with ketchup, some with mustard."

Take a Shot at Analyzing Parallelism and Ellipsis

President John F. Kennedy, in his first inaugural address, relies heavily on the use of parallelism. The purpose of his speech was to address the nation for the first time as president and set the tone for the type of presidency he hoped to establish. The speech, delivered in January 1961, occurred at a time in world history known as the Cold War, when tensions between communist and noncommunist countries threatened peace. It was a time when nuclear war was a possibility, and each nation raced to outpace the other in terms of the manufacture of destructive weapons. At this time it seemed important for President Kennedy to show his intention of keeping the United States strong in the face of challenges from other nations.

Describe which parts of the quotation below are examples of parallelism and ellipsis and analyze the rhetorical effects, considering what you know about the context of the speech.

> Let every nation know, whether it wishes us well or ill, that we shall pay any price, bear any burden, meet any hardship, support any friend, oppose any foes, to assure the survival and the success of liberty. This much we pledge. And more.

Analysis

The grammatical form repeated here is the form of the predicate: a verb plus its object. The first instance of this form follows the subject "we" of the first clause functioning as the object of "that": "we shall pay any price." There are four more predicates that follow, each beginning with a different verb: "bear any burden," "meet any hardship," "support any friend," and "oppose any foes." Notice that each of these verb-plus-object combinations implicitly takes as its subject the word "we," stated only in the first predicate. Therefore, by the rhetorical device of ellipsis, "we" is the subject of each of the subsequent predications. One effect of leaving out the "we" is to stress the verbs and therefore the actions that "we" are willing to take, giving the impression that America will not simply be a passive country but an active one.

Also notice how the piling up of the predicates, one on top of another, gives the impression that the United States will do anything to "assure the survival and the success of liberty."

Therefore, the rhetorical effects here are primarily ethical (suggesting the type of nation America will be) and emotional (suggesting that America is a nation to be feared).

ANALYZING THE RHETORIC OF ANTITHESIS

An *antithesis* is a specific use of parallelism: grammatical forms or parts of speech are repeated in a sentence (or series of sentences in a paragraph) and are used to express opposing or contrary meanings. (Note: Antithesis relies on the parallelism of grammatical forms; it's important to be able to recognize these forms in order to recognize antitheses.)

For example, one of the most well-known antitheses was uttered by astronaut Neil Armstrong, on being the first person to set foot on the moon:

> That's one small step for man, one giant leap for mankind.

There are two grammatical forms repeated in each part of the sentence, before and after the comma. The first grammatical form to be repeated is a noun modified by an adjective: "small step" and "giant leap." The second is a prepositional phrase: "for man" and "for mankind." The meaning of "small step" is the opposite of "giant leap," and, in this context, one man (Neil Armstrong) is opposed to all of "mankind."

One effect of this rhetorical technique in this example is to create a "memorable" saying—repetition helps us to remember words and phrases. For example, the refrains of songs often repeat a phrase, which we can sing even if we can't remember the rest of the song. The repetition also conveys the extent to which Armstrong's landing on the moon is not only an individual achievement, but one representing the ingenuity of humans more generally—his actions speak for all of us. In a way, Armstrong's statement conveys both individual humility (the honor belongs not only to him but to all) as well as pride not merely in himself but all mankind. The device of antithesis creates a balance of opposing elements that conveys an impression of Armstrong's personality as carefully balanced between commitment to self and others.

Take a Shot at Analyzing Antithesis

In President Kennedy's first inaugural address, he also relied heavily on the use of antithesis. Recall that the purpose of his speech was to address the nation for the first time as president and set the tone for the type of presidency he hoped to establish.

Identify and analyze the effects of the rhetorical technique of antithesis in the following passage, taking into account the context of the speech.

> To those nations who would make themselves our adversaries, we offer not a pledge but a request. . . .
>
> Let both sides explore what problems unite us instead of belaboring those problems which divide us.
>
> Let both sides . . . . bring the absolute power to destroy other nations under absolute control of all nations.

Analysis

The second sentence contains the first use of antithesis: the phrase "what problems unite us" is grammatically parallel in form but opposite in meaning to "those problems which divide us." The third sentence contains another antithesis: The phrase "the absolute power to destroy other nations" is grammatically parallel but contrary in meaning to "under absolute control of all nations."

One effect of Kennedy's use of antitheses is to convey the impression that even though nations may be set against other nations at this moment, it is possible to reconcile the differences so the balance of power can be kept as is, without recourse to nuclear war. The use of antitheses creates a logic that implies even opposites can be contained within the same sentence, so perhaps too, opposing powers in the world may be equally contained. The message seems to create the impression that Kennedy will support keeping the nation strong, at the same time he won't over zealously enter into war unless provoked. The ethical perspective created here establishes a personality that seems balanced and fair.

ANALYZING EXCLAMATION AND PARENTHESIS: THE RHETORIC OF INTERRUPTION

Exclamation is a type of interruption in which the speaker or writer stops a sentence midway and addresses an individual who may or may not be present. *Parenthesis* is a type of interruption of a sentence before it has been completed in order to insert some word, phrase, or clause that launches a new idea. One way to easily recognize either of these interruptions is that usually they are set off from the rest of the sentence by some type of punctuation—often a double (or long) dash, a set of commas, or parentheses (or brackets of some sort). Both rhetorical devices temporarily "derail" the sentence and send it in a different direction.

Consider these excerpts from one of the books of the New Testament, Paul's Second Letter to the Corinthians:

> Wherein any man is bold—I am speaking foolishly—I also am bold. . . . Are they ministers of Christ? I—to speak as a fool—am more.

Here the parenthetical technique is marked by long dashes. The phrase "I am speaking foolishly" interrupts the flow of the sentence, which otherwise would have been written as, "Wherein any man is bold, I also am bold." The phrase "to speak as a fool" interrupts the second sentence, which otherwise would have read as, "I am more." The phrases that interrupt each sentence offer commentary on the ideas being expressed by the sentences they have just interrupted. One effect of this technique in this context is to show Paul as self-conscious and wary of not being properly humble. Therefore he keeps interjecting comments that suggest he is aware that to speak so highly of himself is to risk sounding foolish. The parenthetical asides convey this impression of Paul and therefore create ethical effects.

KAPLAN

Take a Shot at Analyzing Interruption

Here is another excerpt from Abraham Lincoln's "Gettysburg Address." Recall that it was delivered in November of 1863 on the field of one of the bloodiest battles of the Civil War, on the occasion of dedicating the battlefield as a national cemetery for the fallen soldiers. The battles at Gettysburg marked the turning point in the war, with huge loses on both the Confederate and Union sides. This historical moment, indeed, must have been one of intense emotion.

Identify any parenthetical rhetorical techniques and analyze their effects, given what you know about the context in which this speech was delivered.

> We have come to dedicate a portion of that field as a final resting place for those who here gave their lives that this nation might live.
> It is altogether fitting and proper that we should do this.
> But, in a larger sense, we cannot dedicate—we cannot consecrate—we cannot hallow this ground.
> The brave men, living and dead, who struggled here have consecrated it.

Analysis

Both sentences 3 and 4 contain parenthetical elements. Notice how the flow (or syntax) of sentence 3 is broken up. One clause begins and then another takes its place, so that it is unclear which clause is the main one of the sentence overall, until it finally ends with "we cannot hallow this ground." In sentence 4, the phrase "living and dead" is a much less unsettling interruption; it clearly expresses a set of terms describing the "brave men." Although the sentence is temporarily derailed or prevented from reaching its completion, the information added is clearly only modifying material, and therefore the main sentence is much more intact, compared to the way the clauses in the previous sentence disrupted its syntax.

In either case, however, the rhetorical effect is emotional. The broken syntax suggests Lincoln struggling to find the right words to do justice to the occasion, or perhaps his emotions are preventing him from completing his thoughts.

Applying Rhetoric

Now that you've learned how to recognize rhetoric, let's move on to *applying* it.

RHETORICAL PATTERNS

Rhetoric is language meant to accomplish a particular purpose or have a particular type of effect on an audience or reader in a particular social situation. There are at least three different types of effects associated with the use of rhetoric:

- Those that contribute to the logical structure of the text
- Those that are responsible for the emotional effect of what we say
- Those that convey to readers the nature of our character or ethical orientation

Rhetoricians recognize hundreds of different rhetorical devices, techniques, or strategies. In practice, a passage from a written text or speech often contains several different rhetorical devices, which combine to create a variety of effects. To recognize the different types of effects of a given rhetorical technique, it's necessary to know a little something about the context of the message: what is actually being said, when, where, and for what purpose.

In this section, we'll examine whole passages of text, try to identify as many different rhetorical devices as possible, and analyze how each contributes to the overall effect of the passages. Keep in mind, however, that to identify and analyze the rhetoric of a given passage, you need to be familiar with the definitions of the most common rhetorical techniques.

The rhetorical techniques you need to be familiar with for this Section are parallelism, antithesis, synecdoche, metonymy, personification, metaphor, analogy, exclamation/parenthesis, and hyperbole.

Practice Set One

President John F. Kennedy, in his first inaugural address, deployed a variety of rhetorical techniques. The purpose of this speech (as with any inaugural address) was to address the nation for the first time as president and set the tone for the type of presidency he hoped to establish. The speech, delivered in January of 1961, occurred at a time in world history known as the Cold War, when tensions between communist and non-communist countries threatened peace. It was a time when nuclear war was a possibility and each nation raced to outpace the other in terms of the manufacture of destructive weapons. At this time it seemed important for the president to show his intention of keeping the United States strong in the face of challenges from other nations, without upsetting the current balance of power among them.

Directions: Read Kennedy's speech and identify the rhetorical techniques listed below (under "hints"). Next, analyze how each contributes to the overall effect of the speech—the logic, emotional impact, or the particular *ethos* (impression of the writer's character or the character of the subject of the speech) they create, taking into consideration the context of the speech.

Hints

You should be able to identify:

- At least one example of repetition and grammatical parallelism
- At least five instances of parallelism with antitheses
- At least three instances of the use of some type of symbolism: personification, metonymy, synecdoche, metaphor, or analogy
- At least one example of hyperbole
- One instance of an exclamation (addressing some intended audience)

Note: For ease of reference, we have numbered each of the sentences in the passage.

(1) We observe today not a victory of [the Democratic] party but a celebration of freedom, symbolizing an end as well as a beginning, signifying renewal as well as change, for I have sworn before you and Almighty God the same solemn oath our forbears prescribed nearly a century and three-quarters ago.

(2) The world is very different now, for man holds in his mortal hands the power to abolish all forms of human poverty and all forms of human life. (3) And yet the same revolutionary beliefs for which our forbears fought are still at issue around the globe—the belief that the rights of man come not from the generosity of the state but from the hand of God. (4) We dare not forget today that we are the heirs of that first revolution.

(5) Let the word go forth from this time and place—to friend and foe alike—that the torch has been passed to a new generation of Americans, born in this century, tempered by war, disciplined by a hard and bitter peace, proud of our ancient heritage, and unwilling to witness or permit the slow undoing of those human rights to which this nation has always been committed, and to which we are committed today, at home and around the world.

(6) Let every nation know, whether it wishes us well or ill, that we shall pay any price, bear any burden, meet any hardship, support any friend, oppose any foe, to assure the survival and the success of liberty. (7) This much we pledge—and more.

(8) To those old allies whose cultural and spiritual origins we share: we pledge the loyalty of faithful friends. (9) United, there is little we cannot do in a host of co-operative ventures. Divided, there is little we can do.

Practice Set One Analysis

How did you do? Were you able to identify all the rhetorical techniques Kennedy used in his address, and analyze how each contributed to the overall effect?

If you're familiar with the basic definitions of rhetorical devices, you should have been able to identify most of the following, after analyzing the excerpt from Kennedy's inaugural address.

Repetition and Grammatical Parallelism

a new generation of Americans *born* in this *century*, / *tempered by war*, / *disciplined by* a hard and bitter *peace*, / *proud of* our ancient *heritage* (5)

The repeated grammatical structures are: the past participle of each verb ("tempered," "disciplined," and "proud"), followed by a preposition ("by," "by," and "of") and a noun ("war," "peace," and "heritage").

pay any price, / bear any burden, / meet any hardship, / support any friend, / oppose any foe (6)

The repeated grammatical structures are: verb ("pay," "bear," "meet," "support," and "oppose") plus modified noun ("any price," "any burden," "any hardship," "any friend," and "any foe". Note how the last pair—"support any friend/oppose any foe"—sets up an antithesis, since the meaning of "support" is the opposite of "oppose," and "friend" is the opposite of "foe."

Parallelism with Antitheses

not a victory of party/but a celebration of freedom (1)

The repeated grammatical structure is noun ("a victory" and "a celebration") plus preposition phrase ("of party" and "of freedom"); the "not" defines "party" as contrary or antithetical to "freedom."

symbolizing *an end*/as well as *a beginning* (1) and signifying *renewal* as well as *change* (1)

The repeated grammatical structures are: the *–ing* verb forms ("symbolizing" and "signifying") followed by nouns ("end/beginning" and "renewal/change"). Each set of nouns are opposite in meaning and parallel in grammatical form.

the power to abolish all forms of human poverty/ and all forms of human life (2)

The repeated grammatical structure is a noun ("all forms") plus prepositional phrase ("of human poverty" and "of human life"); to abolish "poverty" (and save lives) is antithetical in meaning to the abolishment of "human life."

rights of man come not from the generosity of the state/ but from the hand of God (3).

The repeated grammatical structure is prepositional phrase ("from the generosity" and "from the hand") joined with another prepositional phrase ("of the state" and "of God"); "state" is antithetical in meaning to "God."

to *friend* and *foe* alike (5)

The repeated grammatical structure is that of the noun ("friend" and "foe"); "friend" is antithetical in meaning to "foe."

support any friend, / oppose any foe (6)

The repeated grammatical structure is that of verb ("support" and "oppose") plus noun ("friend" and "foe"); "support" is opposite in meaning to "oppose," and "friend" is opposite of "foe."

United, there is little we cannot do in a host of co-operative ventures./Divided, there is little we can do. (9)

The repeated grammatical structure is past participle verb form ("united" and "divided") followed by a "there is" clause ("there is little") joined with another independent clause ("we cannot do" and "we can do"); in meaning, "united" is antithetical to (opposite of) "divided" and "cannot do" is antithetical to "can."

Symbolism: Personification-Metonymy-Synecdoche and Metaphor-Analogy

The world is very different now, for *man holds in his mortal hands* the power to abolish all forms of human poverty (2)

The "man" referred to here is meant to stand for man in the abstract, as a species unique among all others. In this sense, "man" is functioning as a type of synecdoche because this man is also figured as an individual person who has hands and can hold things. Therefore the figure of a man stands for the whole of humankind. "Hands" itself is an instance of metonymy in that it reduces the complex and abstract idea of having control over something to literally having one's hands on it. Power, therefore, is personified by means of a man's literal grip of something with his hands.

the rights of man come not from the generosity of the state but from *the hand of God.* (3)

God is personified as a human being who possesses a hand; and "hand" is an instance of metonymy in that it is meant to refer to the more abstract idea of man being under the influence of God, who is personified as a being with hands, able to bestow the abstract quality of individual rights to all men.

We are the heirs of that first revolution. (4)

The present generation of Americans are implicitly being compared to direct descendents of those who initiated the revolution, which itself is being compared implicitly to a legacy that gets handed down from generation to generation.

Let *the word go forth* from this time and place . . . that *the torch* has been passed to a new generation of Americans (5)

Here "the word" is meant to stand for the entire message of Kennedy's inaugural address, so it is functioning as a synecdoche—it reduces the message to a single word. Note also that the reference to "the word" is a personification, for it can move or "go forth" as a person would. The word "torch" is an instance of metonymy, in that passing a "torch" symbolizes at a more abstract level any passing on of knowledge or responsibility. The reference to "torch" is also a personification, since in the Olympic athletic games, a torch is literally passed from runner to runner to mark the beginning of the games. Here it refers to the transition from one presidency to another.

To those old allies . . . we pledge the loyalty of faithful friends. (8)

Other nations are personified here as friends of the United States.

Hyperbole

a new generation of Americans . . . proud of our ancient heritage (5)

To say that America has an "ancient heritage" (usually meaning before the times of the Roman Empire, before Christ) is a bit of an overstatement, considering that the nation was not even 200 years old at the time of the speech.

Let every nation know. . . that we shall *pay any price, bear any burden.* . . to assure the survival and success of liberty. (6)

The all-encompassing modifier "any" exaggerates to the furthest extreme the extent to which Americans are willing to fight for liberty. There are probably some circumstances—such as the threat of nuclear war and worldwide destruction—that might make us back down from such a commitment.

Exclamation-Parenthesis

Let the word go forth from this time and place—to friend and foe alike—that the torch . . . (5)

The phrase "to friend and foe alike" is an interrupting of the main clause and is an exclamation that addresses the intended audience of the message.

Analyzing the Effects of Kennedy's Rhetorical Techniques

It should be clear from identifying the rhetorical techniques that Kennedy relies heavily on parallelism and especially antitheses. The speech mainly sets up oppositions, such as friend/foe, united/divided, and end/beginning, which seems well suited to the historical situation of the speech. Recall that the United States was engaged in tense relations with the Soviet Union, in a Cold War that pitted communism against capitalism. Nuclear war was considered a real possibility. One effect of all those antitheses is to demonstrate the possibility that even if the world is divided, it is possible to keep those differences in balance, as in each sentence parallel grammatical structures are balanced against differences in meaning. The antitheses set up a logic of balanced oppositions, a logic that also characterized the world at the time. Kennedy's character itself shows awareness of the need for balance—the need to be both strong as well as restrained, so as not to incite unjustifiable aggression.

There are also a fair amount of rhetorical techniques of the symbolic variety—personification, synecdoche, metonymy, and metaphor. Kennedy uses these techniques to portray the nation (and his leadership of it) in terms of vivid, concrete images rather than mere abstract ideas. The concrete images, in other words, give material substance to the ideas he is trying to convey. For example, when he declares, "Let the word go forth," he portrays his speech as able to take action in the world, rather than merely as empty words. Therefore the rhetorical techniques contribute to the ethos of strength conveyed by Kennedy's message. The personifications, metaphors, and other symbolic devices also create emotional effect in that the audience can relate more directly to the vivid images they create than to merely "dry," abstract ideas, such as "freedom," "liberty," and "strength."

Kennedy's use of hyperbole contributes to the emotional effect as well as the ethos, or character of his subject—clearly he means to construct the nation as committed to its principles and willing to fight for them. The use of such extreme assertions as "pay any price, bear any burden," shows the extent to which Kennedy is willing to go to protect the principles on which American government rests.

The use of the exclamation—"to friend and foe alike"—makes it clear the Kennedy means for his speech to address not only the nation and those who supported him, but also those who might question his ability to lead. By directly addressing his "foes," he shows he is not going to shy away from confrontation with his or the nation's enemies.

Overall, these rhetorical techniques portray Kennedy as a strong leader, committed to keeping the nation strong as well as to preserving the principles on which the nation has been founded.

KAPLAN

Practice Set Two

In the following excerpt from *Imaginary Conversations*, written in 1829, Walter Savage Landor expresses his view that the best writers as those who have preserved the harmony, correctness, and energy of older styles of writing and traditional features of the English language, as modeled by the Bible as well as by the works of Milton.

Directions: Read the passage and identify rhetorical techniques and the purposes they seem to be serving in the context of the passage. Test yourself with the questions that follow. Make sure to respond to them on your own before reviewing the correct answers provided.

Note: For ease of reference, we have numbered each of the sentences in the passage.

(1) Let those who look upon style as unworthy of much attention ask themselves how many, in proportion to men of genius, have excelled in it. (2) In all languages, ancient and modern, are there ten prose-writers at once harmonious, correct, and energetic? (3) Harmony and correctness are not uncommon separately, and force is occasionally with each; but where, excepting in Milton, where, among all the moderns, is energy to be found always in the right place? (4) Even Cicero is defective here, and sometimes in the most elaborate of his orations. (5) In the time of Milton it was not customary for men of abilities to address the people at large with what might inflame their passions. (6) The appeal was made to the serious, to the well-informed, to the learned, and was made in the language of their studies. (7) The phraseology of our Bible, on which no subsequent age has improved, was thought to carry with it solemnity and authority; and even when popular feelings were to be aroused to popular interest, the language of the prophets was preferred to the language of the vulgar. . . . (8) Waller, Cowley, and South were resolved to refine what was already pure gold, and threw inadvertently there into the crucible many old family jewels deeply encased within it. (9) Eliot, Pym, Selden, and Milton reverenced their father's house and retained its right language unmodified.

1. In relation to the passage as a whole, the question in sentence 3, "where, excepting in Milton, where among all the moderns, is energy to be found always in the right place," presents
    (A) a metaphor that introduces the subject of the passage
    (B) a proverb that expresses the main theme of the passage
    (C) an antithetical statement that sets up the central question to be explored in the passage
    (D) a rhetorical question that implicitly asserts the author's position on the subject

2. In sentence 6, the author employs which of the following rhetorical techniques?
    (A) A series of antitheses
    (B) Parallelism of grammatical form and theme
    (C) Hyperbole
    (D) Personification

3. The reference in sentence 8 to "pure gold" and "the crucible many old family jewels deeply encased within it" is

    (A) a personification of the way certain writers treasure certain words

    (B) a paradoxical reference to the fact that most writers were sponsored by wealthy patrons

    (C) a metaphor implicitly comparing the language of certain writers to valuable metal, which can be further refined to produce additional gems of language

    (D) an antithetical argument that contrasts worthless language with more valuable language

4. Which of the following best describes the rhetorical function of sentence 9 in the passage?

    (A) Personify the central topic of the passage in morally charged terms

    (B) Establish a counter-argument by means of exemplification

    (C) Create a logical paradox

    (D) Interrupt the deductive logic with a parenthetical exclamation

5. The reference to "father" in sentence 9 is mostly likely meant to suggest in the context of the passage as a whole that

    (A) Eliot, Pym, Selden, and Milton were all examples of brothers who were successful writers

    (B) this group of writers figuratively paid homage to writers who preceded them, which it was their rightful duty to do

    (C) the language of these writers is metonymically a reference to the sacredness of the Church

    (D) the importance in life more generally of the proverb, "Honor thy mother and father"

Practice Set Two Analysis

1. (D)

A rhetorical question that implicitly asserts the author's position on the subject. This is clear, since the author implies immediately before the question that only in Milton is energy to be found.

2. (B)

Parallelism of grammatical form and theme. "The appeal was made *to the* serious, *to the* well-informed, *to the* learned, and was made in the language of their studies." The parallelism is built using the prepositional phrase "to the . . . ."

3. (C)

A metaphor implicitly comparing the language of certain writers to valuable metal, which can be further refined to produce additional gems of language. The direct comparison of two dissimilar things, in this case, pure gold and the writer's use of language, represent the author's use of metaphor.

4. (A)

Personify the central topic of the passage in morally charged terms. The use of "reverenced" and "retained its right language" give this sentence—and the passage—a moral charge.

5. (B)

This group of writers figuratively paid homage to writers who preceded them, which it was their rightful duty to do. Landor is saying that Eliot, Pym, Selden, and Milton "reverenced their father's house" by keeping the original language intact.

Practice Set Three

Read the following paragraph and answer questions 1–3.

> Irony occurs when there is a discrepancy in meaning between what appears to be the case, or what is stated, and the underlying meaning. Types of irony include verbal, dramatic, and situational. Verbal irony occurs when the intended meaning is the opposite of the words that are actually said. Dramatic irony happens when the fact that the audience knows more than a particular character becomes apparent, especially by some statement of the character. Situational irony refers to situations in which what happens is at odds with the audience's expectations. Verbal and dramatic irony are generally intentional, while situational irony may also be unintentional.

1. In the play *Oedipus Rex*, Oedipus is prophesied to kill his father, the king, and to marry his mother. To prevent this occurrence, at birth Oedipus is sent off to be killed, but ends up surviving and being raised by another family. In the course of the play, Oedipus does kill his father, becomes king, and weds his mother. Even after the prophecy is fulfilled, he doesn't know his true identity and sets off to find the king's murderer. At this point, he states, "Now I reign, holding the power which he had held before me, having the selfsame wife and marriage bed—and if his seed had not met barren fortune, we should be linked by offspring from one mother; but as it was, fate leapt upon his Head, [and I shall search] to seize the hand which shed that blood." What type of irony does this statement represent? What are some of the effects of this irony on the play's audience?

2. What type of irony occurs when someone drops a tray in the cafeteria and a classmate calls out, "Nice job!"? What is the effect of this irony on the audience?

3. In his essay "A Modest Proposal," Jonathan Swift proposes a cannibalistic solution to the problem of Irish poverty: He suggests that Irish babies should be eaten as delicacies by the rich. Before he gets to this specific solution, however, he includes the following passage: "There is likewise another great advantage in my scheme, that it will prevent those voluntary abortions, and that horrid practice of women murdering their bastard children, alas, too frequently among us, sacrificing the poor innocent babes, I doubt, more to avoid the expense than the shame." What type of irony does this produce? What are some of the consequences of Swift's irony?

Read the following statements, and then answer questions 4 and 5.

> Rain on your wedding day
> Saying "I love your outfit!" when a friend dons something preposterously ugly
> Feeling ill from eating too much tasty rich food
> A black fly in your Chardonnay

4. People often misunderstand what "irony" means. Which of the examples above is ironic and why?

5. Why are the other examples not ironic?

Practice Set Three Analysis

1. Oedipus's statement here is an example of dramatic irony. While the audience knows of the prophecy and Oedipus's familial origins, Oedipus himself does not. The audience has the pleasure of anticipating the events in the text that are prophesied, and knowing more than the central character. The dramatic irony heightens the tension in the plot as Oedipus comes closer and closer to discovering his own identity.

2. The example here is one of verbal irony. Clearly the bystander is mocking, not praising, the actions of the clumsy student. As for the effects on the audience: This example of verbal irony is also an example of sarcasm, which is a cutting statement. The student who dropped the tray may feel humiliated or may take the opportunity to make fun of himself or herself. The onlookers may feel sorry for the student who dropped the tray, or they may just find the event humorous. Sarcasm usually depends on irony and, in addition, is always cutting; irony, on the other hand, can have many different rhetorical effects.

3. The "Modest Proposal" example shows situational irony. The fact that Swift proposes such a murderous solution throughout the essay is at odds with his apparent condemnation of these women for their "horrid practice." What are the consequences? The juxtaposition of these two kinds of murderous behaviors may cause the reader to question his or her own attitudes toward the poor. It aligns the practices (and so, the impoverished mothers and the wealthy) in a way that doesn't allow easy resolution.

4. The second example—saying "I love your outfit!" when the opposite is true—is ironic. Since the intended meaning is the opposite of the literal meaning, it's an example of verbal irony.

5. Having rain on your wedding day and a black fly in your Chardonnay are simply unfortunate coincidences, not ironies. No ambiguity or movement in meaning exists. Feeling sick is a predictable response from overindulgence in tasty rich foods, and so it doesn't meet the criteria for irony, either.

SATIRE

Satire is a rhetorical strategy that has the purpose of diminishing or ridiculing a subject. Satirical texts function by a variety of rhetorical devices, often including irony, sarcasm, analogies, extended metaphors, hyperbole, understatement, and other figurative language. Becoming familiar with these devices is key to understanding and interpreting satire; the devices are important clues to the meaning implicit in the text. Effective satires also rely on a strong, narrative persona, including a clear and consistent tone (often sarcastic or ironic) and the construction of an immediate relationship between the narrator and the reader. The questions below are based on Jonathan Swift's famous 1729 satire "A Modest Proposal."

After reading on Swift's "A Modest Proposal," you should be able to answer the following study questions.

Study Questions

1. What is this piece about?

2. How is the piece structured?

3. How would you describe the language of the piece?

4. To whom is the piece addressed?

5. What effect does the piece have on the reader?

6. What is the purpose, or goal, of the piece?

7. Is the piece effective at its goal? Why?

Next, answer the following questions about the satirical qualities of Swift's text, then compare your answers with ours, which can be found after the text.

1. Who are the main targets of Swift's satire?

2. How does Swift immediately establish a connection with his audience?

3. What are some metaphors the text uses? What are some of their effects?

4. What other devices does Swift use early in the text to signal the satirical mode of the writing?

5. How does the text use synecdoche? What are the consequences?

A Modest Proposal

Jonathan Swift

FOR PREVENTING THE CHILDREN OF POOR PEOPLE IN IRELAND FROM BEING A BURDEN TO THEIR PARENTS OR COUNTRY, AND FOR MAKING THEM BENEFICIAL TO THE PUBLIC

It is a melancholy object to those who walk through this great town or travel in the country, when they see the streets, the roads, and cabin doors, crowded with beggars of the female-sex, followed by three, four, or six children, all in rags and importuning every passenger for an alms. These mothers, instead of being able to work for their honest livelihood, are forced to employ all their time in strolling to beg sustenance for their helpless infants, who, as they grow up, either turn thieves for want of work, or leave their dear native country to fight for the Pretender in Spain, or sell themselves to the Barbadoes.

I think it is agreed by all parties that this prodigious number of children in the arms, or on the backs, or at the heels of their mothers, and frequently of their fathers, is in the present deplorable state of the kingdom a very great additional grievance; and therefore whoever could find out a fair, cheap, and easy method of making these children sound, useful members of the commonwealth would deserve so well of the public as to have his statue set up for a preserver of the nation.

But my intention is very far from being confined to provide only for the children of professed beggars; it is of a much greater extent, and shall take in the whole number of infants at a certain age who are born of parents in effect as little able to support them as those who demand our charity in the streets.

As to my own part, having turned my thoughts for many years upon this important subject, and maturely weighed the several schemes of other projectors, I have always found them grossly mistaken in their computation. It is true, a child just dropped from its dam may be supported by her milk for a solar year, with little other nourishment; at most not above the value of two shillings, which the mother may certainly get, or the value in scraps, by her lawful occupation of begging; and it is exactly at one year old that I propose to provide for them in such a manner as instead of being a charge upon their parents or the parish, or wanting food and raiment for the rest of their lives, they shall on the contrary contribute to the feeding, and partly to the clothing, of many thousands.

There is likewise another great advantage in my scheme, that it will prevent those voluntary abortions, and that horrid practice of women murdering their bastard children, alas, too frequent among us, sacrificing the poor innocent babes, I doubt, more to avoid the expense than the shame, which would move tears and pity in the most savage and inhuman breast.

The number of souls in this kingdom being usually reckoned one million and a half, of these I calculate there may be about two hundred thousand couple whose wives are breeders; from which number I subtract thirty thousand couples who are able to maintain their own children, although I apprehend there cannot be so many under the present distresses of the kingdom; but this being granted, there will remain all hundred and seventy thousand breeders. I again subtract fifty thousand for those women who miscarry, or whose children die by accident or disease within the year. There only remain all hundred and twenty thousand children of poor parents annually born. The question therefore is, how this number shall be reared and provided for, which, as I have already said, under the present situation of affairs, is utterly impossible by all the methods hitherto proposed. For we can neither employ them in handicraft or agriculture; we neither build houses (I mean in the country) nor cultivate land. They can very seldom pick up a livelihood by stealing till they arrive at six years old, except where they are of towardly parts; although I confess they learn the rudiments much earlier, during which time they can however be looked upon only as probationers, as I have been informed by a principal gentleman in the county of Cavan, who protested to me that he never knew above one or two instances under the age of six, even in a part of the kingdom so renowned for the quickest proficiency in the art.

I am assured by our merchants that a boy or a girl before twelve years old is no salable commodity; and even when they come to this age they will not yield above three pounds, or three pounds and half a crown at most on the Exchange; which cannot turn to account either to the parents or the kingdom, the charge of nutriment and rags having been at least four times that value.

I shall now therefore humbly propose my own thoughts, which I hope will not be liable to the least objection.

I have been assured by a very knowing American of my acquaintance in London, that a young healthy child well nursed is at a year old a most delicious, nourishing, and wholesome food, whether stewed, roasted, baked, or boiled; and I make no doubt that it will equally serve in a fricassee or a ragout.

I do therefore humbly offer it to public consideration that of the hundred and twenty thousand children, already computed, twenty thousand may be reserved for breed, whereof only one fourth part to be males, which is more than we allow to sheep, black cattle, or swine; and my reason is that these children are seldom the fruits of marriage, a circumstance not much regarded by our savages, therefore one male will be sufficient to serve four females.

That the remaining hundred thousand may at a year old be offered in sale to the persons of quality and fortune through the kingdom, always advising the mother to let them suck plentifully in the last month, so as to render them plump and fat for a good table. A child will make two dishes at an entertainment for friends; and when the family dines alone, the fore or hind quarter will make a reasonable dish, and seasoned with a little pepper or salt will be very good boiled on the fourth day, especially in winter.

I have reckoned upon a medium that a child just born will weigh twelve pounds, and in a solar year if tolerably nursed increaseth to twenty-eight pounds.

I grant this food will be somewhat dear, and therefore very proper for landlords, who, as they have already devoured most of the parents, seem to have the best title to the children.

Infant's flesh will be in season throughout the year, but more plentiful in March, and a little before and after. For we are told by a grave author, an eminent French physician, that fish being a prolific diet, there are more children born in Roman Catholic countries about nine months after Lent than at any other season; therefore, reckoning a year after Lent, the markets will be more glutted than usual, because the number of popish infants is at least three to one in this kingdom; and therefore it will have one other collateral advantage, by lessening the number of Papists among us.

I have already computed the charge of nursing a beggar's child (in which list I reckon it cottagers, laborers, and four fifths of the farmers) to be about two shillings per annum, rags included; and I believe no gentleman would repine to give ten shillings for the carcass of a good fat child, which, as I have said, will make four dishes of excellent nutritive meat, when he hath only some particular friend or his own family to dine with him. Thus the squire will learn to be a good landlord, and grow popular among the tenants; the mother will have eight shillings net profit, and be fit for work till she produces another child.

Those who are more thrifty (as I must confess the times require) may flay the carcass; the skin of which artificially dressed will make admirable gloves for ladies, and summer boots for fine gentlemen.

As to our city of Dublin, shambles may be appointed for this purpose in the most convenient parts of it, and butchers we may be assured will not be wanting; although I rather recommend buying the children alive, and dressing them hot from the knife as we do roasting pigs.

A very worthy person, a true lover of his country, and whose virtues I highly esteem, was lately pleased in discoursing on this matter to offer a refinement upon my scheme. He said that many gentlemen of this kingdom, having of late destroyed their deer, he conceived that the want of venison might be well supplied by the bodies of young lads and maidens, not exceeding fourteen years of age nor under twelve, so great a number of both sexes in every county being now ready to starve for want of work and service; and these to be disposed of by their parents, if alive, or otherwise by their nearest relations. But with due deference to so excellent a friend and so deserving a patriot, I cannot be altogether in his sentiments; for as to the males, my American acquaintance assured me from frequent experience that their flesh was generally tough and lean, like that of our schoolboys, by continual exercise, and their taste disagreeable; and to fatten them would not answer the charge. Then as to the females, it would, I think with humble submission, be a loss to the public, because they soon would become breeders themselves: and besides, it is not improbable that some scrupulous people might be apt to censure such a practice (although indeed very unjustly) as a little bordering upon cruelty; which, I confess, hath always been with me the strongest objection against any project, how well soever intended.

But in order to justify my friend, he confessed that this expedient was put into his head by the famous Psalmanazar, a native of the island Formosa, who came from thence to London above twenty years ago, and in conversation told my friend that in his country when any young person happened to be put to death, the executioner sold the carcass to persons of quality as a prime dainty; and that in his time the body of a plump girl of fifteen, who was crucified for an attempt to poison the emperor, was sold to his Imperial Majesty's prime minister of state, and other great mandarins of the court, in joints from the gibbet, at four hundred crowns. Neither indeed can I deny that if the same use were made of several plump young girls in this town, who without one single groat to their fortunes cannot stir abroad without a chair, and appear at the playhouse and assemblies in foreign fineries which they never will pay for, the kingdom would not be the worse.

Some persons of a desponding spirit are in great concern about that vast number of poor people who are aged, diseased, or maimed, and I have been desired to employ my thoughts what course may be taken to ease the nation of so grievous an encumbrance. But I am not in the least pain upon that matter, because it is very well known that they are every day dying and rotting by cold and famine, and filth and vermin, as fast as can be reasonably expected. And as to the younger laborers, they are now in almost as hopeful a condition. They cannot get work, and consequently pine away for want of nourishment to a degree that if at any time they are accidentally hired to common labor, they have not strength to perform it; and thus the country and themselves are happily delivered from the evils to come.

I have too long digressed, all therefore shall return to my subject. I think the advantages by the proposal which I have made are obvious and many, as well as of the highest importance.

For first, as I have already observed, it would greatly lessen the number of Papists, with whom we are yearly overrun, being the principal breeders of the nation as well as our most dangerous enemies; and who stay at home on purpose to deliver the kingdom to the Pretender, hoping to take their advantage by the absence of so many good Protestants, who have chosen rather to leave their country than to stay at home and pay tithes against their conscience to all Episcopal curate.

Secondly, the poorer tenants will have something valuable of their own, which by law may be made liable to distress, and help to pay their landlord's rent, their corn and cattle being already seized and money a thing unknown.

Thirdly, whereas the maintenance of an hundred thousand children, from two years old and upwards, cannot be computed at less than ten shillings a piece per annum, the nation's stock will be thereby increased fifty thousand pounds per annum, besides the profit of a new dish introduced to the tables of all gentlemen of fortune in the kingdom who have any refinement in taste. And the money will circulate among ourselves, the goods being entirely of our own growth and manufacture.

Fourthly, the constant breeders, besides the gain of eight shillings sterling per annum by the sale of their children, will be rid of the charge of maintaining them after the first year.

Fifthly, this food would likewise bring great custom to taverns, where the vintners will certainly be so prudent as to procure the best receipts for dressing it to perfection, and consequently have their houses frequented by all the fine gentlemen, who justly value themselves upon their knowledge in good eating; and a skillful cook, who understands how to oblige his guests, will contrive to make it as expensive as they please.

Sixthly, this would be a great inducement to marriage, which all wise nations have either encouraged by rewards or enforced by laws and penalties. It would increase the care and tenderness of mothers toward their children, when they were sure of a settlement for life to the poor babes, provided in some sort by the public, to their annual profit instead of expense. We should see an honest emulation among the married women, which of them could bring the fattest child to the market. Men would become as fond of their wives during the time of their pregnancy as they are now of their mares in foal, their cows in calf, or sows when they are ready to farrow; nor offer to beat or kick them (as is too frequent a practice) for fear of a miscarriage.

Many, other advantages might be enumerated. For instance, the addition of some thousand carcasses in our exportation of barreled beef, the propagation of swine's flesh, and improvement in the art of making good bacon, so much wanted among us by the great destruction of pigs, too frequent at our tables, which are no way comparable in taste or magnificence to a wellgrown, fat, yearling child, which roasted whole will make a considerable figure at a lord mayor's feast or any other public entertainment. But this and many others I omit, being studious of brevity.

Supposing that one thousand families in this city would be constant customers for infants' flesh, besides others who might have it at merry meetings, particularly weddings and christenings, I compute that Dublin would take off annually about twenty thousand carcasses, and the rest of the kingdom (where probably they will be sold somewhat cheaper) the remaining eighty thousand.

I can think of no one objection that will possibly be raised against this proposal, unless it should be urged that the number of people will be thereby much lessened in the kingdom. This I freely own, and it was indeed one principal design in offering it to the world. I desire the reader will observe, that I calculate my remedy for this one individual kingdom of Ireland and for no other that ever was, is, or I think ever can be upon earth. Therefore let no man talk to me of other expedients: of taxing our absentees at five shillings a pound: of using neither clothes nor household furniture except what is of our own growth and manufacture: of utterly rejecting the materials and instruments that promote foreign luxury: of curing the expensiveness of pride, vanity, idleness, and gaming in our women: of introducing a vein of parsimony, prudence, and temperance: of learning to love our country, in the want of which we differ even from Laplanders and the inhabitants of Topinamboo: of quitting our animosities and factions, nor acting any longer like the Jews, who were murdering one another at the very moment their city was taken: of being a little cautious not to sell our country and conscience for nothing: of teaching landlords to have at least one degree of mercy toward their tenants: lastly, of putting a spirit of honesty, industry, and skill into our shopkeepers; who, if a resolution could now be taken to buy only our native goods, would immediately unite to cheat and exact upon us in the price, the measure, and the goodness, nor could ever yet be brought to make one fair proposal of just dealing, though often and earnestly invited to it.

Therefore I repeat, let no man talk to me of these and the like expedients, till he hath at least some glimpse of hope that there will ever be some hearty and sincere attempt to put them in practice.

But as to myself, having been wearied out for many years with offering vain, idle, visionary thoughts, and at length utterly despairing of success, I fortunately fell upon this proposal, which, as it is wholly new, so it hath something solid and real, of no expense and little trouble, full in our own power, and whereby we can incur no danger in disobliging England. For this kind of commodity will not bear exportation, the flesh being of too tender a consistence to admit a long continuance in salt, although perhaps I could name a country which would be glad to eat up our whole nation without it.

After all, I am not so violently bent upon my own opinion as to reject any offer proposed by wise men, which shall be found equally innocent, cheap, easy, and effectual. But before something of that kind shall be advanced in contradiction to my scheme, and offering a better, I desire the author or authors will be pleased maturely to consider two points. First, as things now stand, how they will be able to find food and raiment for an hundred thousand useless months and backs. And secondly, there being a round million of creatures in human figure throughout this kingdom, whose sole subsistence put into a common stock would leave them in debt two millions of pounds sterling, adding those who are beggars by profession to the bulk of farmers, cottagers, and laborers, with their wives and children who are beggars in effect; I desire those politicians who dislike my overture, and may perhaps be so bold to attempt an answer, that they will first ask the parents of these mortals whether they would not at this day think it a great happiness to have been sold for food at a year old in the manner I prescribe, and thereby have avoided such a perpetual scene of misfortunes as they have since gone through by the oppression of landlords, the impossibility of paying rent without money or trade, the want of common sustenance, with neither house nor clothes to cover them from the inclemencies of the weather, and the most inevitable prospect of entailing the like or greater miseries upon their breed forever.

I profess, in the sincerity of my heart, that I have not the least personal interest in endeavoring to promote this necessary work, having no other motive than the public good of my country, by advancing our trade, providing for infants, relieving the poor, and giving some pleasure to the rich. I have no children by which I call propose to get a single penny; the youngest being nine years old, and my wife past childbearing.

Answers

1. Who are the main targets of Swift's satire?

The main targets are wealthy landowners, the English, people with anti-Catholic sentiments, and the "projectors," cultural commentators who construct schemes to deal with social problems such as poverty.

2. How does Swift immediately establish a connection with his audience?

Swift relies on the shared assumption that the poverty in Ireland is a difficult social problem. For example, he begins the second paragraph with the statement, "I think it is agreed by all parties, that this prodigious number of children in the arms, or on the backs, or at the heels of their mothers, and frequently of their fathers, is in the present deplorable state of the kingdom, a very great additional grievance."

3. What are some of the metaphors the text uses? What are some of their effects?

Swift likens women to breeders, cows, and mares. Children in the text become livestock and gourmet food. Stealing is referred to as an art. The Irish poor are represented as savages. Implicitly, elite society is also represented as barbaric, through the parallel drawn between "the famous Psalmanazar, a [cannibalistic] native of the island Formosa" and those who would feast upon the Irish children in Swift's scheme. Aligning women and children with animals critiques the contemporary practices that dehumanize the poor by exaggeration. In other words, by presenting the connection between women and children and livestock as "reasonable," Swift is taking a societal assumption to its logical conclusion in order to critique it. Because Swift characterizes stealing as an "art" of the poor near the beginning of the essay, it functions to call into question the credibility of the apparently "reasonable" narrator. The equation of everyone with savages and "barbaric" cultures criticizes the moral position of English and Irish societies.

4.   *What other devices does Swift use early in the text to signal the satirical mode of the writing?*

The word "modest" in the title is ironic, given that the entire proposal is actually outlandish. This irony becomes apparent in the third paragraph, where he states, "But my intention if very far from being confined to provide only for the children of professed beggars: it is of a much greater extent." By presenting his intentions as much grander than "modest," this sentence destabilizes the meaning of the title. Additionally, in the eighth and tenth paragraphs, Swift uses repetition of the word "humbly" to further undermine the credibility of the narrator. The repetition calls into question whether or not the narrator is actually "humble" in his proposal. Attention to the tone reveals that he presents himself as anything but "humble." For example, later he boldly states, "I think the advantages by the proposal which I have made are obvious and many, as well as of the highest importance." Also, Swift's mockery of the "projectors," who dispassionately produce and advocate solutions to social problems marks the text as a satire. By putting women and children into an economic framework and characterizing children as "commodities" without taking into account the social and emotional aspects of childbearing and raising children, he parodies Utilitarianism.

5.   *How does the text use synecdoche? What are the consequences?*

In the second to last paragraph, Swift asks his readers to consider, "As things now stand, how they will be able to find food and raiment for a hundred thousand useless mouths and backs." The statement reduces the people who are members of Ireland's poorest classes to "useless mouths and backs." The particular body parts that these people become are significant; as "mouths," they do nothing but consume food, while as "useless . . . backs," they cannot even work, and so are completely unproductive, needy elements of society. Because this statement occurs in a satire, Swift is condemning those who would see the poorest members of society as simply body parts rather than people.

FUNCTIONS OF RHETORIC

Rhetoric is a necessary skill for nearly every writing project. From letters to the editor of a local paper to technical reports describing the construction of a computer system, writers must consider the most appropriate and effective way to get their point across.

But in some instances—a technical manual, for example—the writer has little need to spend a lot of time on rhetorical devices and stylistic considerations. A reader of this material has a predefined reason for reading it—to get the information contained in the text. We read computer manuals because we want information about how a computer works. A writer documenting the facts about a computer system doesn't need to spend a lot of time persuading the reader of the value of the information. However, a writer advocating a new idea or an unpopular opinion might need to spend some time and energy persuading his or her reader of the value of the idea or opinion.

In this section you'll analyze the Preface from Mary Wollstonecraft's *A Vindication of the Rights of Woman*. Before you read this piece, you might want to spend a few minutes thinking about the role society restricted women to during Wollstonecraft's time—the late 18th century. Think about the title of the piece, and speculate about what you think Wollstonecraft's purpose in writing might be. Also consider the audience to whom she was writing. Take notes about the ideas and questions that come to you as you read.

Answer the following list of study questions as you read Wollstonecraft's text. Then answer the "Questions for Further Consideration." The answers to these questions will take some thinking about. They may not be obvious the first time you read this piece, which means you may need to reread part or all of the text to be able to answer the questions fully. Give complete answers to the questions; if you give short answers, you short-change yourself. When you're done, compare your answers with ours.

Study Questions

1. What is this piece about?

2. How is the piece structured?

3. How would you describe the language of the piece?

4. To whom is the piece addressed?

5. What effect does the piece have on the reader?

6. What is the purpose, or goal, of the piece?

7. Is the piece effective at its goal? Why?

Questions for Further Consideration

1. Wollstonecraft addresses this preface to a prominent politician of her time. What do we know about this person? In what ways does she use this very specific audience to her rhetorical advantage?

2. Wollstonecraft makes great use of the rhetoric of interruption. What parts of the text exhibit this device? In what ways does she use the device of interrupting her own train of thought to her advantage?

3. Although Wollstonecraft's message is political, it also has significant moral and ethical overtones. In what way does she establish her moral or ethical authority in this piece?

4. Wollstonecraft realized that there would be a great deal of resistance to her message simply because she was a woman. Because of the prejudices of her day, any idea she put forth would likely be considered as more emotional, and less factual than a man's. How does she overcome this obstacle?

5. Are there any instances of parallel sentence structure that you can see in Wollstonecraft's text? How do these serve her argumentative purpose?

Preface, A Vindication of the Rights of Woman

Mary Wollstonecraft

Dedication

To M. Talleyrand-Perigord, Late Bishop Of Autun.

Sir,

Having read with great pleasure a pamphlet which you have lately published, I dedicate this volume to you; to induce you to reconsider the subject, and maturely weigh what I have advanced respecting the rights of woman and national education: and I call with the firm tone of humanity; for my arguments, Sir, are dictated by a disinterested spirit—I plead for my sex—not for myself.

Independence I have long considered as the grand blessing of life, the basis of every virtue—and independence I will ever secure by contracting my wants, though I were to live on a barren heath.

It is then an affection for the whole human race that makes my pen dart rapidly along to support what I believe to be the cause of virtue: and the same motive leads me earnestly to wish to see woman placed in a station in which she would advance, instead of retarding, the progress of those glorious principles that give a substance to morality. My opinion, indeed, respecting the rights and duties of woman, seems to flow so naturally from these simple principles, that I think it scarcely possible, but that some of the enlarged minds who formed your admirable constitution, will coincide with me.

In France there is undoubtedly a more general diffusion of knowledge than in any part of the European world, and I attribute it, in a great measure, to the social intercourse which has long subsisted between the sexes. It is true, I utter my sentiments with freedom, that in France the very essence of sensuality has been extracted to regale the voluptuary, and a kind of sentimental lust has prevailed, which, together with the system of duplicity that the whole tenour of their political and civil government taught, have given a sinister sort of sagacity to the French character, properly termed finesse; from which naturally flow a polish of manners that injures the substance, by hunting sincerity out of society. And, modesty, the fairest garb of virtue has been more grossly insulted in France than even in England, till their women have treated as PRUDISH that attention to decency, which brutes instinctively observe.

Manners and morals are so nearly allied that they have often been confounded; but, though the former should only be the natural reflection of the latter, yet, when various causes have produced factitious and corrupt manners, which are very early caught, morality becomes an empty name. The personal reserve, and sacred respect for cleanliness and delicacy in domestic life, which French women almost despise, are the graceful pillars of modesty; but, far from despising them, if the pure flame of patriotism have reached their bosoms, they should labour to improve the morals of their fellow-citizens, by teaching men, not only to respect modesty in women, but to acquire it themselves, as the only way to merit their esteem.

Contending for the rights of woman, my main argument is built on this simple principle, that if she be not prepared by education to become the companion of man, she will stop the progress of knowledge and virtue; for truth must be common to all, or it will be inefficacious with respect to its influence on general practice. And how can woman be expected to co-operate unless she know why she ought to be virtuous? Unless freedom strengthen her reason till she comprehend her duty, and see in what manner it is connected with her real good? If children are to be educated to understand the true principle of patriotism, their mother must be a patriot; and the love of mankind, from which an orderly train of virtues spring, can only be produced by considering the moral and civil interest of mankind; but the education and situation of woman, at present, shuts her out from such investigations.

In this work I have produced many arguments, which to me were conclusive, to prove that the prevailing notion respecting a sexual character was subversive of morality, and I have contended, that to render the human body and mind more perfect, chastity must more universally prevail, and that chastity will never be respected in the male world till the person of a woman is not, as it were, idolized, when little virtue or sense embellish it with the grand traces of mental beauty, or the interesting simplicity of affection.

Consider, Sir, dispassionately, these observations, for a glimpse of this truth seemed to open before you when you observed, 'that to see one half of the human race excluded by the other from all participation of government, was a political phenomenon that, according to abstract principles, it was impossible to explain.' If so, on what does your constitution rest? If the abstract rights of man will bear discussion and explanation, those of woman, by a parity of reasoning, will not shrink from the same test: though a different opinion prevails in this country, built on the very arguments which you use to justify the oppression of woman—prescription.

Consider, I address you as a legislator, whether, when men contend for their freedom, and to be allowed to judge for themselves respecting their own happiness, it be not inconsistent and unjust to subjugate women, even though you firmly believe that you are acting in the manner best calculated to promote their happiness? Who made man the exclusive judge, if woman partake with him the gift of reason?

In this style, argue tyrants of every denomination, from the weak king to the weak father of a family; they are all eager to crush reason; yet always assert that they usurp its throne only to be useful. Do you not act a similar part, when you FORCE all women, by denying them civil and political rights, to remain immured in their families groping in the dark? For surely, Sir, you will not assert, that a duty can be binding which is not founded on reason? If indeed this be their destination, arguments may be drawn from reason: and thus augustly supported, the more understanding women acquire, the more they will be attached to their duty—comprehending it—for unless they comprehend it, unless their morals be fixed on the same immutable principle as those of man, no authority can make them discharge it in a virtuous manner. They may be convenient slaves, but slavery will have its constant effect, degrading the master and the abject dependent.

But, if women are to be excluded, without having a voice, from a participation of the natural rights of mankind, prove first, to ward off the charge of injustice and inconsistency, that they want reason—else this flaw in your NEW CONSTITUTION will ever show that man must, in some shape, act like a tyrant, and tyranny, in whatever part of society it rears its brazen front, will ever undermine morality.

I have repeatedly asserted, and produced what appeared to me irrefragable arguments drawn from matters of fact, to prove my assertion, that women cannot, by force, be confined to domestic concerns; for they will, however ignorant, intermeddle with more weighty affairs, neglecting private duties only to disturb, by cunning tricks, the orderly plans of reason which rise above their comprehension.

Besides, whilst they are only made to acquire personal accomplishments, men will seek for pleasure in variety, and faithless husbands will make faithless wives; such ignorant beings, indeed, will be very excusable when, not taught to respect public good, nor allowed any civil rights, they attempt to do themselves justice by retaliation.

The box of mischief thus opened in society, what is to preserve private virtue, the only security of public freedom and universal happiness?

Let there be then no coercion ESTABLISHED in society, and the common law of gravity prevailing, the sexes will fall into their proper places. And, now that more equitable laws are forming your citizens, marriage may become more sacred; your young men may choose wives from motives of affection, and your maidens allow love to root out vanity.

The father of a family will not then weaken his constitution and debase his sentiments, by visiting the harlot, nor forget, in obeying the call of appetite, the purpose for which it was implanted. And, the mother will not neglect her children to practise the arts of coquetry, when sense and modesty secure her the friendship of her husband.

But, till men become attentive to the duty of a father, it is vain to expect women to spend that time in their nursery which they, 'wise in their generation,' choose to spend at their glass; for this exertion of cunning is only an instinct of nature to enable them to obtain indirectly a little of that power of which they are unjustly denied a share: for, if women are not permitted to enjoy legitimate rights, they will render both men and themselves vicious, to obtain illicit privileges.

I wish, Sir, to set some investigations of this kind afloat in France; and should they lead to a confirmation of my principles, when your constitution is revised the Rights of Woman may be respected, if it be fully proved that reason calls for this respect, and loudly demands JUSTICE for one half of the human race.

I am, Sir,

Yours respectfully,

M. W.

Answers to Questions for Further Consideration

1. Although she is certainly writing to the public at large, Wollstonecraft alludes to her specific audience ("M. Talleyrand-Perigord, late bishop of Autun") as having recently published a pamphlet in opposition to her political message regarding the rights of women. By addressing her work to this particular individual, she is able to address the most resistant of all possible audiences her text is likely to encounter. She is also able to anticipate and deal with objections this audience will likely have. By doing this in a respectful and formal manner, she further increases the chance that even the audience most resistant to her message will continue to read her arguments.

2. She frequently interrupts her sentence to address her audience as "Sir," which constantly reinforces the idea that she is presenting her argument with respect. In addition, she uses interruption to make a moral comment on the content of her argument. By breaking out of her sentence to "address you as a legislator," she reminds her audience (both her specific audience and all others who read her text) that legislators are obligated to represent all citizens.

3. Wollstonecraft begins by aligning herself with her (admittedly resistant) audience, pointing out that both she and he are concerned with supporting "the cause of virtue," and that she is speaking out of "an affection for the whole human race." Later in the text, she attributes certain notions regarding the role of women (notions that are the opposite of her own) to "tyrants of every denomination." Finally, in her conclusion she draws upon a respect for "justice for one half of the human race" as a reason for embracing her arguments.

4. Beginning with the first paragraph, she constantly refers to her text as her "arguments" and supports them with evidence she clearly labels "observations." This highly logical language suggests that her position is based not on emotion, but on reason. This is further reinforced when she associates those who oppose her arguments with being "eager to crush reason" and follows this statement with a simple but highly logical summary of her position. She continues to overtly tie her arguments to reason, not emotion, even in the last sentence of this text.

5. Perhaps because she didn't want to be perceived as overly emotional, Wollstonecraft makes little use the kinds of direct parallelism that we often see in political speeches. One pattern that does repeat, however, is the use of rhetorical questions. Throughout her piece she asks her audience direct questions—and in most cases the only logical answer supports her argument. By providing the questions and not the answers, she forces her audience to think further about what she's saying. And by doing so, she furthers her goal of inspiring public thought and debate about her topic.

USING RHETORIC

Answer as many of the following 10 questions as you need to learn the rhetorical devices discussed in this chapter.

1. Make a list of several qualities that, to you, define the character of a good student. Then write a short passage addressing future college students in which you describe these qualities, using **parallelism**.

2. Tell a story from your own life in which you use **hyperbole** in describing the people, places, and events involved. See if you can use hyperbole to enhance the emotional content of your narrative—to make it funnier, sadder, or more exciting.

3. Look around the room you're in right now. Focus on one particular object—a picture on the wall, a piece of furniture, a plant, or some other inanimate object. Describe that object using **personification.** Have a particular rhetorical goal in mind when composing your description—how do you want your audience to feel about this object?

4. One of the most common uses of **irony** is to point out the differences between the ways in which people behave and the ways in which they know they're supposed to behave. Write a brief narrative in which you use irony to point out the inconsistencies between what people say and what they do.

5. Think of a prominent celebrity or political figure. Write a short story (or part of a story) in which you use **satire** to elicit a certain emotional reaction about this person and to communicate some feeling you have about this person—without saying it outright.

6. Think of a news item that you've recently seen on television or read about. Now write a short passage in which you describe the news story and make an **analogy** to some episode from history, mythology, or popular culture. Be sure to use the analogy to make a point about the story—something more than "this is similar to this." Try to convey a specific emotion or attitude about the news item in the analogy you make.

7. Imagine that you're to give a short speech at your high school commencement ceremony. Compose a short passage in which you use **parallelism with antithesis** to describe the road ahead for you and your fellow graduates.

8. Using **metonymy** or **synecdoche** (or both), write a short passage that describes the role the individual plays in governmental decision-making.

9. Write a short passage describing someone you know. Write in the third person point of view, but also use the rhetorical devices of **exclamation** and/or **parenthesis** to interrupt yourself and address your audience directly. In doing so, make sure you convey some feeling you have about this person, without actually coming out and stating the way you feel.

10. Imagine that you're writing a letter to your local newspaper's Op-Ed column. Write a short passage in which you take a position on a local issue or debate (you can make one up if you like), using several **metaphors** to strengthen your argument and elicit an emotional response from your audience.

Analyzing Rhetoric

The ability to detect rhetorical devices is essential for any critical reader. And every writer needs to consider the rhetorical effect of his or her words. One of the best ways to develop your own rhetorical skills is to actively interact with the rhetoric of someone else's writing. As you become more adept at detecting rhetorical devices in the words of others, you'll become more able to produce them on your own. And as you grow to recognize various rhetorical "tricks" in action, you'll find that they become second nature in your own writing.

Remember, rhetoric is just one element of writing. Argument, organization, and convention are all important in their own right. To fully appreciate the effectiveness of any given rhetorical device, you'll need to know how these larger issues work in the piece you're reading. In other words, you'll need to know *what* the author is arguing in order to know *how* he or she is using rhetoric to make that argument more effective.

In the reading for this activity, George Orwell presents an argument about the role that the language we use plays in our thinking about politics and government. Orwell is famous for demonstrating the importance that clear and effective language holds for the citizens of a democracy. His most famous novel, *1984*, portrays a world in which language has degenerated so much that citizens are no longer able to communicate their ideas well enough to question the actions of their government.

As you read his 1946 piece "Politics and the English Language," keep in mind that political speech—something with which Orwell is greatly concerned—is one of the most rhetorically rich genres of speech in today's society. As you develop your own ideas about Orwell's arguments, see if you can relate his ideas to the specific rhetorical devices you've been working with in this lesson.

Directions: Read "Politics and the English Language" by George Orwell. Take notes while reading Orwell's piece. Answer the study questions as you read or after you finish.

Study Questions

1. What is this piece about?

2. How is the piece structured?

3. How would you describe the language of the piece?

4. To whom is the piece addressed?

5. What effect does the piece have on the reader?

6. What is the purpose, or goal, of the piece?

7. Is the piece effective at its goal? Why?

Next, write a response to the following questions; our answers follow the text.

Questions for Further Consideration

1. Orwell claims that the improper use of such devices as metaphors and similes are a symptom of lazy or slovenly language. What are some of the devices Orwell uses in his essay? Can you find any instances of these very rhetorical devices in Orwell's own writing? If so, how do they stand up to his criteria for the appropriate use of language?

2. How does Orwell feel about the role of euphemism in political language? Do you agree or disagree with him? Can you think of any examples of euphemisms from today's world that act the way Orwell is describing?

3. Orwell seems to have very few positive things to say about the use of rhetorical devices. In just a few words, how would you characterize his attitude toward using these devices? Is his attitude absolute? That is, does it apply to every instance in which one might embellish one's language or are there exceptions to his "rules"?

4. Go back into Orwell's text. How would you describe his conception of the relationship between thought and language? How do rhetorical devices play into this relationship?

Politics and the English Language

George Orwell

Most people who bother with the matter at all would admit that the English language is in a bad way, but it is generally assumed that we cannot by conscious action do anything about it. Our civilization is decadent and our language—so the argument runs—must inevitably share in the general collapse. It follows that any struggle against the abuse of language is a sentimental archaism, like preferring candles to electric light or hansom cabs to aeroplanes. Underneath this lies the half-conscious belief that language is a natural growth and not an instrument which we shape for our own purposes.

Now, it is clear that the decline of a language must ultimately have political and economic causes: it is not due simply to the bad influence of this or that individual writer. But an effect can become a cause, reinforcing the original cause and producing the same effect in an intensified form, and so on indefinitely. A man may take to drink because he feels himself to be a failure, and then fail all the more completely because he drinks. It is rather the same thing that is happening to the English language. It becomes ugly and inaccurate because our thoughts are foolish, but the slovenliness of our language makes it easier for us to have foolish thoughts. The point is that the process is reversible. Modern English, especially written English, is full of bad habits which spread by imitation and which can be avoided if one is willing to take the necessary trouble. If one gets rid of these habits one can think more clearly, and to think clearly is a necessary first step toward political regeneration: so that the fight against bad English is not frivolous and is not the exclusive concern of professional writers. I will come back to this presently, and I hope that by that time the meaning of what I have said here will have become clearer. Meanwhile, here are five specimens of the English language as it is now habitually written.

These five passages have not been picked out because they are especially bad—I could have quoted far worse if I had chosen—but because they illustrate various of the mental vices from which we now suffer. They are a little below the average, but are fairly representative examples. I number them so that I can refer back to them when necessary:

KAPLAN

(1) "I am not, indeed, sure whether it is not true to say that the Milton who once seemed not unlike a seventeenth-century Shelley had not become, out of an experience ever more bitter in each year, more alien [*sic*] to the founder of that Jesuit sect which nothing could induce him to tolerate."

—Professor Harold Laski (Essay in *Freedom of Expression*)

(2) "Above all, we cannot play ducks and drakes with a native battery of idioms which prescribes egregious collocations of vocables as the Basic *put up with* for *tolerate, or put at a loss* for *bewilder*."

—Professor Lancelot Hogben (*Interglossia*)

(3) On the one side we have the free personality: by definition it is not neurotic, for it has neither conflict nor dream. Its desires, such as they are, are transparent, for they are just what institutional approval keeps in the forefront of consciousness; another institutional pattern would alter their number and intensity; there is little in them that is natural, irreducible, or culturally dangerous. But *on the other side*, the social bond itself is nothing but the mutual reflection of these self-secure integrities. Recall the definition of love. Is not this the very picture of a small academic? Where is there a place in this hall of mirrors for either personality or fraternity?

—Essay on psychology in *Politics* (New York)

(4) All the "best people" from the gentlemen's clubs, and all the frantic fascist captains, united in common hatred of Socialism and bestial horror at the rising tide of the mass revolutionary movement, have turned to acts of provocation, to foul incendiarism, to medieval legends of poisoned wells, to legalize their own destruction of proletarian organizations, and rouse the agitated petty-bourgeoisie to chauvinistic fervor on behalf of the fight against the revolutionary way out of the crisis.

—Communist pamphlet

(5) If a new spirit is to be infused into this old country, there is one thorny and contentious reform which must be tackled, and that is the humanization and galvanization of the B.B.C. Timidity here will bespeak canker and atrophy of the soul. The heart of Britain may be sound and of strong beat, for instance, but the British lion's roar at present is like that of Bottom in Shakespeare's *Midsummer Night's Dream*—as gentle as any sucking dove. A virile new Britain cannot continue indefinitely to be traduced in the eyes or rather ears, of the world by the effete languors of Langham Place, brazenly masquerading as "standard English." When the Voice of Britain is heard at nine o'clock, better far and infinitely less ludicrous to hear aitches honestly dropped than the present priggish, inflated, inhibited, school-ma'amish arch braying of blameless bashful mewing maidens!

—Letter in *Tribune*

Each of these passages has faults of its own, but, quite apart from avoidable ugliness, two qualities are common to all of them. The first is staleness of imagery; the other is lack of precision. The writer either has a meaning and cannot express it, or he inadvertently says something else, or he is almost indifferent as to whether his words mean anything or not. This mixture of vagueness and sheer incompetence is the most marked characteristic of modern English prose, and especially of any kind of political writing. As soon as certain topics are raised, the concrete melts into the abstract and no one seems able to think of turns of speech that are not hackneyed: prose consists less and less of *words* chosen for the sake of their meaning, and more and more of *phrases* tacked together like the sections of a prefabricated henhouse. I list below, with notes and examples, various of the tricks by means of which the work of prose construction is habitually dodged:

Dying Metaphors. A newly invented metaphor assists thought by evoking a visual image, while on the other hand a metaphor which is technically "dead" (e.g. iron resolution) has in effect reverted to being an ordinary word and can generally be used without loss of vividness. But in between these two classes there is a huge dump of worn-out metaphors which have lost all evocative power and are merely used because they save people the trouble of inventing phrases for themselves. Examples are: *Ring the changes on, take up the cudgel for, toe the line, ride roughshod over, stand shoulder to shoulder with, play into the hands of, no axe to grind, grist to the mill, fishing in troubled waters, on the order of the day, Achilles' heel, swan song, hotbed.* Many of these are used without knowledge of their meaning (what is a "rift," for instance?), and incompatible metaphors are frequently mixed, a sure sign that the writer is not interested in what he is saying. Some metaphors now current have been twisted out of their original meaning without those who use them even being aware of the fact. For example, *toe the line* is sometimes written as *tow the line*. Another example is *the hammer and the anvil*, now always used with the implication that the anvil gets the worst of it. In real life it is always the anvil that breaks the hammer, never the other way about: a writer who stopped to think what he was saying would avoid perverting the original phrase.

Operators or Verbal False Limbs. These save the trouble of picking out appropriate verbs and nouns, and at the same time pad each sentence with extra syllables which give it an appearance of symmetry. Characteristic phrases are *render inoperative, militate against, make contact with, be subjected to, give rise to, give grounds for, have the effect of, play a leading part (role) in, make itself felt, take effect, exhibit a tendency to, serve the purpose of, etc., etc.* The keynote is the elimination of simple verbs. Instead of being a single word, such as *break, stop, spoil, mend, kill*, a verb becomes a *phrase*, made up of a noun or adjective tacked on to some general-purpose verb such as *prove, serve, form, play, render*. In addition, the passive voice is wherever possible used in preference to the active, and noun constructions are used instead of gerunds (by examination of instead of by examining). The range of verbs is further cut down by means of the *-ize* and *de-* formation, and the banal statements are given an appearance of profundity by means of the not *un-*formation. Simple conjunctions and prepositions are replaced by such phrases as *with respect to, having regard to, the fact that, by dint of, in view of, in the interests of, on the hypothesis that*; and the ends of sentences are saved by anticlimax by such resounding commonplaces *as greatly to be desired, cannot be left out of account, a development to be expected in the near future, deserving of serious consideration, brought to a satisfactory conclusion*, and so on and so forth.

Pretentious Diction. Words like *phenomenon, element, individual* (as noun), *objective, categorical, effective, virtual, basic, primary, promote, constitute, exhibit, exploit, utilize, eliminate, liquidate*, are used to dress up a simple statement and give an aire of scientific impartiality to biased judgements. Adjectives like *epoch-making, epic, historic, unforgettable, triumphant, age-old, inevitable, inexorable, veritable*, are used to dignify the sordid process of international politics, while writing that aims at glorifying war usually takes on an archaic color, its characteristic words being: *realm, throne, chariot, mailed fist, trident, sword, shield, buckler, banner, jackboot, clarion*. Foreign words and expressions such as *cul de sac, ancien* *regime, deus ex machina, mutatis mutandis, status quo, gleichschaltung, weltanschauung*, are used to give an air of culture and elegance. Except for the useful abbreviations *i.e., e.g.*, and *etc.*, there is no real need for any of the hundreds of foreign phrases now current in the English language. Bad writers, and especially scientific, political, and sociological writers, are nearly always haunted by the notion that Latin or Greek words are grander than Saxon ones, and unnecessary words like *expedite, ameliorate, predict, extraneous, deracinated, clandestine, subaqueous*, and hundreds of others constantly gain ground from their Anglo-Saxon numbers. The jargon peculiar to Marxist writing (*hyena, hangman, cannibal, petty bourgeois, these gentry, lackey, flunkey, mad dog, White Guard*, etc.) consists largely of words translated from Russian, German, or French; but the normal way of coining a new word is to use Latin or Greek root with the appropriate affix and, where necessary, the *-ize* formation. It is often easier to make up words of this kind (*deregionalize, impermissible, extramarital, non-fragmentary* and so forth) than to think up the English words that will cover one's meaning. The result, in general, is an increase in slovenliness and vagueness.

Meaningless Words. In certain kinds of writing, particularly in art criticism and literary criticism, it is normal to come across long passages which are almost completely lacking in meaning. Words like *romantic, plastic, values, human, dead, sentimental, natural, vitality*, as used in art criticism, are strictly meaningless, in the sense that they not only do not point to any discoverable object, but are hardly ever expected to do so by the reader. When one critic writes, "The outstanding feature of Mr. X's work is its living quality," while another writes, "The immediately striking thing about Mr. X's work is its peculiar deadness," the reader accepts this as a simple difference opinion. If words like *black* and *white* were involved, instead of the jargon words *dead* and *living*, he would see at once that language was being used in an improper way. Many political words are similarly abused. The word *Fascism* has now no meaning except in so far as it signifies "something not desirable." The words *democracy, socialism, freedom, patriotic, realistic, justice* have each of them several different meanings which cannot be reconciled with one another. In the case of a word like *democracy*, not only is there no agreed definition, but the attempt to make one is resisted from all sides. It is almost universally felt that when we call a country democratic we are praising it: consequently the defenders of every kind of regime claim that it is a democracy, and fear that they might have to stop using that word if it were tied down to any one meaning. Words of this kind are often used in a consciously dishonest way. That is, the person who uses them has his own private definition, but allows his hearer to think he means something quite different. Statements like *Marshal Petain was a true patriot, The Soviet Press is the freest in the world, The Catholic Church is opposed to persecution*, are almost always made with intent to deceive. Other words used in variable meanings, in most cases more or less dishonestly, are: *class, totalitarian, science, progressive, reactionary, bourgeois, equality*.

Now that I have made this catalogue of swindles and perversions, let me give another example of the kind of writing that they lead to. This time it must of its nature be an imaginary one. I am going to translate a passage of good English into modern English of the worst sort. Here is a well-known verse from *Ecclesiastes*:

"I returned and saw under the sun, that the race is not to the swift, nor the battle to the strong, neither yet bread to the wise, nor yet riches to men of understanding, nor yet favour to men of skill; but time and chance happeneth to them all."

Here it is in modern English:

"Objective considerations of contemporary phenomena compel the conclusion that success or failure in competitive activities exhibits no tendency to be commensurate with innate capacity, but that a considerable element of the unpredictable must invariably be taken into account."

This is a parody, but not a very gross one. Exhibit (3) above, for instance, contains several patches of the same kind of English. It will be seen that I have not made a full translation. The beginning and ending of the sentence follow the original meaning fairly closely, but in the middle the concrete illustrations—race, battle, bread—dissolve into the vague phrases "success or failure in competitive activities." This had to be so, because no modern writer of the kind I am discussing—no one capable of using phrases like "objective considerations of contemporary phenomena"—would ever tabulate his thoughts in that precise and detailed way. The whole tendency of modern prose is away from concreteness. Now analyze these two sentences a little more closely. The first contains forty-nine words but only sixty syllables, and all its words are those of everyday life. The second contains thirty-eight words of ninety syllables: eighteen of those words are from Latin roots, and one from Greek. The first sentence contains six vivid images, and only one phrase ("time and chance") that could be called vague. The second contains not a single fresh, arresting phrase, and in spite of its ninety syllables it gives only a shortened version of the meaning contained in the first. Yet without a doubt it is the second kind of sentence that is gaining ground in modern English. I do not want to exaggerate. This kind of writing is not yet universal, and outcrops of simplicity will occur here and there in the worst-written page. Still, if you or I were told to write a few lines on the uncertainty of human fortunes, we should probably come much nearer to my imaginary sentence than to the one from *Ecclesiastes*.

As I have tried to show, modern writing at its worst does not consist in picking out words for the sake of their meaning and inventing images in order to make the meaning clearer. It consists in gumming together long strips of words which have already been set in order by someone else, and making the results presentable by sheer humbug. The attraction of this way of writing is that it is easy. It is easier—even quicker, once you have the habit—to say *In my opinion it is not an unjustifiable assumption that* than to say *I think*. If you use ready-made phrases, you not only don't have to hunt about for the words; you also don't have to bother with the rhythms of your sentences since these phrases are generally so arranged as to be more or less euphonious. When you are composing in a hurry—when you are dictating to a stenographer, for instance, or making a public speech—it is natural to fall into a pretentious, Latinized style. Tags like a *consideration which we should do well to bear in mind* or *a conclusion to which all of us would readily assent* will save many a sentence from coming down with a bump. By using stale metaphors, similes, and idioms, you save much mental effort, at the cost of leaving your meaning vague, not only for your reader but for yourself. This is the significance of mixed metaphors. The sole aim of a metaphor is to call up a visual image. When these images clash—as in *The Fascist octopus has sung its swan song, the jackboot is thrown into the melting pot*—it can be taken as certain that the writer is not seeing a mental image of the objects he is naming; in other words he is not really thinking. Look again at the examples I gave at the beginning of this essay. Professor Laski (1) uses five negatives in fifty-three words. One of these is superfluous, making nonsense of the whole passage, and in addition there is the slip—*alien* for akin—making further nonsense, and several avoidable pieces of clumsiness which increase the general vagueness. Professor Hogben (2) plays ducks and drakes with a battery which is able to write prescriptions, and, while disapproving of the everyday phrase *put up with*, is unwilling to look egregious up in the dictionary and see what it means; (3), if one takes an uncharitable attitude towards it, is simply meaningless: probably one could work out its intended meaning by reading the whole of the article in which it occurs. In (4), the writer knows more or less what he wants to say, but an accumulation of stale phrases chokes him like tea leaves blocking a sink. In (5), words and meaning have almost parted company. People who write in this manner usually have a general emotional meaning—they dislike one thing and want to express solidarity with another—but they are not interested in the detail of what they are saying. A scrupulous writer, in every sentence that he writes, will ask himself at least four questions, thus: What am I trying to say? What words will express it? What image or idiom will make it clearer? Is this image fresh enough to have an effect? And he will probably ask himself two more: Could I put it more shortly? Have I said anything that is avoidably ugly?

But you are not obliged to go to all this trouble. You can shirk it by simply throwing your mind open and letting the ready-made phrases come crowding in. They will construct your sentences for you—even think your thoughts for you, to a certain extent—and at need they will perform the important service of partially concealing your meaning even from yourself. It is at this point that the special connection between politics and the debasement of language becomes clear.

In our time it is broadly true that political writing is bad writing. Where it is not true, it will generally be found that the writer is some kind of rebel, expressing his private opinions and not a "party line." Orthodoxy, of whatever color, seems to demand a lifeless, imitative style. The political dialects to be found in pamphlets, leading articles, manifestoes, White Papers and the speeches of undersecretaries do, of course, vary from party to party, but they are all alike in that one almost never finds in them a fresh, vivid, homemade turn of speech. When one watches some tired hack on the platform mechanically repeating the familiar phrases—*bestial, atrocities, iron heel, bloodstained tyranny, free peoples of the world, stand shoulder to shoulder*—one often has a curious feeling that one is not watching a live human being but some kind of dummy: a feeling which suddenly becomes stronger at moments when the light catches the speaker's spectacles and turns them into blank discs which seem to have no eyes behind them. And this is not altogether fanciful. A speaker who uses that kind of phraseology has gone some distance toward turning himself into a machine. The appropriate noises are coming out of his larynx, but his brain is not involved as it would be if he were choosing his words for himself. If the speech he is making is one that he is accustomed to make over and over again, he may be almost unconscious of what he is saying, as one is when one utters the responses in church. And this reduced state of consciousness, if not indispensable, is at any rate favorable to political conformity.

In our time, political speech and writing are largely the defense of the indefensible. Things like the continuance of British rule in India, the Russian purges and deportations, the dropping of the atom bombs on Japan, can indeed be defended, but only by arguments which are too brutal for most people to face, and which do not square with the professed aims of the political parties. Thus political language has to consist largely of euphemism., question-begging and sheer cloudy vagueness. Defenseless villages are bombarded from the air, the inhabitants driven out into the countryside, the cattle machine-gunned, the huts set on fire with incendiary bullets: this is called *pacification*. Millions of peasants are robbed of their farms and sent trudging along the roads with no more than they can carry: this is called *transfer of population* or *rectification of frontiers*. People are imprisoned for years without trial, or shot in the back of the neck or sent to die of scurvy in Arctic lumber camps: this is called *elimination of unreliable elements*. Such phraseology is needed if one wants to name things without calling up mental pictures of them. Consider for instance some comfortable English professor defending Russian totalitarianism. He cannot say outright, "I believe in killing off your opponents when you can get good results by doing so." Probably, therefore, he will say something like this:

"While freely conceding that the Soviet regime exhibits certain features which the humanitarian may be inclined to deplore, we must, I think, agree that a certain curtailment of the right to political opposition is an unavoidable concomitant of transitional periods, and that the rigors which the Russian people have been called upon to undergo have been amply justified in the sphere of concrete achievement."

The inflated style itself is a kind of euphemism. A mass of Latin words falls upon the facts like soft snow, blurring the outline and covering up all the details. The great enemy of clear language is insincerity. When there is a gap between one's real and one's declared aims, one turns as it were instinctively to long words and exhausted idioms, like a cuttlefish spurting out ink. In our age there is no such thing as "keeping out of politics." All issues are political issues, and politics itself is a mass of lies, evasions, folly, hatred, and schizophrenia. When the general atmosphere is bad, language must suffer. I should expect to find—this is a guess which I have not sufficient knowledge to verify—that the German, Russian and Italian languages have all deteriorated in the last ten or fifteen years, as a result of dictatorship.

But if thought corrupts language, language can also corrupt thought. A bad usage can spread by tradition and imitation even among people who should and do know better. The debased language that I have been discussing is in some ways very convenient. Phrases like a *not unjustifiable assumption, leaves much to be desired, would serve no good purpose, a consideration which we should do well to bear in mind*, are a continuous temptation, a packet of aspirins always at one's elbow. Look back through this essay, and for certain you will find that I have again and again committed the very faults I am protesting against. By this morning's post I have received a pamphlet dealing with conditions in Germany. The author tells me that he "felt impelled" to write it. I open it at random, and here is almost the first sentence I see: "[The Allies] have an opportunity not only of achieving a radical transformation of Germany's social and political structure in such a way as to avoid a nationalistic reaction in Germany itself, but at the same time of laying the foundations of a co-operative and unified Europe." You see, he "feels impelled" to write—feels, presumably, that he has something new to say—and yet his words, like cavalry horses answering the bugle, group themselves automatically into the familiar dreary pattern. This invasion of one's mind by ready-made phrases *(lay the foundations, achieve a radical transformation)* can only be prevented if one is constantly on guard against them, and every such phrase anaesthetizes a portion of one's brain.

I said earlier that the decadence of our language is probably curable. Those who deny this would argue, if they produced an argument at all, that language merely reflects existing social conditions, and that we cannot influence its development by any direct tinkering with words and constructions. So far as the general tone or spirit of a language goes, this may be true, but it is not true in detail. Silly words and expressions have often disappeared, not through any evolutionary process but owing to the conscious action of a minority. Two recent examples were *explore every avenue* and *leave no stone unturned*, which were killed by the jeers of a few journalists. There is a long list of flyblown metaphors which could similarly be got rid of if enough people would interest themselves in the job; and it should also be possible to laugh the *not un*-formation out of existence, to reduce the amount of Latin and Greek in the average sentence, to drive out foreign phrases and strayed scientific words, and, in general, to make pretentiousness unfashionable. But all these are minor points. The defense of the English language implies more than this, and perhaps it is best to start by saying what it does *not* imply.

To begin with it has nothing to do with archaism, with the salvaging of obsolete words and turns of speech, or with the setting up of a "standard English" which must never be departed from. On the contrary, it is especially concerned with the scrapping of every word or idiom which has outworn its usefulness. It has nothing to do with correct grammar and syntax, which are of no importance so long as one makes one's meaning clear, or with the avoidance of Americanisms, or with having what is called a "good prose style." On the other hand, it is not concerned with fake simplicity and the attempt to make written English colloquial. Nor does it even imply in every case preferring the Saxon word to the Latin one, though it does imply using the fewest and shortest words that will cover one's meaning. What is above all needed is to let the meaning choose the word, and not the other way around. In prose, the worst thing one can do with words is surrender to them. When yo think of a concrete object, you think wordlessly, and then, if you want to describe the thing you have been visualizing you probably hunt about until you find the exact words that seem to fit it. When you think of something abstract you are more inclined to use words from the start, and unless you make a conscious effort to prevent it, the existing dialect will come rushing in and do the job for you, at the expense of blurring or even changing your meaning. Probably it is better to put off using words as long as possible and get one's meaning as clear as one can through pictures and sensations. Afterward one can choose—not simply *accept*—the phrases that will best cover the meaning, and then switch round and decide what impressions one's words are likely to make on another person. This last effort of the mind cuts out all stale or mixed images, all prefabricated phrases, needless repetitions, and humbug and vagueness generally. But one can often be in doubt about the effect of a word or a phrase, and one needs rules that one can rely on when instinct fails. I think the following rules will cover most cases:

 (i)   Never use a metaphor, simile, or other figure of speech which you are used to seeing in print.
 (ii) Never us a long word where a short one will do.
 (iii) If it is possible to cut a word out, always cut it out.
 (iv) Never use the passive where you can use the active.
 (v)   Never use a foreign phrase, a scientific word, or a jargon word if you can think of an everyday English equivalent.
 (vi) Break any of these rules sooner than say anything outright barbarous.

These rules sound elementary, and so they are, but they demand a deep change of attitude in anyone who has grown used to writing in the style now fashionable. One could keep all of them and still write bad English, but one could not write the kind of stuff that I quoted in those five specimens at the beginning of this article.

I have not here been considering the literary use of language, but merely language as an instrument for expressing and not for concealing or preventing thought. Stuart Chase and others have come near to claiming that all abstract words are meaningless, and have used this as a pretext for advocating a kind of political quietism. Since you don't know what Fascism is, how can you struggle against Fascism? One need not swallow such absurdities as this, but one ought to recognize that the present political chaos is connected with the decay of language, and that one can probably bring about some improvement by starting at the verbal end. If you simplify your English, you are freed from the worst follies of orthodoxy. You cannot speak any of the necessary dialects, and when you make a stupid remark its stupidity will be obvious, even to yourself. Political language—and with variations this is true of all political parties, from Conservatives to Anarchists—is designed to make lies sound truthful and murder respectable, and to give an appearance of solidity to pure wind. One cannot change this all in a moment, but one can at least change one's own habits, and from time to time one can even, if one jeers loudly enough, send some worn-out and useless phrase—*some jackboot, Achilles' heel, hotbed, melting pot, acid test, veritable inferno*, or other lump of verbal refuse—into the dustbin, where it belongs.

Suggested Responses to Questions for Further Consideration

1. Orwell regularly uses simile and metaphor: " . . . there is a huge dump of worn-out metaphors . . . " ; "(modern writing) consists of gumming together long strips of words . . . " He suggests that some words "fall upon the facts like soft snow," while others are like "cavalry horses answering the bugle." While the first device will likely have meaning for many readers, the second may not (especially if the reader is unfamiliar with military history). And Orwell's comparison of stale phrases to "tea leaves blocking a sink" seems to rely on a very particular and somewhat dated knowledge of how tea is prepared. In some cases, then, Orwell might well be vulnerable to the very criticisms he levels at others.

2. Orwell feels that euphemisms too often obscure the truth of what's being said, even to the point of "defending the indefensible." An example is the way in which the word *fascism*, through inaccurate use and overuse " . . . has now no meaning except in so far as it signifies something 'not desirable.'" Although it is certain that sometimes leaders must speak tactfully, Orwell's point is still relevant. The presence in today's language of such phrases as "downsizing" (to describe a corporation's laying off employees to increase profits) suggests that the dynamics Orwell describes are still in action.

3. Orwell's concern is not with rhetorical devices in their own right, but with the problems that come when people use these devices *without thinking critically about them*. He sees nothing wrong with using metaphor, diction, sentence rhythm, or other stylistic devices—so long as a writer (or speaker) thinks about each one that he or she uses. This is why, in his list of "rules" at the conclusion of his essay, he takes care to remind readers that they are free to make their own decisions about when and where to use his guidelines for more effective speech.

4. In Orwell's argument, thought and language are not to be entirely separated. They rely on each other, and obscurity in one leads to obscurity in the other, as he demonstrates in his analogy of a man who "may take to drink because he feels himself to be a failure, then fail all the more completely because he drinks." Rhetorical devices, used improperly, can serve as a substitute for clear language, and because they sound good, they can sometimes be mistaken for clear thinking. This is Orwell's primary concern.

APPLYING RHETORIC

TERMINOLOGY REVIEW: READING TECHNIQUES

rhetorical device	Words used in particular grammatical forms for effect rather than to provide information
deductive argument	Process of reasoning in which a conclusion is determined from a set of given evidence. Moves from general to specific statements.
pun	Two or more words that sound alike but have different meanings
simile	The use of "like" or "as" to compare two different ideas or things
metaphor	An implicit comparison that sets into play the literal meanings of one or more words
analogy	A comparison between two different things that share similar features
personification	Human qualities attributed to an abstract idea, animal, or inanimate object
hyperbole	An exaggeration or overstatement
symbol	Something that refers to or "stands for" an abstract idea
metonymy	The use of a concrete word, rather than an abstract expression, to refer to a more abstract and complex word or idea
synecdoche	A figure of speech in which a part is used to represent the whole
oxymoron	A concise paradox where two contradictory ideas are combined in a single word or phrase
paradox	A situation or concept that juxtaposes two apparently contradictory ideas
irony	The exposed incongruity between what appears to be true and what is actually true
parallelism	The repetition within a sentence of the same grammatical forms
antithesis	The use of opposing or contrasting ideas in parallel grammatical forms or parts of speech
climax	The repetition of words or similar grammatical units in order of increasing importance or of increasing emotional effect

parody	A humorous imitation of a particular style of writing with unusual content or ideas not typically expressed in that style
satire	A mode of writing that mocks characters, events, people, or institutions
metacognition	Monitoring your own thoughts as you encounter ideas and facts presented to you in written form
paraphrase	Summarizing an idea in your own words
critical reading	Actively engaging with a text
inductive argument	At least two statements, one stating a fact, the other making a generalization about the fact, drawing conclusions about a larger group
exclamation	A type of interruption where the speaker or writer stops a sentence midway and addresses an individual who may or may not be present
previewing	Skimming a text to get a general idea of the subject and a general idea of how to approach the text

WRITING TECHNIQUES

Writing Mechanics

CHAPTER 10

KEY TERMS

- convention

GRAMMAR BASICS

When you read your own writing or the writing of your peers, do you often find sentences that just don't sound right? By the time you finish high school, you'll have about 12 years of experience writing grammatically correct sentences. The art of constructing grammatically accurate sentences is something you started developing early in life. You've probably become pretty skilled at writing, and probably apply many of the rules of grammar instinctively.

Whether you're writing a quick email to a friend or submitting a senior project, grammatically correct writing is important. Grammatical mistakes in your writing detract from your content. Errors can also shift your audience's opinion about your subject and, more importantly, affect their opinion about you as a thinker and a writer.

Many books have been written about grammar. Even the most skilled writers have a favorite grammar guide, and consult it regularly. Find a grammar guide you like and refer to it to answer your grammar questions.

Subjects and Predicates

A sentence is made up of one or more words that express a complete thought. Sentences are as varied as the people who write them. Yet for all this variety, the sentence has a clear, easily identifiable structure.

In every sentence there are two basic components: the subject and the predicate. A subject of a sentence is always a noun, or a word or phrase functioning as a noun, and is what the sentence is about. A predicate is the part of the sentence that says something about the subject. The predicate includes the verb, with its objects, complements, and modifiers.

Identify the subjects and predicates in the following sentences. The answers are provided at the end of the chapter.

1. Help!
2. Paul reads.
3. I'm tired.
4. Julia skateboards very poorly.
5. Angry parents yell.
6. High school students study, work on homework, go to work, and play sports after school.
7. My sports car drives fast.

Clauses and Phrases

Two other terms helpful in understanding sentence structure are clause and phrase. A clause is a group of words containing a subject and a predicate. There are two main types of clauses: independent clauses and dependent clauses. Clauses are the key structural elements of sentence architecture. Independent clauses present a complete thought and can stand alone as a sentence. A dependent clause (also called a subordinate clause) cannot stand alone as a sentence.

A phrase is a group of related words that lacks a subject or a predicate, or both. There are many types of phrases: noun phrases, verb phrases, prepositional phrases, appositive phrases, absolute phrases, verbal phrases, gerund phrase, infinitive phrases, and participial phrases. A phrase's main purpose is to add detail or valuable information. Phrases act as modifiers in a sentence.

Examples

The two independent clauses in the following sentence are in italics.

Computers are amazing tools, but good writers need to know basic grammar.

The dependent clause (a clause that can't stand alone) is in italics in this next sentence.

Because my sister advised me to take up a sport, I learned to scuba dive during Spring Break.

An example of a phrase is: *The very fast sailboat.*

Sentence Construction

These are the basic building blocks of sentence construction: subjects, predicates, clauses and phrases. Use these to create different simple and complex sentences. Five kinds of sentences can be created, depending on the mood of the main verb: declarative, interrogative, imperative, exclamatory, and conditional.

Declarative: June 30th is my birthday.

Interrogative: When is your birthday?

Imperative: Read chapter 12 for tomorrow's quiz.

Exclamatory: I simply can't keep up with these long reading assignments!

Conditional: If you do well in the course, you will pass the final exam.

Sentence Structure

There are four different types of sentence structure: simple, compound, complex, and compound-complex.

Simple: My knee hurts. (single subject, single predicate)

Compound: I stretch before I exercise, so why does my knee hurt? (two independent clauses joined by a coordinating conjunction and punctuation)

Complex: If I can squeeze it in before school, I try to run two miles each morning. (contains one independent clause and one or more subordinate clauses)

Compound-Complex: If I'm not late, I run two miles, and I get a latte before school. (two or more independent clauses and one or more subordinate clauses)

Combining Sentences

Using a semicolon, a conjunction, or a conjunctive adverb, combine the sentences in each of the following sets into a single sentence. When you use a conjunction or conjunctive adverb, state in parentheses the relationship it shows. Answer the following questions. (Check them against the answers provided at the end of the chapter.)

1. Harriet Beecher Stowe became widely known with the publication of *Uncle Tom's Cabin* in 1852. Emily Dickinson remained unacclaimed until 50 years after her death.

2. James Joyce was a painstaking writer. He once spent half a day on the composition of a single sentence.

Some of the following entries contain a comma splice (two sentences connected by a comma). If you find one, correct it. If the punctuation is correct, write "correct."

3. Rocinante's head, neck, and muzzle are a single unit made from a small elbow joint; and her body is an L-shaped allen wrench, with the smaller part forming a tail.

4. Welded to the body are four legs, they are made from socket head cap screws.

In some of the following, the punctuation is faulty. Correct any mistakes you find, adding words where necessary. If a sentence is correct as it stands, write "correct."

5. On the coast of Maine is the small town of Pirates Cove it resembles the old New England seaports depicted in paintings hanging in country inns and seafood restaurants.

6. Walking on the beach I collect the shells, they slide and rattle in my bucket as I step over rocks.

MECHANICS AND USAGE

Beyond sentence building, some issues of mechanics are important to use in your writing. Here's a quick review of some of the basics.

Capitalization

Follow the simple rules for capitalization.

- Capitalize first words in every sentence, proper names, names of people, races, languages and places, the names of days, months and holidays.
- Capitalize names of businesses or organizations, names of religions and sacred persons, books, and events. Capitalize titles that precede proper names and familial relationship terms.
- Capitalize A.M., P.M., A.D., and B.C., and the call letters of radio and TV stations.
- Capitalize abbreviated forms of businesses, organizations, and documents names.
- Capitalize the first word of a direct quotation if it stands alone as a sentence, or if it's an interjection that can stand alone.

Italics

Follow the simple rules for italics. Italics, or slanted type, give emphasis to words.

- Italicize the titles of books, periodicals, newspapers, pamphlets, plays, films, TV series, radio programs, long poems, and long musical compositions, as well as the titles of albums, paintings, and sculpture.
- Italicize the names of individual ships, trains, airplanes, and spacecraft.
- Italicize foreign words and phrases.

Of course, on the AP test you needn't worry about italics (unless you have magic handwriting!). In longhand, underlining words that would otherwise be italicized is generally accepted practice.

Quotation Marks

Quotation marks are most commonly used to set off direct quotes in writing, but may also have a mechanical purpose.

- Use quotation marks with the titles of brief works or parts of complete works.
- Quotation marks can also be used to distinguish a word that is being discussed or to indicate that a word is slang.
- Punctuation with quotation marks: Periods and commas are always placed inside quotation marks. Exclamation points and question marks should be placed inside the quote when it punctuates the quoted sentence, and outside the quote when it punctuates the main sentence. Semicolons or colons are always placed outside quotation marks. Any word or punctuation mark that isn't part of the original quotation must be placed inside brackets.
- If more than one paragraph is being quoted, quotation marks should be placed before each paragraph and at the end only of the last paragraph.

Parentheses

Parentheses are used to enclose explanatory or supplemental material that interrupts the regular structure of the sentence. Punctuation is placed within parentheses when the words in the parentheses need punctuation (such as a period or comma).

Brackets

Brackets are used before and after material that a writer adds when quoting another writer.

Apostrophes

An apostrophe is used to show that one or more letters have been left out of a word to form a contraction. An apostrophe is also used to form the plural of a letter, a number, a sign, or a word discussed as a word. The possessive for singular nouns is made by adding an apostrophe and an *s*. This rule also applies to singular nouns ending with an *s* or a *z*. The possessive form of plural nouns ending in *s* is usually made by adding just an apostrophe (the bosses' office).

Hyphens and Dashes

A hyphen is used to divide a word at the end of a line of print. The word must be split between syllables, and the hyphen is always placed after the syllable at the end of the line, not at the beginning of the next line before the next syllable. Use a hyphen also to join two or more words that serve as a single adjective before a noun (example: big-boned woman). There are some exceptions to this rule. Dashes are used to indicate a sudden break or change in a sentence. A dash can also be used to show interrupted or staggering speech in dialogue. A dash is indicated by two hyphens without spacing or with an "em-dash."

Abbreviations

In formal writing only very few words are acceptable to abbreviate. They are Mr., Mrs., Ms., Dr., A.M., and P.M. In informal writing more abbreviations may be used. Many grammar guides have a list of common abbreviations in their glossaries or appendixes.

Common Usage Problems

Usage problems arise when a writer uses a word incorrectly. Most grammar books include a section or glossary that deals with this important issue. For example, *Writing: A College Handbook* has a "Glossary of Usage" near the end of the text. In this glossary you can find the distinction between *accept* and *except,* between *affect* and *effect,* and many of the other commonly confused or misused words.

Mark Twain once said, "The difference between the right word and the nearly right word is the same as that between lightning and the lightning bug." This is a greater issue than simple diction. An expert writer never uses the wrong word of a "plagued pair." Expert writers might not always know the difference between *eminent* and *imminent,* but they're aware there is a difference and consult a reference book to clarify.

Sentence Logic

When a piece has sentence logic, it is, in a word, consistent. Writing that varies in point of view, has shifts in verb tense, or has disagreements in number (singular or plural) needs revision. Other common errors to watch out for include disagreement of a pronoun and its antecedent and shifts from active to passive voice.

In some of the following sentences, the italicized pronoun has been used confusingly. Briefly diagnose what is wrong and then clarify the sentence. If the sentence is correct as it stands, write "correct." (You'll find the answers at the end of the chapter.)

1. Archimedes discovered the principle of displacement while he was taking a bath. *It* made him leap out of the water with excitement.

2. By measuring the water displaced by the crown, and then measuring the water displaced by the ingot, he could easily tell whether *they* matched in volume, and thus whether the crown was pure gold.

In some of the following sentences the verb doesn't agree with its subject. Correct every verb you consider wrong and then explain the correction. If a sentence is correct as it stands, explain why.

3. Members of the city's transportation department is seeking a solution to the traffic problem on Main Street.

4. There has been many complaints from merchants and shoppers.

In some of the following sentences, the tense of one or more verbs doesn't properly correspond to the tense of the italicized verb. Correct those sentences. If a sentence is correct as it stands, write "correct."

5. At that time, inspectors *found* that pollutants have already made the water unsafe to drink.

6. But until the installation was complete, residents *will drink* bottled water.

ANSWERS TO EXERCISES

Subjects and Predicates Exercise

1. The verb *help* is the predicate, and an understood *you* is the subject.

2. The proper noun *Paul* is the subject, and the verb *reads* is the predicate.

3. The pronoun *I* of the contraction *I am* is the subject, and the verb phrase *am tired* is the predicate.

4. The proper noun *Julia* is the subject, and the verb phrase *skateboards very poorly* is the predicate.

5. The noun phrase *Angry parents* is the subject, and the verb *yell* is the predicate.

6. The noun *students* is the subject, and the compound verb clause *work on homework, go to work, and play sports after school* is the predicate.

7. The noun phrase *my sports car* is the subject, and the verb phrase *drives fast* is the predicate.

Combining Sentences Exercise

1. Harriet Beecher Stowe became widely known with the publication of *Uncle Tom's Cabin* in 1852; however, Emily Dickinson remained unacclaimed until fifty years after her death. (contrast)

2. James Joyce was a painstaking writer; in fact, he once spent half a day on the composition of a single sentence. (emphasis)

3. Rocinante's head, neck, and muzzle are a single unit made from a small elbow joint; thus her body is an L-shaped allen wrench, with the smaller part forming a tail.

4. Welded to the body are four legs made from socket head cap screws.

5. On the coast of Maine is the small town of Pirates Cove; it resembles the old New England seaports depicted in paintings that hang in country inns and seafood restaurants.

6. Walking on the beach, I collect the shells; they slide and rattle in my bucket as I step over rocks.

Sentence Logic Exercise

1. Archimedes discovered the principle of displacement while he was taking a bath. *The discovery* made him leap out of the water with excitement. (pronoun antecedent confusion)

2. Correct. ("They" can only refer to ingot and crown because the other nouns are singular or they do not "count.")

3. Members of the city's transportation department are seeking a solution to the traffic problem on Main Street. (The subject, members, is plural, so the verb must be plural.)

4. There have been many complaints from merchants and shoppers. (The "there" refers to a plural noun so the verb must be plural.)

5. At that time, inspectors *found* that pollutants had already made the water unsafe to drink. (The first verb is in the past tense, so the other verb must also be in the past tense.)

6. But until the installation is complete, residents *will drink* bottled water. (Because the second verb is in the future tense, the first verb can't be in the past tense.)

Writing Fundamentals

CHAPTER 11

> **KEY TERMS**
> - thesis statement

THE THESIS

The thesis is the controlling idea of a piece of writing. It helps guide the reader. The thesis is where you begin your essay. The rest of the essay develops, explains, and augments the thesis. Your thesis, then, is the heart of your writing. If it isn't interesting, you'll have a hard time making the rest of the writing compelling.

The thesis statement has two parts, the topic and the comment. These two parts, taken together, provide focus for both the writer and the reader. The topic identifies the subject of the piece; the comment identifies the writer's thoughts about the topic. The thesis helps the reader stay attentive to the writing, and it aids the writer in staying on the topic by reminding him or her about the specific point at issue. By the end of the essay the reader should have a clear understanding of the writer's thoughts on the subject. This is the purpose of the essay—to communicate what the writer thinks about a particular subject to a larger audience.

Strategies for Developing a Thesis

Remember, a thesis statement always has two parts: a topic and a comment that can be developed and explained. The clearer the thesis is in your mind and on paper, the easier it will be to create an essay that flows well and expresses your point to the reader. To make sure you have both parts of the thesis statement, examine the relationship between the two sections of your statement. For the second section to be a comment about the topic, it has to express an opinion, present an interpretation, or raise an interesting point.

If the topic is assigned, do a 10-minute brainstorm session during which you write down all your ideas about the topic. Then examine your brainstorm notes for interesting and arguable points. You need to match your thesis to the length of the writing assignment. An assignment that asks you to write one page demands a much narrower thesis than an assignment that asks you to write five pages.

Once you identify your most intriguing idea, begin to write. You will be writing a first draft, so it's OK if your thesis statement isn't crafted at this point. As you explore your subject and develop your thoughts, you'll come to a clearer understanding of what you're actually saying. Often, at the end of your first draft you'll find material with which to construct your thesis. You'll have written through all the vague and unrelated statements and finally reached what you wanted to say all along.

Now, take this new focus and create a thesis statement with it. Be sure to include both the topic and the commentary. Then you can go back through your draft to add details that support the thesis. You should also delete sections that are unrelated to the thesis. Remember that the thesis is like an umbrella. Everything in the essay should fall under the scope of the thesis. Every detail you provide should develop and support the point or argument you intend to make. Although this method of thesis construction may seem like extra work, it will result in more efficient and coherent writing.

If the topic isn't assigned, go back to your reading notes to generate ideas. Then follow the same procedure you would if your topic were assigned.

Once you've created a thesis, whether through writing into your subject or through another method, think about the kind of writing it will help you produce. The more interesting your thesis is, the more interesting your evidence and developing ideas will be. This, in turn, will help spur you to more interesting writing. To help figure out if you have a good thesis, ask yourself these questions:

- Will my thesis be interesting for my audience?
- Are you writing for an instructor, the general public, a professional in a specialized field? Will the audience expect technical explanations or specialized language?
- Would the average reader be able to follow my points?
- Is my thesis specific to the topic?
- What point do I want to make about the subject?
- What specifically do you want my writing to achieve? Do I intend to inform, persuade, argue, interpret, explain?
- Does my thesis help me with the goal of your writing?
- Is my thesis manageable, given the amount of time I have to write about this topic?
- Do I have enough material to support and develop this thesis? Would it take 10 pages to properly support this thesis?
- Would this thesis require outside research?
- Could I support this thesis if I only had 30 minutes to write?
- In the number of pages you're assigned, can you present your reader with a full understanding of your ideas?

Example

Imagine that you've read the novel *Lolita* by Vladimir Nabokov. Your assignment is to produce one single-spaced, typed page in which you create an interesting thesis about the narrator, Humbert Humbert. You sit down and brainstorm all the fascinating things about Humbert Humbert you can think of and decide that you'd really like to write about how his narrative style is manipulative. This is your topic. Then you think about why it matters that he's a manipulative narrator. You decide this is important because it makes the reader sympathize with him, even though he's a creepy character. This is your comment. Putting these two ideas together, your thesis statement might look something like this:

"In the novel *Lolita*, the manipulative narrative style of Humbert Humbert creates an unexpectedly sympathetic response in the reader."

Then you'd choose three main ideas to develop in your essay.

- What the manipulative narrative style looks like
- Why you'd expect not to sympathize with Humbert Humbert
- Why the reader's sympathetic response is important for the novel

This is a literary example. Using the same process, you could create a thesis for any piece of writing. Once you've constructed the thesis. It's helpful to note the main ideas you need to develop. This will help keep you focused as you write. For example, if you suddenly started to write about Humbert Humbert's wife, Charlotte, the essay would be off topic.

PARAGRAPHS

Paragraphs are important because they guide your reader through your essay. Every time a reader sees a new paragraph, he or she knows that the author is going to develop a new idea. Because your reader expects one idea per paragraph, you need to be sure that each paragraph you write centers on an idea. This doesn't mean that the sentences within the paragraph are repetitive, even though they all talk about the same idea. It means that the sentences need to build on one another to develop the idea you want the paragraph to convey.

Topic Sentence

For each paragraph you should have one sentence that conveys the topic of the paragraph. This sentence, called the topic sentence, is often the first sentence of the paragraph. Placing the topic sentence at the beginning of the paragraph alerts the reader to the idea you'll develop in the paragraph. If the rest of the paragraph doesn't relate to the topic of the first sentence, the reader will be confused.

Evidence

Once you have your topic sentence in place, you have to develop your idea by using evidence. The evidence you use will depend on the kind of essay you're writing. For some essays you might use statistics or facts as evidence. Other types of essays might demand quotations or anecdotes as evidence. However, the function of evidence is the same in all types of writing. Use evidence to prove your point and make your ideas believable to your reader. Evidence helps you show the reader what you're thinking, so it's important that you explain your evidence. In other words, you can't just insert facts, opinions, or quotations into a paragraph. If you just drop evidence into your paragraph without explaining why it's important, you can expect your reader to come up with a different interpretation of that evidence. Remember that everyone has unique ideas when they read. Your job, in presenting evidence to the reader, is to indicate how your evidence supports your argument.

Signal Words

As you present the points of your paragraph, make sure you use signal words to guide your reader. These words or phrases (some examples are *for example, in addition to, therefore, of course*) direct your reader. In other words, they give the reader some preparation for the idea that comes next. The signal phrase *in other words*, at the beginning of the previous sentence, lets you know that the sentence was going to say again, in different words, what came before it. Although as a reader you may not be consciously aware of signal words, the effect they have on your understanding is immense. You can use signal words to help your reader follow your argument by signaling the relationship between your ideas.

Strategies for Developing Paragraphs

Once you've written a paragraph, you should reread it to make sure all your sentences relate back to the first one. Take out sentences that begin to talk about ideas other then those covered by the topic sentence. You don't necessarily have to completely erase those tangential sentences. They might become different topic sentences of their own.

When you've finished developing one idea, it's time to close that paragraph and begin another one. To signal the change of paragraph and indicate the relationship between paragraphs, be sure to use transitions. Just as you need to guide your readers within the paragraph, you also have to guide them between paragraphs.

As you reread your paragraph, ask yourself these questions:

- For each sentence in the paragraph: Does this sentence relate to the topic sentence? How does it help me develop my point?
- For the paragraph as a whole: Does this paragraph say whatever is necessary for the audience to completely understand the topic sentence?
- For the paragraph as a whole: Does the order of the paragraph make sense? Do my ideas flow logically? Is each part of the idea clear before I move on to the next part?

- For the paragraph as a whole: Do I have signal words that help guide the reader through my ideas? Do these signal words accurately signpost the relationships between my ideas?
- As you move between paragraphs: How does the idea in this paragraph relate to the one before it? Do I have a transition that indicates this relationship?

Also as you reread, consider the language you use. Try to be as specific as possible with your word choice. You don't want to make the reader do too much work. That is, the more exact you can be with your words, the less ambiguity there is in your writing, and the more certain you can be about communicating your point. Most words can be interpreted many ways. Not everyone will make the same associations with the same word. For example, the sentence "She was mad" could mean either she was angry or she was mentally ill. Don't worry about being exact when you first pen your paragraphs. Agonizing over word choice during the writing stage might lead to writer's block. Instead, leave the agonizing for the editing stage.

The paragraph below is a sample paragraph, complete with all the components of a well-structured, coherent paragraph. Spend a few minutes examining the paragraph. Identify the topic sentence. Look at the signal words and how they indicate the relationships between the sentences. Examine how each sentence builds on the previous one to develop the main idea of the paragraph.

Example

The use of war metaphors to characterize cancer treatment and research can be traced back to the connection between World War II and the growth in cancer research centers in the 1940s and 1950s. The influence of the war on cancer research was most evident in the mass media of the time. Illustrations for articles in 1950s magazines that celebrated the advances of medical technology relied on war imagery to depict new treatments for cancer. For example, one image from a *Life* magazine article shows the new treatments as pistols used to pump radioactive pellets into tumors. Another illustration, from 1952, portrays an angry cancer cell under an ominous mushroom cloud, demonstrating the connection between the atomic bomb and the importance of technology to new cancer treatments. The relationship was more than symbolic; one of today's most commonly used cancer treatments, chemotherapy, grew out of chemical warfare studies in World War II. The connection between war and cancer continued into the 1970s, when Richard Nixon declared a national "War on Cancer" in 1971, and continues today to affect popular understandings of the treatment of this common disease.

Try It Yourself

Select an article from a newspaper and write a five-paragraph essay about it with a thesis statement, three supporting paragraphs, and one paragraph to wrap-up your point.

Just as you chose the article, it's up to you to choose what you'll write about the article. But keep this in mind: *don't* simply repeat what the article says. If somebody wants to know what the article says, they can read it. You should make your own original point about the article.

For example, you might write about the objectivity of the reporter, the assumptions the article is based on, the type of language the article uses, or important information you feel is left out of the article.

Remember what you've learned here: write a thesis statement that clearly notes what you'll be writing about, and support it in the thesis paragraph with commentary. Be sure the three supporting paragraphs really do relate to your thesis, are logically coherent "units," and have effective transitions from one paragraph to another. Finish your "mini-essay" with a paragraph that sums up what you've stated in the first four paragraphs.

PRACTICE CREATING THESES AND CONSTRUCTING PARAGRAPHS

Directions: Carefully read Edward Arlington Robinson's poem "Richard Cory." Make notes as you read. Then follow the prompts in constructing a thesis and supporting paragraphs about your reaction to the poem. You may not be familiar with writing about poetry. Don't be intimidated; instead, write about it the same way you would any other piece of writing. As you become more familiar with writing about literature, you'll develop a specialized vocabulary for doing so. But that's not what we're looking for here—your grade will be based on the effectiveness of your thesis statement and paragraphs.

Richard Cory
Edward Arlington Robinson

Whenever Richard Cory went down town,
We people on the pavement looked at him:
He was a gentleman from sole to crown,
Clean favored, and imperially slim.

And he was always quietly arrayed,
And he was always human when he talked;
But still he fluttered pulses when he said,
"Good-morning," and he glittered when he walked.

And he was rich,—yes, richer than a king,—
And admirably schooled in every grace:
In fine, we thought that he was everything
To make us wish that we were in his place.

So on we worked, and waited for the light,
And went without the meat, and cursed the bread;
And Richard Cory, one calm summer night,
Went home and put a bullet through his head.

Respond to the following prompts and explain your rationale for each.

1. Develop a **thesis** that describes your reaction to Robinson's poem. Keep in mind that this should be an idea of your own, which you can support and develop by pointing to certain pieces of the poem. Try to limit your thesis to one or two succinct sentences.

2.   Now work out three **supporting statements** that support the thesis you've just written. Keep in mind that you'll need to support these with evidence. Again, limit these statements to one or two succinct sentences.

3.   For each of your three supporting statements, make a list of all the evidence you can think of that can support that statement. This evidence can take many forms, depending on your thesis; just keep in mind that you need to provide your audience with concrete facts and *details* that show them how you've arrived at your idea. Be as specific as possible.

4.   At least some of your evidence should be in the form of **textual citations**, that is, selections from the text that support your idea or ideas. You'll probably want to return to Robinson's poem at this point and find those specific stanzas or phrases that gave you your ideas in the first place.

5.   Organize your three supporting statements, together with your three lists of evidence, into three **paragraphs** by writing out your evidence in sentence form. Give careful consideration to the placement of your supporting statements (which are now **topic sentences**) in each paragraph. For example, you may want to begin each paragraph with its main idea. Or you may want to present some evidence first, and then present the topic sentence at the conclusion of the paragraph.

6.   Now that you have three paragraphs, read each one carefully. Ask yourself of each sentence in which you present evidence—how does this support the topic sentence of this paragraph?

7.   If the answer to that question is unclear, you may want to rethink whether that evidence belongs where it is. Or you may want to add a sentence or two that clearly articulates the relationship between the evidence you've given and the topic sentence of the paragraph to help your reader better understand how your evidence supports the paragraph's main idea. **Revise** your paragraphs, incorporating any changes you've made.

8.   Pick an order in which to present your paragraphs, and write **transitions** that lead your reader from one to the next.

9.   You may want your transition to deal with the main ideas of each paragraph. If you choose this kind of transition, it often helps to begin by writing out a sentence that describes the relationship between the main idea of the first paragraph and the main idea of the next. You can then tailor that sentence to become an effective transition.

10. Or you might use the last piece of evidence presented in the first paragraph as a "jumping off" point to the first sentence of the next paragraph, whether or not that sentence is the topic sentence. But remember—however you choose to structure your transition, keep in mind that **even these sentences need to relate to the topic sentences of the relevant paragraphs.**

Assessing Your Paragraphs

To do this activity you'll have had to write a thesis statement with supporting paragraphs about the Edward Arlington Robinson poem "Richard Cory," as assigned above.

Use the questions below to assess your writing for clarity and effectiveness.

1. What is your thesis?

2. What is the topic sentence of each of your paragraphs?

3. How does each topic sentence relate to your thesis?

4. How do you make transitions between your paragraphs? For example, do you use repetition? Signal phrases? What words in each paragraph function to create paragraph-to-paragraph transitions?

5. Do any of your paragraphs seem to have multiple agendas? In other words, do any seem to have two main ideas rather than one main idea explained in the topic sentence?

6. In each paragraph, does each sentence clearly relate to the topic sentence? If not, can you eliminate it?

7. Write a list of the signal words and phrases that make transitions between the sentences of each paragraph.

8. Does each point have sufficient evidence to explain or illustrate it? Are there any places in the paragraphs where you make interpretations without illustrating them with words or phrases from the poem?

9. Is the significance of each piece of evidence you include clearly explained? Generally, each piece of evidence will require a sentence or two of explanation—are all of these explanatory sentences included in each of your paragraphs?

10. Does each sentence present a slightly different piece of information or elaborate or clarify the previous sentence? Or, on the other hand, are some of your sentences repetitive?

The Writing Process

CHAPTER 12

KEY TERMS
- analytical writing
- transition

WRITING PROCESS SKILLS

The so-called "writing process" can be broken down into five steps: Brainstorming, Outlining, Writing, Revising, and Editing. Let's discuss each step individually.

Brainstorming

Take five minutes and free write about your writing practices. Some people call free writing "nonstop writing"—the idea is that you should just put the pen to paper and write whatever comes into your head for the next five minutes. Don't worry about sentences, punctuation, or spelling. Think about what you do before you write—how do you collect your thoughts? Do you always sit in the same place to write? Do you write on a computer, or on paper first? What seems to work for you as a writer? What things about your writing practices would you consider changing to make your writing habits more effective?

Outlining

Take a look at what you've written. What jumps out at you as important? Do you notice any themes or preoccupations? Underline those points that you repeat or that you think are important. Then, think about how you might put those points into a descriptive paragraph of how you write. You'll probably want to include both what works for you as a writer, and what you might do to change your writing practices to make them more effective. Write a brief vertical outline of a four- or five-sentence paragraph about your writing practices. Don't worry if you come up with more details than you originally came up with in prewriting—that growth in your ideas is the point of the writing process.

Writing

Take the details and phrases in your outline and form them into sentences. Your paragraph should be descriptive—a picture of how you write and how you'd like to change your writing practices to make it easier to write more effectively. If the order of your outline doesn't seem to make sense for your paragraph, change it or add more detail as you go.

Revising

Reread your descriptive paragraph of yourself as a writer, and think about how you can turn it into a plan of action. For this step, you'll be including some of the same details, but really focusing on the types of things you can do to improve the conditions under which you write. Do some more prewriting to develop these ideas or to briefly sketch out a new outline before you write the sentences.

Editing

After you're happy with the ideas in your plan, read the sentences one by one. Make sure that each is one is grammatically sound and clear. Keep your eye out for vagueness and awkwardness in your sentences. Read the paragraph out loud to see how it sounds, and backwards if you want. Make sure each sentence is error-free.

WRITING TECHNIQUES PRACTICE

Now let's practice everything you've learned in this section of the book. Consult our answers, provided after the quiz, only after you've answered the questions on your own.

Sentence Combining Exercise

Using coordination and subordination together, make one sentence from each of the following sets of sentences. Include all the information given, but feel free to change the wording or arrangement of the sentences.

1. The Spaniards came to the region of New Mexico in the early sixteenth century.

   Then they explored the region.

   They conquered the Pueblo Indians.

   They founded Santa Fe.

   Santa Fe is now the state capital.

2. The Pueblo Indians revolted in 1680.

   They drove the Spanish out of the region.

   The Spanish soon reconquered it.

Use parallelism to combine each of the following sets into one or at most two sentences.

3. In different states condemned prisoners have been electrocuted.

   They have been gassed.

   In Utah they can choose to be hanged.

   In Utah they can choose to be shot.

4. The phrase "James brothers" means one thing in the history of the Wild West.

   It has a different meaning in the history of American culture.

   Frank James was a notorious outlaw.

   Jesse James was a notorious outlaw.

   William James was a celebrated writer.

   Henry James was a celebrated writer.

Combine the sentences in each of the following pairs by transforming one sentence into an adjective clause and using it in the other.

5. The steady flow of poppy sap from Afghanistan to neighboring Pakistan is having negative effects on large numbers of people.

   In Pakistan the sap is converted into heroin.

6. Laboratory technicians knowingly flout the laws forbidding the operation.

   The technicians oversee the conversion process.

Combine the sentences in each of the following pairs by changing one of them into an adverb clause. Use a comma as needed.

7. After ten years of fighting, the Trojans were defeated for a reason.

   They failed to guard against Greek trickery.

8. The Greeks hid themselves and their ships behind an island near Troy for a purpose.

   They wanted the Trojans to consider themselves victorious and safe from further attack.

Text Reconstruction Exercise

The order of the sentences in each of the following paragraphs is incorrect. In each paragraph, rearrange the sentences in the sequence you believe is correct. List the numbers of the sentences in the order you believe they should appear.

Paragraph A

(1) They that are the first raisers of their houses, are most indulgent towards their children; beholding them as the continuance, not only of their kind, but of their work; and so both children and creatures. (2) Children sweeten labors; but they make misfortunes more bitter. (3) The perpetuity by generation is common to beasts; but memory, merit, and noble works, are proper to men. (4) They cannot utter the one; nor they will not utter the other. (5) So the care of posterity is most in them that have no posterity. (6) And surely a man shall see the noblest works and foundations have proceeded from childless men; which have sought to express the images of their minds, where those of their bodies have failed. (7) The joys of parents are secret; and so are their griefs and fears. (8) They increase the cares of life; but they mitigate the remembrance of death.

Paragraph B

(1) Is this to be allowed? (2) Not certainly in every case, and yet perhaps in more than rigourists would fancy. (3) There are a thousand different humours in the mind, and about each of them, when it is uppermost, some literature tends to be deposited. (4) It were to be desired that all literary work, and chiefly works of art, issued from sound, human, healthy, and potent impulses, whether grave or laughing, humorous, romantic, or religious. (5) The second duty, far harder to define, is moral.

Paragraph C

(1) Here, like Stevenson in his university days, Huxley seemed to be idle, but in reality, he was always busy on his own private end. (2) Moreover, in his regular courses at Charing Cross, he seems to have done work sufficiently notable to be recognized by several prizes and a gold medal. (3) Self-conducted, also, was his later education at the Charing Cross Hospital. (4) Thomas Henry Huxley was born on May 4, 1825. (5) So constantly did he work over the microscope that the window at which he sat came to be dubbed by his fellow students "The Sign of the Head and Microscope." (6) His autobiography gives a full account of his parents, his early boyhood, and his education. (7) He kept a journal in which he noted thoughts gathered from books, and ideas on the causes of certain phenomena. (8) He read widely; he talked often with older people; he was always investigating the why of things. (9) In this journal he frequently wrote what he had done and had set himself to do in the way of increasing his knowledge. (10) Of formal education, Huxley had little; but he had the richer schooling which nature and life give an eager mind.

For more practice in text reconstruction:

- Write your own paragraph on any subject.
- Rewrite your paragraph with the sentences scrambled in a different order.
- Try to reconstruct your paragraph based on the transition words.
- Did your paragraph provide effective transitions? Would your transitions guide a reader easily through the paragraph?

Answers to Sentence Combining Exercise

1. After the Spaniards came to the region of New Mexico in the early sixteenth century, they explored the region, conquered the Pueblo Indians, and founded Santa Fe, which is now the state capital.

2. Though the Pueblo Indians revolted in 1680 and drove the Spanish out of the region, the Spanish soon reconquered it.

3. In different states condemned prisoners have been electrocuted, hanged, and gassed; but in Utah they can choose to be hanged or shot.

4. The phrase "James brothers" means one thing in the history of the Wild West but another thing in the history of American culture. Frank and Jesse James were notorious outlaws; William and Henry James were celebrated writers.

5. The steady flow of poppy sap from Afghanistan to neighboring Pakistan, where the sap is converted into heroin, is having negative effects on large numbers of people.

6. Laboratory technicians who oversee the conversion process knowingly flout the laws forbidding the operation.

7. After ten years of fighting, the Trojans were defeated because they failed to guard against Greek trickery.

8. The Greeks hid themselves and their ships behind an island near Troy so that the Trojans would consider themselves victorious and safe from further attack.

Answers to Text Reconstruction Exercise

Paragraph A

from "Of Parents and Children," *Essays*, by Francis Bacon

The correct order is: 7, 4, 2, 8, 3, 6, 5, 1, or as follows:

(7) The joys of parents are secret; and so are their griefs and fears. (4) They cannot utter the one; nor they will not utter the other. (2) Children sweeten labors; but they make misfortunes more bitter. (8) They increase the cares of life; but they mitigate the remembrance of death. (3) The perpetuity by generation is common to beasts; but memory, merit, and noble works, are proper to men. (6) And surely a man shall see the noblest works and foundations have proceeded from childless men; which have sought to express the images of their minds, where those of their bodies have failed. (5) So the care of posterity is most in them that have no posterity. (1) They that are the first raisers of their houses, are most indulgent towards their children; beholding them as the continuance, not only of their kind, but of their work; and so both children and creatures.

Paragraph B

from *The Art of Writing*, by Robert Louis Stevenson

The correct order is: 5, 3, 1, 2, 4, or as follows:

(5) The second duty, far harder to define, is moral. (3) There are a thousand different humours in the mind, and about each of them, when it is uppermost, some literature tends to be deposited. (1) Is this to be allowed? (2) Not certainly in every case, and yet perhaps in more than rigourists would fancy. (4) It were to be desired that all literary work, and chiefly works of art, issued from sound, human, healthy, and potent impulses, whether grave or laughing, humorous, romantic, or religious.

Paragraph C

from *Autobiography and Selected Essays*, by Thomas Henry Huxley

The correct order is: 4, 6, 10, 8, 7, 9, 3, 1, 5, 2, or as follows:

(4) Thomas Henry Huxley was born on May 4, 1825. (6) His autobiography gives a full account of his parents, his early boyhood, and his education. (10) Of formal education, Huxley had little; but he had the richer schooling which nature and life give an eager mind. (8) He read widely; he talked often with older people; he was always investigating the why of things. (7) He kept a journal in which he noted thoughts gathered from books, and ideas on the causes of certain phenomena. (9) In this journal he frequently wrote what he had done and had set himself to do in the way of increasing his knowledge. (3) Self-conducted, also, was his later education at the Charing Cross Hospital. (1) Here, like Stevenson in his university days, Huxley seemed to be idle, but in reality, he was always busy on his own private end. (5) So constantly did he work over the microscope that the window at which he sat came to be dubbed by his fellow students "The Sign of the Head and Microscope." (2) Moreover, in his regular courses at Charing Cross, he seems to have done work sufficiently notable to be recognized by several prizes and a gold medal.

TERMINOLOGY REVIEW: WRITING TECHNIQUES

style	How you present your ideas
tone	The "voice" your readers hear as they read your essay
structure	The way an essay is organized and the order in which you present your ideas to the reader
thesis	A one- or two-sentence condensed version of the argument of an essay
topic section	The part of the thesis statement that identifies the topic of the essay
comment section	The part of the thesis statement that makes a point about the topic of the essay
evidence	Details that support an argument or claim
diction	The level of formality exhibited by the specific words chosen
syntax	The grammatical structure of sentences
topic sentence	The sentence that identifies the main point of the paragraph
paragraph	A group of sentences that center on and develop one idea
signal words	Words that help guide the reader through the paragraph. Examples: however, in addition to, similarly, of course, for example.
transitions	Words that function as links between paragraphs. Examples: however, similarly, of course.
outline	A systematic listing of the main points of an essay
deductive argument	A process of reasoning in which a conclusion is determined from a set of given evidence
colloquial	Informal speech or writing, such as a local or regional saying
subject	A word or group of words that identifies a person, place, or thing
predicate	A word or group of words that tells something about what the subject is or does
imperative	A sentence or word that relays a command
fragment sentence	A group of words that do not make a grammatical sentence

clause	A group of structurally related words that have a subject and a verb
dependent clause	This can't stand on its own as a sentence
subordination	An arrangement that makes one or more parts of a sentence secondary to and dependent on another part
independent clause	Can stand on its own as a sentence
subordinate	A clause that begins with a subordinator or a relative pronoun and cannot stand alone as a sentence
subordinating conjunction	Introduces a clause that depends on another clause for its meaning (e.g., *after, although, as, as if*)
run-on	Two or more independent clauses run together with no punctuation or conjunction between them (written as two words, hyphenated)
comma splice	Two independent clauses joined only by a comma (written as two words)
semicolon	Punctuation used to separate complete sentences (not sentence and phrase). Also, to separate elements of series in which items already contain commas.
indefinite pronoun	Refers to unspecified persons or things (e.g., *everyone, someone, anything*)
antecedent	The word to which a pronoun refers

TYPES OF READING ON THE EXAM

Section V

Forms of Prose

CHAPTER 13

KEY TERMS

- ambiguity
- analogy (See also: figurative language)
- analytical writing (See also: evidence, claim, thesis statement)
- appeals to: authority, emotion, logic
- audience
- canon (canonical)
- ethos
- evidence (See also: analytical writing, claim, thesis statement)
- explication
- exposition (See also: expository)
- genre
- imagery
- metaphor (See also: simile, rhetorical device)
- narrative (See also: narrator)
- perspective (See also: point of view)
- reflective
- setting
- simile (See also: metaphor, rhetorical device)
- speaker
- syllogism
- theme
- tone (See also: formal/informal/colloquial)
- voice (See also: narrator)

PERSONAL AND REFLECTIVE WRITING

To get you started thinking about reflective writing, first try this exercise. Write a short personal essay (one page) in which you describe your current college selection process. As part of your writing process, make sure you having a brainstorming session. The session will help you decide the focus of the essay. You might consider writing about a number of things, for example:

- The items that will contribute to your final decision—location, reputation, faculty, cost, etc.
- Any emotional turmoil you might be experiencing as you contemplate the thought of going off to college
- The life changes you'll experience when you go to college
- The kinds of things you imagine yourself learning at college

If you've picked a life path that doesn't include college, write a short personal essay in which you describe what your chosen life path looks like.

For either option, make sure you remember that one goal of personal writing is to convey something about yourself and your experience to the reader. Personal writing doesn't mean informal writing. Your essay needs to have a logical flow, just as with any other piece of writing. Also remember that you're trying to make an impression on your reader. You want your reader to be interested in your experience. Try to make your language and phrasing as colorful as possible, while still keeping your writing clear.

What Is Personal and Reflective Writing?

Much of your college reading and writing will involve texts that follow some disciplinary form; they'll follow the rules of argument of a certain discipline. A report on the Black Plague written by a biologist, for example, will look very different from an essay written on the same topic by a historian. Even though they'd address the same topic, each of these professionals would structure their writing according to the conventions of the discipline in which they're working.

A scholar or a student writing an academic essay in the field of history must adhere to a certain argumentative structure, a certain type of rhetorical stance, and a certain way to organize facts. A scientist must write like scientists. In fact, most professional and academic writing is like this; when we write, we almost always have to follow some kind of pre-established structure.

But in one mode of writing—the personal essay—authors are free to make up their own rules. In a personal essay, writers can tell a story, present a fact (or a whole lot of facts), offer observations, or do just about anything else they find effective or interesting. Because of this, personal essays vary greatly in what they say and how they say it.

But one thing that all personal essays have in common is that, just as in more formally structured forms of writing, every author of a personal essay *has a reason for writing one*. Regardless of the mode of writing or the topic addressed, every piece of writing has a purpose—something that the writer wants the audience to do or to think after they've finished reading.

Effects of Personal/Reflective Writing

To see the effects of personal and reflective writing, read this selection from Mark Twain's *Life on the Mississippi* and answer the questions that follow. Each of your responses should take no less than one, and probably no more than three, full paragraphs.

In responding to the questions, you'll need to do several things. First, you'll need to go back into Twain's text and **isolate specific passages** in which he makes certain rhetorical moves. For most of the questions, you'll then need to continue your response by **analyzing those passages** in terms of what each question is asking. This may mean discussing what you think Twain's intentions were, discussing your own emotional or intellectual reaction to the passage, or both.

Be sure to **refer to and quote from Twain's piece** when answering each of the questions. Remember that your observations about a text are much more powerful if they're supported by actual citations from that text.

Life on the Misssissippi
Mark Twain

When I was a boy, there was but one permanent ambition among my comrades in our village on the west bank of the Mississippi River. That was, to be a steamboatman. We had transient ambitions of other sorts, but they were only transient. When a circus came and went, it left us all burning to become clowns; the first Negro minstrel show that came to our section left us all suffering to try that kind of life; now and then we had a hope that if we lived and were good, God would permit us to be pirates. These ambitions faded out, each in its turn; but the ambition to be a steamboatman always remained.

My father was a justice of the peace, and I supposed he possessed the power of life and death over all men and could hang anybody that offended him. This was distinction enough for me as a general thing; but the desire to be a steamboatman kept intruding, nevertheless. I first wanted to be a cabin-boy, so that I could come out with a white apron on and shake a tablecloth over the side, where all my old comrades could see me; later I thought I would rather be the deckhand who stood on the end of the stage-plank with the coil of rope in his hand, because he was particularly conspicuous. But these were only day-dreams—they were too heavenly to be contemplated as real possibilities. By and by one of our boys went away. He was not heard of for a long time. At last he turned up as apprentice engineer or 'striker' on a steamboat. This thing shook the bottom out of all my Sunday-school teachings. That boy had been notoriously worldly, and I just the reverse; yet he was exalted to this eminence, and I left in obscurity and misery. There was nothing generous about this fellow in his greatness. He would always manage to have a rusty bolt to scrub while his boat tarried at our town, and he would sit on the inside guard and scrub it, where we could all see him and envy him and loathe him.

And whenever his boat was laid up he would come home and swell around the town in his blackest and greasiest clothes, so that nobody could help remembering that he was a steamboatman; and he used all sorts of steamboat technicalities in his talk, as if he were so used to them that he forgot common people could not understand them. He would speak of the "labboard" side of a horse in an easy, natural way that would make one wish he was dead. And he was always talking about "St. Looy" like an old citizen; he would refer casually to occasions when he "was coming down Fourth Street," or when he was "passing by the Planter's House," or when there was a fire and he took a turn on the brakes of "the old Big Missouri;" and then he would go on and lie about how many towns the size of ours were burned down there that day. Two or three of the boys had long been persons of consideration among us because they had been to St. Louis once and had a vague general knowledge of its wonders, but the day of their glory was over now. They lapsed into a humble silence, and learned to disappear when the ruthless "cub"-engineer approached. This fellow had money, too, and hair oil. Also an ignorant silver watch and a showy brass watch chain. He wore a leather belt and used no suspenders. If ever a youth was cordially admired and hated by his comrades, this one was. No girl could withstand his charms. He "cut out" every boy in the village. When his boat blew up at last, it diffused a tranquil contentment among us such as we had not known for months. But when he came home the next week, alive, renowned, and appeared in church all battered up and bandaged, a shining hero, stared at and wondered over by everybody, it seemed to us that the partiality of Providence for an undeserving reptile had reached a point where it was open to criticism.

This creature's career could produce but one result, and it speedily followed. Boy after boy managed to get on the river. The minister's son became an engineer. The doctor's and the post-master's sons became "mud clerks"; the wholesale liquor dealer's son became a barkeeper on a boat; four sons of the chief merchant, and two sons of the county judge, became pilots. Pilot was the grandest position of all. The pilot, even in those days of trivial wages, had a princely salary—from a hundred and fifty to two hundred and fifty dollars a month, and no board to pay. Two months of his wages would pay a preacher's salary for a year. Now, some of us were left disconsolate. We could not get on the river—at least our parents would not let us.

So by and by I ran away. I said I never would come home again till I was a pilot and could come in glory. But somehow I could not manage it. I went meekly aboard a few of the boats that lay packed together like sardines at the long St. Louis wharf, and very humbly inquired for the pilots, but got only a cold shoulder and short words from mates and clerks. I had to make the best of this sort of treatment for the time being, but I had comforting daydreams of a future when I should be a great and honored pilot, with plenty of money, and could kill some of these mates and clerks and pay for them.

Now answer the following questions:

1. This passage is illustrative of Mark Twain's characteristic subtle humor. What are some specific elements of this piece that you find humorous? What effect does that humor have on your reading experience? On your thoughts about Twain as a person?

2. Much of *Life on the Mississippi* is written from an objective, third person point of view. But Twain chooses to write this piece through the eyes of a child, in the manner of his classic novels *Tom Sawyer* and *Huckleberry Finn*. If he didn't begin his piece with the phrase "When I was a boy," what elements of this text would tell you it was written from a child's point of view? Explain each of your answers.

3. Although this piece is written from a child's point of view, there's an obvious element of adult bemusement in this piece. Twain almost seems to be laughing at his own behavior as a child. In which specific elements of this piece does Twain the adult reveal

himself? How does this affect the way you think about the children in the piece? How does it affect the way you think about Twain?

4. Twain doesn't make any direct comment about the town in which he grew up in this piece and yet certain characteristics of this town still seem apparent. Look through the piece again. What can you tell about the town in which these boys lived? In what ways, if any, are Twain the adult's attitudes toward the town different from those of Twain the child? What specific elements of the text tell you this? What kind of emotional reaction do you think Twain wanted his audience to feel toward the town?

5. This piece presents steamboats and their crews in an almost mythological light. In what ways is Twain using this romanticization as a humorous device? In what ways is he using it to comment on life in a small town in the early nineteenth century? Compared to Twain the child, how much do you think Twain the adult sees the steamboat as something more than just a means of transporting cargo and passengers? How can you tell?

More Practice with Personal Writing

To practice personal writing, compose a one-page, single-spaced personal essay on a topic of your choice. If you'd like, you can take this opportunity to write an essay that could serve as a college entrance essay. This kind of college entrance essay is often called a *personal statement*.

If you decide to write a personal statement, imagine the admissions officers at a college you want to attend; they're your audience. Although you won't know exactly who they are, thinking about what they might be looking for in a personal statement will help you in your writing process.

- Who do you think these administrators are?
- What kinds of qualities do you think they want represented in the students at their college?
- What kind of writing are you going to have to do to make them remember your statement in the sea of personal statements and application materials they receive?

If you already have your application materials, see if there's a particular question you have to answer. If so, you can use that question to generate this essay.

If you don't have application materials, or no particular question exists, you'll have to figure out what kind of statement will get you noticed. You might:

- Relate an anecdote
- Talk about your reasons for wanting to attend the college in question
- Describe some of your extra-curricular activities
- Describe the kind of thinker you are
- Describe your intended course of study at college

If you decide to write on another topic, anything you've experienced or thought deeply about is fair game. Remember that whichever option you choose, your reader should finish reading your essay with a vivid picture of you.

Self-Assessment

Looking at your own writing with a critical eye is one way that you can begin to improve your writing. If you can answer questions about what your writing does well and where it needs improvement, you'll become a stronger and more careful writer. In this activity you'll study your own writing by answering questions and generating ideas for revision. Even though you won't actually rewrite, thinking about ways you'd revise your writing will help you see different ways to communicate your ideas.

Choose an essay to work on—it can be the essay from the previous activity. Read your essay and complete the self-assessment workshop below. Make sure that your answers are complete. You shouldn't be able to fully answer these questions with just a yes or a no. Each answer should be at least two or three sentences long. Reading your essay and answering these questions should take you about 45 minutes.

Self-Assessment Workshop

1. Write a five-sentence summary of your essay.

2. What did you intend to communicate in your essay? What methods did you use to do this (personal anecdote, description, dialogue)? Which of these methods do you feel most comfortable using?

3. How successful is your essay at communicating something personal? Pick the one part of your essay that's the most successful. What qualities of this section will make your reader remember it?

4. If your essay responds to a specific question, does it do so adequately? If so, write two sentences that explain why you feel you have done a good job answering the question. If not, write two sentences that explain why you feel you haven't done a good job answering the question.

5. Describe the way you have organized your essay. Are the different sections distinguishable from each other (an introduction, a body, a conclusion)? Is your essay organized in a logical fashion? Do the ideas follow each other such that your reader can understand your point? (Make an outline of your essay to help answer these questions.)

6. What evidence or anecdotes help you communicate something about yourself and develop your main point? Identify your strongest piece of evidence and write two sentences that explain what it helps you communicate. Identify your weakest piece of evidence and write two sentences that explain how it could better help you communicate something about yourself.

7. Do you have transitions between sections of your essay? Do these transitions help guide the reader through your essay? Pick one transition section and write two sentences in which you explain how the transition connects your paragraphs or ideas.

8. Look at the style of your writing. In three sentences describe your writing style. Do you write lengthy sentences or short sentences? Are the sentences complex or simple? Do you use strong and vivid verbs? What kind of vocabulary do you use in your essay? In one phrase identify the stylistic element you would most like to improve.

9. Does this essay represent your best effort? If so, identify your favorite part of the essay and explain why you have picked this part. If not, identify your least favorite part and explain why you don't like this part.

EXPOSITORY WRITING

In this section we'll discuss the skills and styles employed in another important form of prose, expository writing.

Logical Reasoning Skills

Logic is something we use every day, in thinking, speaking, reading, and writing. Logical reasoning helps us come to conclusions about our knowledge and experiences of the world and evaluate the correctness of those conclusions. The two main processes of logical reasoning are *induction* and *deduction*. The key distinction between induction and deduction is that induction moves from the specific to the general, and deduction starts with general principles and moves to specifics.

For example, if you cracked an egg and found it rotten, you might conclude that all the eggs from the carton were rotten, or even that all eggs in this particular shipment were rotten. You'd come to these conclusions *inductively*—that is, by making general conclusions from a specific example. If, on the other hand, you knew that eggs from a particular dairy are always fresh, and your carton of eggs had been delivered from that dairy this morning, you'd probably conclude that the eggs in your carton were fresh. In this case, your conclusion would be *deductive* because it's based on two general premises: eggs from this dairy are always fresh, and your carton was delivered this morning. If the premises are correct, deductive reasoning is more reliable than inductive reasoning. Because inductive reasoning bases general conclusions on individual examples, these conclusions can only be more or less probable.

A *syllogism* is a structured deductive argument with two premises and a conclusion. The following is an example of a syllogism:

- Major Premise: Every new snowboarder will fall on his or her first day on the slopes.
- Minor Premise: George has never snowboarded before, and he plans to go snowboarding on Saturday.
- Conclusion: George will fall on Saturday.

In this example, the conclusion answers the specific question, "What will happen to George on Saturday?" It's based on the general knowledge that new snowboarders always fall and that George is hitting the slopes for the first time on Saturday.

Take a Shot at Analyzing Inductive and Deductive Reasoning

In the following scenarios decide whether the reasoning that takes place in them is inductive or deductive, and explain why. (Our answers are on the next page.)

1. Paul and Jim are planning to spend the day at the beach. Paul says to Jim, "You know, we should make sure we put on sunscreen today. They say that the risk of skin cancer is really high if you don't wear sunscreen regularly, especially in the middle of the day." Jim says to Paul as he applies some sunscreen, "Yeah, you're right. I want to live to be an old man."

2. During the last inning of the final playoff softball game, Angela steps up to the plate. A barely audible groan sweeps through the remainder of the lineup. The score is tied, the team has two outs, and even though she's generally a good player, Angela hasn't yet managed to get on base this game. As the pitcher winds up to pitch, the next batter whispers to her friend, "Ugh. We're going to lose this one for sure."

Modes of Exposition

There are eight modes of exposition: narration, description, definition, comparison and contrast, analogy, classification and division, process analysis, and cause and effect.

- **Narration:** Narration gives details about a topic by telling about a sequence of events. Selecting which details to include and arranging them so that their connections make sense are all part of creating an effective story. Narration is often combined with description.

- **Description:** Description involves including details to illustrate how something appears or acts. Three types of description are external description, analytical description, and evocative description. External description allows the reader to imagine how the object described appears. Analytical description concerns the structure of the object, and evocative description attempts to evoke a feeling or impression made by the object.

- **Definition:** Exposition often involves defining terms. One of the least effective ways to do this is by using a dictionary definition. Effective definitions in essays include details of an object or term that specifically relate to the overall point you want to make. Sometimes expository writing contrasts more than one valid definition of a term to make a statement about a topic. There are numerous ways of defining terms including using synonyms, comparison or contrast, and describing their functions. It's also possible to define terms by classification, by example, or by etymology (examining the roots of words).

- **Comparison and Contrast:** Comparison is a way of presenting information about a topic by focusing on the similarities between two or more things. Contrast highlights the differences between two or more things.

- **Analogy:** Analogy is a form of comparison in which a writer examines similar aspects of things that are otherwise totally dissimilar. The use of analogy is inductive because it enables a reader to understand something abstract, remote, or unknown by comparing it to something specific, concrete, or known.

- **Classification and Division**: Classification involves arranging larger groups of things, people, or ideas into smaller groups, or classes. Division works by cutting a single topic into parts.
- **Process Analysis**: Process analysis presents all the information necessary for a reader to understand how something happens. A process is a sequence of events leading to a particular result. Process analysis can be more or less detailed. If the goal is simply for the reader to understand how an event happens, the analysis can include less detail than if the goal is for the reader to be able to carry out a particular process on his or her own.
- **Cause and Effect**: Analysis of cause and effect shows the causal links between two or more events. An important thing to remember about cause and effect is that one cause may have more than one effect, and one effect may have multiple causes. It's important to keep this complexity in mind during cause and effect analysis.

Answers to Inductive and Deductive Reasoning Exercise

1. In this scenario, Jim is using deductive reasoning. The general principles they know are that not wearing sunscreen increases the risk of skin cancer and that cancer has the potential to shorten one's life. Jim concludes that since he wants to live a long life, he'd rather not increase his risk for the disease, and so will wear sunscreen.

2. In this case, the batter is using inductive reasoning. Even though she knows in general that Angela is a good player, on the specific evidence of her batting attempts during this game, she predicts that Angela won't score any points for the team. Her reasoning may or may not be correct, and the general outcome she anticipates can only be probable.

Expository Styles

Now let's review and practice different expository writing styles to reinforce your knowledge of the styles and gain more insight into the effects or functions of each style.

Each paragraph in this activity is a discrete entity. For some of the expository styles you'll be given a topic; for others you'll construct your own topic. Make sure each paragraph is coherent. Remember that expository writing is writing that presents or explains something to the audience. As you write in different expository styles, think about the different ways you're explaining or presenting. By the end of the activity, you'll have written 10 substantial paragraphs, each of which will model one kind of expository writing.

Definition

Write one paragraph in which you use definition to explain an emotion. Remember that you need to go beyond the dictionary definition. You need to provide an extended definition that will make a specific point about the emotion you choose to define.

Description

Write one paragraph in which you describe a favorite object. This object could be something from your childhood or from your present life. At the end of the paragraph, your reader should have a vivid picture of the object in his or her mind. Remember to use colorful, exact language. To provide description you might write about the appearance of the object, the way it's constructed, or the way it gets used.

Narration

Write one paragraph in which you relate a sequence of events that has affected your life. As well as communicating the sequence, remember to communicate why the events are significant. This will enhance the narration.

Analogy

Write one paragraph in which you use analogy to explain something unfamiliar by likening it to something familiar.

Comparison

Write one paragraph in which you use comparison to show similarities between two ideas or things. For this paragraph you may use either block comparison, in which you present all the information about one item before moving onto the second item, or alternating comparison, in which you go back and forth between the two items.

Contrast

Write one paragraph in which you use contrast to show differences between two ideas or things. For this paragraph you may use either block contrast, in which you present all the information about one item before moving onto the second item, or alternating contrast, in which you go back and forth between the two items.

Classification

Write one paragraph in which you use classification to discuss the types of magazines or books you most frequently read. Classification is an expository method that uses similar characteristics to put many things into a single group.

Division

Write one paragraph in which you use division to discuss your three favorite musical groups or sports teams. Division is an expository method that uses differences to break a single topic into two or more separate parts.

Process Analysis

Write one paragraph in which you use process analysis to explain to your reader how something happens. For this paragraph you may use an informational process method, if you want to explain how an event happens, or an instructional process analysis, if you want your reader to be able to carry out the process on his or her own.

Cause and Effect Analysis

Write one paragraph in which you use cause and effect analysis to show the causal link between one or more events or conditions. Cause and effect analysis uses a linear presentation of events to link causes and effects. For this paragraph you may either describe an event that has already happened, or use cause and effect to predict an outcome based on current conditions.

ANALYTICAL WRITING AND CLOSE READING

Close reading will help you read and write about fiction. (You can close read nonfiction texts as well.) When you practice close reading, you focus on a small part of a text, paying close attention to the language, in order to develop an interpretation of the passage or the text itself. Close reading is both a verb and a noun. You may be asked to do close reading—in other words, study in detail a short work or passage. Or you may be asked to produce a close reading essay, in which you write an essay based on your close reading of a work or passage. Close reading can also be used as one technique within a longer written essay.

Basically, your goal in close reading is to analyze the content of the passage so you can explain its meaning, significance, and function. To do this you'll need to examine how the elements in the passage work in combination to convey a particular meaning.

Close reading begins with noticing. As you study the passage, you need to notice and think about the significance of all the details in the passage. As you take notes on these details, think about which details will matter most to your interpretation. One passage can produce a variety of close readings; different readers will pick up on different elements and details. However, for your close reading to be successful, it has to stay grounded in the passage. In other words, your interpretation must arise from the details in the passage, not from some preconceived notion about what the passage might be saying.

The aim of close reading is to produce an interesting interpretation of the passage by looking at the way the author uses language. If the passage is one section of a longer text and you've read the whole work, you should also discuss the relationship of the passage to the rest of the work. For example, if you close read the first paragraph of a story, besides talking about your interpretation of the paragraph, discuss how that paragraph functions to set the stage for the story. Or, if you close read the last paragraph of a story, besides creating an interpretation of the paragraph, discuss how the paragraph works to close or resolve the events of the story.

Begin with a series of questions about the passage. As you answer these questions and take notes about other interesting details, you develop a reservoir of information about the passage. You won't be able to use all the questions or answers in your close reading, but you can develop your interpretation of the passage from the information in your notes.

- What is the tone of the passage? How is that tone conveyed? How does the narrator's tone affect the passage?

- Whose point of view governs the passage? What do you see—and what is obscured—because of this point of view? What point(s) of view are left out or considered less important?

- Pay attention to the individual words in the passage. What kinds of adjectives, verbs, and adverbs appear? How do they connect the passage to the text as a whole? How does language help build a sense of character, setting, theme? As you attend to the language, circle words that seem particularly important and note the associations or meanings you think they carry. Underline phrases that catch your eye. Make notes to yourself about why you marked these phrases. Underline any repeated words or word sounds and note the effect of this repetition. Identify uses of figurative language. Why might the author use a metaphor or simile? Where do the literal and figurative uses of language collide?

- How do details describing the setting or environment function in the passage? What does the setting say about the text's characters, its themes?

- What facets of different characters/relationships surface in the passage? Does the passage reveal anything surprising or unexpected about the character?

- What does a character's way of speaking reveal about that individual? What about the interactions between characters?

- How is the passage related to the main concerns or issues that arise in the novel?

As you look through your notes about the passage, think about the conclusions you can draw from them. One way to draw conclusions is to think about the function of the passage. Does the passage:

- Describe a scene
- Develop a quality of a particular character
- Reveal the thoughts of a character
- Introduce a theme or idea
- Present an important piece of the plot

You'll have to use your notes and your skill at examining the elements of fiction to help you answer these questions. The answers you produce will help you construct an interpretation of the passage.

Remember that a close reading doesn't consist of a string of answers to all these questions. You need to develop a claim about the passage or interpretation of the passage and choose evidence from your notes to support that claim or interpretation.

Close reading is like being a detective. You have to sort through your notes to determine which details you can put together to develop an interesting and justifiable interpretation of, or claim about, the passage. Taking notes and answering the questions above give you evidence for inclusion in your close reading.

FORMS OF PROSE

Close Reading Exercise

The following two paragraphs are excerpted from Stephen Crane's novella *Maggie, Girl of the Streets*. Published in 1896, the novella is set in turn-of-the-century New York and depicts the downward fortunes of Maggie, a pretty Irish girl who lives in the tenements with her family. Maggie meets Pete, who disgraces her, and her mother kicks her out of the house. Turned onto the streets, Maggie fends for herself by turning to a life of prostitution, the only form of work she can find. Through his portrait of Maggie's limited opportunities, Crane critiques the harshness of tenement life. The passage below comes near the end of the novella, as Maggie walks through the streets toward her death.

Read the passage below, the sample close reading, and the commentary that follows the close reading.

Maggie, Girl of the Streets
Stephen Crane

The girl went into gloomy districts near the river, where the tall black factories shut in the street and only occasional broad beams of light fell across the pavements from the saloons. In front of one of these places, from whence came the sound of a violin vigorously scraped, the patter of feet on boards and the ring of kind laughter, there stood a man with blotched features . . .

She went into the blackness of the final block. The shutters of the tall buildings were closed like grim lips. The structures seemed to have eyes that looked over her, beyond her, at other things. Afar off the lights of avenues glittered as if from impossible distance. Street car bells jingled with a sound of merriment.

The imagery of this passage conveys vividly the grim environment of tenement life. As the girl enters the "gloomy districts," "tall black factories" block the sunlight. The use of this imagery creates for the reader a mental picture of the filthy, foreboding section of the city. Earlier in the story Maggie is referred to as someone who "blossomed in a mud puddle . . . a most rare and wonderful production of a tenement district, a pretty girl." In this scene it is clear that Maggie is no longer a blossom. Wandering through the parts of town where little sunlight reaches the streets, she is, rather, faded and wilted, worn and used up.

Crane uses two literary devices, personification and juxtaposition, to augment the effect of the gloomy imagery. The buildings, with shutters "closed like grim lips" and "eyes that looked over her," seem to disapprove of Maggie and her downfall. In this way the buildings represent her mother, who threw her out onto the street, and the members of the larger society, who look scornfully upon her. The buildings look over and beyond Maggie, "at other things." They notice her only briefly, long enough to register scorn, and then shift their attention to other, more deserving things. This glance at Maggie, which is only momentary, suggests the worthless position she occupies in the eyes of society. Although she is clearly at the end of her line, in the "final block," there is no one to notice or care about her situation. Maggie's isolation is juxtaposed with the laughter in the saloons, the lights of the avenues, and the merriment of the streetcar bells. The contrast between her solitary walk and the merriment of the other locales, where people gather to laugh, shop, and travel, reinforces Maggie's forgotten position within society.

Whereas early in the story she was rare and wonderful, now she is no longer worthy of attention. Maggie's journey from rare to common is indicated in the passage by her namelessness. Although the reader clearly knows that this girl is Maggie, Crane does not call her by name. Her namelessness makes her into a figure larger than just herself. By calling attention to both Maggie's predicament and the fact that others share this dismal life, Crane critiques society's treatment of tenement dwellers. This passage echoes and sharpens the critical project of the novella as a whole.

Commentary

Notice the different sections of the close reading. The first paragraph attends to the language and imagery of the paragraph, concentrating on the gloom and blackness of the city block. The second paragraph discusses how two literary devices, personification and juxtaposition, contribute to the effect of the passage. The final paragraph connects the passage to the entire novella by examining one way Crane makes his critique. Taken together, these paragraphs provide the reader with the author's interpretation of the passage.

Examine which details are taken from the paragraph to help build the close reading. Are these the details you would have chosen? If you were to choose different details, how would the close reading change?

The author of the close reading:

1. Uses direct quotes from the passage:
   - "gloomy districts,"
   - "blossomed in a mud puddle … a most rare and wonderful production of a tenement district, a pretty girl"
   - "closed like grim lips"

2. Makes associations:
   - They notice her only briefly, long enough to register scorn, and then shift their attention to other, more deserving things. This glance at Maggie, which is only momentary, suggests the worthless position she occupies in the eyes of society.
   - Her namelessness makes her into a figure larger than just herself.

3. Shows how parts of the passage are connected to other parts of the story:
   - Earlier in the story Maggie is referred to as someone who "blossomed in a mud puddle … a most rare and wonderful production of a tenement district, a pretty girl." In this scene it is clear that Maggie is no longer a blossom.
   - By calling attention to both Maggie's predicament and the fact that others share this dismal life, Crane critiques society's treatment of tenement dwellers. This passage echoes and sharpens the critical project of the novella as a whole.

These three techniques connect the close reading to the passage and the story, and keep the interpretation from being too abstract or ungrounded. Making associations to concepts or ideas outside the story is the place you can be the most creative, but it is also the place where you run the risk of making unjustifiable conclusions. Be sure the associations you make have some connection to the passage and to the larger themes of the text.

Constructing a Close Reading

In this section you'll practice close reading. Because close reading asks you to look carefully at language, rhetorical techniques, literary devices, and themes, it can take a long time. You have to sift through different details in the passage and different possible associations and meanings, before you arrive at your claim or interpretation.

A close reading is something that you build from the details in the passage, not something that already exists, fully formed, in some abstract literary space. The details you notice, the associations you bring to them, and the way you put them together to form an interpretation or make a claim will make your close reading unique.

Here are the eight steps for close reading.

1. **Read the passage.** Read the selected passage carefully once, making general notes to yourself. Then reread the passage, with the steps 2–8 in mind.

2. **Look at the language.** Circle words that seem important or are repeated. Use the dictionary to look up words you don't know. Underline phrases that draw your attention. Make notes about why you marked these places in the passage.

3. **Brainstorm.** Use individual words or phrases from the passage to free associate. What concepts, ideas, or items outside the story do the words or phrases call to mind? Think about themes that emerge in the story or passage. See if any of your associations match the themes you've identified.

4. **Identify direct quotes.** Write down two or three short quotations (words and phrases) that you can group together; then write one word next to them that explains why they belong together. Do this again for several other sets of quotes. Grouping quotes together in this way will help you think about the paragraphs you'll be writing from this close reading.

5. **Look at the larger framework.** Glance back over the story, essay, or novel in which the passage is set. Write down any quotes from other places in the text that relate to the passage. If these other quotes are linked thematically to the passage, they can help you reinforce your claim about the passage. Looking at the rest of the text can also help you make sure your interpretation of the passage is grounded in the text and not constructed out of thin interpretive air.

6. **Think about function.** What does this passage do for the text? What does it reveal? These questions will help you think about the function of the passage, which is related to what

the passage means or says, but might be less obvious at first. Function is important to think about because understanding what a passage does in a text can help you deepen your interpretation or claim about the passage.

7. **Begin to build.** Look back at all your notes and gather details that seem to go together. From these details, construct a claim about the passage, in which you identify its function or importance. Also create your interpretation of the passage, explaining what you think the passage is saying. These two, claim and interpretation, aren't really separate, but it can be helpful to think about them as separate. An interpretation is a claim about what the passage is saying. You might try out more than one claim or interpretation, depending on the details you select and the way you organize them.

8. **Enhance your claim or interpretation.** Use the quotes and details you gathered from the passage to support your interpretation or claim. A close reading is like a regular essay. You have to support what you're saying with evidence from the passage. A close reading can be different lengths, from a paragraph to an entire essay. Your close reading has to flow logically. You might choose to proceed chronologically through the passage to make your interpretation. You might pick one important detail around which to base your claim. You might talk primarily about how the passage embodies a major theme in the text. You might focus primarily on the mood or tone created by the language of the passage. All these methods are different models for close reading. What they all share is close attention to the language of the passage.

Now it's time to practice writing your own close readings.

Close Reading Practice, Take One

Read Sherwood Anderson's short story "Adventure," from the collection of stories *Winesburg, Ohio*, published in 1919. Then follow the instructions to construct your own close reading.

Adventure
Sherwood Anderson

Alice Hindman, a woman of twenty-seven when George Willard was a mere boy, had lived in Winesburg all her life. She clerked in Winney's Dry Goods Store and lived with her mother, who had married a second husband.

Alice's step-father was a carriage painter, and given to drink. His story is an odd one. It will be worth telling some day.

At twenty-seven Alice was tall and somewhat slight. Her head was large and overshadowed her body. Her shoulders were a little stooped and her hair and eyes brown. She was very quiet but beneath a placid exterior a continual ferment went on.

When she was a girl of sixteen and before she began to work in the store, Alice had an affair with a young man. The young man, named Ned Currie, was older than Alice. He, like George Willard, was employed on the Winesburg Eagle and for a long time he went to see Alice almost every evening. Together the two walked under the trees through the streets of the town and talked of what they would do with their lives. Alice was then a very pretty girl and Ned Currie took her into his arms and kissed her. He became excited and said things he did not intend to say and Alice, betrayed by her desire to have something beautiful come into her rather narrow life, also grew excited. She also talked. The outer crust of her life, all of her natural diffidence and reserve, was torn away and she gave herself over to the emotions of love. When, late in the fall of her sixteenth year, Ned Currie went away to Cleveland where he hoped to get a place on a city newspaper and rise in the world, she wanted to go with him. With a trembling voice she told him what was in her mind. "I will work and you can work," she said. "I do not want to harness you to a needless expense that will prevent your making progress. Don't marry me now. We will get along without that and we can be together. Even though we live in the same house no one will say anything. In the city we will be unknown and people will pay no attention to us."

Ned Currie was puzzled by the determination and abandon of his sweetheart and was also deeply touched. He had wanted the girl to become his mistress but changed his mind. He wanted to protect and care for her. "You don't know what you're talking about," he said sharply; "you may be sure I'll let you do no such thing. As soon as I get a good job I'll come back. For the present you'll have to stay here. It's the only thing we can do."

On the evening before he left Winesburg to take up his new life in the city, Ned Currie went to call on Alice. They walked about through the streets for an hour and then got a rig from Wesley Moyer's livery and went for a drive in the country. The moon came up and they found themselves unable to talk.

In his sadness the young man forgot the resolutions he had made regarding his conduct with the girl. They got out of the buggy at a place where a long meadow ran down to the bank of Wine Creek and there in the dim light became lovers. When at midnight they returned to town they were both glad. It did not seem to them that anything that could happen in the future could blot out the wonder and beauty of the thing that had happened. "Now we will have to stick to each other, whatever happens we will have to do that," Ned Currie said as he left the girl at her father's door.

The young newspaper man did not succeed in getting a place on a Cleveland paper and went west to Chicago. For a time he was lonely and wrote to Alice almost every day. Then he was caught up by the life of the city; he began to make friends and found new interests in life. In Chicago he boarded at a house where there were several women. One of them attracted his attention and he forgot Alice in Winesburg. At the end of a year he had stopped writing letters, and only once in a long time, when he was lonely or when he went into one of the city parks and saw the moon shining on the grass as it had shone that night on the meadow by Wine Creek, did he think of her at all.

In Winesburg the girl who had been loved grew to be a woman. When she was twenty-two years old her father, who owned a harness repair shop, died suddenly. The harness maker was an old soldier, and after a few months his wife received a widow's pension. She used the first money she got to buy a loom and became a weaver of carpets, and Alice got a place in Winney's store. For a number of years nothing could have induced her to believe that Ned Currie would not in the end return to her.

She was glad to be employed because the daily round of toil in the store made the time of waiting seem less long and uninteresting. She began to save money, thinking that when she had saved two or three hundred dollars she would follow her lover to the city and try if her presence would not win back his affections.

Alice did not blame Ned Currie for what had happened in the moonlight in the field, but felt that she could never marry another man. To her the thought of giving to another what she still felt could belong only to Ned seemed monstrous. When other young men tried to attract her attention she would have nothing to do with them. "I am his wife and shall remain his wife whether he comes back or not," she whispered to herself, and for all of her willingness to support herself could not have understood the growing modern idea of a woman's owning herself and giving and taking for her own ends in life.

Alice worked in the dry goods store from eight in the morning until six at night and on three evenings a week went back to the store to stay from seven until nine. As time passed and she became more and more lonely she began to practice the devices common to lonely people. When at night she went upstairs into her own room she knelt on the floor to pray and in her prayers whispered things she wanted to say to her lover. She became attached to inanimate objects, and because it was her own, could not bear to have anyone touch the furniture of her room. The trick of saving money, begun for a purpose, was carried on after the scheme of going to the city to find Ned Currie had been given up. It became a fixed habit, and when she needed new clothes she did not get them. Sometimes on rainy afternoons in the store she got out her bank book and, letting it lie open before her, spent hours dreaming impossible dreams of saving money enough so that the interest would support both herself and her future husband.

"Ned always liked to travel about," she thought. "I'll give him the chance. some day when we are married and I can save both his money and my own, we will be rich. Then we can travel together all over the world."

In the dry goods store weeks ran into months and months into years as Alice waited and dreamed of her lover's return. Her employer, a grey old man with false teeth and a thin grey mustache that drooped down over his mouth, was not given to conversation, and sometimes, on rainy days and in the winter when a storm raged in Main Street, long hours passed when no customers came in. Alice arranged and rearranged the stock. She stood near the front window where she could look down the deserted street and thought of the evenings when she had walked with Ned Currie and of what he had said. "We will have to stick to each other now." The words echoed and re-echoed through the mind of the maturing woman. Tears came into her eyes.

Sometimes when her employer had gone out and she was alone in the store she put her head on the counter and wept. "Oh, Ned, I am waiting," she whispered over and over, and all the time the creeping fear that he would never come back grew stronger within her.

In the spring when the rains have passed and before the long hot days of summer have come, the country about Winesburg is delightful. The town lies in the midst of open fields, but beyond the fields are pleasant patches of woodlands. In the wooded places are many little cloistered nooks, quiet places where lovers go to sit on Sunday afternoons. Through the trees they look out across the fields and see farmers at work about the barns or people driving up and down on the roads. In the town bells ring and occasionally a train passes, looking like a toy thing in the distance.

For several years after Ned Currie went away Alice did not go into the wood with the other young people on Sunday, but one day after he had been gone for two or three years and when her loneliness seemed unbearable, she put on her best dress and set out. Finding a little sheltered place from which she could see the town and a long stretch of the fields, she sat down. Fear of age and ineffectuality took possession of her. She could not sit still, and arose.

As she stood looking out over the land something, perhaps the thought of never ceasing life as it expresses itself in the flow of the seasons, fixed her mind on the passing years. With a shiver of dread, she realized that for her the beauty and freshness of youth had passed. For the first time she felt that she had been cheated. She did not blame Ned Currie and did not know what to blame. Sadness swept over her. Dropping to her knees, she tried to pray, but instead of prayers words of protest came to her lips. "It is not going to come to me. I will never find happiness. Why do I tell myself lies?" she cried, and an odd sense of relief came with this, her first bold attempt to face the fear that had become a part of her everyday life.

In the year when Alice Hindman became twenty-five two things happened to disturb the dull uneventfulness of her days. Her mother married Bush Milton, the carriage painter of Winesburg, and she herself became a member of the Winesburg Methodist Church. Alice joined the church because she had become frightened by the loneliness of her position in life. Her mother's second marriage had emphasized her isolation. "I am becoming old and queer. If Ned comes he will not want me. In the city where he is living men are perpetually young. There is so much going on that they do not have time to grow old," she told herself with a grim little smile, and went resolutely about the business of becoming acquainted with people. Every Thursday evening when the store had closed she went to a prayer meeting in the basement of the church and on Sunday evening attended a meeting of an organization called The Epworth League.

When Will Hurley, a middle-aged man who clerked in a drug store and who also belonged to the church, offered to walk home with her she did not protest. "Of course I will not let him make a practice of being with me, but if he comes to see me once in a long time there can be no harm in that," she told herself, still determined in her loyalty to Ned Currie.

Without realizing what was happening, Alice was trying feebly at first, but with growing determination, to get a new hold upon life. Beside the drug clerk she walked in silence, but sometimes in the darkness as they went stolidly along she put out her hand and touched softly the folds of his coat. When he left her at the gate before her mother's house she did not go indoors, but stood for a moment by the door. She wanted to call to the drug clerk, to ask him to sit with her in the darkness on the porch before the house, but was afraid he would not understand. "It is not him that I want," she told herself; "I want to avoid being so much alone. If I am not careful I will grow unaccustomed to being with people."

During the early fall of her twenty-seventh year a passionate restlessness took possession of Alice. She could not bear to be in the company of the drug clerk, and when, in the evening, he came to walk with her she sent him away. Her mind became intensely active and when, weary from the long hours of standing behind the counter in the store, she went home and crawled into bed, she could not sleep. With staring eyes she looked into the darkness. Her imagination, like a child awakened from long sleep, played about the room. Deep within her there was something that would not be cheated by phantasies and that demanded some definite answer from life.

Alice took a pillow into her arms and held it tightly against her breasts. Getting out of bed, she arranged a blanket so that in the darkness it looked like a form lying between the sheets and, kneeling beside the bed, she caressed it, whispering words over and over, like a refrain. "Why doesn't something happen? Why am I left here alone?" she muttered. Although she sometimes thought of Ned Currie, she no longer depended on him. Her desire had grown vague. She did not want Ned Currie or any other man. She wanted to be loved, to have something answer the call that was growing louder and louder within her.

And then one night when it rained Alice had an adventure. It frightened and confused her. She had come home from the store at nine and found the house empty. Bush Milton had gone off to town and her mother to the house of a neighbor. Alice went upstairs to her room and undressed in the darkness. For a moment she stood by the window hearing the rain beat against the glass and then a strange desire took possession of her. Without stopping to think of what she intended to do, she ran downstairs through the dark house and out into the rain. As she stood on the little grass plot before the house and felt the cold rain on her body a mad desire to run naked through the streets took possession of her.

She thought that the rain would have some creative and wonderful effect on her body. Not for years had she felt so full of youth and courage. She wanted to leap and run, to cry out, to find some other lonely human and embrace him. On the brick sidewalk before the house a man stumbled homeward. Alice started to run. A wild, desperate mood took possession of her. "What do I care who it is. He is alone, and I will go to him," she thought; and then without stopping to consider the possible result of her madness, called softly. "Wait!" she cried. "Don't go away. Whoever you are, you must wait."

The man on the sidewalk stopped and stood listening. He was an old man and somewhat deaf. Putting his hand to his mouth, he shouted. "What? What say?" he called.

Alice dropped to the ground and lay trembling. She was so frightened at the thought of what she had done that when the man had gone on his way she did not dare get to her feet, but crawled on hands and knees through the grass to the house.

When she got to her own room she bolted the door and drew her dressing table across the doorway. Her body shook as with a chill and her hands trembled so that she had difficulty getting into her nightdress. When she got into bed she buried her face in the pillow and wept brokenheartedly. "What is the matter with me? I will do something dreadful if I am not careful," she thought, and turning her face to the wall, began trying to force herself to face bravely the fact that many people must live and die alone, even in Winesburg.

Now read the passage below—excerpted from "Adventure"—and construct your own close reading. Remember to take into account the relationship of this passage to the rest of the story.

In the year when Alice Hindman became twenty-five two things happened to disturb the dull uneventfulness of her days. Her mother married Bush Milton, the carriage painter of Winesburg, and she herself became a member of the Winesburg Methodist Church. Alice joined the church because she had become frightened by the loneliness of her position in life. Her mother's second marriage had emphasized her isolation. "I am becoming old and queer. If Ned comes he will not want me. In the city where he is living men are perpetually young. There is so much going on that they do not have time to grow old," she told herself with a grim little smile, and went resolutely about the business of becoming acquainted with people. Every Thursday evening when the store had closed she went to a prayer meeting in the basement of the church and on Sunday evening attended a meeting of an organization called The Epworth League.

Close Reading Practice, Take Two

To further practice close reading, select a short story (perhaps your favorite one from English class), choose one or two passages from it, perform a close reading on the passages you chose, and write an analytical essay (if you're typing it, it should be one page, single-spaced).

To write an analytical essay based on a close reading, you need to present a summary of the main point or theme of a passage, your thesis about the main point, and evidence supporting your thesis. The evidence in a close reading of literature will be quotes from the text, which illustrate things like tone, style, figurative language, or other rhetorical devices that are significant to your thesis about the passage.

To complete this activity, read the short story you've chosen, making sure to take notes of your interpretations, questions, and reactions to the story as you read. Then, select one or two related passages that interest you, and think about why they do. How is the tone important? The narrative perspective? The characterization? What distinct contribution does each passage make to the text as a whole? Did you find the passage surprising in any way? Why? How does the passage function to create an effect on you, the reader? What words or phrases in the passage seem especially significant?

After you've thought about these questions in relationship to the passage, come up with a tentative thesis statement that states your own point about what specific elements of fiction or rhetorical devices are at work in the passage. Your thesis should also include a commentary on how these elements and devices function toward a larger point in the story.

Then, brainstorm what evidence to use to support your thesis. After you've come up with the evidence you'll include, see if your thesis can use any refining—did your brainstorming come up with any new directions you can incorporate into your thesis? Are there avenues you can't pursue because of a lack of evidence? Hone your thesis statement even more finely, if possible, and then write your essay, using the evidence you've brainstormed to support your thesis.

Good luck, and have fun!

PERSUASIVE WRITING

When we refer to the *argument* of a piece of writing, we're talking about the main idea the author wants to get across, the author's purpose in writing. But argument also implies a logical structure; an argument presents facts in a certain way to convince the audience of the truth of the author's ideas. *Argument relies on logic alone.* Here's a classic three-part argument, or *syllogism*:

> Socrates is a man.
> All men are mortal.
> Therefore, Socrates is mortal.

But in this section we're talking about *persuasive writing*—writing that employs techniques that don't rely strictly on logic to convince an audience. When we supplement the logical content of our writing with psychological content, such as words and phrases intended to invoke emotion in our audience, we're using *persuasion*. For example, an advertiser might appeal to the emotions people feel about children:

> Buy Chamberlain tires. Your children are worth it.

The author of this ad uses parents' concern for their children's safety to sell the idea that they should buy Chamberlain tires. Because no solid information is given about why we should buy Chamberlain tires, we can say that this passage is entirely *persuasive* and not at all *argumentative*.

Take a Shot at Analyzing Argument and Persuasion

Identify each of the following as either argumentative or persuasive. Give specific reasons for your responses. Compare your answers with ours later in this chapter.

1. My house has a wood-burning fireplace, and so does yours. Since both our houses are warm, I'd say that wood-burning fireplaces work pretty well.

2. No one's going to like you if you go to school wearing that jacket.

3. If you're really my friend, you'll loan me ten bucks.

4. A stockbroker friend of mine told me that this stock was going to skyrocket tomorrow. You should buy all you can!

The Rhetorical Triangle

More than two thousand years ago, the ancient Greeks, who were very interested in the role language played in society, spent a great deal of time working out the how's and why's of persuasive speaking and writing. They used the term *rhetoric* to describe the "art of persuasion," and they defined three distinct elements of rhetoric, all of which were important tools for writers and speakers who needed to persuade their audiences of something. This "rhetorical triangle" consists of the following separate elements:

- **Logos** refers to the logical content of communication—that is, the information being presented. It also refers to the organizational structure of the information. The syllogism about Socrates, above, is an example of pure logos, with no ethos or pathos. If a piece of writing is pure logos, we say that it's entirely argumentative and not at all persuasive.

- **Ethos** refers to the character, or persona, of the writer as perceived by the reader. In persuasive writing, it's important to project an ethos that's authoritative, credible, and knowledgeable on your topic.

- **Pathos** refers to the anticipated emotional reaction of the audience to what's being said. When a writer is using pathos, he or she is counting on a making the audience feel a certain emotion, to make the audience more receptive to the writer's argument.

Almost every argument has an element of logos in it—that is, every argument has some factual content. But in many writing situations you may find yourself wanting to supplement the bare facts of your argument with some more emotional, and less informational, elements—to persuade, rather than argue.

Just about every persuasive move you can make in a piece of writing will fall under either ethos or pathos. So let's take a closer look at these two very important rhetorical elements and how they work.

Ethos

In persuasive writing, the primary goal of any writer in developing ethos is to appear knowledgeable and believable. The earlier in your essay you can establish an authoritative persona, or ethos, the better off you'll be—and the more likely your audience will be to accept your argument. Here are a few examples of some of the many ways to establish ethos.

- **Cite a respected scholar or thinker**. If you're writing a paper on physics, for example, you might begin with "According to Steven Hawking, the structure of time is intertwined with the structure of space."

- **Let the audience know of any or your relevant personal experience, study, or credentials**. If you're writing about the conditions in local hospitals, for example, and you'd worked in a hospital in your area, you might begin by stating, "During my time as an intern at Valley Lawn Hospital, I learned many important skills . . . "

- **Mention or cite a respected academic publication**. This is especially effective, and favorite, method of establishing ethos in professional academic writing. A paper on the work of Samuel Johnson, for example, may begin by citing a biographer or critic whose work on Johnson was respected in academic communities: "In Boswell's famous biography of Dr. Samuel Johnson, he observes that . . . "

- **Demonstrate that you've given your topic some serious thought**. This is a less formal but nonetheless effective way of convincing your audience that you know what you're talking about. In writing a paper on news sites on the Internet, for example, you might begin with "When I first began researching newspapers on the web, I didn't now much about them. But as I researched web newspapers, pored over articles about journalism, and read about the web, I grew to appreciate . . . "

Establishing ethos is a subtle, creative process. Use your imagination, and above all, know your audience. Not all kinds of ethos will work on all audiences.

Take a Shot at Analyzing Ethos

1. Which of the following would be the most effective way of establishing an effective *ethos* on the topic of sports medicine? Give specific reasons for your response. (Our answers appear later in this chapter.)

> I have been playing sports since I was a small child, and occasionally I have suffered injuries requiring medical attention.
>
> In my days as a medical student, I did a lot of volunteer work with State University Health Center.

2. In one or two sentences, explain why the following introductory sentence would be effective in establishing an authoritative ethos in a paper written for a history class. (Our response appears later in this chapter.)

> Although it is common knowledge that the Democratic Convention of 1968 was plagued by thousands of protestors and rioting in the streets, what many people don't know is that seven great Americans were arrested as a result of this civil unrest.

3. In one or two sentences, explain why the following introductory sentence would probably not be effective in establishing an authoritative ethos in a report for an English Literature class. Compare your response to ours later in this chapter..

> When Shakespeare wrote his famous play *Dr. Faustus*, the world was introduced for the first time to the dramatic value of a deal with the devil.

Pathos

When you try to make your audience feel happy or sad or scared, you're using the element of pathos. Skillful persuasive writers use pathos to put their audiences in an emotional state that makes them receptive to argument. There are even more ways of using pathos than there are of establishing ethos. Here are a few.

- **Use a tone and style that puts your audience into the mood you want them to be in**. If you're writing a piece arguing that more federal funds be allocated to inner city schools, for example, you might want to use emotionally charged language when discussing the poor conditions in those schools, expecting that your audience will react in a sympathetic way.

- **Use narratives and descriptions to create a certain emotional condition in your audience**. Continuing with the example above, you may want to tell a story about a hardworking student in one of these schools who suffers from a lack of resources (a problem that could be solved if more federal funds were allocated).

- **Appeal to common values**. A value is an idea or principle recognized as important, desirable, or even necessary. For example: Honesty, loyalty, and bravery are all values our society holds to be important. In the example above, you may want to appeal to the commonly held value that "every child deserves a quality education."

- **As with establishing ethos, using pathos effectively requires creativity**. Like any other writing skill, it takes practice. Think carefully about every word and sentence you write, and know your audience. Not all kinds of pathos will work for all audiences.

Take a Shot at Analyzing Pathos

The passage below comes from introduction to Franklin Delano Roosevelt's famous inaugural speech of 1933. Read it with an eye for the kind of emotional reaction you think Roosevelt wanted to elicit in his audience—Americans suffering from the Great Depression. Then answer the questions that follow, writing a sentence or two for each. Compare your answers with ours (later in this chapter.)

Inaugural Speech of 1933
Franklin Delano Roosevelt

This is a day of national consecration, and I am certain that my fellow Americans expect that on my induction into the Presidency I will address them with a candor and a decision which the present situation of our nation impels.

This is pre-eminently the time to speak the truth, the whole truth, frankly and boldly. Nor need we shrink from honestly facing conditions in our country today. This great nation will endure as it has endured, will revive and will prosper.

So first of all let me assert my firm belief that the only thing we have to fear...is fear itself . . . nameless, unreasoning, unjustified terror which paralyzes needed efforts to convert retreat into advance.

In every dark hour of our national life a leadership of frankness and vigor has met with that understanding and support of the people themselves which is essential to victory. I am convinced that you will again give that support to leadership in these critical days.

1. How is Roosevelt using word choice to elicit emotion in this passage?

2. Roosevelt repeatedly refers to "we" in this passage. Who is "we"? How does this use of "we" create pathos?

3. Roosevelt's words seem a bit too formal. Is this tone really appropriate for real-world writing?

Answers to Analyzing Argument and Persuasion Exercise

1. *My house has a wood-burning fireplace, and so does yours. Since both our houses are warm, I'd say that wood-burning fireplaces work pretty well.*

This passage is strictly argumentative, presenting clear premises and a conclusion that follows logically from those premises.

2. *No one's going to like you if you go to school wearing that jacket.*

This is persuasive, playing on the anxiety associated with the need to be accepted socially, which nearly everyone feels.

3. *If you're really my friend, you'll loan me ten bucks.*

While this passage somewhat resembles an argument, the unspoken first premise that "friends loan each other money" serves more as a persuasive device to manipulate emotion than as a valid observation about friendship.

4. *A stockbroker friend of mine told me that this stock was going to skyrocket tomorrow. You should buy all you can!*

The tone of this passage seems excited, even emotional, but the conclusion that buying this stock is advisable does follow logically from the information presented. (This might not be the case, of course, if the friend were a butcher or a musician.) As such, we can say that it's more argumentative than persuasive.

Answers to Analyzing Ethos Exercise

1. *I have been playing sports since I was a small child, and occasionally I have suffered injuries requiring medical attention.*

   In my days as a medical student, I did a lot of volunteer work with State University Health Center.

Although the first quote does suggest that the author might be acquainted with some elements of what sports medicine is about, the second quote, from a former medical student (who is, presumably, now a doctor), suggests a more knowledgeable (and therefore more reliable) point of view than someone who had simply been treated by a sports specialist on a few occasions.

2. *Although it is common knowledge that the Democratic Convention of 1968 was plagued by thousands of protestors and rioting in the streets, what many people don't know is that seven great Americans were arrested as a result of this civil unrest.*

The passage begins by referring to a piece of historical fact that might, in fact, not be common knowledge at all. By presenting this piece of information in this manner, the author has not only let the reader know what the paper is to be about, but has demonstrated that the rest of the paper will probably contain other knowledge about this event that is not so common.

3. *When Shakespeare wrote his famous play* Dr. Faustus, *the world was introduced for the first time to the dramatic value of a deal with the devil.*

This one is a bit of a trick question, because it was in fact Christopher Marlowe, not William Shakespeare, who wrote *Dr. Faustus*. Remember, a factual mistake (or even a grammatical one) early in your essay greatly detracts from your ethos. You don't want to risk losing your credibility before you've even gotten into your argument.

Answers to Analyzing Pathos Exercise

1. How is Roosevelt using word choice to elicit emotion in this passage?

By using such words and phrases as "consecration" (which was also a theme in Lincoln's Gettysburg Address), "impels," "frankly and boldly," and "every dark hour," Roosevelt creates a somber and serious mood in his audience, which is appropriate for the occasion.

2. Roosevelt repeatedly refers to "we" in this passage. Who is "we"? How does this use of "we" create pathos?

"We" refers to the American people. By consistently referring back to this "we" in his discussion of adversity and trial, Roosevelt is able to create a sense of solidarity and perhaps even of patriotism in his audience.

3. Roosevelt's words seem a bit too formal. Is this tone really appropriate for real-world writing?

The tone Roosevelt uses here qualifies as "epideictic," or "highly ceremonial or ritualized language." This kind of tone was very prominent in political and religious speech until recently. But even in the age of television, using a heightened and formal diction can be one way to establish a respectful and receptive state of pathos. As with so many other issues in persuasive writing, it depends mostly on your audience.

TERMINOLOGY REVIEW: FORMS OF PROSE

expository writing	Writing which makes a statement by explaining or giving information.
comparison	Focuses on the similarities between two or more things.
contrast	Focuses on the differences between two or more things.
analogy	A comparison between two different things that share similar features.
analysis	The process of breaking something down into its component parts to better understand what it is or how it works.
argument	Accomplishing a goal through logical means. An argument is a statement that consists of at least one main interpretive assertion that is supported by a series of claims and evidence.
logos	The logical information presented.
ethos	The perceived character or the writer.
pathos	The audience's anticipated emotional reaction.
fallacy	An argument that isn't valid.
faulty	An analogy that compares a fact with a similar point that is still an assumption.
tone	The "voice" your readers hear as they read your essay.
evidence	Details that support a claim or argument.
personal/reflective writing	Writing written to examine and reflect on your own observances, feelings and opinions.
anecdote	A short narrative account of an amusing, revealing, or otherwise interesting event. Anecdotes engage readers, illuminate characters, and present abstract ideas in concrete forms.
persona	The projected identity of the speaker in a literary text or essay.
drama	A composition written for performance by actors. Usually involves a central conflict and builds to a climax and resolution.

FORMS OF PROSE

exposition	The first part of a plot which introduces characters, setting, time and situation.
point of view	The perspective from which a story or poem is told.
narrator	The figure in a text who tells the story.
theme	The central idea or meaning of a story.
imagery	Words or descriptions that evoke the physical setting of the text. Imagery can also refer to illustrative figures of speech.
figurative language	Language which uses stylistic devices such as figures of speech to convey non-literal meanings. Common figures of speech include metaphors and similes.
analytical essay	An essay in which you argue an interpretation of a passage and/or text by closely examining the language in a short selection.

CHAPTER REVIEW

To review your study of types of prose, answer the following study questions.

Study Questions: Forms of Prose

Directions: After carefully reviewing the material covered in this chapter, read the questions below and write one or two sentences in response to each.

1. In literary analysis, specific terms are used to describe the types of third-person narrative point of view and the kinds of knowledge the narrator has. What are these types, and what do they mean?

2. Most academic writing follows certain discipline-specific guidelines. How does the practice of personal writing relate to these guidelines?

3. What is the difference between argument and persuasion?

4. What two major modes of organization do writers usually use in structuring a comparison or contrast essay?

5. What is meant by the term *extended definition*, as it is used in expository writing?

6. What is involved in doing a close reading of a piece of literature?

7. How is argument handled differently in personal writing than in most other types of college or business writing?

8. What are the three elements of Greek rhetoric you should always keep in mind when writing a piece to persuade your audience?

History and Narrative

CHAPTER 14

> **KEY TERMS**
> - antagonist (See also: protagonist)
> - perspective (See also: point of view)
> - protagonist (See also: antagonist)
> - tone
> - transition

ANALYZING BIOGRAPHY AND AUTOBIOGRAPHY

As in all forms of writing, the authors of biographies and autobiographies have a purpose, or agenda. This purpose goes beyond simply relating the facts and events of a life. These facts are the "skeleton" of a complex, subjective presentation of ideas and arguments. Biographies and autobiographies may be factual, but like all history, they make arguments and interpretations about what occurred and can present theses about life, society, and anything else the author chooses to focus on.

In this section, you'll read selections from two biographies: *The Boys' Life of Abraham Lincoln* by Helen Nicolay and the autobiographical *The Life and Adventures of Calamity Jane, by Herself*. These works are considered authoritative accounts of their subjects. Both were written in the early part of the 20th century.

Directions: Read *The Boys' Life of Abraham Lincoln* and *The Life and Adventures of Calamity Jane, by Herself*. Take notes as you read, looking for answers to the study questions. Mark passages, words, or phrases that strike you as significant, and look for differences and similarities between the two texts. Then write responses to the study questions. Each response should be a few sentences to a paragraph long.

Study Questions

Abraham Lincoln Biography

1. How is the text structured?

2. How would I describe the language of the text? How does the author use tone?

3. To whom is the text addressed? How do I know?

4. What issues, above and beyond the events in Lincoln's life, does this text address?

5. Is the author arguing for or against something in this text? What is that argument, if there is one? What specific parts of the text tell me this?

6. Is the author trying to affect me emotionally? What specific parts of the text tell me this?

Calamity Jane Autobiography

1. How is the text structured?

2. How would I describe the language of the text? How does the author use tone?

3. To whom is the text addressed? How do I know?

4. What issues, above and beyond the events in Calamity Jane's life, does this text address?

5. Is the author arguing for or against something in this text? What is that argument, if there is one? What specific parts of the text tell me this?

6. Is the author trying to affect me emotionally? What specific parts of the text tell me this?

The Boys' Life of Abraham Lincoln
Helen Nicolay

Abraham Lincoln's forefathers were pioneers—men who left their homes to open up the wilderness and make the way plain for others to follow them. For one hundred and seventy years, ever since the first American Lincoln came from England to Massachusetts in 1638, they had been moving slowly westward as new settlements were made in the forest. They faced solitude, privation, and all the dangers and hardships that beset men who take up their homes where only beasts and wild men have had homes before; but they continued to press steadily forward, though they lost fortune and sometimes even life itself, in their westward progress. Back in Pennsylvania and New Jersey some of the Lincolns had been men of wealth and influence. In Kentucky, where the future President was born on February 12, 1809, his parents lived in deep poverty. Their home was a small log cabin of the rudest kind, and nothing seemed more unlikely than that their child, coming into the world in such humble surroundings, was destined to be the greatest man of his time. True to his race, he also was to be a pioneer—not indeed, like his ancestors, a leader into new woods and unexplored fields, but a pioneer of a nobler and grander sort, directing the thoughts of men ever toward the right, and leading the American people, through difficulties and dangers and a mighty war, to peace and freedom.

The story of this wonderful man begins and ends with a tragedy, for his grandfather, also named Abraham, was killed by a shot from an Indian's rifle while peaceably at work with his three sons on the edge of their frontier clearing. Eighty-one years later the President himself met death by an assassin's bullet. The murderer of one was a savage of the forest; the murderer of the other that far more cruel thing, a savage of civilization.

When the Indian's shot laid the pioneer farmer low, his second son, Josiah, ran to a neighboring fort for help, and Mordecai, the eldest, hurried to the cabin for his rifle. Thomas, a child of six years, was left alone beside the dead body of his father; and as Mordecai snatched the gun from its resting-place over the door of the cabin, he saw, to his horror, an Indian in his war-paint, just stooping to seize the child. Taking quick aim at a medal on the breast of the savage, he fired, and the Indian fell dead. The little boy, thus released, ran to the house, where Mordecai, firing through the loopholes, kept the Indians at bay until help arrived from the fort.

It was this child Thomas who grew up to be the father of President Abraham Lincoln. After the murder of his father the fortunes of the little family grew rapidly worse, and doubtless because of poverty, as well as by reason of the marriage of his older brothers and sisters, their home was broken up, and Thomas found himself, long before he was grown, a wandering laboring boy. He lived for a time with an uncle as his hired servant, and later he learned the trade of carpenter. He grew to manhood entirely without education, and when he was twenty-eight years old could neither read nor write. At that time he married Nancy Hanks, a good-looking young woman of twenty-three, as poor as himself, but so much better off as to learning that she was able to teach her husband to sign his own name. Neither of them had any money, but living cost little on the frontier in those days, and they felt that his trade would suffice to earn all that they should need. Thomas took his bride to a tiny house in Elizabethtown, Kentucky, where they lived for about a year, and where a daughter was born to them.

Then they moved to a small farm thirteen miles from Elizabethtown, which they bought on credit, the country being yet so new that there were places to be had for mere promises to pay.

Farms obtained on such terms were usually of very poor quality, and this one of Thomas Lincoln's was no exception to the rule. A cabin ready to be occupied stood on it, however; and not far away, hidden in a pretty clump of trees and bushes, was a fine spring of water, because of which the place was known as Rock Spring Farm. In the cabin on this farm the future President of the United States was born on February 12, 1809, and here the first four years of his life were spent. Then the Lincolns moved to a much bigger and better farm on Knob Creek, six miles from Hodgensville, which Thomas Lincoln bought, again on credit, selling the larger part of it soon afterward to another purchaser. Here they remained until Abraham was seven years old.

About this early part of his childhood almost nothing is known.

He never talked of these days, even to his most intimate friends. To the pioneer child a farm offered much that a town lot could not give him—space; woods to roam in; Knob Creek with its running water and its deep, quiet pools for a playfellow; berries to be hunted for in summer and nuts in autumn; while all the year round birds and small animals pattered across his path to people the solitude in place of human companions. The boy had few comrades. He wandered about playing his lonesome little games, and when these were finished returned to the small and cheerless cabin. Once, when asked what he remembered about the War of 1812 with Great Britain, he replied: "Only this: I had been fishing one day and had caught a little fish, which I was taking home. I met a soldier in the road, and having always been told at home that we must be good to soldiers, I gave him my fish." It is only a glimpse into his life, but it shows the solitary, generous child and the patriotic household.

It was while living on this farm that Abraham and his sister Sarah first began going to A-B-C schools. Their earliest teacher was Zachariah Riney, who taught near the Lincoln cabin; the next was Caleb Hazel, four miles away.

Though only seven years old, Abraham was unusually large and strong for his age, and he helped his father in all this heavy labor of clearing the farm. In after years, Mr. Lincoln said that an ax "was put into his hands at once, and from that till within his twenty-third year he was almost constantly handling that most useful instrument—less, of course, in ploughing and harvesting seasons." At first the Lincolns and their seven or eight neighbors lived in the unbroken forest. They had only the tools and household goods they brought with them, or such things as they could fashion with their own hands. There was no sawmill to saw lumber. The village of Gentryville was not even begun. Breadstuff could be had only by sending young Abraham seven miles on horseback with a bag of corn to be ground in a hand grist-mill.

About the time the new cabin was ready, relatives and friends followed from Kentucky, and some of these in turn occupied the half-faced camp. During the autumn a severe and mysterious sickness broke out in their little settlement, and a number of people died, among them the mother of young Abraham. There was no help to be had beyond what the neighbors could give each other. The nearest doctor lived fully thirty miles away. There was not even a minister to conduct the funerals. Thomas Lincoln made the coffins for the dead out of green lumber cut from the forest trees with a whip-saw, and they were laid to rest in a clearing in the woods. Months afterward, largely through the efforts of the sorrowing boy, a preacher who chanced to come that way was induced to hold a service and preach a sermon over the grave of Mrs. Lincoln.

Her death was indeed a serious blow to her husband and children. Abraham's sister, Sarah, was only eleven years old, and the tasks and cares of the little household were altogether too heavy for her years and experience. Nevertheless they struggled bravely through

HISTORY AND NARRATIVE

the winter and following summer; then in the autumn of 1819 Thomas Lincoln went back to Kentucky and married Sarah Bush Johnston, whom he had known, and it is said courted, when she was only Sally Bush. She had married about the time Lincoln married Nancy Hanks, and her husband had died, leaving her with three children. She came of a better station in life than Thomas, and was a woman with an excellent mind as well as a warm and generous heart. The household goods that she brought with her to the Lincoln home filled a four-horse wagon, and not only were her own children well clothed and cared for, but she was able at once to provide little Abraham and Sarah with comforts to which they had been strangers during the whole of their young lives. Under her wise management all jealousy was avoided between the two sets of children; urged on by her stirring example, Thomas Lincoln supplied the yet unfinished cabin with floor, door, and windows, and life became more comfortable for all its inmates, contentment if not happiness reigning in the little home.

The new stepmother quickly became very fond of Abraham, and encouraged him in every way in her power to study and improve himself. The chances for this were few enough. Mr. Lincoln has left us a vivid picture of the situation. "It was," he once wrote, "a wild region, with many bears and other wild animals still in the woods. There I grew up. There were some schools, so-called, but no qualification was ever required of a teacher beyond "readin', writin', and cipherin'" to the Rule of Three. If a straggler supposed to understand Latin happened to sojourn in the neighborhood, he was looked upon as a wizard."

The school-house was a low cabin of round logs, with split logs or "puncheons" for a floor, split logs roughly leveled with an ax and set up on legs for benches, and holes cut out in the logs and the space filled in with squares of greased paper for window-panes. The main light came in through the open door. Very often Webster's "Elementary Spelling-book" was the only text-book. This was the kind of school most common in the middle West during Mr. Lincoln's boyhood, though already in some places there were schools of a more pretentious character. Indeed, back in Kentucky, at the very time that Abraham, a child of six, was learning his letters from Zachariah Riney, a boy only a year older was attending a Catholic seminary in the very next county. It is doubtful if they ever met, but the destinies of the two were strangely interwoven, for the older boy was Jefferson Davis, who became head of the Confederate government shortly after Lincoln was elected President of the United States.

As Abraham had been only seven years old when he left Kentucky, the little beginnings he learned in the schools kept by Riney and Hazel in that State must have been very slight, probably only his alphabet, or at most only three or four pages of Webster's "Elementary Spelling-book." The multiplication-table was still a mystery to him, and he could read or write only the words he spelled. His first two years in Indiana seem to have passed without schooling of any sort, and the school he attended shortly after coming under the care of his stepmother was of the simplest kind, for the Pigeon Creek settlement numbered only eight or ten poor families, and they lived deep in the forest, where, even if they had had the money for such luxuries, it would have been impossible to buy books, slates, pens, ink, or paper. It is worthy of note, however, that in our western country, even under such difficulties, a school-house was one of the first buildings to rise in every frontier settlement. Abraham's second school in Indiana was held when he was fourteen years old, and the third in his seventeenth year. By that time he had more books and better teachers, but he had to walk four or five miles to reach them. We know that he learned to write, and was provided with pen, ink, and a copy-book, and a very small supply of writing-paper, for copies have been printed of several scraps on which he carefully wrote down tables of long measure, land measure, and dry measure, as well as examples in multiplication and compound division, from his arithmetic. He was never able to go to school again after this time, and though the instruction he received from his five teachers—two in Kentucky and three in Indiana—extended over a period of nine years, it must be remembered that it made up in all less than one twelve-month; "that the aggregate of all his schooling did not amount to one year." The fact that he received this instruction, as he himself said, "by littles," was doubtless an advantage. A lazy or indifferent boy would of course have forgotten what was taught him at one time before he had opportunity at another; but Abraham was neither indifferent nor lazy, and these widely separated fragments of instruction were precious steps to self-help. He pursued his studies with very unusual purpose and determination not only to understand them at the moment, but to fix them firmly in his mind. His early companions all agree that he employed every spare moment in keeping on with some one of his studies. His stepmother tells us that "When he came across a passage that struck him, he would write it down on boards if he had no paper, and keep it there until he did get paper. Then he would rewrite it, look at it, repeat it. He had a copy-book, a kind of scrap-book, in which he put down all things, and thus preserved them." He spent long evenings doing sums on the fire-shovel. Iron fire-shovels were a rarity among pioneers. Instead they used a broad, thin clapboard with one end narrowed to a handle, arranging with this the piles of coals upon the hearth, over which they set their "skillet" and "oven" to do their cooking. It was on such a wooden shovel that Abraham worked his sums by the flickering firelight, making his figures with a piece of charcoal, and, when the shovel was all covered, taking a drawing-knife and shaving it off clean again.

The hours that he was able to devote to his penmanship, his reading, and his arithmetic were by no means many; for, save for the short time that he was actually in school, he was, during all these years, laboring hard on his father's farm, or hiring his youthful strength to neighbors who had need of help in the work of field or forest. In pursuit of his knowledge he was on an up-hill path; yet in spite of all obstacles he worked his way to so much of an education as placed him far ahead of his schoolmates and quickly abreast of his various teachers. He borrowed every book in the neighborhood. The list is a short one:

"Robinson Crusoe," "Aesop's Fables," Bunyan's "Pilgrim's Progress," Weems's "Life of Washington," and a "History of the United States." When everything else had been read, he resolutely began on the "Revised Statutes of Indiana," which Dave Turnham, the constable, had in daily use, but permitted him to come to his house and read.

Though so fond of his books; it must not be supposed that he cared only for work and serious study. He was a social, sunny-tempered lad, as fond of jokes and fun as he was kindly and industrious. His stepmother said of him: "I can say, what scarcely one mother in a thousand can say, Abe never gave me a cross word or look, and never refused . . . to do anything I asked him. . . . I must say . . . that Abe was the best boy I ever saw or expect to see."

The Life and Adventures of Calamity Jane
By Herself

My maiden name was Marthy Cannary. I was born in Princeton, Missouri, May 1st, 1852. Father and mother were natives of Ohio. I had two brothers and three sisters, I being the oldest of the children. As a child I always had a fondness for adventure and out-door exercise and especial fondness for horses which I began to ride at an early age and continued to do so until I became an expert rider being able to ride the most vicious and stubborn of horses, in fact the greater portion of my life in early times was spent in this manner.

In 1865 we emigrated from our homes in Missouri by the overland route to Virginia City, Montana, taking five months to make the journey. While on the way the greater portion of my time was spent in hunting along with the men and hunters of the party, in fact I was at all times with the men when there was excitement and adventures to be had. By the time we reached Virginia City I was considered a remarkable good shot and a fearless rider for a girl of my age. I remember many occurrences on the journey from Missouri to Montana. Many times in crossing the mountains the conditions of the trail were so bad that we frequently had to lower the wagons over ledges by hand with ropes for they were so rough and rugged that horses were of no use. We also had many exciting times fording streams for many of the streams in our way were noted for quicksands and boggy places, where, unless we were very careful, we would have lost horses and all. Then we had many dangers to encounter in the way of streams swelling on account of heavy rains. On occasions of that kind the men would usually select the best places to cross the streams, myself on more than one occasion have mounted my pony and swam across the stream several times merely to amuse myself and have had many narrow escapes from having both myself and pony washed away to certain death, but as the pioneers of those days had plenty of courage we overcame all obstacles and reached Virginia City in safety.

Mother died at Black Foot, Montana, 1866, where we buried her. I left Montana in Spring of 1866, for Utah, arriving at Salt Lake city during the summer. Remained in Utah until 1867, where my father died, then went to Fort Bridger, Wyoming Territory, where we arrived May 1, 1868, then went to Piedmont, Wyoming, with U.P. Railway. Joined General Custer as a scout at Fort Russell, Wyoming, in 1870, and started for Arizona for the Indian Campaign. Up to this time I had always worn the costume of my sex. When I joined Custer I donned the uniform of a soldier. It was a bit awkward at first but I soon got to be perfectly at home in men's clothes.

Was in Arizona up to the winter of 1871 and during that time I had a great many adventures with the Indians, for as a scout I had a great many dangerous missions to perform and while I was in many close places always succeeded in getting away safely for by this time I was considered the most reckless and daring rider and one of the best shots in the western country.

After that campaign I returned to Fort Sanders, Wyoming, remained there until spring of 1872, when we were ordered out to the Muscle Shell or Nursey Pursey Indian outbreak. In that war Generals Custer, Miles, Terry and Crook were all engaged. This campaign lasted until fall of 1873.

It was during this campaign that I was christened Calamity Jane. It was on Goose Creek, Wyoming, where the town of Sheridan is now located. Capt. Egan was in command of the Post. We were ordered out to quell an uprising of the Indians, and were out for several days, had numerous skirmishes during which six of the soldiers were killed and several severely wounded. When on returning to the Post we were ambushed about a mile and a half from our destination. When fired upon Capt. Egan was shot. I was riding in advance and on hearing the firing turned in my saddle and saw the Captain reeling in his saddle as though about to fall. I turned my horse and galloped back with all haste to his side and got there in time to catch him as he was falling. I lifted him onto my horse in front of me and succeeded in getting him safely to the Fort. Capt. Egan on recovering, laughingly said: "I name you Calamity Jane, the heroine of the plains." I have borne that name up to the present time. We were afterwards ordered to Fort Custer, where Custer city now stands, where we arrived in the spring of 1874; remained around Fort Custer all summer and were ordered to Fort Russell in fall of 1874, where we remained until spring of 1875; was then ordered to the Black Hills to protect miners, as that country was controlled by the Sioux Indians and the government had to send the soldiers to protect the lives of the miners and settlers in that section. Remained there until fall of 1875 and wintered at Fort Laramie. In spring of 1876, we were ordered north with General Crook to join Gen'ls Miles, Terry and Custer at Big Horn river. During this march I swam the Platte river at Fort Fetterman as I was the bearer of important dispatches. I had a ninety mile ride to make, being wet and cold, I contracted a severe illness and was sent back in Gen. Crook's ambulance to Fort Fetterman where I laid in the hospital for fourteen days. When able to ride I started for Fort Laramie where I met Wm. Hickock, better known as Wild Bill, and we started for Deadwood, where we arrived about June.

During the month of June I acted as a pony express rider carrying the U.S. mail between Deadwood and Custer, a distance of fifty miles, over one of the roughest trails in the Black Hills country. As many of the riders before me had been held up and robbed of their packages, mail and money that they carried, for that was the only means of getting mail and money between these points. It was considered the most dangerous route in the Hills, but as my reputation as a rider and quick shot was well known, I was molested very little, for the toll gatherers looked on me as being a good fellow, and they knew that I never missed my mark. I made the round trip every two days which was considered pretty good riding in that country. Remained around Deadwood all that summer visiting all the camps within an area of one hundred miles. My friend, Wild Bill, remained in Deadwood during the summer with the exception of occasional visits to the camps. On the 2nd of August, while setting at a gambling table in the Bell Union saloon, in Deadwood, he was shot in the back of the head by the notorious Jack McCall, a desperado. I was in Deadwood at the time and on hearing of the killing made my way at once to the scene of the shooting and found that my friend had been killed by McCall. I at once started to look for the assassin and found him at Shurdy's butcher shop and grabbed a meat cleaver and made him throw up his hands; through the excitement on hearing of Bill's death, having left my weapons on the post of my bed. He was then taken to a log cabin and locked up, well secured as every one thought, but he got away and was afterwards caught at Fagan's ranch on Horse Creek, on the old Cheyenne road and was then taken to Yankton, Dak., where he was tried, sentenced and hung.

I remained around Deadwood locating claims, going from camp to camp until the spring of 1877, where one morning, I saddled my horse and rode towards Crook city. I had gone about twelve miles from Deadwood, at the mouth of Whitewood creek, when I met the overland mail running from Cheyenne to Deadwood. The horses on a run, about two hundred yards from the station; upon looking closely I saw they were pursued by Indians. The horses ran to the barn as was their custom. As the horses stopped I rode along side of the coach and found the driver John Slaughter, lying face downwards in the boot of the stage, he having been shot by the Indians. When the stage got to the station the Indians hid in the bushes. I immediately removed all baggage from the coach except the mail. I then took the driver's seat and with all haste drove to Deadwood, carrying the six passengers and the dead driver.

I left Deadwood in the fall of 1877, and went to Bear Butte Creek with the 7th Cavalry. During the fall and winter we built Fort Meade and the town of Sturgis. In 1878 I left the command and went to Rapid city and put in the year prospecting.

In 1879 I went to Fort Pierre and drove trains from Rapid city to Fort Pierre for Frank Witc then drove teams from Fort Pierce to Sturgis for Fred. Evans. This teaming was done with oxen as they were better fitted for the work than horses, owing to the rough nature of the country.

In 1881 I went to Wyoming and returned in 1882 to Miles city and took up a ranch on the Yellow Stone, raising stock and cattle, also kept a way side inn, where the weary traveler could be accommodated with food, drink, or trouble if he looked for it. Left the ranch in 1883, went to California, going through the States and territories, reached Ogden the latter part of 1883, and San Francisco in 1884. Left San Francisco in the summer of 1884 for Texas, stopping at Fort Yuma, Arizona, the hottest spot in the United States. Stopping at all points of interest until I reached El Paso in the fall. While in El Paso, I met Mr. Clinton Burk, a native of Texas, who I married in August 1885. As I thought I had travelled through life long enough alone and thought it was about time to take a partner for the rest of my days. We remained in Texas leading a quiet home life until 1889. On October 28th, 1887, I became the mother of a girl baby, the very image of its father, at least that is what he said, but who has the temper of its mother.

When we left Texas we went to Boulder, Colo., where we kept a hotel until 1893, after which we travelled through Wyoming, Montana, Idaho, Washington, Oregon, then back to Montana, then to Dakota, arriving in Deadwood October 9th, 1895, after an absence of seventeen years.

My arrival in Deadwood after an absence of so many years created quite an excitement among my many friends of the past, to such an extent that a vast number of the citizens who had come to Deadwood during my absence who had heard so much of Calamity Jane and her many adventures in former years were anxious to see me. Among the many whom I met were several gentlemen from eastern cities who advised me to allow myself to be placed before the public in such a manner as to give the people of the eastern cities an opportunity of seeing the Woman Scout who was made so famous through her daring career in the West and Black Hill countries.

An agent of Kohl & Middleton, the celebrated Museum men came to Deadwood, through the solicitation of the gentleman who I had met there and arrangements were made to place me before the public in this manner. My first engagement began at the Palace Museum, Minneapolis, January 20th, 1896, under Kohl and Middleton's management.

Hoping that this little history of my life may interest all readers, I remain as in the older days,

Yours,

Mrs. M. BURK

BETTER KNOWN AS CALAMITY JANE

WRITING ABOUT BIOGRAPHY AND AUTOBIOGRAPHY

In this section, you will write a first draft for an essay comparing *The Boys' Life of Abraham Lincoln* with *The Life and Adventures of Calamity Jane, by Herself*.

Directions: Read the essay directions below, and then read and review the two texts above. Look for ways you could respond to one of the prompts and mark passages you could use as evidence in support of a thesis. Brainstorm a thesis and evidence for your essay. Use all prewriting techniques you find helpful. Next, narrow your thesis and organize your evidence. Now you're ready to write your rough draft. You'll receive 25 points for turning in a complete and developed rough draft. An incomplete or unfinished draft will receive 0 points. Later, you'll share your rough draft with a reviewer, and then rewrite it into final draft form.

Things to Keep in Mind

- Come up with a thesis and the evidence you need to support it, before you begin writing.

- This thesis must be specific and arguable: don't state the obvious. Your goal is to present an original argument about the similarities and differences in these two texts. It should be one or two sentences in length.

- Support your thesis with a close reading and analysis of the text. Remember to refer to and quote the text when presenting your evidence.

- Organize your evidence into paragraphs that each have one controlling idea. Sum up this idea with a topic sentence.

- Make sure your sentences are linked with clear transitions.

- Make sure your summary recounts your thesis and your supporting arguments.

Essay Questions

Choose one of the following prompts and write a two- to four-page essay addressing it. It should make an original argument that compares *The Boys' Life of Abraham Lincoln* with *The Life and Adventures of Calamity Jane, by Herself*.

1. How would you characterize the tone in each of these pieces? Analyze the tone to make an argument about each authors' purpose in writing.

2. How does each text use the literary conventions of characterization or plot development? What is the authors' purpose in using these conventions? How does their use of these conventions differ? How is it similar?

3. What are the cultural and social values described in each text? Do the authors advocate these values? To what degree? What does the description of these values illustrate about the authors' purpose in writing?

THE FINAL DRAFT

Now that you've written a first draft of this essay, it's time to polish it into a final draft.

Ask a friend or family member to read your essay and answer the reviewer questions below. Then, reread your paper and make notes about what needs to be revised. Finally, use your reviewer's notes and your own to rewrite your paper into its final form. It should be two to four pages. (Double-spaced, 12-point Times New Roman or similar font. This measurement is included to give you an idea of the appropriate length for the essay.)

Reviewer Questions

1. Summarize the thesis of this paper.

2. Is the thesis: (a) specific? (b) arguable? (c) a direct response to one of the essay prompts? Explain why or why not. How else could the thesis be improved?

3. Sum up the main idea of each paragraph. Note if the paragraph lacks a controlling idea or has more than one and should be broken into more than one paragraph.

4. Does all the evidence in each paragraph: (a) support, fail to support, or stray from the thesis? (b) include quotes and details from the text? (c) present a convincing, thorough argument? Explain why or why not.

5. Does the author use: (a) topic sentences to sum up the main idea of each paragraph? (b) transitions to link the paragraphs smoothly together?

6. Does the conclusion sum up the thesis and supporting arguments?

7. What are the paper's sentence-level errors and weaknesses?

8. Additional comments?

NEWS AS HISTORY

We don't normally think of the news as a form of history. Rather, we see the news as an objective description of current facts and events. History, in contrast, describes events of the past. It also interprets and analyzes them, rather than simply stating the "facts."

In this section, you'll choose a news story and examine how it's similar to and different from a historical narrative.

Directions: Write an answer to the study question below. Find a news article or television news broadcast that connects in some way to your study question response. It should have elements that are similar to or different from a historical narrative. Do a close reading of the news story. If it's a written text, note in the margins where the writing is similar to historical writing and where it's different. If it's a television news story, write detailed notes of the footage shown, if any, and the language used to describe the event. (*Hint:* It might be helpful to tape the television broadcast so you can take careful notes.) Finally, read and respond to the essay question.

Study Question

Respond to the following question *before* you look for your article or broadcast.

List what you see as the characteristics of historical narrative. For example, what tone do you associate with historical writing—objective or subjective? What kinds of details characterize a piece of writing as "historical"? Does it always have facts and dates? What kinds of diction do you think of as "historical"? Brainstorm as many characteristics as you can; the more you identify, the more developed your analysis will be.

Essay Questions

Now that you've closely read (or watched) and taken notes on a news article (or broadcast), analyze more closely the relationship of the news account to a historical text.

1. Write a paragraph discussing the similarities of the news story to a historical narrative. Support your comparison with examples. Don't merely list similarities; rather, describe the significance of the connections you see.

2. Write another paragraph discussing the *differences* between the news story and a historical narrative. Again, support your comparison with examples. Don't merely list differences; rather, describe the significance of the connections you see.

3. Finally, write a thesis statement that: (a) describes the relationship between news and history, and (b) shows how your analysis of a news story illustrates that relationship.

WRITING HISTORY NARRATIVES

We're all connected with the history of our nation, city, and community in some way. Sometimes we witness or participate in events that are significant to our national or local history—for example, a protest march, a local tragedy, or a strike. Sometimes we belong to a social organization acting to change society. In any case, all of us experience the daily effects of social and cultural change.

Historical narratives can take different forms. They can come from a very personal, or *subjective*, standpoint, or they can also aim to present a factual, or *objective*, version of the event.

READING HISTORICAL ESSAYS

As you may know, historical writing doesn't just state the facts about an event. Even a piece that *seems* "objective" makes an interpretation or argument about the event or describes one side of the story. Like all authors, history writers have an agenda, and they use elements such as evidence, organization, and tone to further that agenda.

For example, when using evidence, writers decide which facts to include and which to ignore. Also, some writers present more facts and events than interpretation and analysis. Others rely mostly on personal reaction and opinion. It all depends on their purpose, and the audience for whom they're writing. When deciding how to organize an essay, writers might decide to present events in chronological order to emphasize cause and effect. They also might organize evidence by the larger themes that they want to make an argument about. Finally, writers use tone to further their purpose: do they want the reader to sympathize with them personally? Are they presenting themselves as an academic or expert?

CHAPTER REVIEW

To review your studies of autobiographies, biographies, and historical writing, answer the following study questions.

Study Questions: History and Narrative

1. What role does language play in writing biography and autobiography? Support your answer by giving one specific example from a text you read in the lesson on autobiographies and biographies.

2. What role does an author's perspective play in determining the structure, style, and organization of a written biography or autobiography? Support your answer by giving one specific example of structure, one example of style, and one example of organization from a text you read in this lesson.

3. How can a reader determine which elements of a biography or autobiography represent historical fact, and which represent the author's perspective? Support your answer by giving one specific example from a text you read in this chapter.

4. What role does language play in recording historical events? Support your answer by giving one specific example from a text you read in the lesson on history writing.

5. What role does an author's perspective play in determining the structure, style, and organization of a piece of history writing? Support your answer by giving one specific example of structure, one example of style, and one example of organization from a text you read in this chapter.

6. How can a reader determine which elements of historical writing represent historical fact, and which represent the author's perspective? Support your answer by giving one specific example from a text you read in this chapter.

7. Is written history primarily objective or subjective? Support your answer by giving three examples from texts you read in this chapter.

The Reading Public: Essays, Politics, and Government

CHAPTER 15

KEY TERMS

- propaganda
- rhetorical device
- tone

ESSAYS AND THE WRITERS WHO SHAPED THEM

In informal, nonacademic essays, authors use other strategies in addition to logic, evidence, and organization to express arguments and ideas, and to connect with or convince the reader. Academic essays present objective arguments that usually leave out much of the writer's personality. You can't use "I" in an academic paper, for example.

In informal, nonacademic essays, however, authors create a *persona* to express their ideas and to establish a relationship with their audience. Don't confuse persona with personality—persona is a consciously crafted voice calculated to have a specific effect on, or produce a specific relationship with, a reader. The intended audience helps determine the persona an author chooses. Consider the essayists in the upcoming activity: the personas created by Francis Bacon and Michel de Montaigne, who wrote in the late 16th and early 17th centuries for a small audience of educated men, differ significantly from the persona created by Mark Twain, who wrote in the 19th century for a much larger and more diverse audience.

In this activity, you'll look at three essays and consider how the authors express ideas and arguments to a specific audience. You'll examine how they establish a relationship with readers by analyzing their use of tone, language, and organization, and you'll think about their argument, or lack of argument.

Directions: Read Francis Bacon's "Of Studies" and "Of Discourse," Michel de Montaigne's "Of Drunkenness," and Mark Twain's "Concerning Tobacco." Take notes as you read, looking for answers to the study questions. Mark passages, words, or phrases that reveal the author's argument. Note the author's use of tone, structure, and other devices that support that argument, and look for ways the author tries to affect his audience. Next, write responses to the study questions for each text. Each response should be a few sentences to a paragraph in length. Then, read and write a response to the essay questions. Each response should be one to two paragraphs in length. Finally, compare your responses to the essay questions with the sample answers provided. Remember that the sample answers provide one, but not the only, correct response.

Study Questions

Write responses to the following questions for each of the essays.

1. Is the author arguing for or against something in this text? What is that argument, if there is one?

2. How would I describe the language of the text? How does the author use tone? What does the language tell me about the culture in which the author lived?

3. Who is the audience being addressed? How do I know?

4. What effect is the author trying to produce on his audience? How does he accomplish this?

5. How does the organization of the essay reflect the author's purpose?

Essay Questions

You should now have a grasp of the arguments in these essays and of how their authors try to convey those arguments and affect their audience. Now you're ready to compare and contrast.

1. Discuss the similarities and differences of the intended audiences of these essays.

2. Compare and contrast how each author uses language and tone to affect his audience.

3. What are the differences in how each essay is organized? Why do they differ?

KAPLAN

Of Studies
Francis Bacon

Studies serve for delight, for ornament, and for ability. Their chief use for delight, is in privateness and retiring; for ornament, is in discourse; and for ability, is in the judgment, and disposition of business. For expert men can execute, and perhaps judge of particulars, one by one; but the general counsels, and the plots and marshalling of affairs, come best, from those that are learned. To spend too much time in studies is sloth; to use them too much for ornament, is affectation; to make judgment wholly by their rules, is the humor of a scholar. They perfect nature, and are perfected by experience: for natural abilities are like natural plants, that need proyning, by study; and studies themselves, do give forth directions too much at large, except they be bounded in by experience. Crafty men contemn studies, simple men admire them, and wise men use them; for they teach not their own use; but that is a wisdom without them, and above them, won by observation. Read not to contradict and confute; nor to believe and take for granted; nor to find talk and discourse; but to weigh and consider. Some books are to be tasted, others to be swallowed, and some few to be chewed and digested; that is, some books are to be read only in parts; others to be read, but not curiously; and some few to be read wholly, and with diligence and attention. Some books also may be read by deputy, and extracts made of them by others; but that would be only in the less important arguments, and the meaner sort of books, else distilled books are like common distilled waters, flashy things. Reading maketh a full man; conference a ready man; and writing an exact man. And therefore, if a man write little, he had need have a great memory; if he confer little, he had need have a present wit: and if he read little, he had need have much cunning, to seem to know, that he doth not. Histories make men wise; poets witty; the mathematics subtile; natural philosophy deep; moral grave; logic and rhetoric able to contend. *Abeunt studia in mores* [Studies pass into and influence matters.] Nay, there is no stond or impediment in the wit, but may be wrought out by fit studies; like as diseases of the body, may have appropriate exercises. Bowling is good for the stone and reins; shooting for the lungs and breast; gentle walking for the stomach; riding for the head; and the like. So if a man's wit be wandering, let him study the mathematics; for in demonstrations, if his wit be called away never so little, he must begin again. If his wit be not apt to distinguish or find differences, let him study the Schoolmen; for they are *cymini sectores* [splitters of hairs]. If he be not apt to beat over matters, and to call up one thing to prove and illustrate another, let him study the lawyers' cases. So every defect of the mind, may have a special receipt.

Of Discourse

Francis Bacon

Some, in their discourse, desire rather commendation of wit, in being able to hold all arguments, than of judgment, in discerning what is true; as if it were a praise, to know what might be said, and not, what should be thought. Some have certain common places, and themes, wherein they are good and want variety; which kind of poverty is for the most part tedious, and when it is once perceived, ridiculous. The honorablest part of talk, is to give the occasion; and again to moderate, and pass to somewhat else; for then a man leads the dance. It is good, in discourse and speech of conversation, to vary and intermingle speech of the present occasion, with arguments, tales with reasons, asking of questions, with telling of opinions, and jest with earnest: for it is a dull thing to tire, and, as we say now, to jade, any thing too far. As for jest, there be certain things, which ought to be privileged from it; namely, religion, matters of state, great persons, any man's present business of importance, and any case that deserveth pity. Yet there be some, that think their wits have been asleep, except they dart out somewhat that is piquant, and to the quick. That is a vein which would be bridled:

Parce, puer, stimulis, et fortius utere loris.

And generally, men ought to find the difference, between saltness and bitterness. Certainly, he that hath a satirical vein, as he maketh others afraid of his wit, so he had need be afraid of others' memory. He that questioneth much, shall learn much, and content much; but especially, if he apply his questions to the skill of the persons whom he asketh; for he shall give them occasion, to please themselves in speaking, and himself shall continually gather knowledge. But let his questions not be troublesome; for that is fit for a poser. And let him be sure to leave other men, their turns to speak. Nay, if there be any, that would reign and take up all the time, let him find means to take them off, and to bring others on; as musicians use to do, with those that dance too long galliards. If you dissemble, sometimes, your knowledge of that you are thought to know, you shall be thought, another time, to know that you know not. Speech of a man's self ought to be seldom, and well chosen. I knew one, was wont to say in scorn, *He must needs be a wise man, he speaks so much of himself*: and there is but one case, wherein a man may commend himself with good grace; and that is in commending virtue in another; especially if it be such a virtue, whereunto himself pretendeth. Speech of touch towards others, should be sparingly used; for discourse ought to be as a field, without coming home to any man. I knew two noblemen, of the west part of England, whereof the one was given to scoff, but kept ever royal cheer in his house; the other would ask, of those that had been at the other's table, *Tell truly, was there never a flout or dry blow given?* To which the guest would answer, *Such and such a thing passed.* The lord would say, *I thought he would mar a good dinner.* Discretion of speech, is more than eloquence; and to speak agreeably to him, with whom we deal, is more than to speak in good words, or in good order. A good continued speech, without a good speech of interlocution, shows slowness: and a good reply or second speech, without a good settled speech, showeth shallowness and weakness. As we see in beasts, that those that are weakest in the course, are yet nimblest in the turn; as it is betwixt the greyhound and the hare. To use too many circumstances, ere one come to the matter, is wearisome; to use none at all, is blunt.

Of Drunkenness
Michel de Montaigne
(translated by Charles Cotton)

The world is nothing but variety and dissemblance: vices are all alike, as they are vices, and peradventure the Stoic understand them so; but although they are equally vices, yet they are not at all equal vices; and he who has transgressed the ordinary bounds of a hundred paces,

Quos ultra, citraque nequit consistere rectum,

should not be in a worse condition than he that has advanced but ten, is not to be believed; or that sacrilege is not worse than stealing a cabbage:

Nec vincet ratio hoc, tantumdem ut peccet, idemque,
Qui teneros caules alieni fregerit horti,
Et qui nocturnus divum sacua legerit.

There is in this as great diversity is in anything whatever. The confounding of the order and measure of sins is dangerous: murderers, traitors, and tyrants get too much by it, and it is not reasonable they should flatter their consciences, because another man is idle, lascivious, or not assiduous at his devotion. Every one lays weight upon the sin of his companions, but lightens his own. Our very instructors themselves rank them sometimes, in my opinion, very ill. As Socrates said that the principal office of wisdom was to distinguish good from evil, we, the best of whom are vicious, ought also to say the same of the science of distinguishing between vice and vice, without which, and that very exactly performed, the virtuous and the wicked will remain confounded and unrecognized.

Now, among the rest, drunkenness seems to me to be a gross and brutish vice. The soul has greater part in the rest, and there are some vices that have something, if a man may so say, of generous in them; there are vices wherein there is a mixture of knowledge, diligence, valor, prudence, dexterity and address; this one is totally corporeal and earthly. And the rudest nation this day in Europe is that alone where it is in fashion. Other vices discompose the understanding: this totally overthrows it and renders the body stupid.

Cum vini vis penetravit . . .
Consequitur gravitas membrorum, praepediuntur
Crura vacillanti, tardescit lingua, madet mens,
Nant oculi; clamor, singultus, jurgia, gliscunt.

The worst state of man is that wherein he loses the knowledge and government of himself. And 'tis said, among other things upon this subject, that, as the must fermenting in a vessel, works up to the top whatever it has in the bottom, so wine, in those who have drunk beyond measure, vents the most inward secrets.

Tu sapientium
Curas et arcanum jocoso
Consilium retegis Lyaeo.

Josephus tells us that by giving an ambassador the enemy had sent to him his full dose of liquor, he wormed out his secrets. And yet, Augustus, committing the most inward secrets of his affairs to Lucius Piso, who conquered Thrace, never found him faulty in the least, no more than Tiberius did Cossus, with whom he intrusted his whole counsels, though we know they were both so given to drink that they have often been fain to carry both the one and the other drunk out of the senate.

Hesterno inflatum venas, de more, Lyaeo.

And the design of killing Caesar was as safely communicated to Cimber, though he would often be drunk, as to Cassius, who drank nothing but water. We see our Germans, when drunk as the devil, know their post, remember the word, and keep to their ranks:

Nec facilis victoria de madidis, et
Blaesis, atque mero titubantibus.

I could not have believed there had been so profound, senseless, and dead a degree of drunkenness had I not read in history that Attalus, having, to put a notable affront upon him, invited to supper the same Pausanias, who upon the very same occasion afterward killed Philip of Macedon, a king who by his excellent qualities gave sufficient testimony of his education in the house and company of Epaminondas, made him drink to such a pitch that he could after abandon his beauty, as of a hedge strumpet, to the muleteers and servants of the basest office in the house. And I have been further told by a lady whom I highly honor and esteem, that near Bordeaux and about Castres where she lives, a country woman, a widow of chaste repute, perceiving in herself the first symptoms of breeding, innocently told her neighbors that if she had a husband she should think herself with child; but the causes of suspicion every day more and more increasing, and at last growing up to a manifest proof, the poor woman was reduced to the necessity of causing it to be proclaimed in her parish church, that whoever had done that deed and would frankly confess it, she did not only promise to forgive, but moreover to marry him, if he liked the motion; whereupon a young fellow that served her in the quality of a laborer, encouraged by this proclamation, declared that he had one holiday found her, having taken too much of the bottle, so fast asleep by the chimney and in so indecent a posture, that he could conveniently do his business without waking her; and they yet live together man and wife.

It is true that antiquity has not much decried this vice; the writings even of several philosophers speak very tenderly of it, and even among the Stoics there are some who advise folks to give themselves sometimes the liberty to drink, nay, to drunkenness, to refresh the soul.

Hoc quoque virtutum quondam certamine, magnum
Socratem palmam promeruisse ferunt.

That censor and reprover of others, Cato, was reproached that he was a hard drinker.

Narratur et prisci Catonis
Saepe mero caluisse virtus.

THE READING PUBLIC: ESSAYS, POLITICS, AND GOVERNMENT

Cyrus, that so renowned king, among the other qualities by which he claimed to be preferred before his brother Artaxerxes, urged this excellence, that he could drink a great deal more than he. And in the best governed nations this trial of skill in drinking is very much in use. I have heard Silvius, an excellent physician of Paris, say that lest the digestive faculties of the stomach should grow idle, it were not amiss once a month to rouse them by this excess, and to spur them lest they should grow dull and rusty; and one author tells us that the Persians used to consult about their most important affairs after being well warmed with wine.

My taste and constitution are greater enemies to this vice than I am; for besides that I easily submit my belief to the authority of ancient opinions, I look upon it indeed as an unmanly and stupid vice, but less malicious and hurtful than the others, which, almost all, more directly jostle public society. And if we cannot please ourselves but it must cost us something, as they hold, I find this vice costs a man's conscience less than the others, besides that it is of no difficult preparation, nor hard to be found, a consideration not altogether to be despised. A man well advanced both in dignity and age, among three principal commodities that he said remained to him of life, reckoned to me this for one, and where would a man more justly find it than among the natural conveniences? But he did not take it right, for delicacy and the curious choice of wines is therein to be avoided. If you found your pleasure upon drinking of the best, you condemn yourself to the penance of drinking of the worst. Your taste must be more indifferent and free; so delicate a palate is not required to make a good toper. The Germans drink almost indifferently of all wines with delight: their business is to pour down and not to taste; and it's so much the better for them; their pleasure is so much the more plentiful and nearer at hand. Secondly, to drink, after the French fashion, but at two meals, and then very moderately, is to be too sparing of the favors of the god. There is more time and constancy required than so. The ancients spent whole nights in this exercise, and ofttimes added the day following to eke it out, and therefore we are to take greater liberty and stick closer to our work. I have seen a great lord of my time, a man of high enterprise and famous success, that without setting himself to it, and after his ordinary rate of drinking at meals, drank not much less than five quarts of wine, and at his going away appeared but too wise and discreet, to the detriment of our affairs. The pleasure we hold in esteem for the course of our lives ought to have a greater share of our time dedicated to it; we should, like shop-boys and laborers, refuse no occasion nor omit any opportunity of drinking, and always have it in our minds. Methinks we every day abridge and curtail the use of wine, and that the after breakfasts, dinner snatches, and collations I used to see in my father's house, when I was a boy, were more usual and frequent then than now.

Is it that we pretend to a reformation? Truly, no; but it may be we are more addicted to Venus than our fathers were. They are two exercises that thwart and hinder one another in their vigor. Lechery weakens our stomach on the one side, and on the other, sobriety renders us more spruce and amorous for the exercise of love.

'Tis not to be imagined what strange stories I have heard my father tell of the chastity of that age wherein he lived. It was for him to say it, being both by art and nature cut out and finished for the service of ladies. He spoke well and little; ever mixing his language with some illustration out of authors most in use, especially in Spanish. Marcus Aurelius was very frequent in his mouth. His behavior was grave, humble, and very modest; he was very solicitous of neatness and propriety both in his person and clothes, whether on horseback or afoot; he was monstrously punctual of his word; and of a conscience and religion generally tending rather toward superstition than otherwise. For a man of little stature, very strong, well proportioned, and well knit; of a pleasing countenance, inclining to brown, and very adroit in all noble exercises. I have yet in the house to be seen canes poured full of lead, with which they say he exercised his arms for throwing the bar or the stone, or in fencing; and shoes with leaden soles to make him lighter for running or leaping. Of his vaulting he has left little miracles behind him; I have seen him when past three score laugh at our exercises, and throw himself in his furred gown into the saddle, make the tour of a table upon his thumbs, and scarce ever mount the stairs into his chamber without taking three or four steps at a time. But as to what I was speaking of before, he said there was scarce one woman of quality of ill fame in a whole province: he would tell of strange privacies, and some of them his own, with virtuous women, free from any manner of suspicion of ill; and for his own part solemnly swore he was a virgin at his marriage; and yet it was after a long practice of arms beyond the mountains, of which wars he left us a journal under his own hand, wherein he has given a precise account from point to point of all passages, both relating to the public and to himself. And he was, moreover, married at a well advanced maturity, in the year 1528, the three-and-thirtieth year of his age, upon his way home from Italy. But let us return to our bottle.

The incommodities of old age, that stand in need of some refreshment and support, might with reason beget in me a desire of this faculty, it being as it were the last pleasure the course of years deprives us of. The natural heat, say the good-fellows, first seats itself in the feet: that concerns infancy; thence it mounts into the middle region, where it makes a long abode and produces, in my opinion, the sole true pleasures of human life; all other pleasures in comparison sleep; toward the end, like a vapor that still mounts upward, it arrives at the throat, where it makes its final residence, and concludes the progress. I do not, nevertheless, understand how a man can extend the pleasure of drinking beyond thirst, and forge in his imagination an appetite artificial and against nature; my stomach would not proceed so far; it has enough to do to deal with what it takes in for its necessity. My constitution is not to care or drink but as following eating and washing down my meat, and for that reason my last draught is always the greatest. And seeing that in old age we have our palate furred with phlegms or depraved by some other ill constitution, the wine tastes better to us as the pores are cleaner washed and laid more open. At least, I seldom taste the first glass well. Anacharsis wondered that the Greeks drank in greater glasses toward the end of a meal than at the beginning; which was, I suppose, for the same reason the Germans do the same, who then begin the battle of drink.

Plato forbids children wine till eighteen years of age, and to get drunk till forty; but, after forty, gives them leave to please themselves, and to mix a little liberally in their feasts the influence of Dionysos, that good deity who restores to younger men their gayety, and to old men their youth; who mollifies the passions of the soul, as iron is softened by fire; and in his laws allows such merry meetings, provided they have a discreet chief to govern and keep them in order, as good and of great utility; drunkenness being, he says, a true and certain trial of every one's nature, and, withal, fit to inspire old men with mettle to divert themselves in dancing and music; things of great use, and that they dare not attempt when sober. He, moreover, says that wine is able to supply the soul with temperance and the body with health. Nevertheless, these restrictions, in part borrowed from the Carthaginians, please him: that men forbear excesses in the expeditions of war; that every judge and magistrate abstain from it when about the administrations of his place or the consultations of the public affairs; that the day is not to be employed with it, that being a time due to other occupations, nor the night on which a man intends to get children.

THE READING PUBLIC: ESSAYS, POLITICS, AND GOVERNMENT

'Tis said that the philosopher Stilpo, when oppressed with age, purposely hastened his end by drinking pure wine. The same thing, but not designed by him, dispatched also the philosopher Arcesilaus.

But, 'tis an old and pleasant question, whether the soul of a wise man can be overcome by the strength of wine?

Si munitae adhibet vim sapientiae.

To what vanity does the good opinion we have of ourselves push us? The most regular and most perfect soul in the world has but too much to do to keep itself upright, and from being overthrown by its own weakness. There is not one of a thousand that is right and settled so much as one minute in a whole life, and that may not very well doubt, whether according to her natural condition she ever can be; but to join constancy to it is her utmost perfection; I mean when nothing should jostle and discompose her, which a thousand accidents may do. 'Tis to much purpose that the great poet Lucretius keeps such a clatter with his philosophy, when, behold! he goes mad with a love philter. Is it to be imagined that an apoplexy will not stun Socrates as well as a porter? Some men have forgotten their own names by the violence of a disease; and a slight wound has turned the judgment of others topsey-turvey. Let him be as wise as he will, after all he is but a man; and than that what is there more frail, more miserable, or more nothing? Wisdom does not force our natural dispositions.

Sudores itaque, et pallorem exsistere toto
Corpore, et infringi linguam, vocemque aboriri,
Caligare oculos, sonere aures, succidere artus,
Denique concidere, ex animi terrore, videmus:

he must shut his eyes against the blow that threatens him; he must tremble upon the margin of a precipice, like a child; nature having reserved these light marks of her authority, not to be forced by our reason and the stoic virtue, to teach man his mortality and our weakness; he turns pale with fear, red with shame, and groans with the cholic, if not with desperate outcry, at least with hoarse and broken voice:

Humani a se nihil alienum putet.

The poets, that feign all things at pleasure, dare not acquit their greatest heroes of tears:

Sic fatur lacrymans, classique immittit habenas.

'Tis sufficient for a man to curb and moderate his inclinations, for totally to suppress them is not in him to do. Even our great Plutarch, that excellent and perfect judge of human actions, when he sees Brutus and Torquatus kill their children, begins to doubt whether virtue could proceed so far, and to question whether these persons had not rather been stimulated by some other passion. All actions exceeding the ordinary bounds are liable to sinister interpretation, forasmuch as our liking no more holds with what is above than with what is below it.

Let us leave that other sect, that sets up an express profession of scornful superiority; but when even in that sect, reputed the most quiet and gentle, we hear these rhodomontades of Metrodorus: *Occupavi te, Fortuna, atque cepi: omnesque aditus tuos interclusi ut ad me aspirare non possess;* when Anaxarchus, by command of Nicocreon the tyrant of Cyprus, was put into a stone mortar, and laid upon with mauls of iron, ceases not to say, "Strike, batter, break, 'tis not Anaxarchus, 'tis but his sheath that you pound and bray so;" when we hear our martyrs cry out to the tyrant in the middle of the flame: "This side is roasted enough, fall to and eat, it is enough done; fall to work with the other;" when we hear the child in Josephus torn piecemeal with pincers, defying Antiochus, and crying out with a constant and assured voice: "Tyrant, thou losest thy labor, I am still at ease; where is the pain, where are the torments with which thou didst so threaten me? Is this all thou canst do? My constancy torments thee more than thy cruelty does me. Oh, pitiful coward, thou faintest, and I grow stronger; make me complain, make me bend, make me yield if thou canst; encourage thy guards, cheer up thy executioners; see, see they faint, and can do no more; arm them, flesh them anew, spur them up;" truly, a man must confess that there is some frenzy, some fury, how holy soever, that at that time possesses those souls. When we come to these Stoical sallies: "I had rather be mad than voluptuous," a saying of Antisthenes; *Maneien mallon e estheien.* When Sextius tells us, "he had rather be fettered with affliction than pleasure;" when Epicurus takes upon him to play with his gout, and, refusing health and ease, defies all torments, and despising the lesser pains, as disdaining to contend with them, he covets and calls out for others sharper, more violent, and more worthy of him;

> *Spumantemque dari, pecora inter inertia, votis*
> *Optat aprum, aut fulvum descendere monte leonem.*

who but must conclude that these are wild sallies pushed on by a courage that has broken loose from its place? Our soul cannot from her own seat reach so high; 'tis necessary she must leave it, raise herself up, and, taking the bridle in her teeth, transport her man so far that he shall afterward himself be astonished at what he has done; as, in war the heat of battle impels generous soldiers to perform things of so infinite danger, as afterward, recollecting them they themselves are the first to wonder at; as it also fares with the poets, who are often rapt with admiration of their own writings, and know not where again to find the track through which they performed so fine a career; which also is in them called fury and rapture. And as Plato says, 'tis no purpose for a sober-minded man to knock at the door of poesy: so Aristotle says that no excellent soul is exempt from a mixture of madness; and he has reason to call all transports, how commendable soever, that surpass our own judgment and understanding, madness; forasmuch as wisdom is a regular government of the soul, which is carried on with measure and proportion, and for which she is to herself responsible. Plato argues thus, that the faculty of the prophesying is so far above us, that we must be out of ourselves when we meddle with it, and our prudence must either be obstructed by sleep or sickness, or lifted from her place by some celestial rapture.

Concerning Tobacco
Mark Twain

As concerns tobacco, there are many superstitions. And the chiefest is this—that there is a STANDARD governing the matter, whereas there is nothing of the kind. Each man's own preference is the only standard for him, the only one which he can accept, the only one which can command him. A congress of all the tobacco-lovers in the world could not elect a standard which would be binding upon you or me, or would even much influence us.

The next superstition is that a man has a standard of his own. He hasn't. He thinks he has, but he hasn't. He thinks he can tell what he regards as a good cigar from what he regards as a bad one—but he can't. He goes by the brand, yet imagines he goes by the flavor. One may palm off the worst counterfeit upon him; if it bears his brand he will smoke it contentedly and never suspect.

Children of twenty-five, who have seven years experience, try to tell me what is a good cigar and what isn't. Me, who never learned to smoke, but always smoked; me, who came into the world asking for a light.

No one can tell me what is a good cigar—for me. I am the only judge. People who claim to know say that I smoke the worst cigars in the world. They bring their own cigars when they come to my house. They betray an unmanly terror when I offer them a cigar; they tell lies and hurry away to meet engagements which they have not made when they are threatened with the hospitalities of my box. Now then, observe what superstition, assisted by a man's reputation, can do. I was to have twelve personal friends to supper one night. One of them was as notorious for costly and elegant cigars as I was for cheap and devilish ones. I called at his house and when no one was looking borrowed a double handful of his very choicest; cigars which cost him forty cents apiece and bore red-and-gold labels in sign of their nobility. I removed the labels and put the cigars into a box with my favorite brand on it—a brand which those people all knew, and which cowed them as men are cowed by an epidemic. They took these cigars when offered at the end of the supper, and lit them and sternly struggled with them—in dreary silence, for hilarity died when the fell brand came into view and started around—but their fortitude held for a short time only; then they made excuses and filed out, treading on one another's heels with indecent eagerness; and in the morning when I went out to observe results the cigars lay all between the front door and the gate. All except one—that one lay in the plate of the man from whom I had cabbaged the lot. One or two whiffs was all he could stand. He told me afterward that some day I would get shot for giving people that kind of cigars to smoke.

Am I certain of my own standard? Perfectly; yes, absolutely—unless somebody fools me by putting my brand on some other kind of cigar; for no doubt I am like the rest, and know my cigar by the brand instead of by the flavor. However, my standard is a pretty wide one and covers a good deal of territory. To me, almost any cigar is good that nobody else will smoke, and to me almost all cigars are bad that other people consider good. Nearly any cigar will do me, except a Havana. People think they hurt my feelings when then come to my house with their life preservers on—I mean, with their own cigars in their pockets. It is an error; I take care of myself in a similar way. When I go into danger—that is, into rich people's houses, where, in the nature of things, they will have high-tariff cigars, red-and-gilt girded and nested in a rosewood box along with a damp sponge, cigars which develop a dismal black ash and burn down the side and smell, and will grow hot to the fingers, and will go on growing hotter and hotter, and go on smelling more and more infamously and unendurably the deeper the fire tunnels down inside below the thimbleful of honest tobacco that is in the front end, the furnisher of it praising it all the time and telling you how much the deadly thing cost—yes, when I go into that sort of peril I carry my own defense along; I carry my own brand—twenty-seven cents a barrel—and I live to see my family again. I may seem to light his red-gartered cigar, but that is only for courtesy's sake; I smuggle it into my pocket for the poor, of whom I know many, and light one of my own; and while he praises it I join in, but when he says it cost forty-five cents I say nothing, for I know better.

However, to say true, my tastes are so catholic that I have never seen any cigars that I really could not smoke, except those that cost a dollar apiece. I have examined those and know that they are made of dog-hair, and not good dog-hair at that.

I have a thoroughly satisfactory time in Europe, for all over the Continent one finds cigars which not even the most hardened newsboys in New York would smoke. I brought cigars with me, the last time; I will not do that any more. In Italy, as in France, the Government is the only cigar-peddler. Italy has three or four domestic brands: the Minghetti, the Trabuco, the Virginia, and a very coarse one which is a modification of the Virginia. The Minghettis are large and comely, and cost three dollars and sixty cents a hundred; I can smoke a hundred in seven days and enjoy every one of them. The Trabucos suit me, too; I don't remember the price. But one has to learn to like the Virginia, nobody is born friendly to it. It looks like a rat-tail file, but smokes better, some think. It has a straw through it; you pull this out, and it leaves a flue, otherwise there would be no draught, not even as much as there is to a nail. Some prefer a nail at first. However, I like all the French, Swiss, German, and Italian domestic cigars, and have never cared to inquire what they are made of; and nobody would know, anyhow, perhaps. There is even a brand of European smoking-tobacco that I like. It is a brand used by the Italian peasants. It is loose and dry and black, and looks like tea-grounds. When the fire is applied it expands, and climbs up and towers above the pipe, and presently tumbles off inside of one's vest. The tobacco itself is cheap, but it raises the insurance. It is as I remarked in the beginning—the taste for tobacco is a matter of superstition. There are no standards—no real standards. Each man's preference is the only standard for him, the only one which he can accept, the only one which can command him.

Sample Answers to Essay Questions

1. Discuss the similarities and differences of the intended audiences of these essays.

2. Compare and contrast how each author uses language and tone to affect his audience.

Montaigne and Bacon wrote during the same time period: the late 16th and early 17th centuries. The printing press had not yet been invented, and education was restricted to the upper classes. Therefore, the audience for their essays was mostly upper-class, educated, and male. One way Montaigne and Bacon use language to reach this audience is by using Latin and Greek quotes. First, the quotes establish a relationship with the audience. Classical authors were central to education at that time. Using classical quotes tells the reader that he and the author have similar educational and socio-economic backgrounds. They establish familiarity with the audience, making the reader feel at home and included. Second, Montaigne and Bacon use Latin and Greek quotes to establish their authority, or ethos. The audience knows that anyone familiar with Latin and Greek must be educated, and therefore trustworthy.

THE READING PUBLIC: ESSAYS, POLITICS, AND GOVERNMENT

In contrast, Twain uses very few terms that include some readers and exclude others. He wrote in 19th century America. By this time the publishing industry and widespread education made his writings accessible to people of varied socioeconomic backgrounds. He uses a "folksy" manner and ordinary speech to establish a bond with his readers.

3. *What are the differences in how each essay is organized? Why do they differ?*

Montaigne structures his piece very loosely, moving from one philosophical statement on drunkenness to another. He also discusses the characteristics of drunkenness in various cultures, and mixes in his own observations. This suggests that he intended to present a meditation, not an argument. Bacon, on the other hand, focuses on a few key points in each of his pieces. These points guide the organization of his essay. This suggests that Bacon intends to make a specific argument, rather than presenting a meditation. Bacon wants to convince his audience to adopt his ideas. In this way, he and Montaigne differ.

Twain's piece might be described as a mixture of these two styles. Like Bacon, he presents an argument. Specifically, he argues that everyone is entitled to enjoy tobacco according to his or her own tastes. Like Montaigne, he allows himself to wander into reflections. However, these meditations always support his general argument, rather than moving away from it. Therefore, he is more like Bacon than Montaigne.

Contrasting Essays Across Time

As we've already discussed, the essay has changed over time. Writers are influenced by their culture, and cultures have changed vastly from the 16th century to today. The audience the writer is trying to reach has also changed. For example, the invention of the printing press widened the audience for written material, and many more people can read today because education is no longer restricted to a privileged few.

Keep this in mind when analyzing the argument, organization, style and audience of writings new and old. However, you'll need to examine essays closely as individual works, not just as products of culture. Essays written during the same time period will have much in common because of the historical and cultural background they share. However, they'll also have many differences.

For example, Montaigne and Bacon were contemporaries, but Montaigne's style is very different from Bacon's. Bacon tries to convince his reader of an argument; Montaigne allows himself to wander and meditate. Montaigne is also very informal: he discusses his personal life, and even ventures into "improper" subjects. Bacon, in contrast, is more formal. Similarly, although many modern essay writers are informal, some, like H.L. Mencken, adopt a more academic tone.

POLITICAL WRITING AND POLITICAL MOVEMENTS

Most political writing is persuasive writing. Because political movements generally need people to join them, political writers use various methods to convince the audience to support their movement. These rhetorical methods include the elements of **logos** (factual information and logical argument), **pathos** (the anticipated emotional reaction from the audience), and **ethos** (the implied personality of the author).

In this section, you'll look at Plato's "The Apology," a political speech given by Socrates after he has been sentenced to die by the Athenian court, to discern the ideas he's trying to convey to his audience and how he tries to persuade his audience of these ideas. This will require analyzing his rhetorical methods of persuasion.

Directions: Read "The Apology" by Plato. Take notes as you read, looking for answers to the study questions. Mark passages, words, or phrases that contribute to a persuasive argument. Then, write responses to the study questions below. Each response should be a few sentences long. Finally, read and write a response to the thesis question.

Study Questions

1. To whom is Socrates speaking? How do you know? How does that influence his writing?

2. What does he want to convince his audience of?

3. Which authorities does Socrates reference? Why these particular authorities?

4. How does he address and anticipate counter-arguments (potential or actual disagreements)?

5. Give one specific example apiece of his use of logos, pathos, and ethos.

6. What reason does he give for his not securing his acquittal?

7. What two examples does he give of ways in which a man could save his life?

8. Where does he make threats? Why? How does he attempt to avoid the problems that usually go along with making threats?

9. What does he mean by discussing the "internal oracle"? Does his reference to this internal oracle represent logos, pathos, or ethos? Why?

10. How does Socrates argue that death is a good? What is the purpose of this argument?

Thesis Question

You should now have a grasp of Socrates's argument and how he tries to reach his audience. Now it's time to create an argument of your own about this document.

Come up with a thesis of one to three sentences that responds to the following prompt:

Prompt: In "The Apology," Socrates addresses a group of judges, some of whom condemned his to death while others voted to acquit him. What is his argument? What strategies does he use to convince his audience of that argument?

When coming up with your thesis, keep the following things in mind:

- Your thesis should *make an argument* about what Socrates wants to convince his audience of and how he attempts to do so. First, summarize what you see as Socrates's main argument. Second, list his persuasive methods.

- Make a list of evidence you could use to support your thesis, specifically textual references.

- Your thesis should be *focused*. That is, it should be narrow enough to write a two- to four-page, double-spaced essay typed in Times New Roman 12-point font.

The Apology

Plato

(translated by Benjamin Jowett)

Not much time will be gained, O Athenians, in return for the evil name which you will get from the detractors of the city, who will say that you killed Socrates, a wise man; for they will call me wise even although I am not wise when they want to reproach you. If you had waited a little while, your desire would have been fulfilled in the course of nature. For I am far advanced in years, as you may perceive, and not far from death. I am speaking now only to those of you who have condemned me to death. And I have another thing to say to them: You think that I was convicted through deficiency of words—I mean, that if I had thought fit to leave nothing undone, nothing unsaid, I might have gained an acquittal. Not so; the deficiency which led to my conviction was not of words—certainly not. But I had not the boldness or impudence or inclination to address you as you would have liked me to address you, weeping and wailing and lamenting, and saying and doing many things which you have been accustomed to hear from others, and which, as I say, are unworthy of me. But I thought that I ought not to do anything common or mean in the hour of danger: nor do I now repent of the manner of my defense, and I would rather die having spoken after my manner, than speak in your manner and live. For neither in war nor yet at law ought any man to use every way of escaping death. For often in battle there is no doubt that if a man will throw away his arms, and fall on his knees before his pursuers, he may escape death; and in other dangers there are other ways of escaping death, if a man is willing to say and do anything. The difficulty, my friends, is not in avoiding death, but in avoiding unrighteousness; for that runs faster than death. I am old and move slowly, and the slower runner has overtaken me, and my accusers are keen and quick, and the faster runner, who is unrighteousness, has overtaken them. And now I depart hence condemned by you to suffer the penalty of death, and they, too, go their ways condemned by the truth to suffer the penalty of villainy and wrong; and I must abide by my award—let them abide by theirs. I suppose that these things may be regarded as fated,—and I think that they are well.

And now, O men who have condemned me, I would fain prophesy to you; for I am about to die, and that is the hour in which men are gifted with prophetic power. And I prophesy to you who are my murderers, that immediately after my death punishment far heavier than you have inflicted on me will surely await you. Me you have killed because you wanted to escape the accuser, and not to give an account of your lives. But that will not be as you suppose: far otherwise. For I say that there will be more accusers of you than there are now; accusers whom hitherto I have restrained: and as they are younger they will be more severe with you, and you will be more offended at them. For if you think that by killing men you can avoid the accuser censuring your lives, you are mistaken; that is not a way of escape which is either possible or honorable; the easiest and noblest way is not to be crushing others, but to be improving yourselves. This is the prophecy which I utter before my departure, to the judges who have condemned me.

Friends, who would have acquitted me, I would like also to talk with you about this thing which has happened, while the magistrates are busy, and before I go to the place at which I must die. Stay then awhile, for we may as well talk with one another while there is time. You are my friends, and I should like to show you the meaning of this event which has happened to me. O my judges—for you I may truly call judges—I should like to tell you of a wonderful circumstance. Hitherto the familiar oracle within me has constantly been in the habit of opposing me even about trifles, if I was going to make a slip or error about anything; and now as you see there has come upon me that which may be thought, and is generally believed to be, the last and worst evil. But the oracle made no sign of opposition, either as I was leaving my house and going out in the morning, or when I was going up into this court, or while I was speaking, at anything which I was going to say; and yet I have often been stopped in the middle of a speech; but now in nothing I either said or did touching this matter has the oracle opposed me. What do I take to be the explanation of this? I will tell you. I regard this as a proof that what has happened to me is a good, and that those of us who think that death is an evil are in error. This is a great proof to me of what I am saying, for the customary sign would surely have opposed me had I been going to evil and not to good.

Let us reflect in another way, and we shall see that there is great reason to hope that death is a good, for one of two things:—either death is a state of nothingness and utter unconsciousness, or, as men say, there is a change and migration of the soul from this world to another. Now if you suppose that there is no consciousness, but a sleep like the sleep of him who is undisturbed even by the sight of dreams, death will be an unspeakable gain. For if a person were to select the night in which his sleep was undisturbed even by dreams, and were to compare with this the other days and nights of his life, and then were to tell us how many days and nights he had passed in the course of his life better and more pleasantly than this one, I think that any man, I will not say a private man, but even the great king, will not find many such days or nights, when compared with the others. Now if death is like this, I say that to die is gain; for eternity is then only a single night. But if death is the journey to another place, and there, as men say, all the dead are, what good, O my friends and judges, can be greater than this? If indeed when the pilgrim arrives in the world below, he is delivered from the professors of justice in this world, and finds the true judges who are said to give judgment there, Minos and Rhadamanthus and Aeacus and Triptolemus, and other sons of God who were righteous in their own life, that pilgrimage will be worth making. What would not a man give if he might converse with Orpheus and Musaeus and Hesiod and Homer? Nay, if this be true, let me die again and again. I, too, shall have a wonderful interest in a place where I can converse with Palamedes, and Ajax the son of Telamon, and other heroes of old, who have suffered death through an unjust judgment; and there will be no small pleasure, as I think, in comparing my own sufferings with theirs. Above all, I shall be able to continue my search into true and false knowledge; as in this world, so also in that; I shall find out who is wise, and who pretends to be wise, and is not. What would not a man give, O judges, to be able to examine the leader of the great Trojan expedition; or Odysseus or Sisyphus, or numberless others, men and women too! What infinite delight would there be in conversing with them and asking them questions! For in that world they do not put a man to death for this; certainly not. For besides being happier in that world than in this, they will be immortal, if what is said is true.

Wherefore, O judges, be of good cheer about death, and know this of a truth—that no evil can happen to a good man, either in life or after death. He and his are not neglected by the gods; nor has my own approaching end happened by mere chance. But I see clearly that to die and be released was better for me; and therefore the oracle gave no sign. For which reason also, I am not angry with my accusers, or my condemners; they have done me no harm, although neither of them meant to do me any good; and for this I may gently blame them.

Still I have a favor to ask of them. When my sons are grown up, I would ask you, O my friends, to punish them; and I would have you trouble them, as I have troubled you, if they seem to care about riches, or anything, more than about virtue; or if they pretend to be something when they are really nothing,—then reprove them, as I have reproved you, for not caring about that for which they ought to care, and thinking that they are something when they are really nothing. And if you do this, I and my sons will have received justice at your hands.

The hour of departure has arrived, and we go our ways—I to die, and you to live. Which is better God only knows.

THE END

Writing About Politics and Government

In this activity, you'll write the first draft of an essay about "The Apology." First, review the thesis you wrote and revised about the essay. Then, review the evidence you brainstormed for your essay and develop it into as much detail as you need to support your thesis—specifically, use references to the text to support your argument. Next, organize your evidence and write your rough draft. It should be two to four pages (double-spaced, 12-point Times New Roman font). Be prepared to share your rough draft with a reviewer, and then rewrite it into final draft form.

Things to Keep in Mind:
- Come up with the evidence you need to support your thesis before you begin writing.
- Organize your evidence into paragraphs that each have one controlling idea. Sum up this idea with a topic sentence.
- Make sure your sentences are linked with clear transitions.
- Make sure your summary recounts your thesis and your supporting arguments.

Essay Question

In "The Apology," Socrates addresses a group of judges, some of whom condemned his to death while others voted to acquit him. What is his argument? What strategies does he use to convince his audience of that argument?

Revision

Now that you've written a first draft of your essay, it's time to polish it into a final draft. Review what your readers said about your writing, especially their suggestions for improvement. Analyze their suggestions. Do they offer specific advice on making the paper better? Are they accurate? Reread your paper and make your own notes about what needs to be revised. Use your notes and your peers' comments to rewrite your paper into its final form. It should be two to four pages (double-spaced, 12-point Times New Roman font).

As you analyze your peers' comments and revise your paper, refer to the peer-review questions from the previous activity. Your final draft will be graded on each of these areas. Here are the peer review questions:

1. Summarize the thesis of this paper.
2. Is the thesis: (a) specific? (b) arguable? (c) a direct response to one of the essay prompts? Explain why or why not. How else could the thesis be improved?
3. Sum up the main idea of each paragraph below. Note if the paragraph lacks a controlling idea or has more than one and should be broken into more than one paragraph.

THE READING PUBLIC: ESSAYS, POLITICS, AND GOVERNMENT

4. Does the evidence in each paragraph: (a) support, fail to support, or stray from the thesis? (b) include quotes and details from the text? (c) present a convincing, thorough argument? Explain why or why not.

5. Does the author use: (a) topic sentences to sum up the main idea of each paragraph? (b) transitions to link the paragraphs smoothly together?

6. Does the conclusion sum up the thesis and supporting arguments?

7. What are the paper's sentence-level errors and weaknesses?

8. Additional comments?

CHAPTER REVIEW

In this section, you'll review your studies of essays and political writing.

Read the study questions, and then review the materials from each lesson, looking for answers to the questions. Your answers should be one to two paragraphs in length.

Study Questions: Essays

1. How has the essay changed over time (from Montaigne to Bacon to the present)? Can you trace a clear progression in terms of purpose, tone, organization, and argument? Why or why not? Support your answer by giving one specific example from three essays you read in this chapter.

2. How do rhetorical devices and strategies function in political writing? Support your answer by examining how a single rhetorical device or strategy works in three political works you read in this chapter.

3. Sum up the arguments of the cultural critics you read in this chapter. How are they similar to, and different from, the piece of cultural criticism you wrote? Consider purpose, organization, tone, and argument.

Philosophy and Religion

CHAPTER 16

> **KEY TERMS**
> - abstract
> - deductive (See also: inductive)
> - inductive (See also: deductive)
> - syllogism
> - utopia (See also: dystopia)

PHILOSOPHICAL TEXTS

Most of our thinking centers on what we can see, touch, taste, smell, and hear: we think about what we had for breakfast, or what we're going to do this Friday night.

Philosophical thinking, however, centers on the abstract. In other words, philosophers try to answer questions about things that often can't be perceived physically or proved empirically. For example: Does God exist? Are human beings naturally good or evil? Do people have free will? Is there a reality outside of our perception?

The Greek philosophers Plato and Socrates tried to address these kinds of abstract questions. For example, Plato argued for the existence of a "world of ideals" in which concepts—such as the concept of perfect goodness, perfect roundness, or the ideal horse—existed even if they didn't exist in the material world (the world we can perceive). For Plato, the ideal world was the "real" world, and the material world was a world of illusion.

In this activity, you'll read a famous example of Platonic thought: "The Allegory of the Cave." This piece gives a good introduction to Plato's theory of the ideal versus the material world. Note that this piece is an allegory, in which Plato uses characters and situations to represent abstract ideas. Unlike much philosophical writing, which uses logic to prove a theory, this piece is intended to *illustrate* a theory. As you read, think about how Plato uses allegory to illustrate his ideas, and pay attention to how and why he uses logic. Finally, give some thought to how persuaded you are by this piece.

Directions: Read Plato's "The Allegory of the Cave" below. Take notes as you read, looking for answers to the reading questions. Mark passages, words, or phrases that sum up Plato's ideas. Then write answers to the reading questions. Each answer should be a few sentences to a paragraph long. Next, reread the essay, looking for answers to the study questions. This time, look for *how* Plato makes his argument. Then write responses to the study questions. Each response should be a few sentences to a paragraph long.

When you've finished writing your responses, look at the sample answers and see how yours compare. In a future assignment, you'll be asked similar questions about a philosophical piece without sample answers. The sample answers give you a sense of how on-target you are in your understanding and analysis of a difficult philosophical piece.

Reading Questions

1. What are the characteristics of life in the cave? Recount the details Plato uses.

2. How does Plato describe the experience of the man who leaves the cave? How does he relate to those trapped in the cave?

3. According to Plato, how does this hypothetical situation represent the human condition?

4. Based on the description (which begins with "This entire allegory . . ."), what can we conclude about Plato's theories about the relationship between "the intellectual world" and "the idea of good"?

Study Questions

Now that you have a grasp of *what* Plato is arguing, you're ready to look at how he argues it.

1. Analyze how Plato makes his argument. How does he use logic? What premises does he base his argument on? Does he use evidence to support his argument?

2. How is an allegory different from an argument that relies strictly on logic? Why would Plato use an allegory to express his ideas rather than a strictly logical argument?

The Allegory of the Cave
Plato
(translated by Benjamin Jowett)

And now, I said, let me show in a figure how far our nature is enlightened or unenlightened: Behold! Human beings living in an underground den, which has a mouth open toward the light and reaching all along the den; here they have been from their childhood, and have their legs and necks chained so that they cannot move, and can only see before them, being prevented by the chains from turning round their heads. Above and behind them a fire is blazing at a distance, and between the fire and the prisoners there is a raised way; and you will see, if you look, a low wall built along the way, like the screen which marionette players have in front of them, over which they show the puppets.

I see.

And do you see, I said, men passing along the wall carrying all sorts of vessels, and statues and figures of animals made of wood and stone and various materials, which appear over the wall? Some of them are talking, others silent.

You have shown me a strange image, and they are strange prisoners.

Like ourselves, I replied; and they see only their own shadows, or the shadows of one another, which the fire throws on the opposite wall of the cave?

True, he said; how could they see anything but the shadows if they were never allowed to move their heads?

And of the objects which are being carried in like manner they would only see the shadows?

Yes, he said.

And if they were able to converse with one another, would they not suppose that they were naming what was actually before them?

Very true.

And suppose further that the prison had an echo which came from the other side, would they not be sure to fancy when one of the passersby spoke that the voice which they heard came from the passing shadow?

No question, he replied.

To them, I said, the truth would be literally nothing but the shadows of the images.

That is certain.

And now look again, and see what will naturally follow if the prisoners are released and disabused of their error. At first, when any of them is liberated and compelled suddenly to stand up and turn his neck round and walk and look toward the light, he will suffer sharp pains; the glare will distress him, and he will be unable to see the realities of which in his former state he had seen the shadows; and then conceive someone saying to him, that what he saw before was an illusion, but that now, when he is approaching nearer to being and his eye is turned toward more real existence, he has a clearer vision—what will be his reply? And you may further imagine that his instructor is pointing to the objects as they pass and requiring him to name them. Will he not be perplexed? Will he not fancy that the shadows which he formerly saw are truer than the objects which are now shown to him?

Far truer.

And if he is compelled to look straight at the light, will he not have a pain in his eyes which will make him turn away to take refuge in the objects of vision which he can see, and which he will conceive to be in reality clearer than the things which are now being shown to him?

True, he said.

And suppose once more, that he is reluctantly dragged up a steep and rugged ascent, and held fast until he is forced into the presence of the sun himself, is he not likely to be pained and irritated? When he approaches the light his eyes will be dazzled, and he will not be able to see anything at all of what are now called realities.

Not all in a moment, he said.

He will require to grow accustomed to the sight of the upper world. And first he will see the shadows best, next the reflections of men and other objects in the water, and then the objects themselves; then he will gaze upon the light of the moon and the stars and the spangled heaven; and he will see the sky and the stars by night better than the sun or the light of the sun by day?

Certainly.

Last of all he will be able to see the sun, and not mere reflections of him in the water, but he will see him in his own proper place, and not in another; and he will contemplate him as he is.

Certainly.

He will then proceed to argue that this is he who gives the season and the years, and is the guardian of all that is in the visible world, and in a certain way the cause of all things which he and his fellows have been accustomed to behold?

Clearly, he said, he would first see the sun and then reason about him.

And when he remembered his old habitation, and the wisdom of the den and his fellow prisoners, do you not suppose that he would felicitate himself on the change, and pity them?

Certainly, he would.

And if they were in the habit of conferring honors among themselves on those who were quickest to observe the passing shadows and to remark which of them went before, and which followed after, and which were together; and who were therefore best able to draw conclusions as to the future, do you think that he would care for such honors and glories, or envy the possessors of them? Would he not say with Homer, "Better to be the poor servant of a poor master," and to endure anything, rather than think as they do and live after their manner?

Yes, he said, I think that he would rather suffer anything than entertain these false notions and live in this miserable manner.

Imagine once more, I said, such a one coming suddenly out of the sun to be replaced in his old situation; would he not be certain to have his eyes full of darkness?

To be sure, he said.

And if there were a contest, and he had to compete in measuring the shadows with the prisoners who had never moved out of the den, while his sight was still weak, and before his eyes had become steady (and the time which would be needed to acquire this new habit of sight might be very considerable), would he not be ridiculous? Men would say of him that up he went and down he came without his eyes; and that it was better not even to think of ascending; and if anyone tried to loose another and lead him up to the light, let them only catch the offender, and they would put him to death.

No question, he said.

This entire allegory, I said, you may now append, dear Glaucon, to the previous argument; the prison house is the world of sight, the light of the fire is the sun, and you will not misapprehend me if you interpret the journey upward to be the ascent of the soul into the intellectual world according to my poor belief, which, at your desire, I have expressed, whether

KAPLAN

rightly or wrongly, God knows. But, whether true or false, my opinion is that in the world of knowledge the idea of good appears last of all, and is seen only with an effort; and, when seen, is also inferred to be the universal author of all things beautiful and right, parent of light and of the lord of light in this visible world, and the immediate source of reason and truth in the intellectual; and that this is the power upon which he who would act rationally either in public or private life must have his eye fixed.

I agree, he said, as far as I am able to understand you.

Moreover, I said, you must not wonder that those who attain to this beatific vision are unwilling to descend to human affairs; for their souls are ever hastening into the upper world where they desire to dwell; which desire of theirs is very natural, if our allegory may be trusted.

Yes, very natural.

And is there anything surprising in one who passes from divine contemplations to the evil state of man, misbehaving himself in a ridiculous manner; if, while his eyes are blinking and before he has become accustomed to the surrounding darkness, he is compelled to fight in courts of law, or in other places, about the images or the shadows of images of justice, and is endeavoring to meet the conceptions of those who have never yet seen absolute justice?

Anything but surprising, he replied.

Anyone who has common sense will remember that the bewilderments of the eyes are of two kinds, and arise from two causes, either from coming out of the light or from going into the light, which is true of the minds eye, quite as much as of the bodily eye; and he who remembers this when he sees anyone whose vision is perplexed and weak, will not be too ready to laugh; he will first ask whether that soul of man has come out of the brighter life, and is unable to see because unaccustomed to the dark, or having turned from darkness to the day is dazzled by excess of light. And he will count the one happy in his condition and state of being, and he will pity the other; or, if he have a mind to laugh at the soul which comes from below into the light, there will be more reason in this than in the laugh which greets him who returns from above out of the light into the den.

That, he said, is a very just distinction.

Answers to Reading Questions

1. What are the characteristics of life in the cave? Recount the details Plato uses.

People in the cave are physically restrained, and can see only shadows thrown on the cave wall. Because they have been this way since childhood, they think that the shadows are reality, when in fact the real world lies just beyond the reach of their perception. Nevertheless, they are accustomed to their version of reality, and would be reluctant to be brought out into the light of Plato's true reality.

2. How does Plato describe the experience of the man who leaves the cave? How does he relate to those trapped in the cave?

The man who has seen the light of the upper world recognizes that the shadows he had perceived as reality are an illusion. After seeing the upper world, returning to the cave causes him pain. He seems foolish and blind to the cave's inhabitants because he cannot see from their perspective anymore. Rather than looking to the enlightened man as a source of truth, they ridicule him, and resist the idea of escape themselves.

3. According to Plato, how does this hypothetical situation represent the human condition?

Plato argues that the world we perceive with our senses is not real, but is merely a shadow of a world that lies beyond the reach of our perception. People think that what they perceive is the only reality, and even if they could see the larger reality, they'd be reluctant to look at it. Plato never defines the "reality" beyond the cave very specifically, but does seem to condemn the reluctance of people to see the truth. Even if someone were to rise above the limits of human perception and see the real world, people would have a hard time believing their account.

4. Based on the description (which begins with, "This entire allegory . . ."), what can we conclude about Plato's theories about the relationship between "the intellectual world" and "the idea of good"?

For Plato, the idea of good is only apprehended through "the ascent of the soul into the intellectual world"; in other words, only the thoughtful, enlightened person can perceive the idea of good. Plato goes on to say that the idea of good is the source of the intellect and rationality that allows for its perception: "in the world of knowledge the idea of good appears last of all . . . and, when seen, is also inferred to be the universal author of all things beautiful and right, parent of light and the lord of light in this visible world, and the immediate source of reason and truth in the intellectual; and that this is the power upon which he who would act rationally . . . must have his eye fixed." This is a positive vision of ultimate reality, and is reinforced by the images Plato uses to describe the world outside the cave (sunlight, moon, stars), as opposed to the world in the cave (darkness, shadows, restraint).

Answers to Study Questions

1. Analyze how Plato makes his argument. How does he use logic? What premises does he base his argument on? Does he use evidence to support his argument?

Plato doesn't use logic in this piece to "prove" his argument. Rather, he uses a process of logical questioning to illustrate the details of a hypothetical situation. For example, he asks Glaucon about the men in the cave: "And if they were able to converse with one another, would they not suppose that what they were naming was actually before them?" and Glaucon replies "Very true." He uses similar questions to draw out details like the cave dwellers' belief that their vision is real and their reluctance to escape their situation. Once Plato has drawn out these details, he states the meaning of the tale, and relates it to his view of human life. He bases his argument on the premise that life is like the situation described. This premise is arguable, and Plato doesn't attempt to prove it here. Thus Plato uses logic to show the details of the allegory rather than to prove that the allegory is true.

2. How is an allegory different from an argument that relies strictly on logic? Why would Plato use an allegory to express his ideas rather than a strictly logical argument?

An allegory is a story that uses characters and events to represent abstract ideas. Plato uses allegory to create persuasive images, rather than trying to prove his point through a drier, more abstract process of logical reasoning (as he does in other dialogues). Plato's images have strong positive and negative associations: the cave dwellers are pitiful, and the world outside the cave is filled with beauty and light. These images give the reader the sense that their own lives are dim, and that they themselves are imprisoned like the men in the cave. Thus Plato convinces the reader that he or she should try to reach for something beyond immediate perception; his allegory is more persuasive than a purely logical argument would be.

RELIGIOUS TEXTS

Sacred texts are the writings upon which religions base themselves. Like philosophical writing, sacred writing focuses on abstract concepts and tries to describe a world that can't be perceived with the senses. However, sacred writing differs from philosophical writing in that it doesn't rely on logic to prove its ideas. When reading sacred writing, it's better to focus on what's being said, (which can be difficult to understand) and how the author tries to connect with their audience.

In this activity, you'll look at selections from the *Tao Te Ching*, an ancient Chinese text, upon which Taoism is based. You'll try to determine the message the text communicates and you'll think about how it functions rhetorically.

Directions: Read selections from the *Tao Te Ching*. Take notes as you read, looking for answers to the reading questions. Mark passages, words, or phrases that sum up the author's main ideas. Then read the piece a second time, looking for answers to the study questions. This time, pay attention to how the author expresses his ideas. Write responses to the study questions; each response should be a few sentences to a paragraph long. Finally, write a response to the short essay question. This response should be a few paragraphs long.

Reading Questions

1. According to this excerpt, what are the characteristics of the Tao?

2. What does this piece argue about opposites? (Pay special attention to "Two.")

3. How does this piece define goodness? Does it mention evil?

4. How does this piece recommend that people should live?

Study Questions

1. How does the illogicality of the piece express and reinforce its main ideas?

2. How does the translator use language for emphasis and poetic effect?

Short Essay Question

Compare and contrast the worldview expressed in the excerpt from the *Tao Te Ching* with the traditional Western view (e.g., American, Judeo-Christian values). How are they similar? How are they different? Compare the traditional Western concept of God to how the *Tao Te Ching* portrays the Tao. Look also at how the two portray opposites, such as good and evil. Finally, how do their recommendations for living differ?

The Tao and Its Characteristics
Lao-Tse
(translated by James Legge)

One

1. The Tao that can be trodden is not the enduring and unchanging Tao. The name that can be named is not the enduring and unchanging name.

2. (Conceived of as) having no name, it is the Originator of heaven and earth; (conceived of as) having a name, it is the Mother of all things.

3. Always without desire we must be found, If its deep mystery we would sound; But if desire always within us be, Its outer fringe is all that we shall see.

4. Under these two aspects, it is really the same; but as development takes place, it receives the different names. Together we call them the Mystery. Where the Mystery is the deepest is the gate of all that is subtle and wonderful.

Two

1. All in the world know the beauty of the beautiful, and in doing this they have (the idea of) what ugliness is; they all know the skill of the skilful, and in doing this they have (the idea of) what the want of skill is.

2. So it is that existence and non-existence give birth the one to (the idea of) the other; that difficulty and ease produce the one (the idea of) the other; that length and shortness fashion out the one the figure of the other; that (the ideas of) height and lowness arise from the contrast of the one with the other; that the musical notes and tones become harmonious through the relation of one with another; and that being before and behind give the idea of one following another.

3. Therefore the sage manages affairs without doing anything, and conveys his instructions without the use of speech.

4. All things spring up, and there is not one which declines to show itself; they grow, and there is no claim made for their ownership; they go through their processes, and there is no expectation (of a reward for the results). The work is accomplished, and there is no resting in it (as an achievement). The work is done, but how no one can see; 'Tis this that makes the power not cease to be.

Three

1. Not to value and employ men of superior ability is the way to keep the people from rivalry among themselves; not to prize articles which are difficult to procure is the way to keep them from becoming thieves; not to show them what is likely to excite their desires is the way to keep their minds from disorder.

2. Therefore the sage, in the exercise of his government, empties their minds, fills their bellies, weakens their wills, and strengthens their bones.

3. He constantly (tries to) keep them without knowledge and without desire, and where there are those who have knowledge, to keep them from presuming to act (on it). When there is this abstinence from action, good order is universal.

PHILOSOPHY AND RELIGION

Four

1. The Tao is (like) the emptiness of a vessel; and in our employment of it we must be on our guard against all fullness. How deep and unfathomable it is, as if it were the Honoured Ancestor of all things!

2. We should blunt our sharp points, and unravel the complications of things; we should attemper our brightness, and bring ourselves into agreement with the obscurity of others. How pure and still the Tao is, as if it would ever so continue!

3. I do not know whose son it is. It might appear to have been before God.

Five

1. Heaven and earth do not act from (the impulse of) any wish to be benevolent; they deal with all things as the dogs of grass are dealt with. The sages do not act from (any wish to be) benevolent; they deal with the people as the dogs of grass are dealt with.

2. May not the space between heaven and earth be compared to a bellows? 'Tis emptied, yet it loses not its power; 'Tis moved again, and sends forth air the more. Much speech to swift exhaustion lead we see; Your inner being guard, and keep it free.

Six

1. The valley spirit dies not, aye the same; the female mystery thus do we name. Its gate, from which at first they issued forth, is called the root from which grew heaven and earth. Long and unbroken does its power remain, Used gently, and without the touch of pain.

Seven

1. Heaven is long-enduring and earth continues long. The reason why heaven and earth are able to endure and continue thus long is because they do not live of, or for, themselves. This is how they are able to continue and endure.

2. Therefore the sage puts his own person last, and yet it is found in the foremost place; he treats his person as if it were foreign to him, and yet that person is preserved. Is it not because he has no personal and private ends, that therefore such ends are realized?

Eight

1. The highest excellence is like (that of) water. The excellence of water appears in its benefiting all things, and in its occupying, without striving (to the contrary), the low place which all men dislike. Hence (its way) is near to (that of) the Tao.

2. The excellence of a residence is in (the suitability of) the place; that of the mind is in abysmal stillness; that of associations is in their being with the virtuous; that of government is in its securing good order; that of (the conduct of) affairs is in its ability; and that of (the initiation of) any movement is in its timeliness.

3. And when (one with the highest excellence) does not wrangle (about his low position), no one finds fault with him.

Nine

1. It is better to leave a vessel unfilled, than to attempt to carry it when it is full. If you keep feeling a point that has been sharpened, the point cannot long preserve its sharpness.

2. When gold and jade fill the hall, their possessor cannot keep them safe. When wealth and honours lead to arrogancy, this brings its evil on itself. When the work is done, and one's name is becoming distinguished, to withdraw into obscurity is the way of Heaven.

WRITING ABOUT PHILOSOPHICAL IDEAS

In this section, you'll write the final draft of an essay about a quote from a philosophical work.

Directions: Read the essay prompt below. Brainstorm a thesis and evidence for your essay, using all prewriting techniques you find helpful. Then narrow your thesis and organize your evidence. Now you're reading to write your rough draft. When you're done, revise your draft for content and clarity and complete your final draft. It should be two to four pages (double-spaced, in 12-point Times New Roman font).

Essay Question

Consider the following quote from Aristotle:

"The man who can live alone is either an animal or a god."

First, sum up the main idea behind the quote, and its implications. Then write a well-organized essay in which you agree with, disagree with, or qualify the assertion. Give logical reasons for your position. Support your thesis with evidence drawn from your reading, personal experience, and/or observation.

CHAPTER REVIEW

Study Questions: Philosophy and Religion

1. What are the characteristics of philosophical writing? Illustrate your definition with examples drawn from the philosophical texts you read in this lesson. Did any of the philosophical pieces you read deviate from the standard definition of philosophical writing? How?

2. What are the characteristics of religious writing? Illustrate your definition with examples drawn from the religious texts you read in this lesson.

KAPLAN

Short Fiction

CHAPTER 17

KEY TERMS

- genre
- narrator
- point of view (See also: perspective)
- setting
- symbolism
- theme
- tone

THE STRUCTURE OF SHORT FICTION

When we read a story for fun, we often read just to find out what happens, or because we're interested in the characters. As with many other types of writing, however, a closer analysis of a piece of short fiction can often reveal a deeper meaning.

It's important to know the structural elements of short stories including plot, character, tone, narrative and language. Learning the meanings of these terms will help you know what to look for when you analyze short stories.

- **Plot** is what happens in a story. The plot can be broken down into several elements: exposition, rising action, climax, falling action, and the conclusion.
- **Exposition** sets the stage and explains the context of the story by introducing the setting, characters, and plot to the reader. Check out this example of an expository paragraph from the beginning of Charles Dickens's "The Ghost of Art":

> I am a bachelor, residing in rather a dreary set of chambers in the Temple. They are situated in a square court of high houses, which would be a complete well, but for the want of water and the absence of a bucket. I live at the top of the house, among the tiles and sparrows. Like the little man in the nursery-story, I live by myself, and all the bread and cheese I get—which is not much—I put upon a shelf. I need scarcely add, perhaps, that I am in love, and that the father of my charming Julia objects to our union.

This paragraph introduces the main character, describes where he lives, and hints at the central conflict in the story. Depending on the length of the story, exposition can be a few paragraphs to a few pages long.

- The term **rising action** describes the events leading up to the high point or main confrontation of the story. For example, the rising action in a mystery story might involve the search for clues that will lead to the solution of a crime. The rising action often creates tension for the reader, who is eager to see what's going to happen next.

- The **climax** is the high point of the story or the part of the story where the conflict leads to a turning point. In a mystery story, the climax might be the criminal's discovery and arrest. Some climaxes involve a confrontation, a revelation about the meaning of events, or an incident related to the conflict. All climaxes, however, represent the culmination of the rising action.

- The **falling action** of a story describes the events that occur after the climax and lead to the conclusion. The conclusion ends the story by offering a resolution to the conflict in the story. It is usually brief, and may contain an element of surprise or irony.

- The **characters** are the people, animals, or sometimes even inanimate objects upon whose thoughts, words, and actions a story is based. Sometimes a story focuses on one major character, and sometimes on several characters. As a story evolves, the author develops his or her characters by revealing more about their thoughts and behavior. As you read a story, ask yourself how the characters change over the course of the story, or whether the characters change at all.

- **Setting** is the time and place in which the story happens. The setting may be established explicitly, or it may have to be inferred from details in the story.

- The **narrator** is the "voice" that tells the story. When he or she sits down to write a story, an author chooses a perspective from which to narrate events. This perspective is called the point of view. Generally, the point of view in the story isn't the author's, but belongs to a character or a persona the author creates. The two most common points of view are **first person** and **third person**.

- A **first-person narrator** is usually signaled by the use of the first person, or "I." For example, when Dickens writes, "I am a bachelor," in the first line of "The Ghost of Art," this tells us that the story has a first person narrator. A first person narrator can be a main character directly involved in the events of the story or a secondary character who is more of an observer.

- A **third-person narrator** tells the story in the third person, using "he," "she," or "it." This narrator isn't a character in the story and isn't directly involved in the action. There are two types of third person narrators: **omniscient** and **limited omniscient**.

- An **omniscient narrator** can see the actions and thoughts of all the characters.

- A **limited omniscient narrator** tells the story through the perspective of one character. For example, in F. Scott Fitzgerald's "Winter Dreams," the narrator says, "Dexter knew there was something dismal about this northern spring, just as he knew there was something gorgeous about the fall." Though the narrator isn't Dexter himself, he has access to his thoughts and feelings. However, the narrator can't see into the minds and hearts of other characters.

- **Theme** is the central idea around which a story is organized. For example, if the events of a story focus on the childhood of a character, ask yourself, What is this story telling me about childhood? Your answer will tell you something about the theme of the story.

- **Language** refers to the way the author uses words in a story. Like any other literary form, short stories use literary and rhetorical devices such as imagery, figurative language, parallelism, and alliteration.

- **Tone** shows the author's attitude toward the subject matter of the story. You can analyze tone by looking closely at the author's style.

- **Style** refers to the distinctive characteristics of an author's writing. To get a sense of the author's style, pay attention to the word choices he or she makes. Does the author use simple or complicated language? Is the diction formal or informal? Does the author use abstract or concrete language? Style can differ widely from author to author, and an author's style can differ from work to work.

LEARNING TO ANALYZE SHORT FICTION

Analyzing a short story requires looking at its formal elements. In this exercise, you'll learn how to analyze plot, character, setting, point of view, symbolism, theme, and tone.

Below are questions to ask yourself about the various elements of a short story. Use your answers to determine how the various elements work together to contribute to the overall effect of the story.

Plot

Plot is the arrangement of the important events in a story.
- How are the events in the story arranged? Do they take place chronologically?
- How does the story begin? Does it begin *in medias res* (in the middle of things)?
- How does the story end? How are the beginning and ending related?
- How would the story be different if it were told in a different order?
- How does the order of events contribute to the meaning of the story? Why is it important?

Character

Character refers to the people (or animals or even objects) who perform the actions in a story.

- Who are the most important characters in the story? What do they seem to represent?
- Who is the protagonist? What character or characters are the antagonist(s)?
- What is each character like? Make a list of their personality traits and significant actions.

Setting

Setting refers to where the action of the story takes place.

- What is the time, place, and social environment of the story? What details indicate this?
- How would the story be different if it were set in a different place, time, or social environment?
- What does the setting contribute to the meaning of the story?

Point of View

Point of view refers to the perspective, values, attitudes, and biases of the narrator.

- Who is telling the story? What is his or her role in the story itself?
- Is it told in the first person ("I"), the second person ("you"), or the third person ("he," "she," or "it")?
- Is the narrator reliable? What evidence do I have for this?
- If the story is told in third person, is he or she omniscient (all-knowing), limited omniscient (can see into the head of one character), or objective (detached from the characters)? What effect does this have on the story itself?

Symbol

A symbol is a person, object, or event that suggests more than its literal meaning.

- What symbols appear in the story? Do they appear more than once? When and where do they appear?
- Are there any similes (comparison using like or as) or metaphors (comparison without like or as)?
- What do the symbols or images seem to represent? What evidence do I have for this?
- How do they contribute to the meaning of the story?

Theme

Theme is the central meaning of a story.

- How do all the elements contribute to the story's central meaning?
- What is the theme or thesis of the story? What statement is it making about its subject? What evidence is there to support this?

Tone

Tone is the author's attitude toward the subject matter of the story.

- What is the attitude of the story?
- What words or images suggest this attitude or tone?
- What feeling am I left with at the end of the story?

PRACTICE ANALYZING SHORT FICTION

Directions: Read Sherwood Anderson's short story "Paper Pills" from his 1919 collection of stories titled *Winesburg, Ohio*. Take notes as you read, looking for answers to the study questions. Your response to each question should be a few sentences to a paragraph long. Then compare your answers to the sample answers provided after the text.

Study Questions

1. How is the plot arranged? Why is the plot arranged in this way?
2. Who is the protagonist? What is he or she like?
3. How is the setting important?
4. What is the point of view of the narrator? How is it important?
5. What symbols are significant in the story? How are they important to the story?
6. How do these elements add up to a theme? What evidence do you have to support this?
7. What is the story's tone? What words or images support this?

Paper Pills
Sherwood Anderson

He was an old man with a white beard and huge nose and hands. Long before the time during which we will know him, he was a doctor and drove a jaded white horse from house to house through the streets of Winesburg. Later he married a girl who had money. She had been left a large fertile farm when her father died. The girl was quiet, tall, and dark, and to many people she seemed very beautiful. Everyone in Winesburg wondered why she married the doctor. Within a year after the marriage she died.

The knuckles of the doctor's hands were extraordinarily large. When the hands were closed they looked like clusters of unpainted wooden balls as large as walnuts fastened together by steel rods. He smoked a cob pipe and after his wife's death sat all day in his empty office close by a window that was covered with cobwebs. He never opened the window. Once on a hot day in August he tried but found it stuck fast and after that he forgot all about it.

Winesburg had forgotten the old man, but in Doctor Reefy there were the seeds of something very fine. Alone in his musty office in the Heffner Block above the Paris Dry Goods Company's store, he worked ceaselessly, building up something that he himself destroyed. Little pyramids of truth he erected and after erecting knocked them down again that he might have the truths to erect other pyramids.

Doctor Reefy was a tall man who had worn one suit of clothes for ten years. It was frayed at the sleeves and little holes had appeared at the knees and elbows. In the office he wore also a linen duster with huge pockets into which he continually stuffed scraps of paper. After some weeks the scraps of paper became little hard round balls, and when the pockets were filled he dumped them out upon the floor. For ten years he had but one friend, another old man named John Spaniard who owned a tree nursery. Sometimes, in a playful mood, old Doctor Reefy took from his pockets a handful of the paper balls and threw them at the nursery man. "That is to confound you, you blathering old sentimentalist," he cried, shaking with laughter.

The story of Doctor Reefy and his courtship of the tall dark girl who became his wife and left her money to him is a very curious story. It is delicious, like the twisted little apples that grow in the orchards of Winesburg. In the fall one walks in the orchards and the ground is hard with frost underfoot. The apples have been taken from the trees by the pickers. They have been put in barrels and shipped to the cities where they will be eaten in apartments that are filled with books, magazines, furniture, and people. On the trees are only a few gnarled apples that the pickers have rejected. They look like the knuckles of Doctor Reefy's hands. One nibbles at them and they are delicious. Into a little round place at the side of the apple has been gathered all of its sweetness. One runs from tree to tree over the frosted ground picking the gnarled, twisted apples and filling his pockets with them. Only the few know the sweetness of the twisted apples.

The girl and Doctor Reefy began their courtship on a summer afternoon. He was forty-five then and already he had begun the practice of filling his pockets with the scraps of paper that became hard balls and were thrown away. The habit had been formed as he sat in his buggy behind the jaded white horse and went slowly along country roads. On the papers were written thoughts, ends of thoughts, beginnings of thoughts.

One by one the mind of Doctor Reefy had made the thoughts. Out of many of them he formed a truth that arose gigantic in his mind. The truth clouded the world. It became terrible and then faded away and the little thoughts began again.

The tall dark girl came to see Doctor Reefy because she was in the family way and had become frightened. She was in that condition because of a series of circumstances also curious.

The death of her father and mother and the rich acres of land that had come down to her had set a train of suitors on her heels. For two years she saw suitors almost every evening. Except two they were all alike. They talked to her of passion and there was a strained eager quality in their voices and in their eyes when they looked at her. The two who were different were much unlike each other. One of them, a slender young man with white hands, the son of a jeweler in Winesburg, talked continually of virginity. When he was with her he was never off the subject. The other, a black-haired boy with large ears, said nothing at all but always managed to get her into the darkness, where he began to kiss her.

KAPLAN

For a time the tall dark girl thought she would marry the jeweler's son. For hours she sat in silence listening as he talked to her and then she began to be afraid of something. Beneath his talk of virginity she began to think there was a lust greater than in all the others. At times it seemed to her that as he talked he was holding her body in his hands. She imagined him turning it slowly about in the white hands and staring at it. At night she dreamed that he had bitten into her body and that his jaws were dripping. She had the dream three times, then she became in the family way to the one who said nothing at all but who in the moment of his passion actually did bite her shoulder so that for days the marks of his teeth showed.

After the tall dark girl came to know Doctor Reefy it seemed to her that she never wanted to leave him again. She went into his office one morning and without her saying anything he seemed to know what had happened to her.

In the office of the doctor there was a woman, the wife of the man who kept the bookstore in Winesburg. Like all old-fashioned country practitioners, Doctor Reefy pulled teeth, and the woman who waited held a handkerchief to her teeth and groaned. Her husband was with her and when the tooth was taken out they both screamed and blood ran down on the woman's white dress. The tall dark girl did not pay any attention. When the woman and the man had gone the doctor smiled. "I will take you driving into the country with me," he said.

For several weeks the tall dark girl and the doctor were together almost every day. The condition that had brought her to him passed in an illness, but she was like one who has discovered the sweetness of the twisted apples, she could not get her mind fixed again upon the round perfect fruit that is eaten in the city apartments. In the fall after the beginning of her acquaintanceship with him she married Doctor Reefy and in the following spring she died. During the winter he read to her all of the odds and ends of thoughts he had scribbled on the bits of paper. After he had read them he laughed and stuffed them away in his pockets to become round hard balls.

Sample Answers to Study Questions

1. How is the plot arranged? Why is the plot arranged in this way?

The story begins in the present; Doctor Reefy is an old man, forgotten by the town. Then it quickly moves back in time to give a brief background on Doctor Reefy and his marriage. Then it moves forward again and tells us that he sits all day in his empty office mourning the death of his wife. Most of the rest of the story is concerned with relating an incident in the past. This is significant because it shows that the past was the most important part of Doctor Reefy's life, specifically his short-lived marriage. His life before and after is empty and largely unknown to the reader, although we know he was already 45 when he met his wife.

2. Who is the protagonist? What is he or she like?

Doctor Reefy is the protagonist. He is old and alone in the present, but we learn that as a younger man he had a beautiful, wealthy wife who saw something in him that others didn't. Though we don't get a lot of information about his past, the narrator suggests that he had a lot of potential. The only other character he has personal contact with is the nurseryman, but the other townspeople seem distant from him. We can also infer that Doctor Reefy isn't concerned with material goods or wealth—we're told that he lives modestly despite having inherited a large amount of money from his wife. The author portrays Doctor Reefy sympathetically, and we get the sense that he is a lonely person.

3. How is the setting important?

The story takes place in a small town in Ohio where Doctor Reefy lives. The story is partly about the repressive conditions of small towns and the isolation of some of the people who live there, so the setting is clearly important.

4. What is the point of view of the narrator? How is it important?

The narrator is omniscient because he can see the thoughts and actions of all the characters. The narrator is not limited to telling the story through the perspective of just one character. The narrator tells part of the story from the girl's perspective, and although he never gives us a detailed account of Dr. Reefy's thoughts, he gives us glimpses of Dr. Reefy's world, and describes his intellectual life.

5. What symbols are significant in the story? How are they important to the story?

The "paper pills" are clearly significant because they appear in the title and reappear throughout the story; they evoke Dr. Reefy's loneliness. Throughout his life he has written his thoughts on small pieces of paper, then stuffed them in his pocket where they become wadded into little balls. When his pockets fill he dumps them on the ground. When his wife was alive; however, he read them aloud to her. The paper pills give the reader a vivid picture of an individual's thoughts and feelings that, when they're not shared with anyone, lose their vitality and get discarded. They are a symbol of the "sweetness" in Dr. Reefy that is unknown by the town.

Also, the author notes that the "gnarled, twisted apples" that the pickers leave behind look like Doctor Reefy's knuckles. This suggests that the apples symbolize Dr. Reefy himself; like the apples that have been rejected by the pickers but nevertheless taste sweet, Dr. Reefy has a side to him that only his wife sees. The narrator extends the apple analogy by suggesting that Dr. Reefy contains "the seeds of something very fine."

6. How do these elements add up to a theme? What evidence do you have to support this?

The theme seems to be that someone's potential for truth and love can be strangled because of their circumstances and isolation. The story's elements, such as the symbol of the "paper pills," the setting, and the characters all support this theme because they show how Doctor Reefy's life has been limited and stunted. His thoughts are contained only in the paper balls that get thrown away, never to be shared with others.

7. What is the story's tone? What words or images support this?

The story has a tragic tone. It's told matter-of-factly, but there are hints of underlying violence and passion. The girl's pregnancy and death, her suitor biting her, and the delicious "twisted little apples" suggest that underneath the everyday realities of small-town life, there are hidden realities and tragic forces that shape peoples' lives.

PREPARING TO WRITE ABOUT SHORT FICTION

When you're getting ready to write about a short story, it's important to look at how the elements of the story work together to create meaning or achieve a specific effect. Consider all the details of the story, including plot, character, setting, point of view, symbols, theme, and tone. You should also make a note of any features of the story that interest you, that don't make sense, or that stand out. Sometimes these features can be clues to the story's meaning.

Directions: Read Nathaniel Hawthorne's "The Minister's Black Veil." Take notes as you read, looking for answers to the study questions. Your response to each study question should be a few sentences to a paragraph long. Once you have answered the questions, draft a thesis for an essay. Gather and list evidence from the story that supports your thesis.

Study Questions

1. How is the plot arranged? Why is this arrangement significant?

2. Who is the protagonist? What is he like? How do you know this from the story? How does the protagonist relate to the other characters in the story? Who are the antagonists?

3. How is the setting important? How does the setting relate to the plot?

4. What is the point of view of the narrator? How is it important?

5. What kinds of figurative language appear in the story? How does this kind of language work to shape the story?

6. What is the story's tone, or attitude toward its subject matter? What words or images support this?

7. Write a sentence that sums up the story's main theme (the point the story makes about its subject matter). Then sum up how the elements in the story contribute to this theme.

Thesis Question

Review your answers to the study questions and draft a thesis that makes an argument about the story.

Things to Remember as You're Drafting Your Thesis:

- Your thesis should explain what you see as a main theme in the story, and how the specific elements in the story contribute to the theme. You can focus on one specific element, like characterization or plot, or you can show how all the elements in the story support the main theme.

- Remember, your interpretation of the story's main theme is just that—an interpretation. That's why you have to back up your thesis with evidence from the story.

- Though you may have to summarize the plot in the body of your essay, avoid doing this in your thesis.

Once you have a thesis, go back to the story and make a list of all the evidence you can use to support your thesis. Does looking at the evidence change your mind or suggest a different approach to the topic? Do you have enough evidence to support your argument? If necessary, redraft your thesis in light of the evidence you've collected.

The Minister's Black Veil: A Parable
Nathaniel Hawthorne

Another clergyman in New England, Mr. Joseph Moody, of York, Maine, made himself remarkable by the same eccentricity that is here related of the Reverend Mr. Hooper. In his case, however, the symbol had a different import. In early life he had accidentally killed a beloved friend, and from that day till the hour of his own death, he hid his face from men.

The sexton stood in the porch of Milford meeting-house, pulling busily at the bell-rope. The old people of the village came stooping along the street. Children, with bright faces, tripped merrily beside their parents, or mimicked a graver gait, in the conscious dignity of their Sunday clothes. Spruce bachelors looked sidelong at the pretty maidens, and fancied that the Sabbath sunshine made them prettier than on week days. When the throng had mostly streamed into the porch, the sexton began to toll the bell, keeping his eye on the Reverend Mr. Hooper's door. The first glimpse of the clergyman's figure was the signal for the bell to cease its summons.

"But what has good Parson Hooper got upon his face?" cried the sexton in astonishment.

All within hearing immediately turned about, and beheld the semblance of Mr. Hooper, pacing slowly his meditative way towards the meeting-house. With one accord they started, expressing more wonder than if some strange minister were coming to dust the cushions of Mr. Hooper's pulpit.

"Are you sure it is our parson?" inquired Goodman Gray of the sexton.

"Of a certainty it is good Mr. Hooper," replied the sexton. "He was to have exchanged pulpits with Parson Shute, of Westbury; but Parson Shute sent to excuse himself yesterday, being to preach a funeral sermon."

The cause of so much amazement may appear sufficiently slight. Mr. Hooper, a gentlemanly person, of about thirty, though still a bachelor, was dressed with due clerical neatness, as if a careful wife had starched his band, and brushed the weekly dust from his Sunday's garb. There was but one thing remarkable in his appearance. Swathed about his forehead, and hanging down over his face, so low as to be shaken by his breath, Mr. Hooper had on a black veil. On a nearer view it seemed to consist of two folds of crape, which entirely concealed his features, except the mouth and chin, but probably did not intercept his sight, further than to give a darkened aspect to all living and inanimate things. With this gloomy shade before him, good Mr. Hooper walked onward, at a slow and quiet pace, stooping somewhat, and looking on the ground, as is customary with abstracted men, yet nodding kindly to those of his parishioners who still waited on the meeting-house steps. But so wonderstruck were they that his greeting hardly met with a return.

SHORT FICTION

"I can't really feel as if good Mr. Hooper's face was behind that piece of crape," said the sexton.

"I don't like it," muttered an old woman, as she hobbled into the meeting-house. "He has changed himself into something awful, only by hiding his face."

"Our parson has gone mad!" cried Goodman Gray, following him across the threshold.

A rumor of some unaccountable phenomenon had preceded Mr. Hooper into the meeting-house, and set all the congregation astir. Few could refrain from twisting their heads towards the door; many stood upright, and turned directly about; while several little boys clambered upon the seats, and came down again with a terrible racket. There was a general bustle, a rustling of the women's gowns and shuffling of the men's feet, greatly at variance with that hushed repose which should attend the entrance of the minister. But Mr. Hooper appeared not to notice the perturbation of his people. He entered with an almost noiseless step, bent his head mildly to the pews on each side, and bowed as he passed his oldest parishioner, a white-haired great grandsire, who occupied an arm-chair in the centre of the aisle. It was strange to observe how slowly this venerable man became conscious of something singular in the appearance of his pastor. He seemed not fully to partake of the prevailing wonder, till Mr. Hooper had ascended the stairs, and showed himself in the pulpit, face to face with his congregation, except for the black veil. That mysterious emblem was never once withdrawn. It shook with his measured breath, as he gave out the psalm; it threw its obscurity between him and the holy page, as he read the Scriptures; and while he prayed, the veil lay heavily on his uplifted countenance. Did he seek to hide it from the dread Being whom he was addressing?

Such was the effect of this simple piece of crape, that more than one woman of delicate nerves was forced to leave the meeting-house. Yet perhaps the pale-faced congregation was almost as fearful a sight to the minister, as his black veil to them.

Mr. Hooper had the reputation of a good preacher, but not an energetic one: he strove to win his people heavenward by mild, persuasive influences, rather than to drive them thither by the thunders of the Word. The sermon which he now delivered was marked by the same characteristics of style and manner as the general series of his pulpit oratory. But there was something, either in the sentiment of the discourse itself, or in the imagination of the auditors, which made it greatly the most powerful effort that they had ever heard from their pastor's lips. It was tinged, rather more darkly than usual, with the gentle gloom of Mr. Hooper's temperament. The subject had reference to secret sin, and those sad mysteries which we hide from our nearest and dearest, and would fain conceal from our own consciousness, even forgetting that the Omniscient can detect them. A subtle power was breathed into his words. Each member of the congregation, the most innocent girl, and the man of hardened breast, felt as if the preacher had crept upon them, behind his awful veil, and discovered their hoarded iniquity of deed or thought. Many spread their clasped hands on their bosoms. There was nothing terrible in what Mr. Hooper said, at least, no violence; and yet, with every tremor of his melancholy voice, the hearers quaked. An unsought pathos came hand in hand with awe. So sensible were the audience of some unwonted attribute in their minister, that they longed for a breath of wind to blow aside the veil, almost believing that a stranger's visage would be discovered, though the form, gesture, and voice were those of Mr. Hooper.

At the close of the services, the people hurried out with indecorous confusion, eager to communicate their pent-up amazement, and conscious of lighter spirits the moment they lost sight of the black veil. Some gathered in little circles, huddled closely together, with their mouths all whispering in the centre; some went homeward alone, wrapt in silent meditation;

some talked loudly, and profaned the Sabbath day with ostentatious laughter. A few shook their sagacious heads, intimating that they could penetrate the mystery; while one or two affirmed that there was no mystery at all, but only that Mr. Hooper's eyes were so weakened by the midnight lamp, as to require a shade. After a brief interval, forth came good Mr. Hooper also, in the rear of his flock. Turning his veiled face from one group to another, he paid due reverence to the hoary heads, saluted the middle aged with kind dignity as their friend and spiritual guide, greeted the young with mingled authority and love, and laid his hands on the little children's heads to bless them. Such was always his custom on the Sabbath day. Strange and bewildered looks repaid him for his courtesy. None, as on former occasions, aspired to the honor of walking by their pastor's side. Old Squire Saunders, doubtless by an accidental lapse of memory, neglected to invite Mr. Hooper to his table, where the good clergyman had been wont to bless the food, almost every Sunday since his settlement. He returned, therefore, to the parsonage, and, at the moment of closing the door, was observed to look back upon the people, all of whom had their eyes fixed upon the minister. A sad smile gleamed faintly from beneath the black veil, and flickered about his mouth, glimmering as he disappeared.

"How strange," said a lady, "that a simple black veil, such as any woman might wear on her bonnet, should become such a terrible thing on Mr. Hooper's face!"

"Something must surely be amiss with Mr. Hooper's intellects," observed her husband, the physician of the village. "But the strangest part of the affair is the effect of this vagary, even on a sober-minded man like myself. The black veil, though it covers only our pastor's face, throws its influence over his whole person, and makes him ghostlike from head to foot. Do you not feel it so?"

"Truly do I," replied the lady; "and I would not be alone with him for the world. I wonder he is not afraid to be alone with himself!"

"Men sometimes are so," said her husband.

The afternoon service was attended with similar circumstances. At its conclusion, the bell tolled for the funeral of a young lady. The relatives and friends were assembled in the house, and the more distant acquaintances stood about the door, speaking of the good qualities of the deceased, when their talk was interrupted by the appearance of Mr. Hooper, still covered with his black veil. It was now an appropriate emblem. The clergyman stepped into the room where the corpse was laid, and bent over the coffin, to take a last farewell of his deceased parishioner. As he stooped, the veil hung straight down from his forehead, so that, if her eyelids had not been closed forever, the dead maiden might have seen his face. Could Mr. Hooper be fearful of her glance, that he so hastily caught back the black veil? A person who watched the interview between the dead and living, scrupled not to affirm, that, at the instant when the clergyman's features were disclosed, the corpse had slightly shuddered, rustling the shroud and muslin cap, though the countenance retained the composure of death. A superstitious old woman was the only witness of this prodigy. From the coffin Mr. Hooper passed into the chamber of the mourners, and thence to the head of the staircase, to make the funeral prayer. It was a tender and heart-dissolving prayer, full of sorrow, yet so imbued with celestial hopes, that the music of a heavenly harp, swept by the fingers of the dead, seemed faintly to be heard among the saddest accents of the minister. The people trembled, though they but darkly understood him when he prayed that they, and himself, and all of mortal race, might be ready, as he trusted this young maiden had been, for the dreadful hour that should snatch the veil from their faces. The bearers went heavily forth, and the mourners followed, saddening all the street, with the dead before them, and Mr. Hooper in his black veil behind.

"Why do you look back?" said one in the procession to his partner.

"I had a fancy," replied she, "that the minister and the maiden's spirit were walking hand in hand."

"And so had I, at the same moment," said the other.

That night, the handsomest couple in Milford village were to be joined in wedlock. Though reckoned a melancholy man, Mr. Hooper had a placid cheerfulness for such occasions, which often excited a sympathetic smile where livelier merriment would have been thrown away. There was no quality of his disposition which made him more beloved than this. The company at the wedding awaited his arrival with impatience, trusting that the strange awe, which had gathered over him throughout the day, would now be dispelled. But such was not the result. When Mr. Hooper came, the first thing that their eyes rested on was the same horrible black veil, which had added deeper gloom to the funeral, and could portend nothing but evil to the wedding. Such was its immediate effect on the guests that a cloud seemed to have rolled duskily from beneath the black crape, and dimmed the light of the candles. The bridal pair stood up before the minister. But the bride's cold fingers quivered in the tremulous hand of the bridegroom, and her deathlike paleness caused a whisper that the maiden who had been buried a few hours before was come from her grave to be married. If ever another wedding were so dismal, it was that famous one where they tolled the wedding knell. After performing the ceremony, Mr. Hooper raised a glass of wine to his lips, wishing happiness to the new-married couple in a strain of mild pleasantry that ought to have brightened the features of the guests, like a cheerful gleam from the hearth. At that instant, catching a glimpse of his figure in the looking-glass, the black veil involved his own spirit in the horror with which it overwhelmed all others. His frame shuddered, his lips grew white, he spilt the untasted wine upon the carpet, and rushed forth into the darkness. For the Earth, too, had on her Black Veil.

The next day, the whole village of Milford talked of little else than Parson Hooper's black veil. That, and the mystery concealed behind it, supplied a topic for discussion between acquaintances meeting in the street, and good women gossiping at their open windows. It was the first item of news that the tavern-keeper told to his guests. The children babbled of it on their way to school. One imitative little imp covered his face with an old black handkerchief, thereby so affrighting his playmates that the panic seized himself, and he well-nigh lost his wits by his own waggery.

It was remarkable that all of the busybodies and impertinent people in the parish, not one ventured to put the plain question to Mr. Hooper, wherefore he did this thing. Hitherto, whenever there appeared the slightest call for such interference, he had never lacked advisers, nor shown himself averse to be guided by their judgment. If he erred at all, it was by so painful a degree of self-distrust, that even the mildest censure would lead him to consider an indifferent action as a crime. Yet, though so well acquainted with this amiable weakness, no individual among his parishioners chose to make the black veil a subject of friendly remonstrance. There was a feeling of dread, neither plainly confessed nor carefully concealed, which caused each to shift the responsibility upon another, till at length it was found expedient to send a deputation of the church, in order to deal with Mr. Hooper about the mystery, before it should grow into a scandal. Never did an embassy so ill discharge its duties. The minister received then with friendly courtesy, but became silent, after they were seated, leaving to his visitors the whole burden of introducing their important business. The topic, it might be supposed, was obvious enough. There was the black veil swathed round Mr. Hooper's forehead, and concealing every feature above his placid mouth, on which, at times, they could perceive the glimmering of a melancholy smile. But that piece of crape, to their imagination, seemed to hang down before his heart, the symbol of a fearful secret between him and them. Were the veil but cast aside, they might speak freely of it, but not till then. Thus they sat a considerable time, speechless, confused, and shrinking uneasily from Mr. Hooper's eye, which they felt to be fixed upon them with an invisible glance. Finally, the deputies returned abashed to their constituents, pronouncing the matter too weighty to be handled, except by a council of the churches, if, indeed, it might not require a general synod.

But there was one person in the village unappalled by the awe with which the black veil had impressed all beside herself. When the deputies returned without an explanation, or even venturing to demand one, she, with the calm energy of her character, determined to chase away the strange cloud that appeared to be settling round Mr. Hooper, every moment more darkly than before. As his plighted wife, it should be her privilege to know what the black veil concealed. At the minister's first visit, therefore, she entered upon the subject with a direct simplicity, which made the task easier both for him and her. After he had seated himself, she fixed her eyes steadfastly upon the veil, but could discern nothing of the dreadful gloom that had so overawed the multitude: it was but a double fold of crape, hanging down from his forehead to his mouth, and slightly stirring with his breath.

"No," said she aloud, and smiling, "there is nothing terrible in this piece of crape, except that it hides a face which I am always glad to look upon. Come, good sir, let the sun shine from behind the cloud. First lay aside your black veil: then tell me why you put it on."

Mr. Hooper's smile glimmered faintly.

"There is an hour to come," said he, "when all of us shall cast aside our veils. Take it not amiss, beloved friend, if I wear this piece of crape till then."

"Your words are a mystery, too," returned the young lady. "Take away the veil from them, at least."

"Elizabeth, I will," said he, "so far as my vow may suffer me. Know, then, this veil is a type and a symbol, and I am bound to wear it ever, both in light and darkness, in solitude and before the gaze of multitudes, and as with strangers, so with my familiar friends. No mortal eye will see it withdrawn. This dismal shade must separate me from the world: even you, Elizabeth, can never come behind it!"

"What grievous affliction hath befallen you," she earnestly inquired, "that you should thus darken your eyes forever?"

"If it be a sign of mourning," replied Mr. Hooper, "I, perhaps, like most other mortals, have sorrows dark enough to be typified by a black veil."

"But what if the world will not believe that it is the type of an innocent sorrow?" urged Elizabeth. "Beloved and respected as you are, there may be whispers that you hide your face under the consciousness of secret sin. For the sake of your holy office, do away this scandal!"

The color rose into her cheeks as she intimated the nature of the rumors that were already abroad in the village. But Mr. Hooper's mildness did not forsake him. He even smiled again— that same sad smile, which always appeared like a faint glimmering of light, proceeding from the obscurity beneath the veil.

"If I hide my face for sorrow, there is cause enough," he merely replied; "and if I cover it for secret sin, what mortal might not do the same?"

And with this gentle, but unconquerable obstinacy did he resist all her entreaties. At length Elizabeth sat silent. For a few moments she appeared lost in thought, considering, probably, what new methods might be tried to withdraw her lover from so dark a fantasy, which, if it had no other meaning, was perhaps a symptom of mental disease. Though of a firmer character than his own, the tears rolled down her cheeks. But, in an instant, as it were, a new feeling took the place of sorrow: her eyes were fixed insensibly on the black veil, when, like a sudden twilight in the air, its terrors fell around her. She arose, and stood trembling before him.

"And do you feel it then, at last?" said he mournfully.

She made no reply, but covered her eyes with her hand, and turned to leave the room. He rushed forward and caught her arm.

"Have patience with me, Elizabeth!" cried he, passionately. "Do not desert me, though this veil must be between us here on earth. Be mine, and hereafter there shall be no veil over my face, no darkness between our souls! It is but a mortal veil—it is not for eternity! O! you know not how lonely I am, and how frightened, to be alone behind my black veil. Do not leave me in this miserable obscurity forever!"

"Lift the veil but once, and look me in the face," said she.

"Never! It cannot be!" replied Mr. Hooper.

"Then farewell!" said Elizabeth.

She withdrew her arm from his grasp, and slowly departed, pausing at the door, to give one long shuddering gaze, that seemed almost to penetrate the mystery of the black veil. But, even amid his grief, Mr. Hooper smiled to think that only a material emblem had separated him from happiness, though the horrors, which it shadowed forth, must be drawn darkly between the fondest of lovers.

From that time no attempts were made to remove Mr. Hooper's black veil, or, by a direct appeal, to discover the secret which it was supposed to hide. By persons who claimed a superiority to popular prejudice, it was reckoned merely an eccentric whim, such as often mingles with the sober actions of men otherwise rational, and tinges them all with its own semblance of insanity. But with the multitude, good Mr. Hooper was irreparably a bugbear. He could not walk the street with any peace of mind, so conscious was he that the gentle and timid would turn aside to avoid him, and that others would make it a point of hardihood to throw themselves in his way. The impertinence of the latter class compelled him to give up his customary walk at sunset to the burial ground; for when he leaned pensively over the gate, there would always be faces behind the gravestones, peeping at his black veil. A fable went the rounds that the stare of the dead people drove him thence. It grieved him, to the very depth of his kind heart, to observe how the children fled from his approach, breaking up their merriest sports, while his melancholy figure was yet afar off. Their instinctive dread caused him to feel more strongly than aught else, that a preternatural horror was interwoven with the threads of the black crape. In truth, his own antipathy to the veil was known to be so great, that he never willingly passed before a mirror, nor stooped to drink at a still fountain, lest, in its peaceful bosom, he should be affrighted by himself. This was what gave plausibility to the whispers, that Mr. Hooper's conscience tortured him for some great crime too horrible to be entirely concealed, or otherwise than so obscurely intimated. Thus, from beneath the black veil, there rolled a cloud into the sunshine, an ambiguity of sin or sorrow, which enveloped the poor minister, so that love or sympathy could never reach him. It was said that ghost and fiend consorted with him there. With self-shudderings and outward terrors, he walked continually in its shadow, groping darkly within his own soul, or gazing through a medium that saddened the whole world. Even the lawless wind, it was believed, respected his dreadful secret, and never blew aside the veil. But still good Mr. Hooper sadly smiled at the pale visages of the worldly throng as he passed by.

Among all its bad influences, the black veil had the one desirable effect, of making its wearer a very efficient clergyman. By the aid of his mysterious emblem—for there was no other apparent cause—he became a man of awful power over souls that were in agony for sin. His converts always regarded him with a dread peculiar to themselves, affirming, though but figuratively, that, before he brought them to celestial light, they had been with him behind the black veil. Its gloom, indeed, enabled him to sympathize with all dark affections. Dying sinners cried aloud for Mr. Hooper, and would not yield their breath till he appeared; though ever, as he stooped to whisper consolation, they shuddered at the veiled face so near their own. Such were the terrors of the black veil, even when Death had bared his visage! Strangers came long distances to attend service at his church, with the mere idle purpose of gazing at his figure, because it was forbidden them to behold his face. But many were made to quake ere they departed! Once, during Governor Belcher's administration, Mr. Hooper was appointed to preach the election sermon. Covered with his black veil, he stood before the chief magistrate, the council, and the representatives, and wrought so deep an impression, that the legislative measures of that year were characterized by all the gloom and piety of our earliest ancestral sway.

In this manner Mr. Hooper spent a long life, irreproachable in outward act, yet shrouded in dismal suspicions; kind and loving, though unloved, and dimly feared; a man apart from men, shunned in their health and joy, but ever summoned to their aid in mortal anguish. As years wore on, shedding their snows above his sable veil, he acquired a name throughout the New England churches, and they called him Father Hooper. Nearly all his parishioners, who were of mature age when he was settled, had been borne away by many a funeral: he had one congregation in the church, and a more crowded one in the churchyard; and having wrought so late into the evening, and done his work so well, it was now good Father Hooper's turn to rest.

Several persons were visible by the shaded candlelight, in the death chamber of the old clergyman. Natural connections he had none. But there was the decorously grave, though unmoved physician, seeking only to mitigate the last pangs of the patient whom he could not save. There were the deacons, and other eminently pious members of his church. There, also, was the Reverend Mr. Clark, of Westbury, a young and zealous divine, who had ridden in haste to pray by the bedside of the expiring minister. There was the nurse, no hired handmaiden of death, but one whose calm affection had endured thus long in secrecy, in solitude, amid the chill of age, and would not perish, even at the dying hour. Who, but Elizabeth! And there lay the hoary head of good Father Hooper upon the death pillow, with the black veil still swathed about his brow, and reaching down over his face, so that each more difficult gasp of his faint breath caused it to stir. All through life that piece of crape had hung between him and the world: it had separated him from cheerful brotherhood and woman's love, and kept him in that saddest of all prisons, his own heart; and still it lay upon his face, as if to deepen the gloom of his darksome chamber, and shade him from the sunshine of eternity.

For some time previous, his mind had been confused, wavering doubtfully between the past and the present, and hovering forward, as it were, at intervals, into the indistinctness of the world to come. There had been feverish turns, which tossed him from side to side, and wore away what little strength he had. But in his most convulsive struggles, and in the wildest vagaries of his intellect, when no other thought retained its sober influence, he still showed an awful solicitude lest the black veil should slip aside. Even if his bewildered soul could have forgotten, there was a faithful woman at this pillow, who, with averted eyes, would have covered that aged face, which she had last beheld in the comeliness of manhood. At length the death-stricken old man lay quietly in the torpor of mental and bodily exhaustion, with an imperceptible pulse, and breath that grew fainter and fainter, except when a long, deep, and irregular inspiration seemed to prelude the flight of his spirit.

The minister of Westbury approached the bedside.

"Venerable Father Hooper," said he, "the moment of your release is at hand. Are you ready for the lifting of the veil that shuts in time from eternity?"

Father Hooper at first replied merely by a feeble motion of his head; then, apprehensive, perhaps, that his meaning might be doubted, he exerted himself to speak.

"Yea," said he, in faint accents, "my soul hath a patient weariness until that veil be lifted."

"And is it fitting," resumed the Reverend Mr. Clark, "that a man so given to prayer, of such a blameless example, holy in deed and thought, so far as mortal judgment may pronounce; is it fitting that a father in the church should leave a shadow on his memory, that may seem to blacken a life so pure? I pray you, my venerable brother, let not this thing be! Suffer us to be gladdened by your triumphant aspect as you go to your reward. Before the veil of eternity be lifted, let me cast aside this black veil from your face!"

And thus speaking, the Reverend Mr. Clark bent forward to reveal the mystery of so many years. But, exerting a sudden energy, that made all the beholders stand aghast, Father Hooper snatched both his hands from beneath the bedclothes, and pressed them strongly on the black veil, resolute to struggle, if the minister of Westbury would contend with a dying man.

"Never!" cried the veiled clergyman. "On earth, never!"

"Dark old man!" exclaimed the affrighted minister, "with what horrible crime upon your soul are you now passing to the judgment?"

Father Hooper's breath heaved; it rattled in his throat; but, with a mighty effort, grasping forward with his hands, he caught hold of life, and held it back till he should speak. He even raised himself in bed; and there he sat, shivering with the arms of death around him, while the black veil hung down, awful, at that last moment, in the gathered terrors of a lifetime. And yet the faint, sad smile, so often there, now seemed to glimmer from its obscurity, and linger on Father Hooper's lips.

"Why do you tremble at me alone?" cried he, turning his veiled face round the circle of pale spectators. "Tremble also at each other! Have men avoided me, and women shown no pity, and children screamed and fled, only for my black veil? What, but the mystery which it obscurely typifies, has made this piece of crape so awful? When the friend shows his inmost heart to his friend; the lover to his best beloved; when man does not vainly shrink from the eye of his Creator, loathsomely treasuring up the secret of his sin; then deem me a monster, for the symbol beneath which I have lived, and die! I look around me, and, lo! on every visage a Black Veil!"

While his auditors shrank from one another, in mutual affright, Father Hooper fell back upon his pillow, a veiled corpse, with a faint smile lingering on the lips. Still veiled, they laid him in his coffin, and a veiled corpse they bore him to the grave. The grass of many years has sprung up and withered on that grave, the burial stone is moss-grown, and good Mr. Hooper's face is dust; but awful is still the thought that it mouldered beneath the Black Veil!

WRITING ABOUT SHORT FICTION

In this section, you'll write the final draft of an essay about Nathaniel Hawthorne's "The Minister's Black Veil."

Directions: Read and review the essay prompt below. If necessary, review Hawthorne's "The Minister's Black Veil" as well as the thesis you wrote about the story. Develop the evidence you brainstormed for your essay so that you have as much detail as you need to support your thesis. Organize your evidence, write a rough draft, and revise as necessary. Lastly, write your final draft. It should be two to four pages (double-spaced, 12-point Times New Roman font).

Things to Keep in Mind:

- Remember, your interpretation of the story's main theme is just that—an interpretation. That's why you have to back up your thesis with evidence from the story.

- Though you may have to summarize the plot in the body of your essay, avoid doing this in your thesis.

- Develop the evidence you need to support your thesis before you begin writing. Be sure to include quotes and examples from the text.

- Organize your evidence into paragraphs that each have one controlling idea. Sum up this idea with a topic sentence.

- Make sure your paragraphs are linked with clear transitions.

- Make sure your summary recounts your thesis and your supporting arguments.

Essay Question

Explain what you see as a main theme in the story, and how the specific elements in the story contribute to the theme. You can focus on one specific element, like characterization or plot, or you can show how all the elements in the story support the main theme.

CHAPTER REVIEW

In this section, you'll review your study of short fiction.

Study Questions: Short Fiction

1. Sum up the theme of the two pieces of short fiction you read in this chapter (Anderson's "Paper Pills" and Hawthorne's "The Minister's Black Veil") in one or two sentences.

2. For each of the two stories, choose three literary elements covered in this lesson and explain how each element contributes to the theme of the story. Don't repeat the same elements for different stories; you should cover six different elements.

PRACTICE TESTS

Practice Test I

How to Take This Test

Before taking this practice test, find a quiet place where you can work uninterrupted for three hours or so. Make sure you have a comfortable desk, several No. 2 pencils for the multiple-choice section, and a few ballpoint pens for the essay section.

This practice test includes a multiple-choice section and a free-response section consisting of three essay questions. Use the answer grid that follows to record your multiple-choice answers. Write the essays on a separate sheet of paper.

Once you start the practice test, don't stop until you've finished the multiple-choice section. You may then take a ten-minute break before proceeding to the essay section.

You'll find the answer key and explanations following the test.

Good luck!

PRACTICE TEST I
ANSWER SHEET

1 Ⓐ Ⓑ Ⓒ Ⓓ Ⓔ   21 Ⓐ Ⓑ Ⓒ Ⓓ Ⓔ   41 Ⓐ Ⓑ Ⓒ Ⓓ Ⓔ

2 Ⓐ Ⓑ Ⓒ Ⓓ Ⓔ   22 Ⓐ Ⓑ Ⓒ Ⓓ Ⓔ   42 Ⓐ Ⓑ Ⓒ Ⓓ Ⓔ

3 Ⓐ Ⓑ Ⓒ Ⓓ Ⓔ   23 Ⓐ Ⓑ Ⓒ Ⓓ Ⓔ   43 Ⓐ Ⓑ Ⓒ Ⓓ Ⓔ

4 Ⓐ Ⓑ Ⓒ Ⓓ Ⓔ   24 Ⓐ Ⓑ Ⓒ Ⓓ Ⓔ   44 Ⓐ Ⓑ Ⓒ Ⓓ Ⓔ

5 Ⓐ Ⓑ Ⓒ Ⓓ Ⓔ   25 Ⓐ Ⓑ Ⓒ Ⓓ Ⓔ   45 Ⓐ Ⓑ Ⓒ Ⓓ Ⓔ

6 Ⓐ Ⓑ Ⓒ Ⓓ Ⓔ   26 Ⓐ Ⓑ Ⓒ Ⓓ Ⓔ   46 Ⓐ Ⓑ Ⓒ Ⓓ Ⓔ

7 Ⓐ Ⓑ Ⓒ Ⓓ Ⓔ   27 Ⓐ Ⓑ Ⓒ Ⓓ Ⓔ   47 Ⓐ Ⓑ Ⓒ Ⓓ Ⓔ

8 Ⓐ Ⓑ Ⓒ Ⓓ Ⓔ   28 Ⓐ Ⓑ Ⓒ Ⓓ Ⓔ   48 Ⓐ Ⓑ Ⓒ Ⓓ Ⓔ

9 Ⓐ Ⓑ Ⓒ Ⓓ Ⓔ   29 Ⓐ Ⓑ Ⓒ Ⓓ Ⓔ   49 Ⓐ Ⓑ Ⓒ Ⓓ Ⓔ

10 Ⓐ Ⓑ Ⓒ Ⓓ Ⓔ   30 Ⓐ Ⓑ Ⓒ Ⓓ Ⓔ   50 Ⓐ Ⓑ Ⓒ Ⓓ Ⓔ

11 Ⓐ Ⓑ Ⓒ Ⓓ Ⓔ   31 Ⓐ Ⓑ Ⓒ Ⓓ Ⓔ

12 Ⓐ Ⓑ Ⓒ Ⓓ Ⓔ   32 Ⓐ Ⓑ Ⓒ Ⓓ Ⓔ

13 Ⓐ Ⓑ Ⓒ Ⓓ Ⓔ   33 Ⓐ Ⓑ Ⓒ Ⓓ Ⓔ

14 Ⓐ Ⓑ Ⓒ Ⓓ Ⓔ   34 Ⓐ Ⓑ Ⓒ Ⓓ Ⓔ

15 Ⓐ Ⓑ Ⓒ Ⓓ Ⓔ   35 Ⓐ Ⓑ Ⓒ Ⓓ Ⓔ

16 Ⓐ Ⓑ Ⓒ Ⓓ Ⓔ   36 Ⓐ Ⓑ Ⓒ Ⓓ Ⓔ

17 Ⓐ Ⓑ Ⓒ Ⓓ Ⓔ   37 Ⓐ Ⓑ Ⓒ Ⓓ Ⓔ

18 Ⓐ Ⓑ Ⓒ Ⓓ Ⓔ   38 Ⓐ Ⓑ Ⓒ Ⓓ Ⓔ

19 Ⓐ Ⓑ Ⓒ Ⓓ Ⓔ   39 Ⓐ Ⓑ Ⓒ Ⓓ Ⓔ

20 Ⓐ Ⓑ Ⓒ Ⓓ Ⓔ   40 Ⓐ Ⓑ Ⓒ Ⓓ Ⓔ

ENGLISH LANGUAGE AND COMPOSITION

Section I: Multiple-Choice Questions

Time: 1 hour

Number of questions: 50

Percent of total grade: 45

Directions: This section contains selections of prose works and questions on their content, style, and form. After reading each passage, select the best answer and fill it in on the corresponding oval on the answer sheet.

Questions 1–13. Read the following passage carefully before you choose your answers.

The passage below is from *"A Plea for Captain John Brown"* by Henry David Thoreau.

When I think of him [John Brown], and his six sons, and his son-in-law, not to enumerate the others, enlisted for this fight,
Line proceeding coolly, reverently, humanely to
(5) work, for months if not years, sleeping and waking upon it, summering and wintering the thought, without expecting any reward but a good conscience, while almost all America stood ranked on the other side—I say again
(10) that it affects me as a sublime spectacle. If he had had any journal advocating "his cause," any organ, as the phrase is, monotonously and wearisomely playing the same old tune, and then passing round the hat, it would have been
(15) fatal to his efficiency. If he had acted in any way so as to be let alone by the government, he might have been suspected. It was the fact that the tyrant must give place to him, or he to the tyrant, that distinguished him from all the
(20) reformers of the day that I know.

It was his peculiar doctrine that a man has a perfect right to interfere by force with the slaveholder, in order to rescue the slave. I agree with him. They who are continually
(25) shocked by slavery have some right to be shocked by the violent death of the slaveholder, but no others. Such will be more shocked by his life than by his death. I shall not be forward to think him mistaken in his

(30) method who quickest succeeds to liberate the slave. I speak for the slave when I say that I prefer the philanthropy of Captain Brown to that philanthropy which neither shoots me nor liberates me. At any rate, I do not think it is
(35) quite sane for one to spend his whole life in talking or writing about this matter, unless he is continuously inspired, and I have not done so. A man may have other affairs to attend to. I do not wish to kill nor to be killed, but I can
(40) foresee circumstances in which both these things would be by me unavoidable. We preserve the so-called peace of our community by deeds of petty violence every day. Look at the policeman's billy and handcuffs! Look at
(45) the jail! Look at the gallows! Look at the chaplain of the regiment! We are hoping only to live safely on the outskirts of this provisional army. So we defend ourselves and our hen-roosts, and maintain slavery. I know
(50) that the mass of my countrymen think that the only righteous use that can be made of Sharp's rifles and revolvers is to fight duels with them, when we are insulted by other nations, or to hunt Indians, or shoot fugitive slaves with
(55) them, or the like. I think that for once the Sharp's rifles and the revolvers were employed in a righteous cause. The tools were in the hands of one who could use them.

GO ON TO THE NEXT PAGE. ➡

The same indignation that is said to have
(60) cleared the temple once will clear it again.
The question is not about the weapon, but the
spirit in which you use it. No man has
appeared in America, as yet, who loved his
fellow-man so well, and treated him so
(65) tenderly. He lived for him. He took up his life
and he laid it down for him. What sort of
violence is that which is encouraged, not by
soldiers, but by peaceable citizens, not so
much by laymen as by ministers of the
(70) Gospel, not so much by the fighting sects as
by the Quakers, and not so much by Quaker
men as by Quaker women?

This event advertises me that there is such
a fact as death—the possibility of a man's
(75) dying. It seems as if no man had ever died in
America before; for in order to die you must
first have lived. I don't believe in the hearses,
and palls, and funerals that they have had.
There was no death in the case, because there
(80) had been no life; they merely rotted or
sloughed off, pretty much as they had rotted or
sloughed along. No temple's veil was rent,
only a hole dug somewhere. Let the dead bury
their dead. The best of them fairly ran down
(85) like a clock. Franklin—Washington—they
were let off without dying; they were merely
missing one day. I hear a good many pretend
that they are going to die; or that they have
died, for aught that I know. Nonsense! I'll
(90) defy them to do it. They haven't got life
enough in them. They'll deliquesce like fungi,
and keep a hundred eulogists mopping the
spot where they left off. Only half a dozen or
so have died since the world began. Do you
(95) think that you are going to die, sir? No!
there's no hope of you. You haven't got your
lesson yet. You've got to stay after school. We
make a needless ado about capital
punishment—taking lives, when there is no
(100) life to take. *Memento mori!* We don't
understand that sublime sentence which some
worthy got sculptured on his gravestone once.

We've interpreted it in a grovelling and
snivelling sense; we've wholly forgotten how
(105) to die.

But be sure you do die nevertheless. Do
your work, and finish it. If you know how to
begin, you will know when to end.

1. The tone of this passage is best described as

   (A) gleeful
   (B) reverent
   (C) indignant
   (D) sarcastic
   (E) plain

2. The first sentence of paragraph 3 (lines
   59–60) contains

   (A) exaggeration
   (B) allusion
   (C) metonymy
   (D) alliteration
   (E) antithesis

3. In line 10, the word "sublime" most likely
   means

   (A) unconscious
   (B) pleasant
   (C) impressive
   (D) cowardly
   (E) noble

4. The rhetorical technique employed by the
   speaker in lines 21–34 is

   (A) appeal to logic
   (B) appeal to emotion
   (C) appeal to authority
   (D) *ad hominem* attack
   (E) hyperbole

5. In lines 84–94, the speaker implies that

   (A) Franklin and Washington are still alive
   (B) death is an illusion
   (C) only cowards die
   (D) in order to truly die, one must truly live
   (E) everyone dies

GO ON TO THE NEXT PAGE. ➡

6. The simile comparing dead men to fungi is best understood to imply

(A) that certain processes of decomposition normally occur at death
(B) some men, as some fungi, have practical purposes
(C) some men are parasites
(D) many fungi are edible
(E) some men live lives as inert and meaningless as fungi

7. "Look at the policeman's billy and handcuffs! Look at the jail! Look at the gallows! Look at the chaplain of the regiment!" These lines (43–46) contain

(A) examples of alliteration
(B) anaphora
(C) antithesis
(D) oxymoron
(E) hyperbole

8. The word "deliquesce" (line 91) in this context most likely means

(A) to melt or rot away
(B) become fibrous
(C) to turn to dust
(D) to become liquid
(E) to decay over a period of many years

9. The violence the speaker refers to in the final sentence of paragraph 3 is most likely

(A) gun violence
(B) violence of the oppressed against the oppressor
(C) violence of putting one's life at risk in a noble cause
(D) violence of slaveholders
(E) warfare

10. Because Quakers were well known to be pacifists, the speaker's use of them as advocates of a certain type of violence could be considered

(A) sarcasm
(B) irony
(C) humor
(D) pathos
(E) antithesis

11. In the last paragraph, the speaker is most likely suggesting

(A) it is useless to continue living
(B) a person who supports injustice should die
(C) it is important to be willing to sacrifice one's life in the name of justice
(D) death is a noble profession
(E) work is death

12. The word "advertises" in line 73 most likely means

(A) suggests to
(B) sells
(C) advises
(D) informs
(E) encourages

13. The expression "*Memento mori!*" (line 100) in this context most likely means

(A) remember more
(B) remember death
(C) human frailty
(D) an object which reminds one of mortality
(E) more souvenirs

Questions 14–23. Read the following passage carefully before you choose your answers.

The passage below is from *"Criticism"* by Edgar Allan Poe.

As I am speaking of poetry, it will not be amiss to touch slightly upon the most singular heresy in its modern history—the heresy of
Line what is called, very foolishly, the Lake
(5) School. Some years ago I might have been induced, by an occasion like the present, to attempt a formal refutation of their doctrine; at present it would be a work of supererogation. The wise must bow to the wisdom of such
(10) men as Coleridge and Southey, but being wise, have laughed at poetical theories so prosaically exemplified.

Aristotle, with singular assurance, has declared poetry the most philosophical of all
(15) writings—but it required a Wordsworth to pronounce it the most metaphysical. He seems to think that the end of poetry is, or should be, instruction; yet it is a truism that the end of our existence is happiness; if so, the end of
(20) every separate part of our existence, everything connected with our existence, should be happiness. Therefore the end of instruction should be happiness; and happiness is another name for pleasure,—therefore the
(25) end of instruction should be pleasure; yet we see the above-mentioned opinion implies precisely the reverse.

To proceed: *ceteris paribus*, he who pleases is of more importance to his fellow-
(30) men than he who instructs, since utility is happiness, and pleasure is the end already obtained while instruction is merely the means of obtaining.

I see no reason, then, why our
(35) metaphysical poets should plume themselves so much on the utility of their works, unless indeed they refer to instruction with eternity in view; in which case, sincere respect for their piety would not allow me to express my
(40) contempt for their judgement; contempt which

it would be difficult to conceal, since their writings are professedly to be understood by the few, and it is the many who stand in need of salvation. In such case I should no doubt be
(45) tempted to think of the devil in "Melmoth," who labours indefatigably, through three octavo volumes, to accomplish the destruction of one or two souls, while any common devil would have demolished one or two thousand.

(50) Against the subtleties which would make poetry a study—not a passion—it becomes the metaphysician to reason—but the poet to protest. Yet Wordsworth and Coleridge are men in years; the one imbued in
(55) contemplating from his childhood, the other a giant in intellect and learning. The diffidence, then, with which I venture to dispute their authority would be overwhelming did I not feel, from the bottom of my heart, that
(60) learning has little to do with the imagination—intellect with the passions—or age with poetry.

Trifles, like straws, upon the surface flow;
He who would search for pearls must dive
(65) below,

are lines which have done much mischief. As regards the greater truths, men oftener err by seeking them at the bottom than at the top; Truth lies in the huge abysses where wisdom
(70) is sought—not in the palpable palaces where she is found. The ancients were not always right in hiding the goddess in a well; witness the light which Bacon has thrown upon philosophy; witness the principles of our
(75) divine faith—that moral mechanism by which the simplicity of a child may overbalance the wisdom of a man.

We see an instance of Coleridge's liability to err, in his *Biographia Literaria*—

GO ON TO THE NEXT PAGE. ➡

(80) professedly his literary life and opinions, but, in fact, a treatise *de omni scibili et quibusdam aliis*. He goes wrong by reason of his very profundity, and of his error we have a natural type in the contemplation of a star. He who

(85) regards it directly and intensely sees, it is true, the star, but it is the star without a ray—while he who surveys it less inquisitively is conscious of all for which the star is useful to us below—its brilliancy and its beauty.

(90)   As to Wordsworth, I have no faith in him. That he had in youth the feelings of a poet I believe—for there are glimpses of extreme delicacy in his writings—(and delicacy is the poet's own kingdom—his El Dorado)—but

(95) they have the appearance of a better day recollected; and glimpses, at best, are little evidence of present poetic fire—we know that a few straggling flowers spring up daily in the crevices of the glacier.

(100)   He was to blame in wearing away his youth in contemplation with the end of poetizing in his manhood.

    With the increase of his judgment the light which should make it apparent has faded

(105) away. His judgment consequently is too correct. This may not be understood,—but the old Goths of Germany would have understood it, who used to debate matters of importance to their State twice, once when drunk, and

(110) once when sober—sober that they might not be deficient in formality—drunk lest they should be destitute of vigour. The long wordy discussions by which he tries to reason us into admiration of his poetry, speak very little in

(115) his favour: they are full of such assertions as this (I have opened one of his volumes at random)—"Of genius the only proof is the act of doing well what is worthy to be done, and what was never done before";—indeed? then

(120) it follows that in doing what is unworthy to be done, or what has been done before, no genius can be evinced; yet the picking of pockets is an unworthy act, pockets have been picked time immemorial and Barrington, the

(125) pickpocket, in point of genius, would have thought hard of a comparison with William Wordsworth, the poet.

14. In the first paragraph, Coleridge and Southey can be inferred to be

  (A) journalists
  (B) bad poets
  (C) members of "the Lake School"
  (D) playwrights
  (E) professors

15. The term "a work of supererogation" (line 8) most likely means

  (A) more than is necessary
  (B) superfluous
  (C) extra
  (D) greatly needed
  (E) thoroughly understood

16. In lines 9–12 ("The wise must . . . so prosaically exemplified."), the speaker's tone is

  (A) humorous
  (B) bitter
  (C) angry
  (D) ironic
  (E) laconic

17. The speaker presents Wordsworth's position that poetry should be instructional as

  (A) the opposite of his own position
  (B) reasonable
  (C) identical with Aristotle's position
  (D) purely rational
  (E) understood

18. The predominant rhetorical device used by the speaker in this passage is

  (A) appeal to reason
  (B) appeal to emotion
  (C) appeal to authority
  (D) hyperbole
  (E) *ad hominem* attack

GO ON TO THE NEXT PAGE. ➡

19. One method the speaker uses to establish himself as an expert is

    (A) frequent use of oxymoron
    (B) frequent use of Latin phrases
    (C) praising other critics
    (D) repeated use of puns
    (E) quoting Shakespeare

20. The speaker seems to have the most respect for the poet

    (A) Wordsworth
    (B) Southey
    (C) Coleridge
    (D) Barrington
    (E) Aristotle

21. The speaker seems to have the least respect for the poet

    (A) Wordsworth
    (B) Southey
    (C) Coleridge
    (D) Barrington
    (E) Aristotle

22. What is the speaker's point when he states in lines 107–112 that " . . . the old Goths of Germany would have understood it, who used to debate matters of importance to their State twice, once when drunk, and once when sober—sober that they might not be deficient in formality—drunk lest they should be destitute of vigour"?

    (A) the old Goths would have understood the poetry of Wordsworth
    (B) the old Goths would have composed poetry only when drunk
    (C) the old Goths would have recognized the need for poetry to have both good form and passion
    (D) the old Goths were historically considered first-rate poets
    (E) the old Goths participated in the oral tradition

23. "The ancients were not always right in hiding the goddess in a well" (lines 71–72) is an example of

    (A) alliteration
    (B) allusion
    (C) hyperbole
    (D) oxymoron
    (E) metaphor

GO ON TO THE NEXT PAGE. ➡

KAPLAN

Questions 24–33. Read the following passage carefully before you choose your answers.

The passage below is from *"Self Reliance"* by Ralph Waldo Emerson.

There is a time in every man's education when he arrives at the conviction that envy is ignorance; that imitation is suicide; that he
Line must take himself for better, for worse, as his
(5) portion; that though the wide universe is full of good, no kernel of nourishing corn can come to him but through his toil bestowed on that plot of ground which is given to him to till. The power which resides in him is new in
(10) nature, and none but he knows what that is which he can do, nor does he know until he has tried. Not for nothing one face, one character, one fact, makes much impression on him, and another none. This sculpture in the
(15) memory is not without pre-established harmony. The eye was placed where one ray should fall, that it might testify of that particular ray. We but half express ourselves, and are ashamed of that divine idea which
(20) each of us represents. It may be safely trusted as proportionate and of good issues, so it be faithfully imparted, but God will not have his work made manifest by cowards. A man is relieved and gay when he has put his heart
(25) into his work and done his best; but what he has said or done otherwise, shall give him no peace. It is a deliverance which does not deliver. In the attempt his genius deserts him; no muse befriends; no invention, no hope.
(30) Trust thyself: every heart vibrates to that iron string. Accept the place the divine providence has found for you, the society of your contemporaries, the connection of events. Great men have always done so, and confided
(35) themselves childlike to the genius of their age, betraying their perception that the absolutely trustworthy was seated at their heart, working through their hands, predominating in all their being. And we are now men, and must accept
(40) in the highest mind the same transcendent

destiny; and not minors and invalids in a protected corner, not cowards fleeing before a revolution, but guides, redeemers, and benefactors, obeying the Almighty effort, and
(45) advancing on Chaos and the Dark.

What pretty oracles nature yields us on this text, in the face and behaviour of children, babes, and even brutes! That divided and rebel mind, that distrust of a sentiment because our
(50) arithmetic has computed the strength and means opposed to our purpose, these have not. Their mind being whole, their eye is as yet unconquered, and when we look in their faces, we are disconcerted. Infancy conforms to
(55) nobody: all conform to it, so that one babe commonly makes four or five out of the adults who prattle and play to it. So God has armed youth and puberty and manhood no less with its own piquancy and charm, and made it
(60) enviable and gracious and its claims not to be put by, if it will stand by itself. Do not think the youth has no force, because he cannot speak to you and me. Hark! in the next room his voice is sufficiently clear and emphatic. It
(65) seems he knows how to speak to his contemporaries. Bashful or bold, then, he will know how to make us seniors very unnecessary.

24. The main idea of the first paragraph can BEST be summed up as

(A) God is not happy with mankind
(B) Unless we discover who we are within ourselves we cannot be fulfilled
(C) We must till the soil that surrounds us, in order to reap the corn
(D) Our memories are pre-ordained to be harmonious
(E) We must be wary of envy, ignorance, imitation and suicide

GO ON TO THE NEXT PAGE. ➡

25. The first paragraph contains all of the following rhetorical devices EXCEPT

    (A) analogy
    (B) contradiction
    (C) onomatopoeia
    (D) alliteration
    (E) parallel structure

26. Lines 2–3 utilize examples of the following rhetorical device

    (A) metaphors
    (B) similes
    (C) analogies
    (D) apostrophes
    (E) personification

27. The best summary of lines 18–27 is

    (A) God is ashamed of us humans
    (B) We are ashamed of God's divine ideal of us
    (C) God does not like cowards
    (D) God is not pleased with man's half-hearted efforts
    (E) We should not be concerned with God's expectations of us

28. A significant grammatical shift can be seen from the first to the second paragraph when the author

    (A) does not mention God as often
    (B) mentions Chaos and the Dark (line 45)
    (C) suddenly addresses the reader as "you" (line 32)
    (D) talks about children, babies, and animals (lines 47–48)
    (E) refers to youth versus old age

29. In the second paragraph, Emerson tells us that great men have always been

    (A) child geniuses
    (B) invalids hiding in protected corners
    (C) betrayed by their contemporaries
    (D) creative with their hands
    (E) accepting of the place found for them by divine providence

30. In the final sentence of the second paragraph, the author stresses his point through the use of

    (A) apostrophe
    (B) onomatopoeia
    (C) antithesis
    (D) anaphora
    (E) allusion

31. We are disconcerted when we look into the eyes of children or babes because

    (A) their behavior disturbs us
    (B) they are demanding of our time and energy
    (C) we distrust their sentiments
    (D) their eyes have not yet been conquered
    (E) four or five adults prattle and play

32. In this passage Emerson seems to be

    (A) complimenting those who refuse to live according to the expectations of others
    (B) extolling man to obtain harmony by conforming to the group
    (C) praising those who wisely follow the teachings of others
    (D) reminding man that he is not central to the universe
    (E) exhorting man to believe in himself and live up to his own ideals

33. This passage could BEST be described as

    (A) a stirring call for us to hold firmly to our own particular understanding of what is right and true
    (B) a supreme argument for us to improve our own divinity by joining the community of man
    (C) a forceful call for us to become totally independent and unconcerned by those who depend upon us
    (D) a plea for us to recognize God within each other
    (E) a philosophical musing about our own individual position within the universe

GO ON TO THE NEXT PAGE. ➡

KAPLAN

Questions 34–42. Read the following passage carefully before you choose your answers.

The passage below is from *"A Vindication of the Rights of Woman"* by Mary Wollstonecraft.

Dedication
To M. Talleyrand-Perigord, Late Bishop Of Autun.

Line Sir,

(5)   Having read with great pleasure a pamphlet which you have lately published, I dedicate this volume to you; to induce you to reconsider the subject, and maturely weigh what I have advanced respecting the rights of

(10) woman and national education: and I call with the firm tone of humanity; for my arguments, Sir, are dictated by a disinterested spirit—I plead for my sex—not for myself.

     Independence I have long considered as

(15) the grand blessing of life, the basis of every virtue—and independence I will ever secure by contracting my wants, though I were to live on a barren heath.

     It is then an affection for the whole human

(20) race that makes my pen dart rapidly along to support what I believe to be the cause of virtue: and the same motive leads me earnestly to wish to see woman placed in a station in which she would advance, instead of

(25) retarding, the progress of those glorious principles that give a substance to morality. My opinion, indeed, respecting the rights and duties of woman, seems to flow so naturally from these simple principles, that I think it

(30) scarcely possible, but that some of the enlarged minds who formed your admirable constitution, will coincide with me.

     In France there is undoubtedly a more general diffusion of knowledge than in any

(35) part of the European world, and I attribute it, in a great measure, to the social intercourse which has long subsisted between the sexes. It is true, I utter my sentiments with freedom, that in France the very essence of sensuality

(40) has been extracted to regale the voluptuary, and a kind of sentimental lust has prevailed,

which, together with the system of duplicity that the whole tenour of their political and civil government taught, have given a sinister

(45) sort of sagacity to the French character, properly termed finesse; from which naturally flow a polish of manners that injures the substance, by hunting sincerity out of society. And, modesty, the fairest garb of virtue has

(50) been more grossly insulted in France than even in England, till their women have treated as PRUDISH that attention to decency, which brutes instinctively observe.

     Manners and morals are so nearly allied

(55) that they have often been confounded; but, though the former should only be the natural reflection of the latter, yet, when various causes have produced factitious and corrupt manners, which are very early caught,

(60) morality becomes an empty name. The personal reserve, and sacred respect for cleanliness and delicacy in domestic life, which French women almost despise, are the graceful pillars of modesty; but, far from

(65) despising them, if the pure flame of patriotism have reached their bosoms, they should labour to improve the morals of their fellow-citizens, by teaching men, not only to respect modesty in women, but to acquire it themselves, as the

(70) only way to merit their esteem.

     Contending for the rights of woman, my main argument is built on this simple principle, that if she be not prepared by education to become the companion of man,

(75) she will stop the progress of knowledge and virtue; for truth must be common to all, or it will be inefficacious with respect to its influence on general practice. And how can woman be expected to co-operate unless she

(80) know why she ought to be virtuous? Unless freedom strengthen her reason till she comprehend her duty, and see in what manner

GO ON TO THE NEXT PAGE. ➡

it is connected with her real good? If children
are to be educated to understand the true
(85) principle of patriotism, their mother must be a
patriot; and the love of mankind, from which
an orderly train of virtues spring, can only be
produced by considering the moral and civil
interest of mankind; but the education and
(90) situation of woman, at present, shuts her out
from such investigations.

In this work I have produced many
arguments, which to me were conclusive, to
prove that the prevailing notion respecting a
(95) sexual character was subversive of morality,
and I have contended, that to render the
human body and mind more perfect, chastity
must more universally prevail, and that
chastity will never be respected in the male
(100) world till the person of a woman is not, as it
were, idolized, when little virtue or sense
embellish it with the grand traces of mental
beauty, or the interesting simplicity of
affection.

(105) Consider, Sir, dispassionately, these
observations-for a glimpse of this truth
seemed to open before you when you
observed, 'that to see one half of the human
race excluded by the other from all
(110) participation of government, was a political
phenomenon that, according to abstract
principles, it was impossible to explain.' If so,
on what does your constitution rest? If the
abstract rights of man will bear discussion and
(115) explanation, those of woman, by a parity of
reasoning, will not shrink from the same test:
though a different opinion prevails in this
country, built on the very arguments which
you use to justify the oppression of woman—
(120) prescription.

Consider, I address you as a legislator,
whether, when men contend for their freedom,
and to be allowed to judge for themselves
respecting their own happiness, it be not
(125) inconsistent and unjust to subjugate women,
even though you firmly believe that you are

acting in the manner best calculated to
promote their happiness? Who made man the
exclusive judge, if woman partake with him
(130) the gift of reason?

34. The paragraphs in this passage are but an
introduction to a longer discourse that can
BEST be described as

(A) cause and effect
(B) personal narrative
(C) comparison and contrast
(D) extended definition
(E) rhetorical argumentation

35. In the first three paragraphs, Wollstonecraft
flatters her audience by

(A) assuring Talleyrand that she has read his
pamphlet (lines 5–6)
(B) considering independence a grand
blessing of life (lines 14–15)
(C) appealing to Talleyrand's "admiral
constitution" (lines 31–32)
(D) "respecting the rights and duties of
women" (lines 27–28)
(E) wishing "to see woman placed in a
station in which she would advance"
(lines 23–24)

36. In the second paragraph, the word
"independence" is used twice in the same
sentence, and in each case it is used as a(n)

(A) subject of the independent clause
(B) object of a preposition phrase
(C) predicate nominative of the independent
clause
(D) object of the independent clause verbs
(E) antecedent of a pronoun

37. The tone of the third paragraph could BEST
be described as

(A) hesitantly sanguine
(B) somewhat pessimistic
(C) somberly lugubrious
(D) reluctantly submissive
(E) willingly compromising

GO ON TO THE NEXT PAGE. ➡

38. In the fourth paragraph, the author argues that

    (A) the French people are morally conservative
    (B) the French and English are warm allies
    (C) Americans have had an influence on French manners
    (D) the French character has been damaged by excessive attention to sensual matters
    (E) in France certain types of behavior are illegal

39. In the fourth and fifth paragraphs, the author's position on chastity seems to be that

    (A) the women of France are models of chastity
    (B) the women of England are morally inferior
    (C) all men and women should have sexual liberty
    (D) women do not respect men who are chaste
    (E) until men behave chastely, women should not respect them

40. In the fifth paragraph, the author argues that

    (A) manners and morality are mutually exclusive
    (B) it is possible to be moral and have poor manners
    (C) it is impossible to be moral and have poor manners
    (D) poor manners reflect badly on moral people
    (E) manners are the outward images of morality

41. In line 58, the word "factitious" most closely means

    (A) factual
    (B) fictitious
    (C) produced by artificial means
    (D) false or inauthentic
    (E) competitive

42. In paragraphs 6 through 10, the author argues that

    (A) in order to participate fully in society, women must be educated in virtue
    (B) it is unfair for women to be subordinate to men
    (C) men are naturally superior to women
    (D) (A), (B), and (C)
    (E) (A) and (B) only

GO ON TO THE NEXT PAGE. ➡

Questions 43–50. Read the following passage carefully before you choose your answers.

The passage below is from *"Of Truth"* by Francis Bacon.

What is truth? said jesting Pilate, and would not stay for an answer. Certainly there be that delight in giddiness, and count it a bondage to
Line fix a belief; affecting free-will in thinking, as
(5) well as in acting. And though the sects of philosophers, of that kind be gone, yet there remain certain discoursing wits, which are of the same veins, though there be not so much blood in them as was in those of the ancients.
(10) But it is not only the difficulty and labor which men take in finding out of truth, nor again that when it is found it imposeth upon men's thoughts, that doth bring lies in favor; but a natural though corrupt love of the lie itself. One
(15) of the later school of the Grecians examineth the matter and is at a stand to think what should be in it, that men should love lies, where neither they make for pleasure, as with poets, nor for advantage, as with the merchant; but for the lie's
(20) sake. But I cannot tell; this same truth is a naked and open day-light, that doth not show the masks and mummeries and triumphs, of the world, half so stately and daintily as candle-lights. Truth may perhaps come to the price of a
(25) pearl, that showeth best by day; but it will not rise to the price of a diamond or carbuncle, that showeth best in varied lights. A mixture of a lie doth ever add pleasure. Doth any man doubt, that if there were taken out of men's minds vain
(30) opinions, flattering hopes, false valuations, imaginations as one would, and the like, but it would leave the minds of a number of men poor shrunken things, full of melancholy and indisposition, and unpleasing to themselves?
(35) One of the fathers, in great severity, called poesy *vinum doemonum* [devils' wine], because it filleth the imagination; and yet, it is but with the shadow of a lie. But it is not the lie that passeth through the mind, but the lie that sinketh
(40) in, and settleth in it, that doth the hurt; such as we spake of before. But howsoever these things are thus in men's depraved judgments and affections, yet truth, which only doth judge itself, teacheth that the inquiry of truth, which is
(45) the love-making or wooing of it, the knowledge of truth, which is the presence of it, and the belief of truth, which is the enjoying of it, is the sovereign good of human nature. The first creature of God, in the works of the days, was
(50) the light of the sense; the last was the light of reason; and his sabbath work ever since is the illumination of his Spirit. First he breathed light upon the face of the matter or chaos; then he breathed light into the face of man; and still he
(55) breatheth and inspireth light into the face of his chosen. The poet that beautified the sect that was otherwise inferior to the rest, saith yet excellently well: It is a pleasure to stand upon the shore and to see ships tossed upon the sea; a
(60) pleasure to stand in the window of a castle and to see a battle and the adventures thereof below: but no pleasure is comparable to the standing upon the vantage ground of truth (a hill not to be commanded, and where the air is always
(65) clear and serene), and to see the errors and wanderings and mists and tempests in the vale below; so always that this prospect be with pity, and not with swelling or pride. Certainly, it is heaven upon earth, to have a man's mind move
(70) in charity, rest in providence, and turn upon the poles of truth.

To pass from theological and philosophical truth to the truth of civil business; it will be acknowledge, even by those that practise it not,
(75) that clear and round dealing, is the honor of man's nature; and that mixture of falsehoods is like alloy in coin of gold and silver, which may make the metal work the better, but it embaseth it. For these winding and crooked courses are
(80) the goings of the serpent; which goeth basely upon the belly, and not upon the feet. There is no vice that doth so cover a man with shame as to be found false and perfidious. And therefore Montaigne saith prettily, when he inquired the

GO ON TO THE NEXT PAGE. ➡

(85) reason why the word of the lie should be such a disgrace and such an odious charge. Saith he, If it be well weighed, to say that a man lieth, is as much to say as that he is brave towards God, and a coward towards men. For a lie faces God, *(90)* and shrinks from man. Surely the wickedness of falsehood and breach of faith cannot possibly be so highly expressed, as in that it shall be the last peal to call the judgments of God upon the generations of men; it being foretold that when *(95)* Christ cometh, he shall not find faith upon the earth.

43. In the second sentence, "there be" refers to

(A) a certain delight in giddiness
(B) people who fix beliefs
(C) people who take pleasure in truth
(D) people who enjoy telling lies and find truth restrictive
(E) criminals

44. In the phrase "And though the sects of philosophers of that kind be gone" (lines 5–6), "that kind" refers to

(A) philosophers who like to lie for fun
(B) Stoics
(C) believers in "free-will in thinking"
(D) ancient Greek doctors
(E) Bacon's contemporaries

45. The tone of the passage is BEST described as

(A) sarcastic
(B) confident and didactic
(C) depressed
(D) humorous
(E) combative

46. In the last two sentences of paragraph 1 (lines 27–34), the author implies that

(A) there are degrees of lies
(B) some lies can be beneficial
(C) a lie is always preferable to the truth
(D) the truth is always preferable to a lie
(E) (A) and (B)

47. From lines 62–71 ("no pleasure is comparable . . . upon the poles of truth."), it can be inferred that

(A) while the author may find some lies important, truth is superior
(B) truth allows one to see clearly
(C) truth engenders pity
(D) looking upon the world with an understanding of truth leads to peace
(E) all of the above

48. The phrase " . . . and that mixture of falsehoods, is like alloy in coin of gold and silver, which may make the metal work the better, but it embaseth it" (lines 76–79) is an example of

(A) high diction
(B) simile
(C) metaphor
(D) alliteration
(E) satire

49. The word "embaseth" (line 78) most likely means

(A) to improve
(B) to steal
(C) to enrich
(D) to edify
(E) to lessen the value by introducing impurities

50. "For these winding and crooked courses, are the goings of the serpent; which goeth basely upon the belly, and not upon the feet." This sentence (lines 79–81) is an example of

(A) alliteration
(B) simile
(C) metaphor
(D) antithesis
(E) metonymy

END OF SECTION I

GO ON TO THE NEXT PAGE. ➡

Section II: Free-Response Questions

Time: 2 hours

Number of questions: 3

Percent of total grade: 55

Directions: This section contains three essay questions. Answer all three questions, budgeting your time carefully.

GO ON TO THE NEXT PAGE. ➡

KAPLAN

Question One

(Suggested Time—40 minutes. Your response will count toward
one-third of your total score on this section of the exam.)

Read the following passage from Mark Twain's *Is Shakespeare Dead?* Then write an essay that analyzes how Twain uses rhetorical strategies and stylistic devices to convey his attitude toward Shakespeare's literary reputation.

For seven years after Shakespeare's death nobody seems to have been interested in him. Then the quarto was published, and Ben
Line Jonson awoke out of his long indifference and
(5) sang a song of praise and put it in the front of the book. Then silence fell AGAIN.

For sixty years. Then inquiries into Shakespeare's Stratford life began to be made, of Stratfordians. Of Stratfordians who had
(10) known Shakespeare or had seen him? No. Then of Stratfordians who had seen people who had known or seen people who had seen Shakespeare? No. Apparently the inquiries were only made of Stratfordians who were not
(15) Stratfordians of Shakespeare's day, but later comers; and what they had learned had come to them from persons who had not seen Shakespeare; and what they had learned was not claimed as FACT, but only as legend—dim
(20) and fading and indefinite legend;
legend of the calf-slaughtering rank, and not worth remembering either as history or fiction.

Has it ever happened before—or since— that a celebrated person who had spent exactly
(25) half of a fairly long life in the village where he was born and reared, was able to slip out of this world and leave that village voiceless and gossipless behind him—utterly voiceless, utterly gossipless? And permanently so? I
(30) don't believe it has happened in any case except Shakespeare's. And couldn't and wouldn't have happened in his case if he had been regarded as a celebrity at the time of his death.

(35) When I examine my own case—but let us do that, and see if it will not be recognizable as exhibiting a condition of things quite likely to result, most likely to result, indeed substantially SURE to result in the case of a
(40) celebrated person, a benefactor of the human race. Like me.

My parents brought me to the village of Hannibal, Missouri, on the banks of the Mississippi, when I was two and a half years
(45) old. I entered school at five years of age, and drifted from one school to another in the village during nine and a half years. Then my father died, leaving his family in exceedingly straitened circumstances; wherefore my book-
(50) education came to a standstill forever, and I became a printer's apprentice, on board and clothes, and when the clothes failed I got a hymn-book in place of them. This for summer wear, probably. I lived in Hannibal fifteen and
(55) a half years, altogether, then ran away, according to the custom of persons who are intending to become celebrated. I never lived there afterward. Four years later I became a "cub" on a Mississippi steamboat in the St.
(60) Louis and New Orleans trade, and after a year and a half of hard study and hard work the U.S. inspectors rigorously examined me through a couple of long sittings and decided that I knew every inch of the Mississippi—
(65) thirteen hundred miles—in the dark and in the day—as well as a baby knows the way to its mother's paps day or night. So they licensed me as a pilot—knighted me, so to speak—and I rose up clothed with authority, a responsible
(70) servant of the United States government.

GO ON TO THE NEXT PAGE. ➡

Now then. Shakespeare died young—he was only fifty-two. He had lived in his native village twenty-six years, or about that. He died celebrated (if you believe everything you (75) read in the books). Yet when he died nobody there or elsewhere took any notice of it; and for sixty years afterward no townsman remembered to say anything about him or about his life in Stratford. When the inquirer (80) came at last he got but one fact—no, LEGEND—and got that one at second hand, from a person who had only heard it as a rumor, and didn't claim copyright in it as a production of his own. He couldn't, very well, (85) for its date antedated his own birth-date. But necessarily a number of persons were still alive in Stratford who, in the days of their youth, had seen Shakespeare nearly every day in the last five years of his life, and they (90) would have been able to tell that inquirer some first-hand things about him if he had in those last days been a celebrity and therefore a person of interest to the villagers. Why did not the inquirer hunt them up and interview them? (95) Wasn't it worth while? Wasn't the matter of sufficient consequence? Had the inquirer an engagement to see a dog-fight and couldn't spare the time?

It all seems to mean that he never had any (100) literary celebrity, there or elsewhere, and no considerable repute as actor and manager.

Now then, I am away along in life—my seventy-third year being already well behind me—yet SIXTEEN of my Hannibal (105) schoolmates are still alive to-day, and can tell—and do tell—inquirers dozens and dozens of incidents of their young lives and mine together; things that happened to us in the morning of life, in the blossom of our (110) youth, in the good days, the dear days, "the days when we went gipsying, a long time ago." Most of them creditable to me, too. One child to whom I paid court when she was five years old and I eight still lives in Hannibal,

(115) and she visited me last summer, traversing the necessary ten or twelve hundred miles of railroad without damage to her patience or to her old-young vigor. Another little lassie to whom I paid attention in Hannibal when she (120) was nine years old and I the same, is still alive—in London—and hale and hearty, just as I am. And on the few surviving steamboats—those lingering ghosts and remembrancers of great fleets that plied the (125) big river in the beginning of my water-career—which is exactly as long ago as the whole invoice of the life-years of Shakespeare number—there are still findable two or three river-pilots who saw me do creditable things (130) in those ancient days; and several white-headed engineers; and several roustabouts and mates; and several deck-hands who used to heave the lead for me and send up on the still night air the "six—feet—SCANT!" that made (135) me shudder, and the "M-a-r-k—twain!" that took the shudder away, and presently the darling "By the d-e-e-p—four!" that lifted me to heaven for joy.

They know about me, and can tell. And so (140) do printers, from St. Louis to New York; and so do newspaper reporters, from Nevada to San Francisco. And so do the police. If Shakespeare had really been celebrated, like me, Stratford could have told things about (145) him; and if my experience goes for anything, they'd have done it.

GO ON TO THE NEXT PAGE. ➡

Question Two

(Suggested Time—40 minutes. Your response will count toward
one-third of your total score on this section of the exam.)

Read the following fictional narrative from *Mary Barton* by Elizabeth Gaskell (1810–1865), written in 1848
when she was a minister's wife in Manchester, England. In a well-organized essay, analyze how rhetorical
devices (such as language, imagery, diction, and syntax) used in the description of John Barton enable the
reader to understand Gaskell's attitude toward the plight of the English mill workers.

Among these few was John Barton. At all
times it is a bewildering thing to the poor
weaver to see his employer removing from
Line house to house, each one grander than the last,
(5) till he ends in building one more magnificent
than all, or withdraws his money from the
concern, or sells his mill, to buy an estate in
the country, while all the time the weaver, who
thinks he and his fellows are the real makers
(10) of this wealth, is struggling on for bread for
his children, through the vicissitudes of
lowered wages, short hours, fewer hands
employed, etc. And when he knows trade is
bad, and could understand (at least partially)
(15) that there are not buyers enough in the market
to purchase the goods already made, and
consequently that there is no demand for
more; when he would bear and endure much
without complaining, could he also see that
(20) his employers were bearing their share; he is, I
say, bewildered and (to use his own word)
"aggravated" to see that all goes on just as
usual with the millowners. Large houses are
still occupied, while spinners' and weavers'
(25) cottages stand empty, because the families that
once filled them are obliged to live in rooms
or cellars. Carriages still roll along the streets,
concerts are still crowded by subscribers, the
shops for expensive luxuries still find daily
(30) customers, while the workman loiters away
his unemployed time in watching these things,
and thinking of the pale, uncomplaining wife
at home, and the wailing children asking in
vain for enough of food—of the sinking
(35) health, of the dying life of those near and dear

to him. The contrast is too great. Why should
he alone suffer from bad times?

John Barton's parents had suffered; his
mother had died from absolute want of the
(40) necessaries of life. He himself was a good,
steady workman, and, as such, pretty certain
of steady employment. But he spent all he got
with the confidence (you may also call it
improvidence) of one who was willing, and
(45) believed himself able, to supply all his wants
by his own exertions. And when his master
suddenly failed, and all hands in the mill were
turned back, one Tuesday morning, with the
news that Mr. Hunter had stopped, Barton had
(50) only a few shillings to rely on; but he had
good heart of being employed at some other
mill, and accordingly, before returning home,
he spent some hours in going from factory to
factory, asking for work. But at every mill was
(55) some sign of depression of trade! some were
working short hours, some were turning off
hands, and for weeks Barton was out of work,
living on credit. It was during this time that
his little son, the apple of his eye, the
(60) cynosure of all his strong power of love, fell
ill of the scarlet fever. They dragged him
through the crisis, but his life hung on a
gossamer thread. Everything, the doctor said,
depended on good nourishment, on generous
(65) living, to keep up the little fellow's strength,
in the prostration in which the fever had left
him. Mocking words! when the commonest
food in the house would not furnish one little
meal. Barton tried credit; but it was worn out
(70) at the little provision shops, which were now

GO ON TO THE NEXT PAGE. ➡

suffering in their turn. He thought it would be
no sin to steal, and would have stolen; but he
could not get the opportunity in the few days
the child lingered. Hungry himself, almost to

(75) an animal pitch of ravenousness, but with the
bodily pain swallowed up in anxiety for his
little sinking lad, he stood at one of the shop
windows where all edible luxuries are
displayed; haunches of venison, Stilton

(80) cheeses, moulds of jelly—all appetising sights
to the common passer-by. And out of this shop
came Mrs. Hunter! She crossed to her
carriage, followed by the shopman loaded
with purchases for a party. The door was

(85) quickly slammed to, and she drove away; and
Barton returned home with a bitter spirit of
wrath in his heart to see his only boy a corpse!

GO ON TO THE NEXT PAGE.

Question Three

(Suggested Time—40 minutes. Your response will count toward
one-third of your total score on this section of the exam.)

Few leaders have had as much impact upon the American consciousness as the late civil rights leader Martin Luther King Jr. Dr. King was, perhaps, the major influence on the Civil Rights movement of the late '50s and the '60s. Tragically assassinated in 1968, his legacy lives on. The following is one of many of King's strong beliefs:

"The ultimate measure of a man is not where he stands in moments of comfort and convenience, but where he stands in times of challenge and controversy."

In a well-organized essay, defend, challenge, or qualify King's belief that controversy and/or challenge are what bring out the true side of us. Base your response on your reading, experience, or observations.

END OF EXAMINATION

Practice Test I
Answers and Explanations

ANSWER KEY

1. C	21. B	41. D
2. B	22. C	42. E
3. E	23. B	43. D
4. B	24. B	44. C
5. D	25. C	45. B
6. E	26. C	46. E
7. B	27. D	47. E
8. A	28. C	48. B
9. C	29. E	49. E
10. B	30. C	50. C
11. C	31. D	
12. A	32. E	
13. B	33. A	
14. C	34. E	
15. B	35. A	
16. D	36. D	
17. A	37. A	
18. A	38. D	
19. B	39. E	
20. C	40. E	

PRACTICE TEST I
COMPUTE YOUR SCORE

Remember not to take any score on the practice test too literally. There is no way to determine precisely what your AP grade will be because:

- The conditions under which you take the practice test will not exactly mirror real test conditions.
- While the multiple-choice questions are scored by computer, the free-response questions are graded manually by faculty consultants. You will not be able to accurately grade your own essays.

Section I: Multiple-Choice

Number Correct ☐ – (¼ × Number Wrong*) ☐ = ☐ × 1.296 = ☐ = Multiple-Choice Raw Score

*Do not include questions left blank.

Section II: Free-Response

Question 1: (out of 9 points possible) ☐ × 2.933 = ☐

Question 2: (out of 9 points possible) ☐ × 2.933 = ☐

Question 3: (out of 9 points possible) ☐ × 2.933 = ☐

Total Questions 1, 2, and 3 = ☐ = Free-Response Raw Score

Composite Score

Section I Multiple-Choice Score ☐ + Section II Free-Response Score ☐ = ☐ = Composite Score

CONVERSION CHART	
Composite Score Range**	**AP Grade**
114–144	5
88–113	4
67–87	3
40–66	2
0–39	1

Section I: Multiple-Choice Questions

Questions 1–13

1. (C)

The speaker is clearly indignant at the condition of slavery and the general perception of John Brown as crazy or a criminal. There is nothing gleeful or sarcastic in the tone, and the language is sophisticated, not plain. The speaker is quite respectful to John Brown, but not reverent.

2. (B)

The speaker alludes to Christ's clearing the temple of moneylenders.

3. (E)

The speaker is impressed with Brown's ability to proceed and plan for months, "without expecting any reward but a good conscience, while almost all America stood ranked on the other side." Of all the choices, noble (E) is the most appropriate.

4. (B)

The primary appeal is to the emotions: "They who are continually shocked by slavery have some right to be shocked by the violent death of the slaveholder, but no others. Such will be more shocked by his life than by his death."

5. (D)

The speaker's argument is that very few men live fully, including some American heroes. A true death can only be had by living fully and fighting for a just cause.

6. (E)

The simile comparing men to fungi is a thorough one; like fungi, many men accomplish very little, breaking down rather than building up, and living off the dead.

7. (B)

Anaphora is a form of repetition in which a word or phrase is repeated at the beginning of a series of poetic lines or sentences. The repeated use of "Look at the . . . " in a series of sentences is anaphora.

8. (A)

While all of the words may seem to apply well either to man or to fungus, only (A) contains the sense of both decomposing and liquefying that would carry through the analogy for both.

9. (C)

The groups listed as supporting the kind of violence the speaker discusses are groups known for being nonviolent, but also committed to ending injustice. The only violence that could be supported by such people would be putting one's life at risk in a noble cause.

10. (B)

Because the speaker respects the Quakers, his rhetorical intention cannot be sarcasm (A) or humor (C). However, there is an intentional use of irony (B): the irony of the nonviolent advocating a form of violence. This is not antithesis (E), which would require the direct use of two opposites.

11. (C)

The speaker addresses those who would wish to follow the example of living fully and standing up to injustice.

12. (A)

Although the most familiar definition of the word "advertise" is *to sell*, this meaning is clearly not intended in this context. Of the others, only (A) makes sense in the context of the sentence.

13. (B)

The Latin phrase *"Memento mori!"* means "Remember death!" Reading the two sentences that follow the expression should put it in context ("we've forgotten how to die").

Questions 14–23

14. (C)

While it is true that Coleridge and Southey are generally known to be poets, it cannot be inferred from this passage that they, for example, are not merely critics of poetry associated with "what is called, very foolishly, the Lake School." It is clear that they are associated with it from the first paragraph. There is nothing in the paragraph to indicate that they are associated with any of the other categories.

15. (B)

The speaker implies that, although at one time he would have found it necessary to formally refute the doctrine of the Lake School, now it would be unnecessary.

16. (D)

The speaker presents contrary ideas in the same sentence: that while "the wise must bow to the wisdom of such men as Coleridge and Southey, but being wise, have laughed at poetical theories so prosaically exemplified." While some in the critical community apparently recognize Coleridge and Southey as "wise," the speaker is apparently not among this group. The laughter suggested in this passage appears to be more sardonic than humorous, because it is at the expense of the two poetic critics.

17. (A)

The speaker implies that Wordsworth's opinion that the end (objective) of poetry should be instruction, while the speaker's opinion is that the end of poetry should be pleasure.

18. (A)

The speaker uses logic to reach the conclusions that the opinions of Wordsworth and Coleridge are erroneous and outdated.

19. (B)

The speaker frequently uses Latin phrases to indicate a certain level of education. The speaker does not use puns (D) or oxymorons (A), quote Shakespeare (E), or praise other critics (C).

20. (C)

While he has some praise and criticism for both Wordsworth and Coleridge, he states that Coleridge "goes wrong by reason of his very profundity . . ." whereas "as to Wordsworth, I have no faith in him." He does not mention Southey other than as a reference; Aristotle is a philosopher, not a poet; Barrington is a master pickpocket, not a poet.

21. (B)

The speaker mentions Southey only in passing, while he discusses Wordsworth and Coleridge in detail.

22. (C)

The speaker's reference to the old Goths illustrates his main complaint against Wordsworth: the poet lacks, in the speaker's opinion, depth of passion; his judgment is "too correct."

23. (B)

The speaker here uses a mythological allusion to support his claim that truth and wisdom are not found in the same way: poetical truth is to be found in the "huge abysses where wisdom is sought—not in the palpable palaces where she (wisdom) is found." According to the speaker, poetical truth is found through passion, not through contemplation.

Questions 24–33

24. (B)

Choice (B) best summarizes the intent of the first paragraph. Lines 3–5, 10–12, and 23–27 best support this as the BEST response. All of the other possible responses have a bit of validity, but none is the *best* response. In many questions such as this, the AP test will rarely offer you responses that are ridiculously not correct. Instead, you must choose from bits of truth to discover the one response that *best* answers the question.

25. (C)

Onomatopoeia, or words whose pronunciation sounds like the noise they are naming—such as *buzz, zip, whir*, etc.—is not present in paragraph one. Analogy (A) can be found in lines 6–9 in the discussion of corn, or goodness, only being available through the proper treatment of that "plot of ground," our own life, that we are given to till. In other words, we must make the best of what we are given in order to enjoy the goodness that is available everywhere. Antithesis, or contradiction (B), is most obvious in lines 27–28 when Emerson talks about the "deliverance that does not deliver." Alliteration (D) is present within several lines of this passage, including the "n" sound in lines 9–10 as well as in other lines. Parallel structure (E) can be found early in the paragraph with the repetition of short choppy clauses in lines 3–5. Parallel syntax is also evident within the last sentence of the first paragraph.

26. (C)

In lines 2–3 analogies appear: "envy is ignorance" and "imitation is suicide." These are neither metaphors nor similes, which require a figurative comparison between two seemingly different things, usually between abstract ideas and concrete objects, with similes using "like" or "as." The speaker implies a more direct relationship than either metaphor or simile.

27. (D)

When the speaker claims that "God will not have his work made manifest by cowards," he is referring to the cowardly way in which "we but half express ourselves." Doing one's best leads to being "relieved and gay . . ." but doing less than that "shall give him no peace."

28. (C)

The only *grammatical* shift among the choices is when the speaker begins to refer to the reader as "you." Frequency of mentioning God (A) or discussing Chaos and Dark (B), children, babies, and animals (D), or youth against old age (E) are not grammatical shifts.

29. (E)

The "so" in the third sentence of the second paragraph refers to what is done, or rather the action performed in the second sentence, which is accepting the place found for oneself by divine providence. It cannot refer to what follows. The great men have "confided themselves childlike to the genius of their age"; in other words, they have accepted their place in time, trusting, "childlike," or as a child would, in the outcome. The phrase "betraying their perception that the absolutely trustworthy was seated at their heart, working through their hands" means that the great men show to the world their confidence in their virtue, and that virtue shows in the work of their hands. They are definitely "not minors and invalids in a protected corner," but "guides, redeemers, and benefactors, obeying the Almighty effort, and advancing on Chaos and the Dark."

30. (C)

Antithesis is a figure of speech in which one term or series of terms is balanced against an opposing term or series of terms. In this case the three negative images that great men are not (minors, invalids, and cowards) are balanced against the positive images that truly represent great men (guides, redeemers, and benefactors). There is no onomatopoeia (words that sound like the sounds they represent), apostrophe (direct address of a person or a personified concept), or allusion (historical or literary reference). Antithesis and anaphora are both types of parallelism, with anaphora lacking the opposing nature.

31. (D)

Lines 52–53 state that a child's "eye is as yet unconquered" because children's minds are whole, not divided, as the minds of adults are. Children, according to the speaker, have not yet learned distrust and doubt as adults have. Children, babies, and animals are still capable of trust.

32. (E)

Emerson is exhorting, or encouraging, men to trust their own genius, to seek for answers within themselves, to trust their own ideas. Choices (B) and (C) are antithetical to the general philosophy of Emerson, and while (A) is in accordance with his transcendental philosophy, it is not the subject of this particular passage. (D) could be considered to be mentioned in the final paragraph when Emerson states "Bashful or bold, then, he [youth, personified as a single child] will know how to make us seniors very unnecessary." However, this is not the essence of this passage.

33. (A)

Emerson intends to encourage us to trust our individual vision and genius, or our own particular understanding of what is right and true. This piece has nothing to do with joining the community of man (B) or being totally independent and unconcerned by those who depend on us (C); nor is it a plea for us to recognize God within each other (D). It is also more specific than a philosophical musing about our own individual position within the universe (E).

Questions 34–42

34. (E)

This discourse could best be described as rhetorical argumentation (E). In it, the author, Mary Wollstonecraft, argues that there is no rational justification for the oppression of women. In the passage, she uses cause and effect (A), among other rhetorical devices, to establish her argument. Although she speaks presumably from personal experience when she describes the character of the French people, she does not use personal narrative (B) in the form of anecdotes to do so. She certainly uses comparison and contrast (C) to help establish her argument, by comparing the immorality of the French with the virtue of more "civilized" groups, as well as her discussion of manners and morals. There is no use of extended definition (D) in the passage.

35. (A)

In the opening line of her letter, Wollstonecraft assures Talleyrand that she has read "with great pleasure a pamphlet which you have recently published" and subsequently dedicates her volume to him. (C) is the only other choice which might possibly be construed as flattering Talleyrand, but it is actually directed not at his, but at France's, "admirable constitution." Choices (B), (D), and (E) have nothing to do with flattery.

36. (D)

The subject of each of the independent clauses containing the word "independence" is "I." If the syntax is more traditionally arranged, this becomes clear: "I have long considered independence as the grand blessing of life . . . I will ever secure independence by contracting my wants . . ." Therefore, the word "independence" is used in both cases as the direct object, or object of the verb.

KAPLAN

37. (A)

Wollstonecraft's tone seems somewhat hopeful; the key to this is the last sentence of the paragraph: "My opinion, indeed, respecting the rights and duties of woman, seems to flow so naturally from these simple principles, that I think it scarcely possible, but that some of the enlarged minds who formed your admirable constitution, will coincide with me."

38. (D)

Wollstonecraft makes several references to the sophistication of the French in sensual matters to the detriment of their national character—for example, read the last sentence: "And, modesty, the fairest garb of virtue has been more grossly insulted in France than even in England, till their women have treated as prudish that attention to decency, which brutes instinctively observe." There is no mention of the political relationship between England and France (B), or of Americans at all (C). There is no discussion of the French penal code (E), and Wollstonecraft finds the French people the opposite of morally conservative (A).

39. (E)

Wollstonecraft spends these paragraphs establishing the value of what she considers "moral behavior" in men and women. Choices (A) through (D) are all opposites of her position. In the last sentence of the paragraph, she states "if the pure flame of patriotism have reached their bosoms, they [women] should labour to improve the morals of their fellow-citizens, by teaching men, not only to respect modesty in women, but to acquire it themselves, as the only way to merit their esteem."

40. (E)

Wollstonecraft states that "Manners and morals are so nearly allied that they have often been confounded; but, though the former [manners] should only be the natural reflection of the latter,

yet, when various causes have produced factitious and corrupt manners, which are very early caught, morality becomes an empty name." Thus, manners, which may develop from poor morals, serve to reinforce and propagate those morals.

41. (D)

Both (C) and (D) are literal definitions of the word "factitious," but (D) makes more sense in the context of the reading. (A) and (B) are partial homophones, and (E) is not related in any way.

42. (E)

Wollstonecraft seems to feel in this piece that women are generally morally superior to men, although the women of France have fallen prey to the general licentiousness of French culture. She explicitly makes points (A) and (B) in the last paragraph: "Consider, I address you as a legislator, whether, when men contend for their freedom, and to be allowed to judge for themselves respecting their own happiness, it be not inconsistent and unjust to subjugate women, even though you firmly believe that you are acting in the manner best calculated to promote their happiness? Who made man the exclusive judge, if woman partake with him the gift of reason?"

Questions 43–50

43. (D)

The subject of the sentence should be a collective noun that describe the group of individuals "that delight in giddiness, and count it a bondage to fix a belief; affecting free-will in thinking, as well as in acting." These individuals delight in the giddiness of lying; "fixing a belief" is a form of bondage to these individuals.

44. (C)

Bacon claims that, while sects philosophers who believe in free will in thinking are gone, individuals continue to argue similar things, although not as forcefully as the ancients. (A) is similar in meaning, but (C) is more specific. There is no mention of Stoics, ancient Greek doctors, or Bacon's contemporaries.

45. (B)

The tone is that of an individual who is certain of his position, and is delivered in an instructive manner. There is no use of sarcasm (A) or humor (D). It is not combative (E), because Bacon does not give his opponents the consideration of equal combatants.

46. (E)

Neither (C) nor (D) is correct, since Bacon implies that lies, especially the petty self-deceptions that fuel our egos, can be beneficial (B), and that there is a difference between the lie that passes through the mind does not damage it and the lie that sinks in the mind, which does real damage. This difference in degree supports (A).

47. (E)

Read the cited lines carefully. Here, Bacon is inferring that truth is superior to falsehood (A), and brings with it clarity (B) and pity (C). He also discusses the peace (D) and serenity felt when "standing upon the vantage ground of truth." So all of the statements are correct (E).

48. (B)

The "mixture of falsehoods" is set into a comparison with an "alloy . . . of gold and silver," using "like," which makes it a simile. If the same comparison had been used without "like," it would be a metaphor. There is no use of satire (E), the diction is not particularly elevated (A), and there is no alliteration (D).

49. (E)

An alloy is a mixture of different types of metals. Since gold and silver are considered to be the most valuable metals, any other metal alloyed with gold and silver would decrease their value, by introducing impurities. Although "embaseth" is an archaic word, it shares a root with the word "debase," and is synonymous with it.

50. (C)

The metaphor is the direct comparison of the "winding and crooked courses" with "the goings of the serpent." There is no alliteration, antithesis, or metonymy. A simile would require the use of the words "like" or "as."

SECTION II: FREE-RESPONSE QUESTIONS

Question One: Twain's Evaluation of Shakespeare

Analysis of Question One

Students should delight in exploring this passage by Mark Twain. True to Twain's literary style, there is far more here than what can be seen on the surface of the passage. Twain lures us in subtly and cleverly. He first mentions that Shakespeare passed from this world without much interest from anyone save a brief mention by Ben Jonson about seven years after Shakespeare's death. Then there was silence for sixty years! Like a good mystery writer, Twain tweaks our curiosity with this casual mention of Shakespeare's apparent anonymity. In fact, it was only long after his death that people who seemingly knew nothing about him finally began creating the Shakespeare legend. And if Twain is to be believed, what we know about Shakespeare is much like Greek mythology—less than 10% fact and the rest complete fabrication.

Much of the rest of this passage is pure Mark Twain—his humor, his competent control of language, his clever, egotistical self. Only once in the middle of the passage does Twain return to Shakespeare, and that is only to say that no one really knows anything about him. He sums it up by saying "It all seems to mean that he never had any literary celebrity, there or elsewhere, and no considerable repute as actor and manager." He concludes his passage by returning to his favorite subject, Mark Twain.

At face value, students might be tempted to say that Twain didn't think much of Shakespeare as a literary giant at all. Some students might choose that route, and from this passage, they could develop this thesis with support and references. Others, however, may realize that it is the very fact that little is known about Shakespeare that makes him the literary celebrity that he has become. Mark Twain does not ever disappoint. Hopefully, successful AP English Language students will succeed as well.

Scoring Guide for Question One

9 Points: Essays scoring a 9 meet all the criteria for 8-point papers and are also particularly full or apt in analysis or demonstrate particular stylistic command.

8 Points: Essays earning a score of 8 effectively analyze how the rhetorical strategies and stylistic devices Twain uses convey his view of Shakespeare's literary reputation. The writer should recognize how specific strategies (such as tone, syntax, and diction) contribute to the writer's purpose. The prose of these essays demonstrates an ability to control a wide range of the elements of effective writing, but it is not flawless.

7 Points: Essays earning a score of 7 fit the description of 6-point essays but employ more complete analysis or more mature prose style.

6 Points: Essays earning a score of 6 adequately analyze how the rhetorical strategies and stylistic devices Twain uses achieve his purpose and make a persuasive case. They may discuss rhetorical elements such as diction or tone that contribute to the essay's effect, but their discussion may be incomplete. A few lapses in diction or syntax may be present, but in general the prose of 6 essays conveys their writers' ideas clearly.

5 Points: Essays earning a score of 5 develop their analysis of Twain's rhetorical strategies in a limited or inconsistent manner. The focus of these essays may be unclear or their analysis insufficiently developed. A few lapses in diction or syntax may be present, but usually the prose will convey their writers' ideas more or less clearly

4 Points: Essays earning a score of 4 inadequately respond to the task. Their analysis of rhetorical strategies and effectiveness is limited in accuracy or purpose. They may misunderstand the purpose of or paraphrase Twain's essay more than analyze it. The prose of 4-point essays may convey their writers' ideas adequately, but may suggest immature control over organization, diction, or syntax.

3 Points: Essays earning a score of 3 meet the criteria for 4-point essays but are less perceptive about how rhetorical strategies connect to purpose in Twain's essay or are less consistent in their control of elements of writing.

2 Points: Essays earning a score of 2 achieve little success in analyzing how rhetorical strategies contribute to the effectiveness of Twain's essay. These essays pay little attention to rhetorical features and generalize about, or seriously misread, tone or purpose. They may simply paraphrase or comment on Twain's essay without analyzing his strategies. The prose of 2-point papers often reveals consistent weakness in writing, a lack of development or organization, grammatical problems, or lack of control.

1 Point: Essays earning a score of 1 meet the criteria for a score of 2-point essays, but in addition are especially simplistic in their discussion or weak in controlling elements of language.

Sample Student Response to Question One

When we hear the name Mark Twain we often think of the clever writer who gave us Huck and Jim, Tom and Betsy. I remember reading a bit about him, though, and I recall that besides being a newspaper man for many years, he was somewhat the equivalent of today's stand-up comedian. All of those traits—fine writer, journalist (and a bit yellow at that), and comedian—come across in this passage. I think I detect at least one other trait as well.

The original piece was titled Is Shakespeare Dead? I do not think this has anything to do with the demise of Shakespeare's person. It is a question about whether as a celebrity, a "hero" possibly, is there any chance that he (Shakespeare) still lives. That is the question that Twain seems to be trying to answer.

Actually, Twain spends most of this essay talking about himself. Apparently he is one of his own favorite subjects. He assures us that HE must certainly be a "celebrated person, a benefactor of the human race."

He spends much time giving us his autobiography. He seeks our empathy when he tells us that his family was poor, especially after his father died. He was so poor, in fact, that when his clothes wore out, he "got a hymn-book in place of them." He amuses us by assuring us, that this was probably "for summer wear," not necessarily a year round condition. In this humorous vein he then tells us that at fifteen he ran away, "according to the custom of the persons who are intending to become celebrated." Again and again he reminds us, not so modestly, that he, at least, should be considered celebrated.

But what, then, is his attitude towards William Shakespeare's literary reputation? Well, to borrow from this so-called nobody of a writer, Shakespeare, I think that Twain "doth protest too much!" It is precisely because William Shakespeare lived a rather anonymous life, and that made him the literary giant that he has become. We know not when he was born, but I remember that there are records in Stratford of his baptism. Also, I can remember being amused that he left his wife for long periods of time, but they still managed to have children. At least I've never read or heard that he ever questioned their paternity. I also remember giggling over the fact that he willed this somewhat estranged wife his second-best bed—how odd. But someone wrote all those plays. Someone acted and owned part of the theaters he acted in. Someone also wrote a lot of sonnets with only numbers for titles. Maybe Shakespeare was a shy person growing up. Like many people, perhaps it was only through his writing and acting that he could express himself. Whatever the case, Shakespeare, the Bard of Avon, is certainly very much alive. His plays are presented all over the world in many formats. They've been written into novels and rewritten as movies, and they've even become the basis of Star Trek TV episodes. Shakespeare's work will always be alive, so Shakespeare is very definitely NOT dead.

I think that Mark Twain was a fine writer. His work is also read worldwide, but he will never be considered the universal bard that he so tries to deny. In fact, I think Twain new he would never, ever be as Alive as William Shakespeare. That's why he spends so much time trying to convince us, or at least convince himself, that Shakespeare was a nobody.

Commentary on Sample Student Response to Question One

Whether this student is an aspiring psychoanalyst or just a perceptive AP English student, he has truly written a successful essay in response to this first prompt.

The fact that Twain spends so much time NOT talking about Shakespeare is the very reason why Shakespeare is a living entity for Twain. In fact, this student indicates that there is a jealousy here, professional rivalry that poor Shakespeare can't even respond to! Most of the stylistic devices are implied. Very few specific strategies are discussed. Nevertheless, this is a successful response to this prompt.

The prose of this composition demonstrates outstanding composition skills. Tone is implied as Twain's humor is emphasized, and a clever perception of the possible truth of Twain's feelings are highlighted by the Shakespearean quote about protesting too much.

Although this response is heavy on analyzing Twain's underlying motive, the implicit discussion of the manipulation of rhetorical strategies by Twain cannot be ignored. The voice of this young writer is strong, and she demonstrates competent understanding and expression.

Some may say the most it might earn from the scoring guide would be a 6 since it lacks explicit discussion of specific rhetorical strategies. Others might argue that the implicit understanding and recognition of these strategies are so obvious as to certainly earn this response at least a 7. There is a lesson here for potential AP English writers. You do not have to spell everything out, but you always take a chance if you assume that the reader will automatically pick up on your intrinsic understanding. Doubtlessly, however, this is a very adequate response to this prompt, and this student has presented herself well.

Question Two: Describing John Barton

Analysis of Question Two

Students should have little trouble identifying Gaskell's (a la *Mary Barton*) attitude towards the plight of English mill workers in the middle of the 19th century. Manipulating the reader's emotion with the cathartic pathos reminiscent of Charles Dickens's *A Christmas Carol* (1843) or Victor Hugo's *Les Miserables* (1862), Gaskell makes it clear that it was a time of haves and have-nots. John Barton, hardworking weaver, was a have-not. By describing the extreme difficulties of just one man who finds himself out of work and desperate to save his family from starvation, Gaskell clearly demonstrates how unconscionable life was for the common mill workers whose very livelihood depended upon the whims of the rich and the realities of the alleyways.

Gaskell uses rich description in this fictional narrative. Strong verbs engage the reader in the struggle to survive. We can easily imagine one grand house after another on the fine avenues juxtaposed with overcrowded hovels overflowing with sick and starving children. Gaskell tells us "the contrast is too great."

John's life was never easy, but he was a "good, steady workman" who felt certain that he could always provide for himself and his family. He never anticipated the day when his willingness "to supply all his wants by his own exertions" would no longer be enough. His mill was closed, and others quickly showed "some sign of depression of trade." And so the sad story went. Gaskell uses this inside look into John Barton's despair to show readers the hopelessness pervasive during that time.

Though this is not a difficult prompt nor a particularly imperceptive reading, students must remember not only are they to analyze the John Barton story, but they are also to explain how this insight into one is actually insight into the lives of far too many. It is impossible not to be moved by such description. It is important, however, to see beyond the maudlin to the overall purpose of the passage. Gaskell uses a variety of rhetorical devices to develop this narrative, and AP English students should find this a challenging but very doable essay question.

Scoring Guide for Question Two

9 Points: Essays scoring a 9 meet all the criteria for 8-point papers and are also particularly full or apt in analysis or demonstrate particular stylistic command.

8 Points: Essays earning a score of 8 effectively analyze how the imagery, diction, tone, and other stylistic devices Gaskell employs effectively achieves her purpose of establishing a warm and sympathetic tone towards the mill workers. These essays are likely to recognize how specific strategies (such as tone, syntax, and diction) contribute to the reader's understanding of the writer's attitude. The prose of these essays demonstrates an ability to control a wide range of the elements of effective writing, but it is not flawless.

7 Points: Essays earning a score of 7 fit the description of 6-point essays but use more complete analysis or more mature prose style.

6 Points: Essays earning a score of 6 adequately analyze how the imagery, diction, tone, and other stylistic devices Gaskell uses to depict John Barton, help to establish her attitude towards mill workers of that era. They may discuss rhetorical elements such as diction or tone that contribute to the essay's effect, but their discussion may be incomplete. A few lapses in diction or syntax may be present, but in general the prose of 6-point essays conveys their writers' ideas clearly.

5 Points: Essays earning a score of 5 recognize Gaskell's attitude, but their development of the strategies she uses is limited or inconsistent. Their focus may be unclear or their analysis insufficiently developed. A few lapses in diction or syntax may be present, but usually the prose in 5-point essays conveys their writers' ideas more or less clearly.

4 Points: Essays earning a score of 4 inadequately respond to the task. Their analysis of rhetorical strategies and effectiveness in establishing attitude is limited in accuracy or purpose. They may misunderstand purpose or paraphrase Gaskell's writing more than analyze it. The prose of 4-point essays may convey their writers' ideas adequately, but may suggest immature control over organization, diction, or syntax.

3 Points: Essays earning a score of 3 meet the criteria for score of 4-point essays, but are less perceptive about how rhetorical strategies connect to purpose in Gaskell's essay or are less consistent in their control of elements of writing.

2 Points: Essays earning a score of 2 achieve little success in analyzing how rhetorical strategies contribute to establishing Gaskell's attitude. These essays pay little attention to rhetorical features and generalize about, or seriously misread, tone or purpose. They may simply paraphrase or comment on Gaskell's essay without analyzing her strategies or purpose. The prose of 2-point papers often reveals consistent weakness in writing, a lack of development or organization, grammatical problems, or lack of control.

1 Point: Essays earning a score of 1 meet the criteria for a 2-point essay, but in addition are especially simplistic in their discussion or weak in controlling elements of language.

Sample Student Response to Question Two

How can we not be touched by Tiny Tim at Christmas time? How can we not be moved by the street ruffian Oliver who gets adopted by a wealthy gentleman? And how can we not notice the contrasts between Oliver's before and after circumstances? In this fictional narrative passage outlining the desperate life a John Barton, Elizabeth Gaskell makes it clear to everyone that such a situation is unexcusable. She personalizes these deplorable conditions by detailing the terrible situation of just one mill employee.

Contrast is the most obvious stylistic device Gaskell uses. She talks about the mill owners moving from one house to another yet more grand. While "spinners' and weavers' cottages stand empty." John Barton sees the glutted market. In his peasant wisdom he recognizes that "there are not buyers enough," but he is not able to anticipate the consequences. In the beginning he feels secure that he is a good man, willing to work hard to provide for himself and his family. He was "one who was willing, and believed himself able, to supply all his wants by his own exertions."

When the mill closes and John finds himself out of work and desperate to save his starving family, the sense of contrast increases. He is ravenous, but there is not enough to feed even his failing son. In the meantime, he stares into the shops of the rich, "where all edible luxuries are displayed." Everything is there to feed him and save his child. However, the shops that might have given him credit during "good times" are themselves suffering from lack of provisions and having to close. Of course the shops of the wealthy would not even let him in the back door. A wealthy lady buys fancy foods for a party and Barton returns home to find his starving son has died. Contrast is a strong stylistic device in this passage by Gaskell.

In the description itself, Gaskell's choice of language and images is also very powerful. She likes to use a series of noun adjectives such as "lowered wages," "short hours," "fewer hands." Later she talks about "expensive luxuries," "daily customers" and so on.

The images evoked by contrast are also strong. The unemployed loiter about in misery. Over-large poor families must abandon crowded hovels for single, damp basement rooms because they are so desperate. In the meantime, the rich still attend parties and concerts, ride in carriages and shop for luxuries. Rich women sweep into luxury shops while pale, uncomplaining wives try to make one more meal from yesterday's soup bone.

Irony exists when John Barton's very frail son's only hope for survival is "good nourishment and generous living." Gaskell even tells us these are "mocking words." The mill owner's wife shops for luxury foods for a party that John Barton can only look at through the window. She goes home "loaded with purchases for a party." He goes home and finds his son has died. What stronger message could have been written than the one we get from this heart-wrenching story. As the passage says, "the contrast is too great."

For years people have been told stories or taught lessons from Bible parables, Greek myths, American folklore. Elizabeth Gaskell has created a similar instructional opportunity. Her attitude is one that says we ought to be ashamed that such inequities are allowed to exist. She skillfully demonstrates this attitude with John Barton's poignant story.

Commentary on Sample Student Response to Question Two

The prompt directs students to analyze how some of the rhetorical devices used to describe John Barton enable the reader to understand Gaskell's attitude towards the plight of the English mill workers in the mid-19th century. This essay successfully fulfills the tasks of the prompt.

The student's response begins by telling us that Gaskell's attitude was that conditions were deplorable, downright "unexcusable." (Even the best student essays are not without flaws.) Later in the composition, the essay discusses how this attitude can be seen in the contrasts that are described and by the story of one such mill worker, John Barton.

KAPLAN

This student has identified the strongest of the contrasts. He recognizes the irony of John's starving stare into the shop window where the wealthy mill owner's wife stocks up on party supplies. The essay even notes that John cannot even stoop to stealing, for the only shops he might steal from (shops of the common man) are in dire straights themselves—what irony!

Discussion of tone is implicit, while specific references to language are made. The essay response is also supported by appropriate references from the passage. An interesting point is made about John Barton's sense that the world of supply and demand is awry, but in his ignorance he is not able to anticipate how this will affect him and his family. Another notable feature of this essay is when the student notes that Gaskell's use of John Barton is not unlike the lessons one can learn from myths, folklore and Bible tales. Although this student does not take this analogy further, it nevertheless indicates that he recognizes that it is not really John Barton about whom Gaskell is concerned. There is a bigger picture that Gaskell wishes us to consider.

This student response fulfills all the characteristics of a 6 paper on the Scoring Rubric. In addition, this "analysis is fairly complete," furthermore it does "suggest a mature prose style" on the part of the student. Without a doubt this is an essay response that would garner at least a 7 from AP readers; some might even boost it up to an 8.

Question Three: Dr. King's Beliefs

Analysis of Question Three

Although most students will probably agree with Martin Luther King Jr. in their responses, the prompt does not insist on such compliance. Students may decide to challenge King's statement with arguments backed with experience or observation, or possibly from their reading. Regardless, most students will find quotation challenging, but not so difficult they will be unable to develop a response.

Students may find the easiest support for their essays by looking to their history lessons at some of the great leaders—George Washington did not shine until the Revolution loomed; Lincoln showed his best side while struggling with our nation's Civil War. Martin Luther King honed his own character when he confronted the social order that stood in the way of civil rights. New York City Mayor Giuliani demonstrated his mettle during the aftermath of September 11th. Countless leaders seem to have forged their character within the fires of the controversy or challenge that surrounded them.

Many outstanding writers such as Nathaniel Hawthorne, Jonathan Swift, Aldous Huxley, and George Orwell created their best writing in response to the controversy and challenge around them. Students will easily be able to think of many other examples with which to buttress their responses.

Scoring Guide for Question Three

9 Points: Essays earning a score of 9 meet the criteria for 8 responses, and, in addition, are especially sophisticated in their argument or demonstrate particularly impressive control of language.

8 Points: Essays earning a score of 8 successfully establish and support their position on whether or not a person's ultimate measure is best seen in times of challenge and controversy, using appropriate evidence. The prose of these essays demonstrates an ability to control a wide range of the elements of effective writing but is not flawless.

7 Points: Essays earning a score of 7 fit the description of 6 essays but are distinguished by more complete or more purposeful argumentation or by a more mature prose style.

6 Points: Essays earning a score of 6 adequately establish and support their position on whether a person's best measure is seen when he or she is amidst challenge and controversy. These arguments are generally sound and provide sufficient evidence, but they are less developed or less coherent than essays earning higher scores. The writing may contain lapses in diction or syntax, but generally the prose is clear.

5 Points: Essays earning a score of 5 establish and support their position on whether a person's character is best seen when he or she is amidst challenge and controversy, but their arguments may be inconsistent or unevenly developed. While the writing may contain lapses in diction or syntax, it usually conveys ideas adequately.

4 Points: Essays earning a score of 4 respond to the prompt inadequately. They may have difficulty establishing a position about a person's measure in times of challenge and controversy; they may use unconvincing evidence, or may be insufficiently developed. The prose generally conveys the writer's ideas but may suggest immature control of writing.

3 Points: Essays earning a score of 3 meet the criteria for the score of 4 but are less successful in developing their position or less consistent in controlling the elements of writing.

2 Points: Essays earning a score of 2 demonstrate little success in developing their position. These essays may fail to present an argument, substitute a simpler task such as summary, or respond with unrelated ideas or inappropriate evidence. The prose often demonstrates consistent weaknesses in writing.

1 Point: Essays earning a score of 1 meet the criteria for the score of 2 but are undeveloped, especially simplistic in their argument, or weak in their control of writing.

Sample Student Response to Question Three

Mary Shelley has always been my favorite author. In fact, I did my senior research project on her and her infamous <u>Frankenstein</u>. When I first read the quote by Martin Luther King in this prompt, I thought of using historical people to support my response. I considered FDR, or Churchill, or possibly even Anne Frank. Then I remembered my favorite author and realized that it was challenge and controversy that prompted Mary Shelley to write her famous book as well as to make a name for herself. Some even call her the mother of science fiction writing. Actually, more accurately, authors tend to call Frankenstein the father of science fiction. In fact it is this very mother vs. father contrast that is the root of all that made Mary Shelley what she was.

Mary Shelley was the daughter of a truly liberated mother, Mary Wollstonecraft, who married William Godwin only a couple months before the birth of their child. Since this was the late 1700s, Mary realized that having an illegitimate child would be unacceptable in that day and age. Nevertheless, Mary Wollstonecraft was a woman before her time, and although she died soon after her daughter's birth, apparently baby Mary inherited her mother's liberated genes. Her father was an indulgent parent who encouraged his daughter's independence and allowed her far more intellectual leeway than most women had during that era.

Mary was still a teenager when she ran away with her husband Percy Shelley. Not long after that she and her husband became friends with Lord Byron. The story goes that she was not to be left out of a writing contest between the men, a contest to see who could write the most horrific tale. She was not to be dissuaded from this venture. Remember, this was a time when women were to be seen and not heard. Whatever thoughts they had (if they even had any) were supposed to reflect the beliefs of their husbands. Mary Shelley lived a little before the time that the Bronte sisters gave themselves men's names to protect their own reputations when they published their first books, so for Mary to take on this project was out of character for a woman of her era.

The story itself can also be interpreted as an analogy for Mary's frustrated spirit. Frankenstein's creation is seen by many to be the monster nobody will appreciate (just as Mary's great talent unappreciated due to social conventions of her time). She creates the book—like Frankenstein did the monster—and it takes on a life of its own. But, it is not of that time and place so it finds itself alone and unloved, just as Mary's great intellectual spirit was not appreciated. Nevertheless, the monster had to be created—both Frankenstein's creature and Mary's book.

Challenge and controversy prompted Mary to write. She was not to be outdone by the men, and, in fact, hers was the only successful piece to come out of the writing contest. To add some insulting icing to this cake, her husband even wrote a preface to the first edition, and some interpret his words as a bit of an apology for the forwardness of this woman to have written such a book as Frankenstein. In fact, many early readers were sure that he had written the majority of the book while the "little woman" might have had something to do with the final copying. It is an attitude such as this that King meant when he said that a person's measure is best seen under challenge and controversy. For Mary Shelley, this is certainly the case. Many may call Frankenstein the father of science fiction, but, in reality, the truth is that Mary Shelley is the *mother* of science fiction.

Commentary on Sample Student Response to Question Three

Students could answer this prompt using any of a wide range of figures from history, fiction, or their own lives to support their arguments. Some might even choose to challenge Martin Luther King's belief, or, perhaps, qualify his statement. Nevertheless, this is a prompt that offers students the opportunity to be reflective and practical as well as creative. This particular student has done all of this and more.

The choice that this student made is unusual. Many great people have proven themselves in times of conflict, challenge, and controversy. The tragedy of September 11th certainly has shown us many such characters. History and literature are also rife with similar characters. Nevertheless, this student has chosen to write about an author who would ordinarily NOT be the first choice to come to most people's minds when applying King's quote, and it works.

One might ask how anyone would know such details to answer in this manner. The student quickly explains this in the introduction when she tells us about her research project. Any AP student will tell you that if you have researched someone for a paper, usually you end up feeling like you know the person and haven't simply read about him or her. And, indeed, Mary Shelley was a woman before her time who insisted on prevailing despite the social limitations placed upon women in that era. Even her husband was less than enthusiastic about her accomplishments. This student even gives us an historical perspective with the mentioning of the Bronte sisters.

The student essay carefully lays the groundwork for Mary Shelley as an example of what Martin Luther King may have been talking about. Mary Shelley's mother and father are mentioned, as is her elopement to Percy Shelley. This student response cleverly draws us into the argument by providing us with just enough background and information about Mary Shelley to pique our interest without bogging us down with too many details.

The student then talks about the story-writing contest, and how she was the only one of the three (the other two accomplished *male* writers) who created anything memorable as a result of the contest—so memorable, in fact, that *Frankenstein* is generally considered the watershed of science fiction literature. Challenge, controversy, and conflict seemed to have fueled Mary Shelley's creative muse, demonstrating her "ultimate measure."

The student's fourth paragraph is cleverly presented. She hints at the allegory of the story, teasing the reader with this analogy, but she refrains from rehashing what was probably a very strong section of her research project. Instead, she leaves us with something to think about without causing us to become distracted.

This student has also written a very successful conclusion to this essay. Unfortunately, under the time restraints of the AP exam, conclusions are often short-changed, but that is not the case here. Not only does this conclusion pull everything together, the student herself comes through with creative spirit by emphasizing that it is not *Frankenstein* who is the father of science fiction, but Mary Shelley who is its *mother*. This cleverly brings the reader back to the focus of the introductory paragraph.

Most AP readers would agree that this is a very successful student response essay. It would easily score an 8, for it successfully establishes and supports the argumentative position by using appropriate evidence about Mary Shelley the writer and a bit about her novel. In addition, this essay successfully demonstrates effective writing. Some AP readers might even consider this response good enough to earn a score of 9. This AP student has created not a monster, as did Dr. Frankenstein, but rather a very fine response to a challenging and thought-provoking prompt.

Practice Test II

How to Take This Test

Before taking this practice test, find a quiet place where you can work uninterrupted for three hours or so. Make sure you have a comfortable desk, several No. 2 pencils for the multiple-choice section, and a few ballpoint pens for the essay section.

This practice test includes a multiple-choice section and a free-response section consisting of three essay questions. Use the answer grid that follows to record your multiple-choice answers. Write the essays on a separate sheet of paper.

Once you start the practice test, don't stop until you've finished the multiple-choice section. You may then take a ten-minute break before proceeding to the essay section.

You'll find the answer key and explanations following the test.

Good luck!

PRACTICE TEST II
ANSWER SHEET

1 (A)(B)(C)(D)(E)   21 (A)(B)(C)(D)(E)   41 (A)(B)(C)(D)(E)

2 (A)(B)(C)(D)(E)   22 (A)(B)(C)(D)(E)   42 (A)(B)(C)(D)(E)

3 (A)(B)(C)(D)(E)   23 (A)(B)(C)(D)(E)   43 (A)(B)(C)(D)(E)

4 (A)(B)(C)(D)(E)   24 (A)(B)(C)(D)(E)   44 (A)(B)(C)(D)(E)

5 (A)(B)(C)(D)(E)   25 (A)(B)(C)(D)(E)   45 (A)(B)(C)(D)(E)

6 (A)(B)(C)(D)(E)   26 (A)(B)(C)(D)(E)   46 (A)(B)(C)(D)(E)

7 (A)(B)(C)(D)(E)   27 (A)(B)(C)(D)(E)   47 (A)(B)(C)(D)(E)

8 (A)(B)(C)(D)(E)   28 (A)(B)(C)(D)(E)   48 (A)(B)(C)(D)(E)

9 (A)(B)(C)(D)(E)   29 (A)(B)(C)(D)(E)   49 (A)(B)(C)(D)(E)

10 (A)(B)(C)(D)(E)   30 (A)(B)(C)(D)(E)   50 (A)(B)(C)(D)(E)

11 (A)(B)(C)(D)(E)   31 (A)(B)(C)(D)(E)

12 (A)(B)(C)(D)(E)   32 (A)(B)(C)(D)(E)

13 (A)(B)(C)(D)(E)   33 (A)(B)(C)(D)(E)

14 (A)(B)(C)(D)(E)   34 (A)(B)(C)(D)(E)

15 (A)(B)(C)(D)(E)   35 (A)(B)(C)(D)(E)

16 (A)(B)(C)(D)(E)   36 (A)(B)(C)(D)(E)

17 (A)(B)(C)(D)(E)   37 (A)(B)(C)(D)(E)

18 (A)(B)(C)(D)(E)   38 (A)(B)(C)(D)(E)

19 (A)(B)(C)(D)(E)   39 (A)(B)(C)(D)(E)

20 (A)(B)(C)(D)(E)   40 (A)(B)(C)(D)(E)

ENGLISH LANGUAGE AND COMPOSITION

Section I: Multiple-Choice Questions

Time: 1 hour

Number of questions: 50

Percent of total grade: 45

Directions: This section contains selections of prose works and questions on their content, style, and form. After reading each passage, select the best answer and fill it in on the corresponding oval on the answer sheet.

Questions 1–13. Read the following passage carefully before you choose your answers.

The passage below is from *"Concerning the Deity"* by Mark Twain.

. . . We may now skip eleven hundred and thirty or forty years, which brings us down to enlightened Christian times and the troubled days
Line of King Stephen of England. The augur
(5) [soothsayer] has had his day and has been long ago forgotten; the priest had fallen heir to his trade.

King Henry is dead; Stephen, that bold and outrageous person, comes flying over from Normandy to steal the throne from Henry's
(10) daughter. He accomplished his crime, and Henry of Huntington, a priest of high degree, mourns over it in his Chronicle. The Archbishop of Canterbury consecrated Stephen: "wherefore the Lord visited the Archbishop with the same judgment which he
(15) had inflicted upon him who struck Jeremiah the great priest: he died with a year."

Stephen's was the greater offense, but Stephen could wait; not so the Archbishop, apparently.

The kingdom was a prey to intestine wars;
(20) slaughter, fire, and rapine spread ruin throughout the land; cries of distress, horror, and woe rose in every quarter.

That was the result of Stephen's crime. These unspeakable conditions continued during nineteen
(25) years. Then Stephen died as comfortably as any man ever did, and was honorably buried. It makes one pity the poor Archbishop, and wish that he, too, could have been let off as leniently. How did Henry of Huntington know that the Archbishop

(30) was sent to his grave by judgment of God for consecrating Stephen? He does not explain. Neither does he explain why Stephen was awarded a pleasanter death than he was entitled to, while the aged King Henry, his predecessor, who had ruled
(35) England thirty-five years to the people's strongly worded satisfaction, was condemned to close his life in circumstances most distinctly unpleasant, inconvenient, and disagreeable. His was probably the most uninspiring funeral that is set down in
(40) history. There is not a detail about it that is attractive.

It seems to have been just the funeral for Stephen, and even at this far-distant day it is matter of just regret that by an indiscretion the wrong man
(45) got it. Whenever God punishes a man, Henry of Huntington knows why it was done, and tells us; and his pen is eloquent with admiration; but when a man has earned punishment, and escapes, he does not explain. He is evidently puzzled, but he
(50) does not say anything. I think it is often apparent that he is pained by these discrepancies, but loyally tries his best not to show it. When he cannot praise, he delivers himself of a silence so marked that a suspicious person could mistake it for suppressed
(55) criticism. However, he has plenty of opportunities to feel contented with the way things go—his book is full of them.

GO ON TO THE NEXT PAGE. ➡

King David of Scotland ". . . under color of religion caused his followers to deal most
(60) barbarously with the English. They ripped open women, tossed children on the points of spears, butchered priests at the altars, and, cutting off the heads from the images on crucifixes, placed them on the bodies of the slain, while in exchange they
(65) fixed on the crucifixes the heads of their victims. Wherever the Scots came, there was the same scene of horror and cruelty: women shrieking, old men lamenting, amid the groans of the dying and the despair of the living."
(70)   But the English got the victory.

"Then the chief of the men of Lothian fell, pierced by an arrow, and all his followers were put to flight. For the Almighty was offended at them and their strength was rent like a cobweb."
(75)   Offended at them for what? For committing those fearful butcheries? No, for that was the common custom on both sides, and not open to criticism. Then was it for doing the butcheries "under cover of religion"? No, that was not it;
(80) religious feeling was often expressed in that fervent way all through those old centuries. The truth is, He was not offended at "them" at all; He was only offended at their king, who had been false to an oath. Then why did not He put the punishment
(85) upon the king instead of upon "them"? It is a difficult question. One can see by the Chronicle that the "judgments" fell rather customarily upon the wrong person, but Henry of Huntington does not explain why. Here is one that went true; the
(90) chronicler's satisfaction in it is not hidden:

"In the month of August, Providence displayed its justice in a remarkable manner; for two of the nobles who had converted monasteries into fortifications, expelling the monks, their sin being
(95) the same, met with a similar punishment. Robert Marmion was one, Godfrey de Mandeville the other. Robert Marmion, issuing forth against the enemy, was slain under the walls of the monastery, being the only one who fell, though he was
(100) surrounded by his troops. Dying excommunicated, he became subject to death everlasting. In like manner Earl Godfrey was singled out among his followers, and shot with an arrow by a common foot-soldier. He made light of the wound, but he
(105) died of it in a few days, under excommunication. See here the like judgment of God, memorable through all ages!"

The exaltation jars upon me; not because of the death of the men, for they deserved that, but
(110) because it is death eternal, in white-hot fire and flame. It makes my flesh crawl. I have not known more than three men, or perhaps four, in my whole lifetime, whom I would rejoice to see writhing in those fires for even a year, let alone forever. I
(115) believe I would relent before the year was up, and get them out if I could. I think that in the long run, if a man's wife and babies, who had not harmed me, should come crying and pleading, I couldn't stand it; I know I should forgive him and let him
(120) go, even if he had violated a monastery. Henry of Huntington has been watching Godfrey and Marmion for nearly seven hundred and fifty years, now, but I couldn't do it, I know I couldn't. I am soft and gentle in my nature, and I should have
(125) forgiven them seventy-and-seven times, long ago. And I think God has; but this is only an opinion, and not authoritative, like Henry of Huntington's interpretations. I could learn to interpret, but I have never tried; I get so little time.
(130)   All through his book Henry exhibits his familiarity with the intentions of God, and with the reasons for his intentions. Sometimes—very often, in fact—the act follows the intention after such a wide interval of time that one wonders how Henry
(135) could fit one act out of a hundred to one intention out of a hundred and get the thing right every time when there was such abundant choice among acts and intentions. Sometimes a man offends the Deity with a crime, and is punished for it thirty years
(140) later; meantime he has committed a million other crimes: no matter, Henry can pick out the one that brought the worms. Worms were generally used in those days for the slaying of particularly wicked people. This has gone out, now, but in old times it
(145) was a favorite. It always indicated a case of "wrath." For instance:

GO ON TO THE NEXT PAGE. ➡

" . . . the just God avenging Robert Fitzhilderbrand's perfidy, a worm grew in his vitals, which gradually gnawing its way through his
(150) intestines fattened on the abandoned man till, tortured with excruciating sufferings and venting himself in bitter moans, he was by a fitting punishment brought to his end."

It was probably an alligator, but we cannot tell;
(155) we only know it was a particular breed, and only used to convey wrath. Some authorities think it was an ichthyosaurus, but there is much doubt.

However, one thing we do know; and that is that that worm had been due years and years.
(160) Robert F. had violated a monastery once; he had committed unprintable crimes since, and they had been permitted—under disapproval—but the ravishment of the monastery had not been forgotten nor forgiven, and the worm came at last.

(165) Why were these reforms put off in this strange way? What was to be gained by it? Did Henry of Huntington really know his facts, or was he only guessing? Sometimes I am half persuaded that he is only a guesser, and not a good one. The divine
(170) wisdom must surely be of the better quality than he makes it out to be.

1. The tone of this passage is best described as

    (A) somber
    (B) didactic
    (C) bitter
    (D) pathetic
    (E) satiric

2. In the first sentence, the author uses the word "enlightened"

    (A) as a synonym for "instructive"
    (B) as a synonym for "intelligent"
    (C) in an ironic sense
    (D) as an adjective modifying "Christianity"
    (E) (C) and (D) only

3. "The augur [soothsayer] has had his day and has been long ago forgotten; the priest had fallen heir to his trade." This sentence (lines 4–6) implies that

    (A) all augurs are dead
    (B) priests are the children of augurs
    (C) priests perform the same function that once belonged to augurs
    (D) no one relies on augurs in the time of which the author speaks
    (E) both (C) and (D)

4. The first paragraph

    (A) sets a serious tone
    (B) represents a transition in the discussion from a much earlier historical period to a later one
    (C) suggests ignorance of history on the part of the author
    (D) describes a period in which superstition has been forgotten
    (E) none of the above

5. The author's attitude toward Henry of Huntington is

    (A) that he is an accurate historian
    (B) that he unfairly favors King Stephen
    (C) that he wrongly attributes the Archbishop of Canterbury as a historical source
    (D) that he alters the facts for the benefit of the rulers
    (E) that he arbitrarily attributes some deaths to divine retribution, while being unable to justify the unpunished existence of greater criminals

6. In line 47, the use of the word "pen" is an example of

(A) metonymy
(B) synecdoche
(C) metaphor
(D) symbol
(E) personification

7. According to Twain in lines 52–55,

(A) Henry of Huntington finds fault with kings who are cruel
(B) Henry of Huntington's silences on God's lack of punishment of certain unrighteous persons are suppressed criticism of God
(C) Henry of Huntington criticizes other historians' silences on injustice
(D) Henry of Huntington feels he cannot condone the brutality of God's vengeance
(E) Henry of Huntington is evidently satisfied with the outcome

8. In lines 80–81, what is the intent of the phrase "expressed in that fervent way"?

(A) To indicate that church services have been more energetic
(B) Kings have been stirring up followers of the faith
(C) Twain refers to "butcheries 'under cover of religion'"
(D) To demonstrate that evangelism was on the rise during this period
(E) Religious faith of the soldiers was strong

9. The fate that Robert Marmion and Godfrey de Mandeville met was

(A) defeat in battle
(B) being eaten internally by worms
(C) dying of disease
(D) dying excommunicated
(E) being attacked by eagles

10. Marmion's and Godfrey's crimes were

(A) exacting fines against the church
(B) killing women and children
(C) decapitating priests and defiling crucifixes
(D) converting monasteries into fortifications and expelling the monks
(E) torturing enemy soldiers

11. The aspect of the episode of Marmion and Godfrey that bothers Twain most is

(A) the punishments in these cases were too light
(B) the punishments in these cases were too severe
(C) the chronicler's evident glee in reporting the punishment
(D) the punishments in these cases were inconsistent
(E) the fact that Godfrey was shot by a common foot soldier

12. In paragraph 13, Twain uses the following literary device(s)

(A) hyperbole
(B) understatement
(C) litotes
(D) alliteration
(E) (A) and (B)

13. The overall message of this entire passage seems to be

(A) Henry of Huntington is a poor historian
(B) Henry of Huntington frequently discusses the intentions of God, and conveniently fits certain deaths with certain punishments
(C) in Henry of Huntington's Chronicle, the punishment does not always fit the crime
(D) Henry of Huntington rejoices in punishments that seem excessive to Twain
(E) (B), (C), and (D)

GO ON TO THE NEXT PAGE.

Questions 14–26. Read the following passage carefully before you choose your answers.

The passage below is from *"The Subjection of Women"* by John Stuart Mill.

The object of this Essay is to explain as clearly as I am able the grounds of an opinion which I have held from the very earliest period
Line when I had formed any opinions at all on social
(5) or political matters, and which, instead of being weakened or modified, has been constantly growing stronger by the progress reflection and the experience of life. That the principle which regulates the existing social relations between the
(10) two sexes—the legal subordination of one sex to the other—is wrong itself, and now one of the chief hindrances to human improvement; and that it ought to be replaced by a principle of perfect equality, admitting no power or privilege on the
(15) one side, nor disability on the other.

The very words necessary to express the task I have undertaken, show how arduous it is. But it would be a mistake to suppose that the difficulty of the case must lie in the insufficiency or
(20) obscurity of the grounds of reason on which my convictions. The difficulty is that which exists in all cases in which there is a mass of feeling to be contended against. So long as opinion is strongly rooted in the feelings, it gains rather than loses
(25) instability by having a preponderating weight of argument against it. For if it were accepted as a result of argument, the refutation of the argument might shake the solidity of the conviction; but when it rests solely on feeling, the worse it fares
(30) in argumentative contest, the more persuaded adherents are that their feeling must have some deeper ground, which the arguments do not reach; and while the feeling remains, it is always throwing up fresh entrenchments of argument to
(35) repair any breach made in the old. And there are so many causes tending to make the feelings connected with this subject the most intense and most deeply-rooted of those which gather round and protect old institutions and custom, that we
(40) need not wonder to find them as yet less undermined and loosened than any of the rest by

the progress of the great modern spiritual and social transition; nor suppose that the barbarisms to which men cling longest must be less
(45) barbarisms than those which they earlier shake off.

In every respect the burthen is hard on those who attack an almost universal opinion. They must be very fortunate as well as unusually
(50) capable if they obtain a hearing at all. They have more difficulty in obtaining a trial, than any other litigants have in getting a verdict. If they do extort a hearing, they are subjected to a set of logical requirements totally different from those exacted
(55) from other people. In all other cases, burthen of proof is supposed to lie with the affirmative. If a person is charged with a murder, it rests with those who accuse him to give proof of his guilt, not with himself to prove his innocence. If there
(60) is a difference of opinion about the reality of an alleged historical event, in which the feelings of men general are not much interested, as the Siege of Troy example, those who maintain that the event took place are expected to produce their
(65) proofs, before those who take the other side can be required to say anything; and at no time are these required to do more than show that the evidence produced by the others is of no value. Again, in practical matters, the burthen of proof is
(70) supposed to be with those who are against liberty; who contend for any restriction or prohibition either any limitation of the general freedom of human action or any disqualification or disparity of privilege affecting one person or kind of
(75) persons, as compared with others. The *a priori* presumption is in favour of freedom and impartiality. It is held that there should be no restraint not required by the general good, and that the law should be no respecter of persons but
(80) should treat all alike, save where dissimilarity of treatment is required by positive reasons, either of justice or of policy. But of none of these rules of

evidence will the benefit be allowed to those who maintain the opinion I profess. It is useless for me (85) to say that those who maintain the doctrine that men have a right to command and women are under an obligation obey, or that men are fit for government and women unfit, on the affirmative side of the question, and that they are bound to (90) show positive evidence for the assertions, or submit to their rejection. It is equally unavailing for me to say that those who deny to women any freedom or privilege rightly allowed to men, having the double presumption against them that (95) they are opposing freedom and recommending partiality, must held to the strictest proof of their case, and unless their success be such as to exclude all doubt, the judgment ought to be against them. These would be thought good pleas (100) in any common case; but they will not be thought so in this instance. Before I could hope to make any impression, I should be expected not only to answer all that has ever been said by those who take the other side of the question, but to imagine (105) that could be said by them—to find them in reasons, as I as answer all I find: and besides refuting all arguments for the affirmative, I shall be called upon for invincible positive arguments to prove a negative. And even if I could do all and (110) leave the opposite party with a host of unanswered arguments against them, and not a single unrefuted one on [their] side, I should be thought to have done little; for a cause supported on the one hand by universal usage, and on the (115) other by so great a preponderance of popular sentiment, is supposed to have a presumption in its favour, superior to any conviction which an appeal to reason has power to produce in any intellects but those of a high class.

(120)   I do not mention these difficulties to complain of them; first, because it would be useless; they are inseparable from having to contend through people's understandings against the hostility their feelings and practical tendencies: and truly the (125) understandings of the majority of mankind would need to be much better cultivated than has ever

yet been the case, before they be asked to place such reliance in their own power of estimating arguments, as to give up practical principles in (130) which have been born and bred, and which are the basis of much existing order of the world, at the first argumentative attack which they are not capable of logically resisting. I do not therefore quarrel with them for having too little faith in (135) argument, but for having too much faith in custom and the general feeling. It is one of the characteristic prejudices of the reaction of the nineteenth century against the eighteenth, to accord to the unreasoning elements in human (140) nature the infallibility which the eighteenth century is supposed to have ascribed to the reasoning elements. For the apotheosis of Reason we have substituted that of Instinct; and we call thing instinct which we find in ourselves and for (145) which we cannot trace any rational foundation. This idolatry, infinitely more degrading than the other, and the most pernicious of the false worships of the present day, of all of which it is now the main support, will probably hold its (150) ground until it gives way before a sound psychology laying bare the real root of much that is bowed down to as the intention of Nature and ordinance of God. As regards the present question, I am willing to accept the unfavourable (155) conditions which the prejudice assigns to me. I consent that established custom, and the general feelings, should be deemed conclusive against me, unless that custom and feeling from age to age can be shown to have owed their existence to (160) other causes than their soundness, and to have derived their power from the worse rather than the better parts of human nature. I am willing that judgment should go against me, unless I can show that my judge has been tampered with. The (165) concession is not so great as it might appear; for to prove this, is by far the easiest portion of my task.

GO ON TO THE NEXT PAGE. ➡

14. The "object of this Essay," as outlined by Mill in the first paragraph, is

   (A) to demonstrate the proper methods of subjection of women
   (B) to illustrate how women are subjected to harassment
   (C) to report on the condition of women in other countries
   (D) to argue that the system legally legitimizing the inferiority of women is morally wrong and must be replaced
   (E) to suggest ways in which legislation could be introduced changing labor conditions for women

15. Mill's argument in the second paragraph is that

   (A) it is extremely difficult to argue using reason against deeply rooted emotions
   (B) emotional arguments are far superior to those based in reason
   (C) opinionated arguments must always be wrong
   (D) a well-reasoned argument to a deeply held conviction tends to strengthen, rather than weaken, that conviction
   (E) both (A) and (D)

16. In the second paragraph, the statement "it is always throwing up fresh entrenchments of argument to repair any breach made in the old" is best understood as a metaphor for

   (A) the way in which rational argument successfully undermines and weakens emotionally held beliefs
   (B) the way in which stale beliefs crumble under the weight of emotion
   (C) the way in which strongly held emotional beliefs put up resistance to rational argument
   (D) the way in which rationality crushes all resistance
   (E) the way in which physical labor can overcome obstacles

17. In paragraph 3, Mill's use of the metaphor of a trial is best interpreted as

   (A) the way evidence is normally presented to support emotional arguments
   (B) the way in which the burden of proof normally lies with the party that seeks to impose restrictions, such as limits on freedom
   (C) the murdering of Mill's belief in the equal treatment of women
   (D) demonstrating the way in which evidence is presented to a jury
   (E) indicating the legal challenges facing his argument

18. The example of the Siege of Troy is given

   (A) as further proof of the equality of women
   (B) to demonstrate that during the Trojan War women enjoyed special privileged status
   (C) to demonstrate how when feelings are not deeply engaged in an issue, one must merely furnish proof of one's position, which the other side can merely refute and dismiss
   (D) to indicate that the issue Mill puts forth is of little interest to most people
   (E) as an analysis of the history of patriarchal hierarchy

19. From the context of its use in paragraph 3, the Latin phrase *a priori* (line 75) can be inferred to mean

   (A) working from an established assumption
   (B) false
   (C) unrelated
   (D) natural
   (E) undetermined

GO ON TO THE NEXT PAGE. ➡

20. In lines 77–84, Mills proposes

    (A) that all things being equal, it is the duty of all citizens to conform to the laws of the land
    (B) the very nature of law is highly determinate
    (C) that although the law is normally structured to allow the maximum amount of liberty, that standard does not apply to women
    (D) God determines the law of the land, and so women are excluded by God
    (E) Mill is aware that his position is unnatural

21. Although Mill may not use them, examples that could be used to demonstrate Mill's argument might include

    (A) a man on trial for murder
    (B) an argument in favor of equal treatment of black and white men
    (C) the attempt to disprove a commonly held historical belief
    (D) a common property dispute
    (E) (A), (B), and (C)

22. In lines 101–113, Mill is best understood to mean

    (A) Mill is confident he could make an airtight case for the equal treatment of women
    (B) Mill understands he is arguing against the weight of tradition
    (C) Mill understands that even if he makes a flawless case against the arguments of the opposition and leaves none of their arguments unanswered, he could not hope to convince his opponents that he is right.
    (D) (B) and (C)
    (E) (A), (B), and (C)

23. Lines 113–119 ("for a cause . . . high class.") could best be rephrased as

    (A) a cause generally accepted is easily shaken
    (B) a cause that is unpopular is as difficult to overturn as one that is popular
    (C) truth is intuitively understood by all
    (D) a universally supported popular belief is presumed to be true, and is held above common rational standards by all but the brightest minds
    (E) none of the above

24. What rhetorical intention does Mill have with his statement concerning "intellects . . . of a high class" (line 119)?

    (A) Mill is demonstrating deep humility
    (B) Mill demonstrates a lack of understanding of his audience
    (C) Mill implies that in order to accept his argument, one must be especially intelligent, with the related implication that one who does not accept Mill's argument is of a lesser degree of intelligence
    (D) Mill flatters the intelligence of his detractors
    (E) Mill attempts to impress his adherents with his own deep intelligence

25. In the last paragraph, Mill states that he does not "mention these difficulties to complain of them" but because of all of the following EXCEPT

    (A) he feels the reason of mankind in general is not sufficiently developed
    (B) the cause he argues against is the basis for much of the existing order in the world
    (C) too many people are deeply hostile to his cause
    (D) most men have too much faith in custom
    (E) he knows his argument is weak

26. The "idolatry" Mills refers to in the last paragraph is

    (A) the valuing of Instinct over Reason
    (B) the valuing of Reason over Instinct
    (C) respect for the thinking of the eighteenth century
    (D) the infallibility of Reason
    (E) the deepest held beliefs of Christianity

GO ON TO THE NEXT PAGE. ➡

Questions 27–39. Read the following passage carefully before you choose your answers.

The passage below is from *"An Essay Concerning Human Understanding"* by John Locke.

1. Idea is the object of thinking. Every man
being conscious to himself that he thinks; and that
which his mind is applied about whilst thinking
Line being the ideas that are there, it is past doubt that
(5) men have in their minds several ideas,—such as
are those expressed by the words whiteness,
hardness, sweetness, thinking, motion, man,
elephant, army, drunkenness, and others: it is in
the first place then to be inquired, How he comes
(10) by them?

I know it is a received doctrine, that men have
native ideas, and original characters, stamped
upon their minds in their very first being. This
opinion I have at large examined already; and, I
(15) suppose what I have said in the foregoing Book
will be much more easily admitted, when I have
shown whence the understanding may get all the
ideas it has; and by what ways and degrees they
may come into the mind;—for which I shall
(20) appeal to every one's own observation and
experience.

2. All ideas come from sensation or reflection.
Let us then suppose the mind to be, as we say,
white paper, void of all characters, without any
(25) ideas:—How comes it to be furnished? Whence
comes it by that vast store which the busy and
boundless fancy of man has painted on it with an
almost endless variety? Whence has it all the
materials of reason and knowledge? To this I
(30) answer, in one word, from EXPERIENCE. In that
all our knowledge is founded; and from that it
ultimately derives itself. Our observation
employed either, about external sensible objects,
or about the internal operations of our minds
(35) perceived and reflected on by ourselves, is that
which supplies our understandings with all the
materials of thinking. These two are the fountains
of knowledge, from whence all the ideas we have,
or can naturally have, do spring.

3. The objects of sensation one source of ideas.
(40) First, our Senses, conversant about particular
sensible objects, do convey into the mind several
distinct perceptions of things, according to those
various ways wherein those objects do affect
(45) them. And thus we come by those ideas we have
of yellow, white, heat, cold, soft, hard, bitter,
sweet, and all those which we call sensible
qualities; which when I say the senses convey into
the mind, I mean, they from external objects
(50) convey into the mind what produces there those
perceptions. This great source of most of the ideas
we have, depending wholly upon our senses, and
derived by them to the understanding, I call
SENSATION.

(55) *4. The operations of our minds, the other source
of them.* Secondly, the other fountain from which
experience furnisheth the understanding with
ideas is,—the perception of the operations of our
own mind within us, as it is employed about the
(60) ideas it has got;—which operations, when the
soul comes to reflect on and consider, do furnish
the understanding with another set of ideas, which
could not be had from things without. And such
are perception, thinking, doubting, believing,
(65) reasoning, knowing, willing, and all the different
actings of our own minds;—which we being
conscious of, and observing in ourselves, do from
these receive into our understandings as distinct
ideas as we do from bodies affecting our senses.
(70) This source of ideas every man has wholly in
himself; and though it be not sense, as having
nothing to do with external objects, yet it is very
like it, and might properly enough be called
internal sense. But as I call the other
(75) SENSATION, so I call this REFLECTION, the
ideas it affords being such only as the mind gets
by reflecting on its own operations within itself.
By reflection then, in the following part of this
discourse, I would be understood to mean, that
(80) notice which the mind takes of its own operations,

GO ON TO THE NEXT PAGE. ➡

and the manner of them, by reason whereof there
come to be ideas of these operations in the
understanding. These two, I say, viz. external
material things, as the objects of SENSATION,
(85) and the operations of our own minds within, as
the objects of REFLECTION, are to me the only
originals from whence all our ideas take their
beginnings. The term operations here I use in a
large sense, as comprehending not barely the
(90) actions of the mind about its ideas, but some sort
of passions arising sometimes from them, such as
is the satisfaction or uneasiness arising from any
thought.

     5. All our ideas are of the one or the other of
(95) *these.* The understanding seems to me not to have
the least glimmering of any ideas which it doth
not receive from one of these two. External
objects furnish the mind with the ideas of sensible
qualities, which are all those different perceptions
(100) they produce in us; and the mind furnishes the
understanding with ideas of its own operations.

     These, when we have taken a full survey of
them, and their several modes, combinations, and
relations, we shall find to contain all our whole
(105) stock of ideas; and that we have nothing in our
minds which did not come in one of these two
ways. Let any one examine his own thoughts, and
thoroughly search into his understanding; and
then let him tell me, whether all the original ideas
(110) he has there, are any other than of the objects of
his senses, or of the operations of his mind,
considered as objects of his reflection. And how
great a mass of knowledge soever he imagines to
be lodged there, he will, upon taking a strict view,
(115) see that he has not any idea in his mind but what
one of these two have imprinted;—though
perhaps, with infinite variety compounded and
enlarged by the understanding, as we shall see
hereafter.

(120)   *6. Observable in children.* He that attentively
considers the state of a child, at his first coming
into the world, will have little reason to think him
stored with plenty of ideas, that are to be the
matter of his future knowledge. It is by degrees he
(125) comes to be furnished with them. And though the
ideas of obvious and familiar qualities imprint
themselves before the memory begins to keep a
register of time or order, yet it is often so late
before some unusual qualities come in the way,
(130) that there are few men that cannot recollect the
beginning of their acquaintance with them. And if
it were worth while, no doubt a child might be so
ordered as to have but a very few, even of the
ordinary ideas, till he were grown up to a man.
(135) But all that are born into the world, being
surrounded with bodies that perpetually and
diversely affect them, variety of ideas, whether
care be taken of it or not, are imprinted on the
minds of children. Light and colours are busy at
(140) hand everywhere, when the eye is but open;
sounds and some tangible qualities fail not to
solicit their proper senses, and force an entrance
to the mind;—but yet, I think, it will be granted
easily, that if a child were kept in a place where
(145) he never saw any other but black and white till he
were a man, he would have no more ideas of
scarlet or green, than he that from his childhood
never tasted an oyster, or a pine-apple, has of
those particular relishes.

GO ON TO THE NEXT PAGE. ➡

27. In paragraph 1, Locke uses the words "whiteness, hardness, sweetness, thinking, motion, man, elephant, army, drunkenness"

    (A) to represent a set of images men dream of
    (B) to indicate the extreme reaches of thought in certain men
    (C) as expressions of ideas which exist in men's minds
    (D) as examples of common vocabulary
    (E) (A) and (D)

28. In paragraph 2, when he refers to "native ideas" (line 12), Locke means

    (A) primitive men have a certain philosophy that civilized men reject
    (B) civilized concepts of unique complexity
    (C) simplistic beliefs that are easily dismissed
    (D) innate ideas universal to all men, present at birth
    (E) a fragile belief system

29. Which of the following sentences is most likely to be the thesis statement of the entire essay?

    (A) "Idea is the object of thinking."
    (B) "All ideas come from sensation or reflection."
    (C) "And thus we come by those ideas we have of yellow, white, heat, cold, soft, hard, bitter, sweet, and all those which we call sensible qualities; which when I say the senses convey into the mind, I mean, they from external objects convey into the mind what produces there those perceptions."
    (D) "All our ideas are of the one or the other of these."
    (E) "It is by degrees he comes to be furnished with them."

30. "White paper" (line 24) is a metaphor for

    (A) illiteracy
    (B) the condition of the uneducated mind
    (C) the state of the mind free of ideas
    (D) the human condition
    (E) it is not a metaphor

31. According to Locke, which of the following furnishes the mind with the raw materials needed to form ideas?

    (A) Experience
    (B) Reason
    (C) The operation of our minds
    (D) Original characters
    (E) None of the above

32. Which of the following best describes the process described in paragraph 5?

    (A) The mind receives certain sensations
    (B) Through conversation with others, the mind forms opinions
    (C) Certain operations take place entirely within the mind to produce ideas, which cannot be received from sensations
    (D) Sensations are taken within the mind and processed further into more refined ideas
    (E) (A) and (B)

33. For Locke the term "reflection"

    (A) encompasses the entire realm of thought
    (B) applies only to that which occurs in the mind
    (C) excludes analysis of that received by the senses
    (D) both (B) and (C)
    (E) none of the above

GO ON TO THE NEXT PAGE. ➡

 309

34. In the beginning of paragraph 7, the word "several" means

    (A) various
    (B) separate
    (C) many
    (D) diverse
    (E) intended

35. Locke's observations of children support the idea that

    (A) we are not innately possessed of ideas
    (B) children come to a gradual gathering of ideas
    (C) many things that seem obvious to adults are gradually learned by children
    (D) children begin receiving sensation from the beginning
    (E) all of the above

36. In the last part of the passage (lines 143–149), Locke

    (A) proves that certain colors are naturally deduced
    (B) shows that the understanding of colors, in exception to his general rule, is innate
    (C) concedes that an understanding of certain concepts may be unnecessary
    (D) demonstrates that certain concepts must be received through sensation to be understood
    (E) none of the above

37. The chief rhetorical strategy used by Locke in this essay is

    (A) appeal to authority
    (B) appeal to emotion
    (C) appeal to logic
    (D) rhetorical questions
    (E) use of irony

38. The audience for Locke's essay is most likely to be

    (A) children
    (B) educated persons who assume that at least some ideas are innate
    (C) serious philosophers
    (D) the working class
    (E) government officials

39. It could be inferred from Locke's argument that ideas could NOT originate from which sources?

    (A) The senses
    (B) The instincts
    (C) Divine providence
    (D) Experience
    (E) (B) and (C)

GO ON TO THE NEXT PAGE. ➡

Questions 40–50. Read the following passage carefully before you choose your answers.

The passage below is from *"Teaching Hamlet to Adolescents in the 21st Century"* by Steve Burby.

Although I'm no big fan of Harold Bloom,
like him, I consider myself to be a "Bardolator"—
a serious devotee of the study of the life and
Line works of William Shakespeare. In *Shakespeare:*
(5) *The Invention of the Human*, Bloom holds up
Falstaff and Hamlet, in that order, as the Bard's
two greatest creations. I would quibble, at the
very least, with the order. The task of making an
elitist, misogynist, procrastinating prince teetering
(10) on the edge of madness a sympathetic, indeed, a
noble (in the most catholic sense of the word)
character is a feat of mastery. That this portrayal
should be able to endure the centuries is proof
positive of Shakespeare's genius.

(15) Trying to teach Shakespeare—any
Shakespeare—to the 21st century adolescent is a
truly daunting challenge. Many of today's high
school students are sophisticated beyond the
ability of most adults to truly appreciate. These
(20) are students well-educated in the school of life,
part of a culture raised from early childhood on a
diet of *Jerry Springer*, MTV, Howard Stern, and
South Park. Many of my students are parents, and
some, as teenagers, have multiple children.
(25) Visually oriented and overstimulated, they have
little patience with the written word. "Break it
down, Mr. Burby," is what I frequently hear when
I confront them with a passage of Shakespearean
text. They want it spoon-fed, a temptation that I
(30) (usually) resist.

Regardless of our personal feelings about the
culture of adolescents, their precocious
sophistication and overstimulation, their lifestyle
choices and use of the vernacular, we as teachers
(35) must continually reach out to our students, and
pick our battles. We can instill more positive
values in small doses without alienating them,
partly by accepting them as wholly as we are
able.

(40) How does this apply to the teaching of
Hamlet? In many ways, I believe that *Hamlet* is
an ideal play to impart to our sophisticated
students. Many of the themes of *Hamlet* lie at the
outer boundaries of society, much as the media
(45) the students are familiar with, *videlicet South Park*
and *Jerry Springer*. *Hamlet* deals with the
corruption of government and family, suicide,
betrayal, the generation gap, misogyny, spying,
and incest.

(50) One of the problems with presenting *Hamlet*
to a high-school audience is the use of old
textbooks containing somewhat bowdlerized
versions of the play. In the textbooks I use for this
course, which are twenty years old, some crucial
(55) lines are cut, undermining accurate understanding
of the motivations of some of the characters.
Indeed, many earlier critics, hampered by the
general lack of sophistication of their eras,
seemed unable to either conceive of, or to accept,
(60) Shakespeare's more worldly meanings. Ironically,
our 21st-century teenagers may be better able to
appreciate Shakespeare's richness.

I believe the best way to teach any
Shakespeare work is as a whole. Our students
(65) deserve this. Using bowdlerized versions or
modern-language translations robs the plays of
much of their entertainment value, as well as
usurping at least part of the role of the teacher.
We should not talk down to our students, and
(70) sometimes this can feel awkward. We have an
altogether appropriate desire, as adults, to want to
"protect" our students from some of the harsher
aspects of a play like *Hamlet*. But by 12th grade,
it is inappropriate to do so. High school seniors,
(75) from the most to the least sophisticated, can
handle the touchy moral issues and mature themes
of *Hamlet*.

GO ON TO THE NEXT PAGE. ➡

One example of an issue that is both simpler and more complex than it seems is the issue of
(80) Hamlet's treatment of the two women in the play, whose roles suggest they should deserve better: Gertrude, his mother, and Ophelia, his sometime beloved. Some critics have suggested that Hamlet has an Oedipus complex, because he is obsessed
(85) with his mother's sex life. Many critics feel that innocent Ophelia is treated so harshly by Hamlet that sympathy for his character is undermined. Both of these interpretations are quite obviously flawed, as a close reading of the most complete
(90) versions of the play reveals.

Earlier in this piece I alluded to my sanitized textbooks. If left to the version of the play presented in my text, the single most important issue in Hamlet's treatment of Ophelia is left
(95) unresolved, and indeed this has seriously been debated by earlier critics: *In her madness, Ophelia clearly admits to having had a sexual relationship with Prince Hamlet.* There can be no doubt. The following crucial song by Ophelia is
(100) omitted from my textbook:

Tomorrow is Saint Valentine's day,
All in the morning betime,
And I a maid at your window,
To be your Valentine.

(105) *Then up he rose and donned his clothes*
And dupped the chamber door;
Let in the maid that out a maid
Never departed more . . .

By Gis and by Saint Charity,
(110) *Alack and fie for shame,*
Young men will do't if they come to't,
By Cock they are to blame.

Quoth she, "Before you tumbled me,
You promised me to wed" . . .
(115) *"So would I ha' done by yonder sun*
An thou hadst not come to my bed." (IV, v)

Not only is this perhaps the single most poignant moment in the play, it both condemns and excuses Hamlet, and gives our 21st-century
(120) high schoolers a moral issue they can readily and eagerly relate to. In the plays of Shakespeare, the mad character always speaks the hidden truth. It makes clear Ophelia's earlier confusing behavior in the prelude to Hamlet's nunnery speech: when
(125) she confronts Hamlet, redelivering his love letters, accusing him of being "unkind." Hamlet, according to Ophelia, and also according to her father and brother, has indeed been unkind. But that is only one side of the story: Hamlet, too,
(130) feels abandoned and betrayed by Ophelia, in his hour of greatest need. Her father, whom Hamlet clearly detests, is Lord Chamberlain to the usurper king, his "uncle-father." But the key reason for Hamlet's distrust of Ophelia is his
(135) mother's betrayal of his father, her adulterous incest.

Some critics, such as T.S. Eliot, blame Hamlet for not being equal to the task of revenge, but I am indebted to John Dover Wilson's *What*
(140) *Happens in Hamlet* for my understanding of the magnitude of Gertrude's sin, especially in Shakespeare's time, and its effect on Hamlet. My students invariably enter into a discussion of the ramifications of this incest. Discussion always
(145) comes around to various episodes of *Springer* and Woody Allen's relationship with, and marriage to, his longtime companion's adopted daughter. This emotional incest is something they can easily relate to, having been exposed to examples in the
(150) entertainment media. Hamlet feels "sullied" and corrupted by this act of his mother's: because of his biological source, he cannot escape this corruption. To paraphrase Wilson, the fruit of a rotten tree carries the tree's rottenness, so Hamlet
(155) is inextricably bound to his mother's corruption. Many of my students realize the moral implications of this before I raise it in discussion; others subsequently reevaluate the values presented to them by our adolescent culture.
(160) Hamlet the tragic hero is intrinsically flawed. His

GO ON TO THE NEXT PAGE. ➡

tragic flaw is not, as many critics have speculated, procrastination, but contamination by association. His mother's crimes have infected him and are consuming him like a terminal cancer. His tragic
(165) communication breakdown with Ophelia is partly a result of his distrust of his mother, and by extension, all women ("Frailty, thy name is woman!"). In this, Hamlet is mistaken. He suspects that Ophelia has a lover, but not that her
(170) father and brother have attempted to protect her honor. Compounded by this is Ophelia's complicity in spying on Hamlet during the nunnery scene, in which Ophelia, in proving herself willing to lie to Hamlet for her father,
(175) proves she cannot be trusted.

Teaching the plays of Shakespeare, unadulterated, to our culturally sophisticated teenagers gives us a wonderful opportunity to introduce them to a more rigorous moral code
(180) than they may be accustomed to from watching MTV. In the tragedies of Shakespeare, as in life, actions have inescapable consequences.

40. In the first paragraph, Burby claims to concur with Harold Bloom on the point that

  (A) the works of Shakespeare are deserving of serious study
  (B) Falstaff is Shakespeare's greatest creation
  (C) Hamlet is both misogynist and insane
  (D) Shakespeare's Hamlet is a noble character
  (E) Hamlet, and by inference, Shakespeare himself, is Catholic

41. In the first paragraph the word "catholic" is used to mean

  (A) Roman Catholic
  (B) religious in a general sense
  (C) Christian
  (D) universal
  (E) immortal

42. In the second paragraph, Burby argues that

  (A) most adults would have difficulty appreciating Shakespeare
  (B) as a result of various cultural and media influences, many adolescents of the 21st century are easily bored and dislike reading
  (C) students of today are trained to be good listeners
  (D) *South Park, Jerry Springer*, and MTV contain frequent allusions to Shakespeare
  (E) Shakespeare is not really relevant to the 21st century

43. Burby applies the word "sophisticated" (line 18) to adolescents to mean

  (A) intellectual
  (B) conscious of protocol
  (C) well-educated
  (D) possessing knowledge and experience beyond what is generally expected for adolescence
  (E) ready for college

44. In line 52, the word "bowdlerized" can be inferred to mean

  (A) accurate
  (B) ignorant
  (C) censored
  (D) humorous
  (E) unabridged

GO ON TO THE NEXT PAGE. ➡

45. The argument of paragraph 5 is that

    (A) incomplete versions of Shakespeare's texts leads to incomplete or erroneous understanding of the plays and the characters

    (B) students come to care deeply about the characters in *Hamlet*

    (C) old textbooks tend to be more accurate than current ones

    (D) scholars of other eras believed in teaching the plays only to college students

    (E) Shakespearean scholars are now generally in agreement about interpretation of the texts

46. In paragraph 6, Burby argues that

    (A) the plays of Shakespeare should be taught as a whole

    (B) modern-language translations detract from the entertainment value of the play

    (C) all 12th graders can deal with the issues in *Hamlet*, regardless of their level of sophistication

    (D) it can feel awkward for adults to discuss some of the mature themes of *Hamlet* with adolescents

    (E) all of the above

47. According to this article, an issue debated by many critics has been

    (A) Hamlet's misogyny

    (B) the identity of King Hamlet's murderer

    (C) the role of Prince Fortinbras

    (D) Horatio's character

    (E) the fates of Rosencrantz and Guildenstern

48. According to Burby, the justification(s) for his argument that Ophelia and Hamlet have had a sexual relationship include(s)

    (A) a song of Ophelia omitted from some versions of the play

    (B) the madness of Ophelia

    (C) the tendency of mad characters in Shakespeare's plays to speak the hidden truth

    (D) Hamlet's treatment of Ophelia during the Mousetrap scene

    (E) (A), (B), and (C)

49. According to John Dover Wilson, Hamlet's distrust of Ophelia is caused in part by

    (A) his inability to carry out revenge

    (B) his dislike of Polonius

    (C) her return of Hamlet's letters in the nunnery scene

    (D) his mother's adulterous, incestuous relationship with his uncle

    (E) none of the above

50. According to Burby, the connection between Hamlet's distrust of Ophelia and his feeling of contamination by his mother is demonstrated by

    (A) the Ghost's demand for revenge

    (B) the death of Polonius

    (C) Hamlet's utterance of the phrase "Frailty, thy name is woman!"

    (D) Hamlet's knowledge that Ophelia had had other lovers

    (E) none of the above

END OF SECTION I

GO ON TO THE NEXT PAGE. ➡

SECTION II: FREE-RESPONSE QUESTIONS

Time: 2 hours

Number of questions: 3

Percent of total grade: 55

Directions: This section contains three essay questions. Answer all three questions, budgeting your time carefully.

GO ON TO THE NEXT PAGE. ➡

Question One

(Suggested Time—40 minutes. Your response will count toward
one-third of your total score on this section of the exam.)

The following passage is taken from *The Rambler* by Samuel Johnson. Read the passage; then, in a well-organized essay, discuss the various rhetorical strategies Johnson uses to develop his extended definition of envy. In addition, discuss which rhetorical devices (such as tone, attitude, diction, and syntax) Johnson employs in developing his definition.

The empire of envy has no limits, as it requires to its influence very little help from external circumstances. Envy may always be
Line produced by idleness and pride, and in what place
(5) will they not be found?

Envy is almost the only vice which is practicable at all times, and in every place; the only passion which can never lie quiet for want of irritation: its effects therefore are everywhere
(10) discoverable, and its attempts always to be dreaded.

It is impossible to mention a name which any advantageous distinction has made eminent, but some latent animosity will burst out. The wealthy
(15) trader, however he may abstract himself from publick affairs, will never want those who hint, with Shylock, that ships are but boards. The beauty, adorned only with the unambitious graces of innocence and modesty, provokes, whenever
(20) she appears, a thousand murmurs of detraction. The genius, even when he endeavours only to entertain or instruct, yet suffers persecution from innumerable criticks, whose acrimony is excited merely by the pain of seeing others pleased, and
(25) of hearing applauses which another enjoys.

The frequency of envy makes it so familiar, that it escapes our notice; nor do we often reflect upon its turpitude or malignity, till we happen to feel its influence. When he that has given no
(30) provocation to malice, but by attempting to excel, finds himself pursued by multitudes whom he never saw, with all the implacability of personal resentment; when as a publick enemy, and incited by every stratagem of defamation; when he hears
(35) the misfortunes of his family, or the follies of his

youth, exposed to the world; and every failure of conduct, or defect of nature, aggravated and ridiculed; he then learns to abhor those artifices at which he only laughed before, and discovers how
(40) much the happiness of life would be advanced by the eradication of envy from the human heart.

Envy is, indeed, a stubborn weed of the mind, and seldom yields to the culture of philosophy. There are, however, considerations, which, if
(45) carefully implanted and diligently propagated, might in time overpower and repress it, since no one can nurse it for the sake of pleasure, as its effects are only shame, anguish, and perturbation.

It is above all other vices inconsistent with
(50) the character of a social being, because it sacrifices truth and kindness to very weak temptations. He that plunders a wealthy neighbour gains as much as he takes away, and may improve his own condition in the same
(55) proportion as he impairs another's; but he that blasts a flourishing reputation, must be content with a small dividend of additional fame, so small as can afford very little consolation to balance the guilt by which it is obtained.

(60) I have hitherto avoided that dangerous and empirical morality, which cures one vice by means of another. But envy is so base and detestable, so vile in its original, and so pernicious in its effects, that the predominance of almost any other quality
(65) is to be preferred. It is one of those lawless enemies of society, against which poisoned arrows may honestly be used. Let it therefore be constantly remembered, that whoever envies another, confesses his superiority, and let those be
(70) reformed by their pride who have lost their virtue.

GO ON TO THE NEXT PAGE. ➡

It is no slight aggravation of the injuries
which envy incites, that they are committed
against those who have given no intentional
provocation; and that the sufferer is often marked
(75) out for ruin, not because he has failed in any duty,
but because he has dared to do more than was
required.

Almost every other crime is practised by the
help of some quality which might have produced
(80) esteem or love, if it had been well employed; but
envy is mere unmixed and genuine evil; it pursues
a hateful end by despicable means, and desires
not so much its own happiness as another's
misery. To avoid depravity like this, it is not
(85) necessary that any one should aspire to heroism
or sanctity, but only that he should resolve not to
quit the rank which nature assigns him, and wish
to maintain the dignity of a human being.

GO ON TO THE NEXT PAGE. ➡

Question Two

(Suggested Time—40 minutes. Your response will count toward
one-third of your total score on this section of the exam.)

The following is the final inaugural address of Franklin D. Roosevelt, given in January of 1945, the last year
of World War II. Paying particular attention to the rhetorical strategies that he uses, such as tone, diction,
and syntax, analyze FDR's attitude about the war and the necessity of working for a just, honorable, and
durable peace. In addition, comment on the probable effect of his words upon his listeners.

Mr. Chief Justice, Mr. Vice President, my
friends, you will understand and, I believe, agree
with my wish that the form of this inauguration be
Line simple and its words brief.
(5)   We Americans of today, together with our
allies, are passing through a period of supreme test.
It is a test of our courage—of our resolve—of our
wisdom—our essential democracy.
        If we meet that test—successfully and
(10) honorably—we shall perform a service of historic
importance which men and women and children
will honor throughout all time.
        As I stand here today, having taken the solemn
oath of office in the presence of my fellow
(15) countrymen—in the presence of our God—I know
that it is America's purpose that we shall not fail.
        In the days and in the years that are to come we
shall work for a just and honorable peace, a durable
peace, as today we work and fight for total victory
(20) in war.
        We can and we will achieve such a peace.
        We shall strive for perfection. We shall not
achieve it immediately—but we still shall strive. We
may make mistakes—but they must never be
(25) mistakes which result from faintness of heart or
abandonment of moral principle.
        I remember that my old schoolmaster, Dr.
Peabody, said, in days that seemed to us then to be
secure and untroubled: "Things in life will not
(30) always run smoothly. Sometimes we will be rising
toward the heights—then all will seem to reverse
itself and start downward. The great fact to
remember is that the trend of civilization itself is
forever upward; that a line drawn through the
(35) middle of the peaks and the valleys of the centuries
always has an upward trend."

        Our Constitution of 1787 was not a perfect
instrument; it is not perfect yet. But it provided a
firm base upon which all manner of men, of all
(40) races and colors and creeds, could build our solid
structure of democracy.
        And so today, in this year of war, 1945, we
have learned lessons—at a fearful cost—and we
shall profit by them.
(45)   We have learned that we cannot live alone, at
peace; that our own well-being is dependent on the
well-being of other nations far away. We have
learned that we must live as men, not as ostriches,
nor as dogs in the manger.
(50)   We have learned to be citizens of the world,
members of the human community.
        We have learned the simple truth, as Emerson
said, that "The only way to have a friend is to be
one."
(55)   We can gain no lasting peace if we approach it
with suspicion and mistrust or with fear. We can
gain it only if we proceed with the understanding,
the confidence, and the courage which flow from
conviction.
(60)   The Almighty God has blessed our land in
many ways. He has given our people stout hearts
and strong arms with which to strike mighty blows
for freedom and truth. He has given to our country
a faith which has become the hope of all peoples in
(65) an anguished world.
        So we pray to Him now for the vision to see
our way clearly—to see the way that leads to a
better life for ourselves and for all our fellow
men—to the achievement of His will to peace on
(70) earth.

GO ON TO THE NEXT PAGE. ➡

KAPLAN

Question Three

(Suggested Time—40 minutes. Your response will count toward
one-third of your total score on this section of the exam.)

Read the paragraph below from Henry David Thoreau's essay "Walking." Consider Thoreau's statement that sometimes we are heedless or stupid in our decisions; sometimes we find it difficult to choose the correct direction because it is not clear to us just what our direction should be. Drawing on your experience, your reading, and/or your observations, consider what Thoreau has said. In a well-organized essay, defend, challenge, or qualify Thoreau's sentiments.

What is it that makes it so hard sometimes to determine
whither we will walk? I believe that there is a subtle magnetism
in Nature, which, if we unconsciously yield to it, will direct us
Line aright. It is not indifferent to us which way we walk. There is a
(5) right way; but we are very liable from heedlessness and
stupidity to take the wrong one. We would fain take that walk,
never yet taken by us through this actual world, which is
perfectly symbolical of the path which we love to travel in the
interior and ideal world; and sometimes, no doubt, we find it
(10) difficult to choose our direction, because it does not yet exist
distinctly in our idea.

END OF EXAMINATION

Practice Test II
Answers and Explanations

ANSWER KEY

1.	E	21.	E	41.	D
2.	E	22.	D	42.	B
3.	E	23.	D	43.	D
4.	B	24.	C	44.	C
5.	E	25.	E	45.	A
6.	A	26.	A	46.	E
7.	B	27.	C	47.	A
8.	C	28.	D	48.	E
9.	D	29.	B	49.	D
10.	D	30.	C	50.	C
11.	C	31.	A		
12.	E	32.	C		
13.	E	33.	D		
14.	D	34.	B		
15.	E	35.	E		
16.	C	36.	D		
17.	B	37.	C		
18.	C	38.	B		
19.	A	39.	E		
20.	C	40.	A		

PRACTICE TEST II
COMPUTE YOUR SCORE

Remember not to take any score on the practice test too literally. There is no way to determine precisely what your AP grade will be because:

- The conditions under which you take the practice test will not exactly mirror real test conditions.
- While the multiple-choice questions are scored by computer, the free-response questions are graded manually by faculty consultants. You will not be able to accurately grade your own essays.

Section I: Multiple-Choice

Number Correct [   ] − (¼ × Number Wrong*) [   ] = [   ] × 1.296 = [   ] = Multiple-Choice Raw Score

*Do not include questions left blank.

Section II: Free-Response

Question 1: (out of 9 points possible) [   ] × 2.933 = [   ]

Question 2: (out of 9 points possible) [   ] × 2.933 = [   ]

Question 3: (out of 9 points possible) [   ] × 2.933 = [   ]

Total Questions 1, 2, and 3 = [   ] = Free-Response Raw Score

Composite Score

Section I Multiple-Choice Score [   ] + Section II Free-Response Score [   ] = [   ] = Composite Score

CONVERSION CHART

Composite Score Range**	AP Grade
114–144	5
88–113	4
67–87	3
40–66	2
0–39	1

Section I: Multiple-Choice Questions

Questions 1–13

1. (E)

Twain's tone is highly satiric, bordering at times on what some readers might consider irreverent. Consider the first sentence of the passage: "We may now skip eleven hundred and thirty or forty years, which brings us down to enlightened Christian times and the troubled days of King Stephen of England." His use of the word "skip" to dismiss "eleven hundred and thirty or forty years." In addition, the very slippery nature of the time period skipped seems satirical of the normal precision of historians, as if somehow exact dates do not matter. Because the tone is satiric, it cannot be somber (A); it lacks the precision to be truly didactic (B); pathos is presented in the sufferings of victims of unjust persecution, but the tone itself is not pathetic (D); and, while Twain is known for being acerbic, the tone is not bitter (C).

2. (E)

Here Twain uses the phrase "enlightened Christianity" in ironic juxtaposition with examples of barbarity committed by nominally Christian rulers, and the vicious judgments of a Christian chronicler. "Enlightened" is also an adjective modifying "Christianity."

3. (E)

Twain describes a time when augurs, who generally read signs in nature (for example, the entrails of birds or other animals), are no longer in use, or indeed even remembered. Their function, that of prediction, had been taken over by priests. While (A), all augurs are dead, is true, it is not the best answer. There is nothing in the passage to suggest that (B) is the case, and the passage of more than a millennium refutes it.

4. (B)

The transition in the discussion is suggested by the ellipsis and the temporal shift forward by "eleven hundred and thirty or forty years." Twain amply proves his in-depth knowledge of history (C) throughout the passage. Superstition has not been forgotten (D), merely transferred from augurs to priests.

5. (E)

Twain provides several examples of Henry of Huntington's willingness to attribute various agonizing deaths to the punishment of a just God. At one point Twain states: "Whenever God punishes a man, Henry of Huntington knows why it was done, and tells us; and his pen is eloquent with admiration; but when a man has earned punishment, and escapes, he does not explain."

6. (A)

Metonymy is the use of a word related to the term intended. In this case, the word *pen* represents the act of writing. Synecdoche is the use of an important part to represent a whole, for example, describing ranch workers as *hands* because they work with their hands. Neither symbol, nor metaphor, nor personification is present.

7. (B)

According to Twain, Henry of Huntington does not explain when an evil person, such as King Stephen, escapes a punishment as severe as that which is received by someone guilty of a lesser evil, such as the Archbishop of Canterbury, who is guilty only of consecrating Stephen as king. On these points, Henry of Huntington is silent, and Twain interprets these silences as "suppressed criticism."

8. (C)

The use of this phrase is irony indicated by the use of understatement. Twain is outraged by the injustice of the judgments of God as expressed by Henry of Huntington, and uses irony, a typical Twain literary device, to express that outrage.

9. (D)

Reread the second half of paragraph 11: "Robert Marmion, issuing forth against the enemy, was slain under the walls of the monastery, being the only one who fell, though he was surrounded by his troops. Dying excommunicated, he became subject to death everlasting. In like manner Earl Godfrey was singled out among his followers, and shot with an arrow by a common foot-soldier. He made light of the wound, but he died of it in a few days, under excommunication."

10. (D)

Again, turn to paragraph 11 to answer this question: "In the month of August, Providence displayed its justice in a remarkable manner; for two of the nobles who had converted monasteries into fortifications, expelling the monks, their sin being the same, met with a similar punishment."

11. (C)

At the beginning of paragraph 12, Twain says: "The exaltation jars upon me; not because of the death of the men, for they deserved that, but because it is death eternal, in white-hot fire and flame. It makes my flesh crawl."

12. (E)

Hyperbole is a form of exaggeration. For example, "meantime he has committed a *million other crimes* . . ." Twain uses understatement with his use of the word *generally* in paragraph 13. Litotes is a particular form of understatement in which the grammatically correct use of a double negative indicates a positive, for example, "the weather was not unpleasant." Twain does not use litotes in this passage. Alliteration is most often used in poetry,

and although sometimes employed effectively in prose, it does not appear here.

13. (E)

Twain uses several examples to demonstrate situations in which the punishment does not fit the crime, and a greater criminal receives no punishment. In his Chronicle, Twain shows how Henry of Huntington also relates that specific crimes are connected seemingly arbitrarily to deaths many years after the fact. At one point, Twain takes Henry of Huntington to task for rejoicing excessively.

Questions 14–26

14. (D)

Mill states that "the principle which regulates the existing social relations between the two sexes—the legal subordination of one sex to the other—is wrong itself, and now one of the chief hindrances to human improvement; and that it ought to be replaced by a principle of perfect equality, admitting no power or privilege on the one side, nor disability on the other."

15. (E)

Mill states that his task is "arduous" precisely because he argues against a strongly held belief possessed by nearly all persons, and that the strength of belief leads to a denial of rational argument: "So long as opinion is strongly rooted in the feelings, it gains rather than loses instability by having a preponderating weight of argument against it. For if it were accepted as a result of argument, the refutation of the argument might shake the solidity of the conviction; but when it rests solely on feeling, the worse it fares in argumentative contest, the more persuaded adherents are that their feeling must have some deeper ground, which the arguments do not reach; and while the feeling remains, it is always throwing up fresh entrenchments of argument to repair any breach made in the old."

16. (C)

Mill is referring to the way in which deeply held emotional convictions become stronger and less rational when confronted with logical arguments; in this case, the argument that women and men should be treated as equals under the law and by custom. The emotional belief is undermined, but that undermining is turned into entrenchment which repairs breaches made by reason in the old belief.

17. (B)

In a court, the burden of proof lies with the party trying to limit liberty: "If a person is charged with a murder, it rests with those who accuse him to give proof of his guilt, not with himself to prove his innocence." However, this is the opposite of the case in which Mill is trying to refute a commonly held belief.

18. (C)

Mill compares this with his own position of having to refute a commonly held, deeply emotional falsehood, which cannot be easily dislodged by merely presenting factual evidence in a rational manner.

19. (A)

In this case, *a priori* means working from the established assumption of "freedom and impartiality"—in other words, one should assume that these are the standard conditions from which all decisions proceed, and any circumstance requiring restriction of liberty or a lack of impartiality must be argued for: precisely the opposite of Mill's position.

20. (C)

Because the opinion is universally held that women are not the equals of men, the same standards of law do not apply to women and men.

21. (E)

Answers (A), (B), and (C) could all be used in various ways to demonstrate Mill's argument. He does use variations on (A) and (C), in his discussions of ways in which the burden of proof normally falls on the side that wishes to impose restrictions on liberty. Although Mill does not argue here for equal rights for black people, a similar case could be made on the basis of a universally held belief that flies in the face of custom. However, as for (D), it would be difficult to use a common property dispute to demonstrate either side of Mill's argument, since the issues raised, and the emotions involved, are more complex.

22. (D)

Mill does not state that he is confident that he could make an airtight case, but that even if he could, he could not shake his opponents' irrational belief in their position.

23. (D)

Mill restates the difficulty of arguing against a position that is held by all and is presumed to be true. According to Mill, only "intellects . . . of a high class"—the brightest minds—can rise above such an irrational mode of thought.

24. (C)

Mill's unstated point is that in order to accept his rational argument in opposition to custom and popular sentiment, one must be uncommonly intelligent. Furthermore, he uses language suggesting elitism ("high class") to make those who disagree with his position seem more commonplace.

25. (E)

Mill feels his argument is strong, but because it flies in the face of common practice and custom (B), in which men have too much faith (D), it results in a deep hostility to his cause (C), and the vast majority of men are not sufficiently cultivated to appreciate an argument based solely on reason (A).

26. (A)

The intellectual movement away from rationality and towards instinct that marked the transition from the so-called "Age of Reason" of the 18th century towards the "Romantic" movement of the 19th century, and the subsequent elevation of the nonrational understanding over rational argument is what Mill deplores as "idolatry" and the "most pernicious of false worships."

Questions 27–39

27. (C)

In the first paragraph, Lock is establishing the various types of ideas that exist simultaneously in the minds of men, and the words he lists represent those ideas.

28. (D)

Locke is setting up an argument to refute the notion that there is an *a priori* set of ideas present in all men from the beginning, so he mentions this belief as "received doctrine," or generally accepted understanding.

29. (B)

Locke's argument is best expressed by this sentence. It is both concise and complete. It makes a very good thesis statement for this essay. Statement (A) lays the groundwork of the argument, the starting assumption. It is not the argument itself. Statement (C) is a supporting statement for one portion of the argument, namely that external perceptions contribute to our ideas. Statement (D) is a restatement of the thesis, but is not sufficient in itself because the terms are not defined. Statement (E) is likewise too vague.

30. (C)

Since Locke is attempting to prove that the mind has no innate ideas, he must prove that the ideas come from somewhere. In this case, the ideas come from either sensation or reflection. Therefore, the state of the mind before the ideas are either received through sensation or produced through reflection is compared metaphorically to a sheet of white paper.

31. (A)

Experience, as received through sensation, furnishes our minds with the raw materials of ideas. Those ideas are shaped by reason, in the form of the operations of our minds. "Original characters" are akin to the "native ideas" which some early philosophers supposed the mind to be imbued with.

32. (C)

Locke reserves the term "reflection" for "perception, thinking, doubting, believing, reasoning, knowing, willing, and all the different actings of our own minds;—which we being conscious of, and observing in ourselves, do from these receive into our understandings as distinct ideas as we do from bodies affecting our senses." In other words, the operations of our minds which occur completely separate form our sensations.

33. (D)

While a modern reader might interpret "reflection" to include analysis of data received by the senses, Locke explicitly eliminates sensation from his concept of reflection.

34. (B)

Locke here uses "several" in the archaic meaning of "separate" or "distinct," not the current definition, "many." Neither "diverse" nor "intended" are acceptable definitions of "several." This supports his notion that sensation and perception are two distinct processes.

35. (E)

Locke indicates that while children have no ideas in the beginning, they gradually begin to accumulate sensations and over time develop the quality of reflection, and that most men, looking back at their own childhoods, can usually recollect at what time they began to form certain complex ideas.

36. (D)

According to Locke, it is intuitively clear that certain experiences must be received through the senses, such as the experience of red or green, or the taste of oysters or pineapples. This position supports his arguments that all ideas must originate from either sensation or reflection.

37. (C)

Locke creates a structured, rational argument that moves from premise through supporting arguments to a well-reasoned conclusion. He does not present himself as an authority by presenting his credentials (A) or appealing to the emotions by using sentimentality (B). The questions that appear are not rhetorical in nature, but are used to frame the argument (D). There is no irony used in the essay at all (E).

38. (B)

Locke's arguments would have been attended to by an educated audience. Because the ideas he presented were new at the time, it is relatively safe to assume that most of his audience would have accepted the notion that at least some ideas were innate. It is unlikely that Locke would have written for either the narrow groups of serious philosophers (C) or government officials (E); children (A) and the working class (D) would not have sufficient experience, training, or education to analyze his arguments.

39. (E)

Locke argues that ideas do indeed originate from the senses and experience (sensation). By inference, an idea cannot be divinely inspired, or originating from the instincts (innate).

Questions 40–50

40. (A)

By using Bloom's term "bardolator," Burby concurs with Bloom on the importance of studying the life and works of Shakespeare. He "quibbles"—disagrees—with Bloom on the greatness of Falstaff (B); there is no concurrence on the mental state (C), character (D), or religion (E) of Hamlet in the paragraph.

41. (D)

The original meaning of the word *catholic* (lowercase "c") is "universal." There is nothing in the paragraph itself to suggest any religious meaning, or the concept of immortality. Here the meaning is that Hamlet's character is noble, not merely that he is a member of the nobility or an elite social group.

42. (B)

Through the media and culture, adolescents of the 21st century have become "visually oriented and overstimulated." As a result, "they have little patience with the written word." While shows like *South Park* or *Jerry Springer* may or may not have frequent allusions to Shakespeare, it is not relevant to the argument of this paragraph. (D) There is nothing in the second paragraph to suggest that adults cannot appreciate Shakespeare (A) or that Shakespeare is not currently relevant (E).

43. (D)

As Burby states, shows like *South Park* and *Springer* routinely explore themes that would generally have been considered taboo a decade ago, and teen parents—and teen parents of multiple children—are more common and more accepted than a decade ago. It is difficult, then, to argue that adolescents should not be exposed to *Hamlet* as Shakespeare's audience would have experienced it.

44. (C)

Read the sentence following the line reference. Here, Burby refers to crucial lines being cut from the texts previously referred to as "bowdlerized." This eliminates choices (A) and (E), and strongly suggests (C). There is no evidence in text to suggest either humorous (D) or ignorant (B).

45. (A)

Deletion of certain lines or scenes can leave the student with incomplete information to make an accurate judgment about the motivations of characters.

46. (E)

Burby opens paragraph 6 by saying that the plays should be taught "as a whole" (A). Then he continues his argument that "modern-language translations rob the plays of much of their entertainment value" (B), and that while adults may feel "awkward" (D), all 12th graders "can handle the touchy moral issues" of *Hamlet* (C).

47. (A)

Hamlet's treatment of the two women in the play, Gertrude and Ophelia, has been justifiably labeled misogynistic, particularly his treatment of the seemingly innocent Ophelia. While some of the other issues have been debated by critics, none is discussed in the article.

48. (E)

Burby discusses all of the reasons given in the question as evidence that Ophelia and Hamlet have had a sexual relationship, except for Hamlet's treatment of Ophelia during the Mousetrap scene, which, while it could be construed as evidence, is not included in this discussion.

49. (D)

According to Wilson, Hamlet feels "sullied" or contaminated by his mother's sin against his father. T.S. Eliot is the critic who claims that Hamlet is not up to the task of revenge. Wilson is not mentioned as discussing Hamlet's hatred of Polonius or Ophelia's return of Hamlet's letters.

50. (C)

When Hamlet, heartbroken by his mother's perfidy, utters "Frailty, thy name is woman," he extends Gertrude's flaw to cover all women. In fact, Ophelia has had no other lovers, but feels abandoned by Hamlet. The Ghost's call for revenge is not mentioned; Hamlet has given up on Ophelia long before he kills Polonius.

SECTION II: FREE-RESPONSE QUESTIONS

Question One: Johnson's Definition of Envy

Analysis of Question One

Johnson's definition of envy can be classified as a formal or extended definition. AP Language and Composition students should not be unfamiliar with this mode of discourse, and will find much to comment about in Johnson's rich and challenging essay.

It is easy to recognize that envy is one of those intangible concepts best defined by what it does, how it affects not only those who possess it but also those who must suffer as the often innocent victims of these possessors.

Students will recognize that Johnson accomplishes his definition by using synonyms and connotations for an abstract concept—envy. He relies upon clever analogy and numerous examples to develop his ideas. Envy is so powerful it is an empire unto itself. It's an easy vice to nourish because it is practicable any time, any place. It is a frequent visitor, often bursting out with "latent animosity." It is a "stubborn weed of the mind," says Johnson, and it is "a vice inconsistent with the character of a social being." Finally, he assures the reader that to suffer any other vice is preferable to suffer from the vice of envy.

Johnson discusses the despicable behavior that is typical of one who envies. Very bluntly he tells us that envy is evil, and will only result in the possessor of envy feeling "shame, anguish and perturbation." What student could not find something to talk about after reading this provocative passage by Samuel Johnson?

Scoring Guide for Question One

9 Points: Essays scoring a 9 meet all the criteria for 8-point papers and are also particularly full or apt in analysis or demonstrate particular stylistic command.

8 Points: Essays earning a score of 8 effectively analyze how the rhetorical strategies and stylistic devices Johnson employs effectively achieve his definition of the envy. They are like to recognize how specific devices (such as tone, syntax, and diction) contribute to the writer's definition. The prose of these essays demonstrates an ability to control a wide range of the elements of effective writing, but it is not flawless.

7 Points: Essays earning a score of 7 fit the description of 6-point essays but employ more complete analysis or more mature prose style.

6 Points: Essays earning a score of 6 adequately analyze how the rhetorical strategies and stylistic devices Johnson uses to define his concept of envy. They may discuss rhetorical elements such as diction or tone that contribute to the essay's effect, but their discussion may be incomplete. They may skirt around the idea that Johnson has attempted to create a definition of the term. A few lapses in diction or syntax may be present, but in general the prose of 6 essays conveys their writers' ideas clearly.

5 Points: Essays earning a score of 5 fit the description of 6-point essays but their development of these strategies is limited or inconsistent. Their focus may be unclear or their analysis insufficiently or developed. A few lapses in diction or syntax may be present, but usually the prose in 5-point essays conveys their writers' ideas more or less clearly.

4 Points: Essays earning a score of 4 inadequately respond to the task. Their analysis of rhetorical strategies and discussion of the effectiveness of stylistic is limited in accuracy or purpose. They may misunderstand the purpose of prompt or paraphrase Johnson's definition more than analyze it. The prose of 4-point essays may convey their writers' ideas adequately, but may suggest immature control over organization, diction, or syntax.

3 Points: Essays earning a score of 3 meet the criteria for 4-point essays but are less perceptive about how rhetorical strategies connect to purpose in Johnson's definition or are less consistent in their control of elements of writing.

2 Points: Essays earning a score of 2 achieve little success in analyzing how rhetorical strategies contribute to the effectiveness of Johnson's definition. These essays pay little attention to rhetorical features and generalize about, or seriously misread, tone or purpose. They may simply paraphrase or comment on Johnson's definition without analyzing his strategies. The prose of 2-point papers often reveals consistent weakness in writing, a lack of development or organization, grammatical problems, or lack of control.

1 Point: Essays earning a score of 1 meet the criteria for a score of 2-point essays, but in addition are especially simplistic in their discussion or weak in controlling elements of language.

Sample Student Response to Question One

Who among us hasn't fancied what someone else had—new running shoes, a nifty car, the best looking girl? Which of us has not yearned to be on the first string, make the winning touch down or earn a 5 on the AP English Language and Composition Exam? Not many, would be my guess. I think it is human nature to want what another has. The classic movie, 2001, A Space Odyssey opens with one cave man contentedly going about his business. This peacefulness is suddenly shattered when another caveman wants what the other has and they start beating each other up. The reason for this? Envy.

Samuel Johnson says that envy is so very powerful that it is an empire that is out of control. It has no limits. Wherever there is idleness and pride, there will be envy. With something so powerful, it is no wonder that Johnson utilizes so many strategies to develop his ideas.

Johnson strains the vocabulary of any reader with the words he uses to illustrate envy. Even if a reader does not know every word Johnson chooses, it is easy to figure out that they all have very negative connotations, and most have to do with hatred, evil and anger.

First Johnson warns us that envy is everywhere. He sets up a suspicious tone in the second paragraph. He warns us that envy is a passion, but not a good passion. It is something always irritated and therefore readily present whether we acknowledge its existence or not. By setting up this warning, Johnson seems to be drawing us all in, telling us "reader beware."

In the third paragraph Johnson seems to be telling us what envy is not. We might expect something really obvious, and he even throws out the name of a literary villain, Shylock. But it is not someone like that who triggers envy. It is those who mean others nothing but the best. Those who are truly innocent, who only wish to "see others pleased" that excite acrimony (hate?) in those who "suffer" from envy. The envious are those who are angered when "seeing others pleased" and those upset by "hearing applauses which another enjoys." By setting up opposites like this, Johnson gets his point across. Envy is a cruel taskmaster.

Then Johnson talks about the <u>frequency</u> of envy, meaning its characteristic of being everywhere, all the time. One does not usually think of a vice as necessarily keeping a schedule, but Johnson tells us that it is so everywhere that we often don't even notice it. This reminds me of the arguments about TV violence. Critics often say that violence on TV and in video games is so pervasive that we don't even recognize that it is there. Maybe Johnson understood more about psychology and one's unconscious learning than we give him credit for. Using alliteration and wonderful word choice Johnson says of anyone who finally sees the truth of envy's lurking presence "he then learns to abhor those artifices at which he only laughed before and discovers how much the happiness of life would be advanced by the eradication of envy from the human heart."

Johnson uses analogy in his definition of envy. He tells us it is a "stubborn weed of the mind." Now everyone knows how hard it is to get rid of the common dandelion, so this is part of the definition even common folk can understand. It does not yield to the culture of philosophy (weed killer?) so we must find other ways to combat it. No one wants to grow a garden of dandelions, and no one wants to harbor envy. It only brings us "shame, anguish and perturbation." Later on in the definition Johnson suggests that we might want to harbor any other vice rather than envy. Perhaps, by extending his analogy, one might be happy with a garden made up of some kinds of weeds, just not this one.

Finally, Johnson hits everyone at their most sensitive level. He says that envy is inconsistent with the character of a social being. No one wants to not be a social being, that would take away our very humanity. It is an anti-social vice because of the injuries that it incites. These injuries are especially hateful because they are committed "against those who have given no intentional provocation." Who wants to be accused of that? If Johnson hasn't convinced the reader before, by appealing to the reader's very humanness, he truly gets his message across.

Johnson finishes by asserting that envy is unmixed and genuine evil. He calls the shots as he sees them. He does not mince words. His sentence structure is straightforward, and his language is angry and every descriptor seems negative and bad. Without a doubt Johnson's definition tells us that of all "diseases" humans are susceptible to, envy is the one thing we should avoid at all costs.

Commentary on Sample Student Response to Question One

This AP English Language and Comp student has obviously had some experience with formal, extended definition. This student recognizes that with a concept as abstract as envy, Johnson had to develop his definition using a variety of rhetorical strategies. The student has rightly recognized comparison and analogy—definition by what the concept does and indirectly by what it does not do.

The prompt also directs students to also address whatever rhetorical devices Johnson has used to develop his definition. Again this student recognizes Johnson's use of balance and contrast. She also mentions Johnson's vocabulary, correctly identifying the gist of the words as relevant to evil and malice. In addition, Johnson's straightforward sentence structure is noticed as well as several observations on Johnson's methods of involving his reader. Tone is implicitly addressed as being seductive, reproachful, and pleading.

Yes, this response lacks the sophistication usually found in 8–9 papers. The near paragraph-by-paragraph analysis is rather mundane. Nevertheless, this student has succeeded in effectively, though not brilliantly responding to tasks of the prompt. In conclusion, this is certainly a high 6 to a 7 response. Some might even push it up into the strata of a low 8 response. This young writer obviously understands most of what Samuel Johnson is saying. The definition is not only comprehended, but this student seems to have heeded the underlying warning of that Johnson shares with the reader, warning us of the very malevolent characteristics of envy.

Question Two: FDR's Fourth Inaugural Address

Analysis of Question Two

It is impossible to imagine that any student responding to this prompt and passage will not have at least a cursory knowledge of FDR as a critical influence upon America's participation in World War II. Those students with a strong U.S. history background must be careful not to substitute historical or biographical information for an appropriate response to this prompt.

This fourth inaugural address is a very straightforward speech, lending itself to ready understanding by any Advanced Placement student. The prompt directs students to consider FDR's feelings about war and the inevitable struggle to obtain peace that is bound to follow the war. Students are asked to consider how Roosevelt used specific rhetorical devices to get his point across. In addition, students are reminded that they must also consider what effect this address may have had, and whether or not there may be a discrepancy between his intended effect and the probable effect of his words upon his audience.

Successful responses will include references to specific rhetorical strategies such as tone, diction, syntax, etc. Perceptive students will note how FDR engages his audience by reaching out to them not just as their president, but as a fellow countryman, a citizen, a friend who wants as much as they to see the end of this war and to work together towards a "just and honorable peace, a durable peace."

It will be evident to most that syntax is critical to the success of FDR's message: his words are powerful and moving, and he uses the dash liberally for emphasis, highlighting those sentiments he most wants to convey to his listeners. In addition, FDR's clever use of repetition certainly emphasizes his message to his people.

Tone within this address cannot be overlooked. After embracing his listeners with the constant use of "we must," "we have learned," "we can gain," etc.—thereby uniting everyone to these common goals—he turns to God for help in these endeavors. Who could argue with this?

A wise student will consider the 1945 war-weary audience who were receiving FDR's message. America was more than ready for peace, and they would surely have welcomed Roosevelt's heartfelt sentiments. Nevertheless, it was seven long months before the end, and FDR did not live to see the peace he so fervently anticipated.

Students should find much to say about this historical passage. The challenge, however, will be to respond to the tasks of the prompt. It is not incorrect or disadvantageous for a student to include additional information, but the tasks of the prompt must be fulfilled for a student to receive a satisfactory score.

Scoring Guide for Question Two

9 Points: Essays scoring a 9 meet all the criteria for 8-point papers and are also particularly full or apt in their analysis, or they demonstrate impressive stylistic control.

8 Points: Essays earning a score of 8 effectively analyze the rhetorical strategies and stylistic devices that demonstrate Franklin D Roosevelt's attitudes within his inaugural address. They refer to the text, directly or indirectly, and are likely to clearly describe how strategies such as tone, syntax and diction contribute to this attitude. In addition, they successfully address the effect of this address on the audience. Their prose demonstrates an ability to control a wide range of the elements of effective writing, but they will not necessarily be flawless.

7 Points: Essays earning a score of 7 fit the description of 6-point essays, but they demonstrate a more complete analysis or more mature prose style.

6 Points: Essays earning a score of 6 adequately analyze how rhetorical strategies help convey FDR's attitude in his inaugural address as well as how this address would be received by its audience. They refer to the text, directly or indirectly, and they may discuss or implicitly recognize features and devices such as tone and syntax and use examples appropriately. Explanations of how specific strategies work may be less effective or less developed. A few lapses in diction or syntax may be present, but generally the prose of 6 essays conveys their writers' ideas clearly.

5 Points: Essays earning a score of 5 understand the task and analyze rhetorical strategies used by FDR to express his attitude and indicate its effect upon his audience. The development of the 5 response is limited or inconsistent. They may treat strategies in superficial ways or develop their ideas inconsistently. A few lapses in diction or syntax may be present, but the writer's ideas are usually clearly evident.

4 Points: Essays earning a score of 4 inadequately respond to the question's tasks. They may misunderstand, misrepresent, or oversimplify Roosevelt's attitude or its probable effect upon his audience. They may use evidence inappropriately or they may identify strategies without clearly or appropriately connecting them to Roosevelt's attitude within his address. They may fail to comment upon the effect of Roosevelt's speech upon his listeners. They may suggest immaturity in terms of control over organization of ideas, diction, or syntax.

3 Points: Essays earning a score of 3 meet the criteria for a 4-point essay, but are less perceptive about the ways in which rhetorical strategies help convey Roosevelt's attitude or its effect upon his audience. They are often less consistent in their control of elements of good writing

2 Points: Essays earning a score of 2 achieve little success in analyzing the rhetorical strategies employed by Roosevelt to convey his attitude. They may substitute simpler tasks for the one at hand, often paraphrasing the passage extensively. They may overlook the probable effect of the passage upon its audience. The purpose of these papers often reveals consistent weaknesses in writing, a lack of organization, grammatical problems, or control.

1 Point: Essays earning a score of 1 meet the criteria for a score of 2-point essays, but in addition are especially simplistic in their response to the quotation or weak in their control of language.

Sample Student Response to Question Two

January 1945: more than 6 months before the U.S. bombed Hiroshima but over 3 years since Pearl Harbor. How could any war weary American not be encouraged and energized by Franklin D. Roosevelt's strong, sincere fourth inaugural address? Through a clever use of words and sentence structure, as well as an earnest tone, it is clear that FDR truly believes that although the end of the war is near, the establishment of an honorable and durable peace is going to take some time to accomplish.

As in probably all U.S. presidential inaugural addresses, FDR addresses dignitaries and his fellow countrymen, embracing everyone as if his ideals and sentiments would naturally be everyone else's as well. He says that "men, women and children" will be acting honorable and with all-time importance. He assures all that America "shall not fail." Who could not warm to such a message?

Throughout his speech, FDR keeps repeating the pronoun "we." He talks about ending war and striving for peace, but that this will not be an easy task. He admits that we may make mistakes along the way (a sure way of engaging his audience), but we shall persevere. There is no doubt that he feels that war is near completion. However, he spends most of his speech looking beyond war to the long struggle ahead as America attempts to establish a durable peace. FDR not only uses repetition and parallel structure to get his point across, but he also effectively uses the dash. The dashes help emphasize and clarify points he wishes to make. One can almost here him take a slight pause, for instance in lines 14–15, when he says "my fellow countrymen—in the presence of our God—" reminding everyone that this is not a task that we mortals can handle without some divine assistance. Later, the dash is used for contrast such as in lines 30–32 when he says, "rising to the heights—then all will seem to reverse itself and start downward." Finally, he expresses sorrow with the dashes in lines 42–44: "we have learned lessons—at a fearful cost—and we shall profit by them."

One other rhetorical devise FDR relies upon in this address is allusion. First he mentions his former schoolmaster, who long before taught FDR that not everything will go smoothly (lines 29–30) and then to Emerson, the famous American poet, who spoke of the necessity of friends (lines 53–54). Finally, FDR makes reference, in line 37, to our Constitution in 1787.

He admits that it is not perfect, that we are still working on it, but it still provides "a firm base upon which all manner of men, of all races and colors and creeds, could build our solid structure of democracy."

From lines 45 through about 51 FDR echoes John Donne's message that no man is an island. FDR says that we have learned some lessons from this war. The tone of the parent or schoolmaster can almost be heard within these lines—a "learning experience" from a bad thing (war). America cannot live in isolation. It is interdependent with its allies. He reminds all of us that "we must live as men, not as ostriches, nor as dogs in the manger." Instead we must become "citizens of the world, members of the human community." I personally find the Emerson quote a bit simplistic, something that Mr. Rogers would be apt to say on his TV show for children. Nevertheless, it is a true statement. World War II certainly taught the U.S. the importance of strong allies.

Finally, I imagine that this speech was well received. I happen to know from U.S. History class that, indeed, America looked to FDR as its father figure throughout the war. His famous Fireside Chats were what kept many people from despair. But aside from this, his words are positive in that he anticipates an end to the war, but also realistic when he reminds all that peace is not going to be a snap. It will be an ongoing struggle. One, in fact, that we are still working on today.

Commentary on Sample Student Response to Question Two

This student clearly understands FDR's fourth inaugural address. He adequately analyzes several rhetorical strategies and how they help to convey FDR's message. This student does not just tell us that the president uses a lot of dashes (a common comment on many student responses, unfortunately), but continues by describing just how these dashes are used—to express sentiments, to contrast points, to emphasize meaning. That is what makes this an "upper-half" response. The student tells us what rhetorical device the passage has, and then goes on to explain how this device is used.

Tone is addressed, and diction and its significance are certainly implicitly discussed. In addition, this student brings in the concept of allusion and how FDR makes reference to other people and things to express himself.

Finally, the student remembers to comment on the probable effect of this passage upon the audience. In fact, audience is implicitly mentioned prior to the final paragraph where it is addressed directly.

Although this essay response is not without flaws—it doesn't flow as well as it might—this student obviously has all the tools. It is a response that could easily work its way into the 8–9 range upon revision. As it stands now, however, it is clearly a 7 response. It is certainly stronger than an adequate 6, but it does not demonstrate the flair and stylistic control of an 8 paper.

Not only does this student know his history, he has avoided the pitfall of substituting this knowledge for a response to the tasks of the prompt. Instead he uses the information to enhance his answer, resulting in a very satisfactory composition.

Question Three: Thoreau—Choosing the Right Direction

Analysis of Question Three

This single paragraph is excerpted from a much longer essay by Thoreau. Like other essays by Thoreau, "Nature" allegorically becomes the vehicle for his philosophy. The entire essay actually talks about certain physical walks he takes, directions he meanders, and destinations in which he finds himself. None of this, however, is necessary for students to know in order to respond successfully to this prompt. In fact, this prompt is very open-ended for students. They should easily be able to understand what Thoreau is saying and readily apply it to their own lives or to something else they have observed or read about.

In responding to this prompt, the more successful student should avoid the pitfalls of answering with the most trite response. Not accepting a date from a certain someone or ordering the wrong thing at the local restaurant are not the type of regrets that are apt to garner much praise from essay scorers. It is true that students are encouraged to include experiences; it is a wise student who takes a broader approach when responding to a question such as this one. It would be better, perhaps, to reference situations from literature or from history as support in responding to this prompt.

Another tendency to avoid is to oversimplify the interpretation of Thoreau. Yes, he is talking about the direction one might take in a physical walk, but rarely is anything Thoreau wrote as straightforward as that. Students should think in more metaphysical terms when considering how heedless and stupid humans can be in their actions. Also, we must realize that "right answers" do not always exist because we have not yet formulated such a path within our imagination.

Although the piece seems simple from a surface reading, upon analysis and reflection, Thoreau actually offers students a thought-provoking passage with which to grapple.

Scoring Guide for Question Three

9 points: Essays earning a score of 9 meet all of the criteria for 8 papers and in addition are especially thorough in their analysis or demonstrate a particularly impressive control of argumentative style.

8 points: Essays earning a score of 8 effectively interpret Thoreau's comments about the difficulties we face in choosing and following the right direction. These essays present a carefully reasoned argument in support of their position and enlist appropriate evident from outside readings and observation that support it. Their prose demonstrates an impressive control of the elements of effective argumentative writing, though it is not flawless.

7 points: Essays earning a score of 7 fit the description of 6 essays but feature either more purposeful arguments or a greater command of prose style.

6 points: Essays scoring six accurately interpret Thoreau's comments about finding and following the right direction. These arguments, while generally sound in nature and adequately supported, are nevertheless not as persuasive as essays earning scores of 7 because they are often less developed or less cogent. Though these papers may demonstrate lapses in diction or syntax, they do reflect an adequate level of competence.

5 points: Essays scoring 5 generally understand the task but are either limited in scope or insufficiently developed. Though they may be marked by errors in syntax or diction, they nevertheless reflect a certain level of competence.

4 points: Essays scoring 4 respond inadequately to the question's task, often misunderstanding, misrepresenting, or oversimplifying Thoreau's comments about the difficulties in recognizing and following the appropriate direction. They often lack sufficient evidence to support their claims. Though their prose is often adequate enough to convey the writers' claims, it generally suggests a limited control over organization, diction, or syntax.

3 points: Essays earning a score of 3 meet the criteria for a score of 4, but are either less persuasive in interpreting Thoreau's comments, or display a more limited control over the elements of effective composition.

2 points: Essays scoring 2 achieve little success in illustrating Thoreau's comments about the difficulties in recognizing and following the appropriate direction. They may misread Thoreau, or fail to develop their argument to any substantive level. They summarize rather than analyze the material they choose to affirm or negate Thoreau's position, or display significant weaknesses in organization, clarity, fluency, or mechanics.

1 point: Essays earning a score of 1 meet the criteria for a score of 2 but are either overly simplistic or marred by severe deficiencies in the elements of composition.

Sample Student Response to Question Three

Henry David Thoreau, American poet and essayist, always makes things seem more simple than they are. In this short passage from "Walking" he seems to be discussing where he might go to exercise today. In reality, I think he is using nature (he had a thing about being outdoors, living on ponds and stuff) to represent more than a mere afternoon stroll.

There's no doubt that many of us are heedless of the "right way" and instead we make stupid decisions (directions), which we often live to regret. Also, we sometimes make decisions prematurely, maybe because we haven't really considered all the factors, or something is thrust at us from the outside, and we never considered thinking about "that direction" until it is introduced by someone else.

Every one of us has made a bad decision. Sometimes it's just a little, inconsequential thing, like staying out after our curfew and trying to sneak back into the house. Other times "heedless" or "stupid" decisions can lead to greater consequences, like being coerced to go to a college you don't really want to, but you agree because of family pressure, or worse yet, peer pressure.

Such situations are actually the basis of most any literary or dramatic tragedy. Macbeth is what comes to my mind. There he was, minding his own business, happy to be the new Thane of Cowder when bam, three ugly witches suggest a direction (being king) he had never even thought of before. He just about dismisses the suggestion as a "bad idea" by the time he gets home, but then he encounters Lady Macbeth. That's when his trouble really began.

Not only does he ignore the "right way" to go, but his wife convinces him to take the "wrong one (direction)." Not only does she also introduce a thought that did "not yet exist distinctly in (his) idea" as the witches had, but she compounds it with even more wrong directions. Before he knows it he not only considers this new direction as the one he thinks he wants, he's ready to kill to get there. His own "heedlessness and stupidity" is evident, however, because he does not act rashly. In fact he thinks long and hard about what he is to do. He sees a bloody dagger before him, a sure sign that he's taken the wrong turn (direction). Finally he urges himself on by saying whatever he's going to do, he'd better do it quickly. This too seems like he recognizes that he is definitely going in the wrong direction.

Later in the play, the reality of his misdirection takes the shape of a ghost of someone else he had killed, his former friend and aid, Banquo. I believe that these hallucinations are the best proof that the direction (or better yet, misdirection) that Macbeth took had not "existed distinctly in (his) idea." He knew he had really messed up, but by then he was so far in the wrong direction there was no turning back for him.

I wonder if Thoreau might have had Macbeth in mind when he wrote his essay. Probably not. Nevertheless, I have to agree with him that it is often very hard for us to determine "whither we will walk."

Commentary on Sample Student Response to Question Three

Not only does this successful essay avoid the temptation to limit its response to the personal, this student has very successfully utilized a well-chosen Shakespearean tragedy to prove her point.

Immediately we can see that this student not only understands the short Thoreau passage, but also recognizes it as more than what it seems. The essay uses *Macbeth* as its main resource for developing the argument, and this student has done this very successfully. Not only does she demonstrate understanding of the passage, but she applies it to Macbeth and his own misdirection in an exceptionally well-developed manner for the very limited time the student had to respond. This is a sign of a student who can decode the task of the prompt, use appropriate resources for developing her argument, and support the points effectively.

The prose of this response is good. Although the student sometimes lapses into informality, that is not a drawback to the success of the essay. It certainly allows the voice of this very competent writer to be heard. This essay demonstrates an impressive control of the elements of successful composition. Without a doubt this response merits an 8, or possibly a very high 7, as a score.

Remember that every score contains a range of papers. There is not just a single type of "8 paper." Many responses can show characteristics of "8-ness." Looking at the rubric, this student has successfully responded to the tasks of this prompt and has developed an interesting and competent essay to express her ideas.

Practice Test III

How to Take This Test

Before taking this practice test, find a quiet place where you can work uninterrupted for three hours or so. Make sure you have a comfortable desk, several No. 2 pencils for the multiple-choice section, and a few ballpoint pens for the essay section.

This practice test includes a multiple-choice section and a free-response section consisting of three essay questions. Use the answer grid that follows to record your multiple-choice answers. Write the essays on a separate sheet of paper.

Once you start the practice test, don't stop until you've finished the multiple-choice section. You may then take a ten-minute break before proceeding to the essay section.

You'll find the answer key and explanations following the test.

Good luck!

PRACTICE TEST III
ANSWER SHEET

1 Ⓐ Ⓑ Ⓒ Ⓓ Ⓔ   21 Ⓐ Ⓑ Ⓒ Ⓓ Ⓔ   41 Ⓐ Ⓑ Ⓒ Ⓓ Ⓔ

2 Ⓐ Ⓑ Ⓒ Ⓓ Ⓔ   22 Ⓐ Ⓑ Ⓒ Ⓓ Ⓔ   42 Ⓐ Ⓑ Ⓒ Ⓓ Ⓔ

3 Ⓐ Ⓑ Ⓒ Ⓓ Ⓔ   23 Ⓐ Ⓑ Ⓒ Ⓓ Ⓔ   43 Ⓐ Ⓑ Ⓒ Ⓓ Ⓔ

4 Ⓐ Ⓑ Ⓒ Ⓓ Ⓔ   24 Ⓐ Ⓑ Ⓒ Ⓓ Ⓔ   44 Ⓐ Ⓑ Ⓒ Ⓓ Ⓔ

5 Ⓐ Ⓑ Ⓒ Ⓓ Ⓔ   25 Ⓐ Ⓑ Ⓒ Ⓓ Ⓔ   45 Ⓐ Ⓑ Ⓒ Ⓓ Ⓔ

6 Ⓐ Ⓑ Ⓒ Ⓓ Ⓔ   26 Ⓐ Ⓑ Ⓒ Ⓓ Ⓔ   46 Ⓐ Ⓑ Ⓒ Ⓓ Ⓔ

7 Ⓐ Ⓑ Ⓒ Ⓓ Ⓔ   27 Ⓐ Ⓑ Ⓒ Ⓓ Ⓔ   47 Ⓐ Ⓑ Ⓒ Ⓓ Ⓔ

8 Ⓐ Ⓑ Ⓒ Ⓓ Ⓔ   28 Ⓐ Ⓑ Ⓒ Ⓓ Ⓔ   48 Ⓐ Ⓑ Ⓒ Ⓓ Ⓔ

9 Ⓐ Ⓑ Ⓒ Ⓓ Ⓔ   29 Ⓐ Ⓑ Ⓒ Ⓓ Ⓔ   49 Ⓐ Ⓑ Ⓒ Ⓓ Ⓔ

10 Ⓐ Ⓑ Ⓒ Ⓓ Ⓔ   30 Ⓐ Ⓑ Ⓒ Ⓓ Ⓔ   50 Ⓐ Ⓑ Ⓒ Ⓓ Ⓔ

11 Ⓐ Ⓑ Ⓒ Ⓓ Ⓔ   31 Ⓐ Ⓑ Ⓒ Ⓓ Ⓔ

12 Ⓐ Ⓑ Ⓒ Ⓓ Ⓔ   32 Ⓐ Ⓑ Ⓒ Ⓓ Ⓔ

13 Ⓐ Ⓑ Ⓒ Ⓓ Ⓔ   33 Ⓐ Ⓑ Ⓒ Ⓓ Ⓔ

14 Ⓐ Ⓑ Ⓒ Ⓓ Ⓔ   34 Ⓐ Ⓑ Ⓒ Ⓓ Ⓔ

15 Ⓐ Ⓑ Ⓒ Ⓓ Ⓔ   35 Ⓐ Ⓑ Ⓒ Ⓓ Ⓔ

16 Ⓐ Ⓑ Ⓒ Ⓓ Ⓔ   36 Ⓐ Ⓑ Ⓒ Ⓓ Ⓔ

17 Ⓐ Ⓑ Ⓒ Ⓓ Ⓔ   37 Ⓐ Ⓑ Ⓒ Ⓓ Ⓔ

18 Ⓐ Ⓑ Ⓒ Ⓓ Ⓔ   38 Ⓐ Ⓑ Ⓒ Ⓓ Ⓔ

19 Ⓐ Ⓑ Ⓒ Ⓓ Ⓔ   39 Ⓐ Ⓑ Ⓒ Ⓓ Ⓔ

20 Ⓐ Ⓑ Ⓒ Ⓓ Ⓔ   40 Ⓐ Ⓑ Ⓒ Ⓓ Ⓔ

ENGLISH LANGUAGE AND COMPOSITION

Section I: Multiple-Choice Questions

Time: 1 hour

Number of questions: 50

Percent of total grade: 45

Directions: This section contains selections of prose works and questions on their content, style, and form. After reading each passage, select the best answer and fill it in on the corresponding oval on the answer sheet.

Questions 1–13. Read the following passage carefully before you choose your answers.

The passage below is from *"A Liberal Education"* by Thomas Huxley.

What is education? Above all things, what is our ideal of a thoroughly liberal education?—of that education which, if we could begin life again,
Line we would give ourselves—of that education
(5) which, if we could mould the fates to our own will, we would give our children? Well, I know not what may be your conceptions upon this matter, but I will tell you mine, and I hope I shall find that our views are not very discrepant.
(10)   Suppose it were perfectly certain that the life and fortune of every one of us would, one day or other, depend upon his winning or losing a game of chess. Don't you think that we should all consider it to be a primary duty to learn at least
(15) the names and the moves of the pieces; to have a notion of a gambit, and a keen eye for all the means of giving and getting out of check? Do you not think that we should look with a disapprobation amounting to scorn, upon the
(20) father who allowed his son, or the state which allowed its members, to grow up without knowing a pawn from a knight?
    Yet it is a very plain and elementary truth, that the life, the fortune, and the happiness of
(25) every one of us, and, more or less, of those who are connected with us, do depend upon our knowing something of the rules of a game infinitely more difficult and complicated than chess. It is a game which has been played for

(30) untold ages, every man and woman of us being one of the two players in a game of his or her own. The chessboard is the world, the pieces are the phenomena of the universe, the rules of the game are what we call the laws of Nature. The
(35) player on the other side is hidden from us. We know that his play is always fair, just, and patient. But also we know, to our cost, that he never overlooks a mistake, or makes the smallest allowance for ignorance. To the man who plays
(40) well, the highest stakes are paid, with that sort of overflowing generosity with which the strong shows delight in strength. And one who plays ill is checkmated—without haste, but without remorse.
(45)   My metaphor will remind some of you of the famous picture in which Retzsch has depicted Satan playing at chess with man for his soul. Substitute for the mocking fiend in that picture a calm, strong angel who is playing for love, as we
(50) say, and would rather lose than win—and I should accept it as an image of human life.
    Well, what I mean by Education is learning the rules of this mighty game. In other words, education is the instruction of the intellect in the
(55) laws of Nature, under which name I include not merely things and their forces, but men and their ways; and the fashioning of the affections and of the will into an earnest and loving desire to move

in harmony with those laws. For me, education
(60) means neither more nor less than this. Anything
which professes to call itself education must be
tried by this standard, and if it fails to stand the
test, I will not call it education, whatever may be
the force of authority, or of numbers, upon the
(65) other side.

It is important to remember that, in strictness,
there is no such thing as an uneducated man. Take
an extreme case. Suppose that an adult man, in
the full vigour of his faculties, could be suddenly
(70) placed in the world, as Adam is said to have been,
and then left to do as he best might. How long
would he be left uneducated? Not five minutes.
Nature would begin to teach him, through the eye,
the ear, the touch, the properties of objects. Pain
(75) and pleasure would be at his elbow telling him to
do this and avoid that; and by slow degrees the
man would receive an education which, if narrow,
would be thorough, real, and adequate to his
circumstances, though there would be no extras
(80) and very few accomplishments.

And if to this solitary man entered a second
Adam or, better still, an Eve, a new and greater
world, that of social and moral phenomena, would
be revealed. Joys and woes, compared with which
(85) all others might seem but faint shadows, would
spring from the new relations. Happiness and
sorrow would take the place of the coarser
monitors, pleasure and pain; but conduct would
still be shaped by the observation of the natural
(90) consequences of actions; or, in other words, by
the laws of the nature of man.

To every one of us the world was once as
fresh and new as to Adam. And then, long before
we were susceptible of any other modes of
(95) instruction, Nature took us in hand, and every
minute of waking life brought its educational
influence, shaping our actions into rough
accordance with Nature's laws, so that we might
not be ended untimely by too gross disobedience.
(100) Nor should I speak of this process of education as
past for any one, be he as old as he may. For
every man the world is as fresh as it was at the
first day, and as full of untold novelties for him

who has the eyes to see them. And Nature is still
(105) continuing her patient education of us in that
great university, the universe, of which we are all
members—Nature having no Test-Acts.

Those who take honours in Nature's
university, who learn the laws which govern men
(110) and things and obey them, are the really great and
successful men in this world. The great mass of
mankind are the "Poll," who pick up just enough
to get through without much discredit. Those who
won't learn at all are plucked; and then you can't
(115) come up again. Nature's pluck means
extermination.

1. The first paragraph indicates that the primary
   mode of discourse for this passage will probably
   be

   (A) argumentation
   (B) extended definition
   (C) explication
   (D) description
   (E) narration

2. The first sentence of paragraph 2 (lines 10–13)
   constructs a hypothetical statement by using

   (A) past tense
   (B) the word "suppose"
   (C) conditional tense
   (D) the words "depend upon"
   (E) unclear pronoun reference

3. Paragraph 2 contains all of the following stylistic
   devices EXCEPT

   (A) metaphor
   (B) alliteration
   (C) asyndeton
   (D) rhetorical question
   (E) hyperbole

4. The antecedent of the pronoun "his" in line 12 is

   (A) life
   (B) one
   (C) it
   (D) us
   (E) fortune

GO ON TO THE NEXT PAGE. ➡

5. The game of chess, the metaphor that encompasses paragraphs 2 and 3, is a stylistic device known as

  (A) simile
  (B) hyperbole
  (C) litote
  (D) conceit
  (E) chiasmus

6. The syntax of the triple metaphors in lines 32–34 utilizes a sentence structure known as

  (A) antithesis
  (B) run-on sentence
  (C) assonance
  (D) polysyndeton
  (E) asyndeton

7. The reader can infer that Retzsch (line 46) was a(n)

  (A) angel
  (B) devil
  (C) artist
  (D) educator
  (E) philosopher

8. The definitive paragraph of this passage that best states the author's point of view is paragraph

  (A) 1
  (B) 3
  (C) 5
  (D) 7
  (E) 9

9. "This standard" (line 62) refers to

  (A) nature
  (B) harmony
  (C) intellect
  (D) education
  (E) the game

10. Paragraph 6 contains all of the following stylistic devices EXCEPT

  (A) hypothetical statement
  (B) asyndeton
  (C) personification
  (D) parallel structure
  (E) oxymoron

11. One may draw all of the following conclusions from this passage EXCEPT

  (A) our life, fortune, and happiness depend upon our knowing the rules of a game more difficult than the game of chess
  (B) education is the instruction of the intellect in the laws of nature
  (C) successful people are those who have learned the laws which govern men and things, and obey them
  (D) we are all like Adam and Eve every time we face a situation that we have not yet experienced
  (E) it is not until we have learned all the rules of the universal game that education can be truly complete

12. The BEST clarification for the words "poll" (line 112) and "pluck" (line 115) as they are used in the final paragraph is

  (A) poll means "a tally"; pluck means "to pull out from the rest"
  (B) poll refers to the minimally educated; pluck refers to those who have no education
  (C) poll refers to the well-educated; pluck refers to the minimally educated
  (D) poll refers to those without education; pluck refers to those who cannot be educated
  (E) poll refers to the non-educated; pluck refers to the minimally educated

13. The tone of this passage can BEST be described as

  (A) ominously realistic
  (B) ironically emotional
  (C) persuasive and prophetic
  (D) metaphorical and erudite
  (E) sympathetic and discursive

GO ON TO THE NEXT PAGE. ➡

Questions 14–26. Read the following passage carefully before you choose your answers.

The passage below, *"The Plague," is from Giovanni Boccaccio's* Decameron, *which he wrote between 1348 and 1351.*

DURING these times there was a pestilence, by which the whole human race came near to being annihilated. Now in the case of all other
Line scourges sent from heaven some explanation of a
(5) cause might be given by daring men, such as the many theories propounded by those who are clever in these matters; for they love to conjure up causes which are absolutely incomprehensible to man, and to fabricate outlandish theories of
(10) natural philosophy knowing well that they are saying nothing sound but considering it sufficient for them, if they completely deceive by their argument some of those whom they meet and persuade them to their view. But for this calamity
(15) it is quite impossible either to express in words or to conceive in thought any explanation, except indeed to refer it to God. For it did not come in a part of the world nor upon certain men, nor did it confine itself to any season of the year, so that
(20) from such circumstances it might be possible to find subtle explanations of a cause, but it embraced the entire world, and blighted the lives of all men, though differing from one another in the most marked degree, respecting neither sex
(25) nor age.

They were taken in the following manner. They had a sudden fever, some when just roused from sleep, others while walking about, and others while otherwise engaged, without any
(30) regard to what they were doing. And the body showed no change from its previous color, nor was it hot as might be expected when attacked by a fever, nor indeed did any inflammation set in, but the fever was of such a languid sort from its
(35) commencement and up till evening that neither to the sick themselves nor to a physician who touched them would it afford any suspicion of danger. It was natural, therefore, that not one of those who had contracted the disease expected to
(40) die from it. But on the same day in some cases, in others on the following day, and in the rest not many days later, a bubonic swelling developed; and this took place not only in the particular part of the body which is called boubon, that is,
(45) "below the abdomen," but also inside the armpit, and in some cases also beside the ears, and at different points on the thighs.

Up to this point, then, everything went in about the same way with all who had taken the
(50) disease. But from then on very marked differences developed; and I am unable to say whether the cause of this diversity of symptoms was to be found in the difference in bodies, or in the fact that it followed the wish of Him who
(55) brought the disease into the world. For there ensued with some a deep coma, with others a violent delirium, and in either case they suffered the characteristic symptoms of the disease. For those who were under the spell of the coma forgot
(60) all those who were familiar to them and seemed to lie sleeping constantly. And if anyone cared for them, they would eat without waking, but some also were neglected, and these would die directly through lack of sustenance. But those who were
(65) seized with delirium suffered from insomnia and were victims of a distorted imagination; for they suspected that men were coming upon them to destroy them, and they would become excited and rush off in flight, crying out at the top of their
(70) voices. And those who were attending them were in a state of constant exhaustion and had a most difficult time of it throughout. For this reason everybody pitied them no less than the sufferers, not because they were threatened by the
(75) pestilence in going near it (for neither physicians nor other persons were found to contract this malady through contact with the sick or with the dead, for many who were constantly engaged either in burying or in attending those in no way
(80) connected with them held out in the performance

GO ON TO THE NEXT PAGE. ➡

of this service beyond all expectation, while with many others the disease came on without warning and they died straightway); but they pitied them because of the great hardships which they were
(85) undergoing. For when the patients fell from their beds and lay rolling upon the floor, they kept putting them back in place, and when they were struggling to rush headlong out of their houses, they would force them back by shoving and
(90) pulling against them. And when water chanced to be near, they wished to fall into it, not so much because of a desire for drink (for the most of them rushed into the sea), but the cause was to be found chiefly in the diseased state of their minds.
(95) They had also great difficulty in the matter of eating, for they could not easily take food. And many perished through lack of any man to care for them, for they were either overcome by hunger, or threw themselves down from a height.
(100) And in those cases where neither coma nor delirium came on, the bubonic swelling became mortified and the sufferer, no longer able to endure the pain, died. And one would suppose that in all cases the same thing would have been
(105) true, but since they were not at all in their senses, some were quite unable to feel the pain; for owing to the troubled condition of their minds they lost all sense of feeling.
　　　So it was that in this disease there was no
(110) cause which came within the province of human reasoning; for in all cases the issue tended to be something unaccountable. For example, while some were helped by batlling, others were harmed in no less degree. And of those who
(115) received no care many died, but others, contrary to reason, were saved. And again, methods of treatment showed different results with different patients. Indeed the whole matter may be stated thus, that no device was discovered by man to
(120) save himself, so that either by taking precautions he should not suffer, or that when the malady had assailed him he should get the better of it; but suffering came without warning and recovery was due to no external cause.

14. All of the following syntactical structures can be found in the first paragraph of this passage EXCEPT
   (A) introductory subordinate clause
   (B) compound sentence with two independent clauses
   (C) use of infinitives
   (D) complex sentence structure
   (E) simple sentence

15. The possessive adjective "their" in line 14 refers to
   (A) victims of the plague
   (B) people who are persuaded
   (C) clever, daring men
   (D) learned medical professionals
   (E) revered philosophers

16. Lines 34–42 set up a contradiction that can BEST be described as a(n)
   (A) dramatic irony
   (B) situational irony
   (C) verbal irony
   (D) antithesis
   (E) situational paradox

17. The syntax of paragraph 2 demonstrates an abundance of
   (A) complex sentence structure with ample use of transitions
   (B) simple and compound sentence structure with numerous prepositional phrases
   (C) fragmented sentences and wordiness
   (D) hypothetical description and figurative imagery
   (E) pessimistic tone and little energy

18. "Languid" as it is used in line 34 means
   (A) lazy and indolent
   (B) ill and out of sorts
   (C) infected and contagious
   (D) unsuspecting and subtle
   (E) virulent and deadly

19. Lines 70–80 can BEST be interpreted as meaning

    (A) those who buried the dead feared for their lives
    (B) attendants of the ill were at risk to become infected
    (C) infected patients were not pitied by those who were well
    (D) those who tended the ill became carriers of the plague
    (E) caregivers were not more susceptible to contagion than any others

20. The parallel repetition of the "for when"/"and when" structure in paragraph 3 is known as

    (A) oxymoron
    (B) apostrophe
    (C) antithesis
    (D) anaphora
    (E) apposition

21. Lines 55–66 indicate that those suffering from the plague generally experienced which of the following symptoms

    (A) a coma so deep they were unable to eat
    (B) delirium that made them unaware of basics such as eating
    (C) a coma that caused patients to experience distorted imagination
    (D) either a deep coma or violent delirium
    (E) behavior so bizarre that men had to come and take them away

22. The last paragraph can BEST be summarized as saying

    (A) human reasoning could understand this disease
    (B) certain treatment methods worked on the majority of those treated
    (C) no person was able to recover once infected
    (D) those who received care had a better chance of surviving
    (E) man had no device with which to save himself from the pestilence

23. The tone of this passage can BEST be interpreted as

    (A) dispassionate and analytical
    (B) discursive and clinical
    (C) resigned and emotional
    (D) lyrical and convincing
    (E) erudite and melancholy

24. The language of this passage can BEST be described as

    (A) formal
    (B) academic
    (C) technical
    (D) clinical
    (E) colloquial

25. The attitude of the writer can BEST be described as

    (A) regretful but resigned to the inevitable
    (B) vehement but cautious
    (C) somber but optimistic
    (D) apprehensive and pessimistic
    (E) despondent and mournful

26. The mode of discourse employed by the writer of this passage is predominantly

    (A) argumentation
    (B) explication
    (C) comparison and contrast
    (D) extended definition
    (E) description

GO ON TO THE NEXT PAGE. ➡

KAPLAN

<u>Questions 27–39.</u> Read the following passage carefully before you choose your answers.

The passage below is from *"Shakespearean Tragedy"* (1904) by A. C. Bradley.

Othello is, in one sense of the word, by far the most romantic figure among Shakespeare's heroes; and he is so partly from the strange life of
Line war and adventure which he has lived from
(5) childhood. He does not belong to our world, and he seems to enter it we know not whence—almost as if from wonderland. There is something mysterious in his descent from men of royal siege; in his wanderings in vast deserts and
(10) among marvellous peoples; in his tales of magic handkerchiefs and prophetic Sibyls; in the sudden vague glimpses we get of numberless battles and sieges in which he has played the hero and has borne a charmed life; even in chance references to
(15) his baptism, his being sold to slavery, his sojourn in Aleppo.

And he is not a merely romantic figure; his own nature is romantic. He has not, indeed, the meditative or speculative imagination of Hamlet;
(20) but in the strictest sense of the word he is more poetic than Hamlet. . . . And this imagination, we feel, has accompanied his whole life. He has watched with a poet's eye the Arabian trees dropping their med'cinable gum, and the Indian
(25) throwing away his chance-found pearl; and has gazed in a fascinated dream at the Pontic sea rushing, never to return, to the Propontic and the Hellespont; and has felt as no other man ever felt (for he speaks of it as none other ever did) the
(30) poetry of the pride, pomp, and circumstance of glorious war.

So he comes before us, dark and grand, with a light upon him from the sun where he was born; but no longer young, and now grave, self-
(35) controlled, steeled by the experience of countless perils, hardships and vicissitudes, at once simple and stately in bearing and in speech, a great man naturally modest but fully conscious of his worth, proud of his services to the State, unawed by
(40) dignitaries and unelated by honours, secure, it

would seem, against all dangers from without and all rebellion from within. And he comes to have his life crowned with the final glory of love, a love as strange, adventurous and romantic as any
(45) passage of his eventful history, filling his heart with tenderness and his imagination with ecstasy. For there is no love, not that of Romeo in his youth, more steeped in imagination than Othello's.

(50) The sources of danger in this character are revealed but too clearly by the story. In the first place, Othello's mind, for all its poetry, is very simple. He is not observant. His nature tends outward. He is quite free from introspection, and
(55) is not given to reflection. Emotion excites his imagination, but it confuses and dulls his intellect. On this side he is the very opposite of Hamlet, with whom, however, he shares a great openness and trustfulness of nature. In addition, he has little
(60) experience of the corrupt products of civilised life, and is ignorant of European women.

In the second place, for all his dignity and massive calm (and he has greater dignity than any other of Shakespeare's men), he is by nature full
(65) of the most vehement passion. Shakespeare emphasises his self-control, not only by the wonderful pictures of the First Act, but by references to the past. . . .

Lastly, Othello's nature is all of one piece.
(70) His trust, where he trusts, is absolute. Hesitation is almost impossible to him. He is extremely self-reliant, and decides and acts instantaneously. If stirred to indignation, as "in Aleppo once," he answers with one lightning stroke. Love, if he
(75) loves, must be to him the heaven where either he must leave or bear no life. If such a passion as jealousy seizes him, it will swell into a well-night incontrollable flood. He will press for immediate conviction or immediate relief. Convinced, he will
(80) act with the authority of a judge and the swiftness

GO ON TO THE NEXT PAGE. ➡

of a man in mortal pain. Undeceived, he will do like execution on himself.

(85)   This character is so noble, Othello's feelings and actions follow so inevitably from it and from the forces brought to bear on it, and his sufferings are so heart-rending, that he stirs, I believe, in most readers a passion of mingled love and pity which they feel for no other hero in Shakespeare, and to which not even Mr. Swinburne can do (90) more than justice. Yet there are some critics and not a few readers who cherish a grudge against him. They do not merely think that in the later stages of his temptation he showed a certain obtuseness, and that, to speak pedantically, he (95) acted with unjustifiable precipitance and violence; no one, I suppose, denies that. But, even when they admit that he was not of a jealous temper, they consider that he *was* "easily jealous"; they seem to think that it was inexcusable in him to (100) feel any suspicion of his wife at all; and they blame him for never suspecting Iago or asking him for evidence.

27. In the first two paragraphs the author indicates that the character Othello is all of the following EXCEPT

(A) much more poetic than the character Hamlet
(B) mysterious and somewhat mythical
(C) more introspective than Hamlet
(D) a former slave
(E) a successful soldier

28. In lines 7–14, the series of prepositional phrases with no connecting conjunction between them is a rhetorical device known as

(A) asyndeton
(B) anadiplosis
(C) anaphora
(D) anachronism
(E) antithesis

29. In discussing Othello's "poet's eye" in lines 22–28, the author employs

(A) metaphor and simile
(B) parenthesis and understatement
(C) parallelism and alliteration
(D) hyperbole and apostrophe
(E) personification and allusion

30. The author explains Othello's "simple" mind in paragraph 4 using syntax that is primarily

(A) long, periodic sentences
(B) extensive subordination of ideas
(C) simple sentences and short clauses
(D) numerous coordinated ideas
(E) inverted sentence order

31. Paragraph 3 employs all of the following rhetorical devices EXCEPT

(A) anadiplosis
(B) isocolon
(C) assonance
(D) hyperbole
(E) synecdoche

32. The author describes the character Othello as all of the following EXCEPT

(A) being a mature man, inexperienced in love
(B) having royal ancestors
(C) being imaginative
(D) possessing a romantic nature
(E) being self-possessed

33. The description of Othello's nature in paragraph 6 can BEST be described as a series of

(A) hyperboles
(B) conditional tenses
(C) sentimental images
(D) similes and metaphors
(E) understatements

GO ON TO THE NEXT PAGE. ➡

34. Based on the description of Othello's nature given in paragraph 6, he is capable of being all of the following EXCEPT

    (A) completely trusting
    (B) romantically passionate
    (C) quick-acting
    (D) calm and unflappable
    (E) self-reliant

35. One could summarize paragraph 7 BEST by saying Othello is a character

    (A) so fearsome that viewers are in awe of him
    (B) so pitiable one cannot but feel sorry for him
    (C) so noble his heart-rending sufferings make him unique among Shakespeare's creations
    (D) so jealous his wife caused him to act without thinking
    (E) so pedantic that his very actions cause the viewer to feel jealous rage

36. Based on the entire passage, the author's description of the character Othello is that he is

    (A) shallow but confident
    (B) vain but insecure
    (C) insolent and naïve
    (D) romantic and self-assured
    (E) gullible and regretful

37. The overall tone in this passage can BEST be described as

    (A) analytical
    (B) realistic
    (C) philosophical
    (D) ironic
    (E) clinical

38. The author's attitude towards the character Othello is

    (A) critically empathetic
    (B) subjectively haughty
    (C) contemptuously emotional
    (D) respectfully cynical
    (E) disgustedly disappointed

39. The author's primary purpose in this passage seems to be to

    (A) justify the reasons for Othello's behavior
    (B) explain to the reader why Othello is the most notable of Shakespeare's heroes
    (C) demonstrate how a great man like Othello can fall so far from grace
    (D) qualify the author's criticism of the character Othello
    (E) remonstrate with critics such as Swinburne about what they have written

<u>Questions 40–50.</u> Read the following passage carefully before you choose your answers.

The speech below was given on August 14, 1947 by Jawaharlal Nehru upon India's independence from Great Britain.

Long years ago we made a tryst with destiny, and now the time comes when we shall redeem our pledge, not wholly or in full measure, but
Line very substantially. At the stroke of midnight hour,
(5) when the world sleeps, India will awake to life and freedom.

A moment comes which comes but rarely in history, when we step out from the old to the new, then an age ends, and when the soul of a nation,
(10) long suppressed, finds utterance. It is fitting that at this solemn moment we take the pledge of dedication to India and her people and to the still larger cause of humanity. At the dawn of history India started on her unending quest, and trackless
(15) centuries are filled with her striving and the grandeur of her successes and her failures. Through good and ill fortune alike she has never lost sight of that quest or forgotten the ideals which gave her strength. We end today a period of
(20) ill fortune and India discovers herself again.

The achievement we celebrate today is but a step, an opening of opportunity, to the greater triumphs and achievements that await us. Are we brave enough and wise enough to grasp this
(25) opportunity and accept the challenge of the future? Freedom and power bring responsibility. That responsibility rests upon this assembly, a sovereign body representing the sovereign people of India. Before the birth of freedom we have
(30) endured all the pains of labour and our hearts are heavy with the memory of this sorrow. Some of those pains continue even now.

Nevertheless, the past is over and it is the future that beckons to us now. That future is not
(35) one of ease or resting but of incessant striving so that we might fulfill the pledges we have so often taken and the one we shall take today. The service of India means the service of the millions who suffer. It means the ending of poverty and
(40) ignorance and disease and inequality of

opportunity. The ambition of the greatest man of our generation has been to wipe every tear from every eye. That may be beyond us but so long as there are tears and suffering, so long our work
(45) will not be over. And so we have to labour and to work, and work hard, to give reality to our dreams. Those dreams are for India, but they are also for the world, for all the nations and peoples are too closely knit together today for any one of
(50) them to imagines that it can live apart.

Peace has been said to be indivisible, so is freedom, so is prosperity now, and so also is disaster in this one world that can no longer be split into isolated fragments. To the people of
(55) India whose representatives we are, we make appeal to join us with faith and confidence in this great adventure. This is no time for petty and destructive criticism, no time for ill-will or blaming others. We have to build the noble
(60) mansion of free India where all her children may dwell.

40. The purpose of the paragraph 2 in relationship to paragraph 1 is to

  (A) continue the argument
  (B) contradict details
  (C) define terms
  (D) narrate situation
  (E) explicate introduction

41. The word "tryst" as it is used in line 1 can BEST be described as a(n)

  (A) romantic liaison
  (B) clandestine meeting
  (C) contract with providence
  (D) arrangement to meet
  (E) solemn oath

GO ON TO THE NEXT PAGE. ➡

42. India's freedom is described using the analogy of

    (A) romantic appointment
    (B) labor and birth
    (C) pledge with destiny
    (D) brave triumphant steps
    (E) responsibility of the assembly

43. Paragraph 3 contains all of the following rhetorical devices EXCEPT

    (A) rhetorical question
    (B) anadiplosis
    (C) personification
    (D) metaphor
    (E) litote

44. In the phrase "incessant striving" (line 35) refers to

    (A) the past
    (B) the future
    (C) India, the country
    (D) labor pains
    (E) honored pledges

45. The sentence "And so we have to labour and to work, and work hard, to give reality to our dreams" (lines 45–47) contains an unusual syntactical word repetition known as

    (A) zeugma
    (B) isocolon
    (C) chiasmus
    (D) polysyndeton
    (E) alliteration

46. Paragraph 4 contains all of the following rhetorical devices EXCEPT

    (A) antithesis
    (B) alliteration
    (C) repetition
    (D) chiasmus
    (E) understatement

47. The first sentence of the final paragraph (lines 51–54) contains a repetitive structure without conjunctions. This rhetorical device is known as

    (A) oxymoron
    (B) asyndeton
    (C) chiasmus
    (D) parallelism
    (E) anaphor

48. This speech concludes with the reference to free India as a "noble mansion" wherein "all her children may dwell" (lines 59–61). This sentence utilizes the rhetorical device known as

    (A) simile
    (B) hyperbole
    (C) analogy
    (D) apostrophe
    (E) antithesis

49. The final paragraph of this speech can BEST be described as a(n)

    (A) prayer to ensure India's success
    (B) entreaty to put differences aside
    (C) appeal to India's people to build mansions
    (D) criticism of petty annoyances and disagreements
    (E) comparison of freedom and prosperity

50. The overall tone of this speech can BEST be described as

    (A) optimistic and cautionary
    (B) triumphant and celebratory
    (C) joyful and exalted
    (D) philosophical and poetic
    (E) objective and fatalistic

END OF SECTION I

GO ON TO THE NEXT PAGE. ➡

Section II: Free-Response Questions

Time: 2 hours
Number of questions: 3
Percent of total grade: 55

Directions: This section contains three essay questions. Answer all three questions, budgeting your time carefully.

GO ON TO THE NEXT PAGE. ➡

Question One

(Suggested Time—40 minutes. Your response will count toward
one-third of your total score on this section of the exam.)

The following passage is taken from President William Jefferson Clinton's Inaugural Address in 1993. Read the passage carefully. Then write a well-organized essay in which you briefly summarize the points Clinton makes and analyze the rhetorical strategies Clinton uses to present his argument. Identify and analyze the use of tone, organization, rhetorical appeals, and other such devices.

When George Washington first took the oath I have just sworn to uphold, news traveled slowly across the land by horseback, and across the
Line ocean by boat. Now the sights and sounds of this
(5) ceremony are broadcast instantaneously to billions around the world. Communications and commerce are global. Investment is mobile. Technology is almost magical, and ambition for a better life is now universal.

(10) We earn our livelihood in America today in peaceful competition with people all across the Earth. Profound and powerful forces are shaking and remaking our world, and the URGENT question of our time is whether we can make
(15) change our friend and not our enemy. This new world has already enriched the lives of MILLIONS of Americans who are able to compete and win in it. But when most people are working harder for less, when others cannot work
(20) at all, when the cost of health care devastates families and threatens to bankrupt our enterprises, great and small; when the fear of crime robs law abiding citizens of their freedom; and when millions of poor children cannot even imagine the
(25) lives we are calling them to lead, we have not made change our friend.

We know we have to face hard truths and take strong steps, but we have not done so. Instead we have drifted, and that drifting has eroded our
(30) resources, fractured our economy, and shaken our confidence. Though our challenges are fearsome, so are our strengths. Americans have ever been a restless, questing, hopeful people, and we must bring to our task today the vision and will of
(35) those who came before us. From our Revolution

to the Civil War, to the Great Depression, to the Civil Rights movement, our people have always mustered the determination to construct from these crises the pillars of our history. Thomas
(40) Jefferson believed that to preserve the very foundations of our nation we would need dramatic change from time to time. Well, my fellow Americans, this is OUR time. Let us embrace it.

GO ON TO THE NEXT PAGE. ➡

Question Two

(Suggested Time—40 minutes. Your response will count toward
one-third of your total score on this section of the exam.)

The following letter, addressed to Dr. Lanyon, is urging him to the aid of his friend, Henry Jekyll. Read the letter carefully. Then, in a well-organized essay, explain how various rhetorical devices such as tone, word choice, imagery, and syntax create the letter's overwhelming sense of urgency.

10th December, 18—

Dear Lanyon, You are one of my oldest friends; and although we may have differed at times on
Line scientific questions, I cannot remember, at least on
(5) my side, any break in our affection. There was never a day when, if you had said to me, 'Jekyll, my life, my honour, my reason, depend upon you,' I would not have sacrificed my left hand to help you. Lanyon, my life, my honour my reason, are all at
(10) your mercy; if you fail me to-night I am lost. You might suppose, after this preface, that I am going to ask you for something dishonourable to grant. Judge for yourself.

I want you to postpone all other engagements
(15) for to-night—ay, even if you were summoned to the bedside of an emperor; to take a cab, unless your carriage should be actually at the door; and with this letter in your hand for consultation, to drive straight to my house. Poole, my butler, has his
(20) orders; you will find, him waiting your arrival with a locksmith. The door of my cabinet is then to be forced: and you are to go in alone; to open the glazed press (letter E) on the left hand, breaking the lock if it be shut; and to draw out, with all its
(25) contents as they stand, the fourth drawer from the top or (which is the same thing) the third from the bottom. In my extreme distress of wind, I have a morbid fear of misdirecting you; but even if I am in error, you may know the right drawer by its
(30) contents: some powders, a phial and a paper book. This drawer I beg of you to carry back with you to Cavendish Square exactly as it stands.

That is the first part of the service: now for the second. You should be back, if you set out at once
(35) on the receipt of this, long before midnight; but I will leave you that amount of margin, not only in the fear of one of those obstacles that can neither be prevented nor foreseen, but because an hour when your servants are in bed is to be preferred for what
(40) will then remain to do. At midnight, then, I have to ask you to be alone in your consulting-room, to admit with your own hand into the house a man who will present himself in my name, and to place in his hands the drawer that you will have brought
(45) with you from my cabinet. Then you will have played your part and earned my gratitude completely. Five minutes afterwards, if you insist upon an explanation, you will have understood that these arrangements are of capital importance; and
(50) that by the neglect of one of them, fantastic as they must appear, you might have charged your conscience with my death or the shipwreck of my reason.

Confident as I am that you will not trifle with
(55) this appeal, my heart sinks and my hand trembles at the bare thought of such a possibility. Think of me at this hour, in a strange place, labouring under a blackness of distress that no fancy can exaggerate, and yet well aware that, if you will but punctually
(60) serve me, my troubles will roll away like a story that is told.

Serve me, my dear Lanyon, and save,
Your friend,
H. J.

(65) P.S. I had already sealed this up when a fresh terror struck upon my soul. It is possible that the postoffice may fail me, and this letter not come into your hands until to-morrow morning. In that case, dear Lanyon, do my errand when it shall be most
(70) convenient for you in the course of the day; and once more expect my messenger at midnight. It may then already be too late; and if that night passes without event, you will know that you have seen the last of Henry Jekyll.

GO ON TO THE NEXT PAGE. ➡

Question Three

(Suggested Time—40 minutes. Your response will count toward
one-third of your total score on this section of the exam.)

Margaret Thatcher, former Prime Minister of Great Britain, once said, "In politics, if you want anything said, ask a man; if you want anything done, ask a woman."

Many would agree that this quote could apply not just to politics but to life in general. In a well-organized essay, consider Thatcher's quote and defend, qualify, or challenge her opinion that men are more likely to talk while women are more likely to do. Base your response on your reading, observations, and experiences.

END OF EXAMINATION

Practice Test III
Answers and Explanations

ANSWER KEY

1. B	21. D	41. C
2. C	22. E	42. B
3. E	23. A	43. E
4. B	24. D	44. B
5. D	25. A	45. C
6. E	26. B	46. E
7. C	27. C	47. B
8. C	28. A	48. C
9. E	29. E	49. B
10. E	30. C	50. A
11. E	31. E	
12. B	32. B	
13. D	33. B	
14. A	34. D	
15. C	35. C	
16. B	36. D	
17. B	37. A	
18. D	38. A	
19. E	39. B	
20. D	40. E	

PRACTICE TEST III
COMPUTE YOUR SCORE

Remember not to take any score on the practice test too literally. There is no way to determine precisely what your AP grade will be because:

- The conditions under which you take the practice test will not exactly mirror real test conditions.
- While the multiple-choice questions are scored by computer, the free-response questions are graded manually by faculty consultants. You will not be able to accurately grade your own essays.

Section I: Multiple-Choice

Number Correct ☐ − (¼ × Number Wrong*) ☐ = ☐ × 1.296 = ☐ = Multiple-Choice Raw Score

*Do not include questions left blank.

Section II: Free-Response

Question 1: (out of 9 points possible) ☐ × 2.933 = ☐

Question 2: (out of 9 points possible) ☐ × 2.933 = ☐

Question 3: (out of 9 points possible) ☐ × 2.933 = ☐

Total Questions 1, 2, and 3 = ☐ = Free-Response Raw Score

Composite Score

Section I Multiple-Choice Score ☐ + Section II Free-Response Score ☐ = ☐ = Composite Score

CONVERSION CHART

Composite Score Range**	AP Grade
114–144	5
88–113	4
67–87	3
40–66	2
0–39	1

Section I: Multiple-Choice Questions

Questions 1–13

1. (B)

The phrase "mode of discourse" refers to the type of writing in a passage. A mode might be descriptive (paints a picture), narrative (tells a story), argumentative (persuades the audience), etc. This passage is basically an extended definition. It is the author's attempt to characterize the concept of education. It is rare that a passage is written in a single mode, for writers switch in and out of several modes in order to express themselves. Nevertheless, based on the introductory paragraph, it seems that this passage is primarily going to be an extended definition (B).

2. (C)

Hypothetical sentences express something which "might happen" or "might have happened," usually stating a condition under which something may take place, and then usually expressing the action or the consequence (i.e., what would happen). Lines 10–13 set up such a hypothesis: "Suppose it were perfectly certain that the life and fortune of every one of us would, one day or other, depend upon his winning or losing a game of chess." Of course the word "suppose" (B) alerts us to the hypothesis, but what most clinches the hypothetical structure is the use of the conditional tense, "it were" (C). Notice that the conditional takes a plural verb even though the subject is singular. Conditional tense (sometimes referred to as subjunctive mood) is used for a hypothetical statement, or a wish or statement contrary to fact; for example, "If I were a rich person, I would take a trip around the world. I wish I were a rich person."

3. (E)

Paragraph 2 contains many stylistic devices. Metaphor (A) is obvious as the life to a game of chess comparison evolves. Line 17 offers the alliterative (B) "giving and getting." Asyndeton (C)

is present in lines 15–16, where the conjunction is omitted between " . . . moves of the pieces" and "to have a notion of a gambit." The sentence in lines 17–22 is a rhetorical question (D). Nowhere in this paragraph is there hyperbole—exaggeration used for stylistic effect (E).

4. (B)

The antecedent of the pronoun "his" in line 12 is the word "one" (B). At first glance, you might be tempted to answer "us" (D), but the "us" is actually the object of the preposition "of," and the pronoun "one" is the word the prepositional phrase is modifying. In fact, to some ears, the word "our" sounds better than the correct "his." You have to be very careful when faced with an occasional picky grammar question such as this one. Although you might also be distracted by answer choices (A), (C), and (E), closer scrutiny should lead you to (B) or (D), with (B) being the correct response.

5. (D)

Because the game of chess as a metaphor for life is extended throughout two paragraphs, it becomes more than a mere metaphor, but is actually a conceit. Perhaps the most famous conceit is that found in a John Donne poem of the compass and the lovers, where one is constant (the center point) while the other travels afar, always drawn back by the stable partner. None of the other answer choices offered is a viable option.

6. (E)

Reread the lines in question. "The chessboard is the world, the pieces are the phenomena of the universe, the rules of the game are what we call the laws of Nature." Notice the absence of conjunctions in this series. Asyndeton (E) is a rhetorical device wherein the writer consciously omits conjunctions for stylistic effect. Antithesis (A) is the juxtaposition of opposing ideas. You might be tempted to answer (B), run-on sentence, but this omission of conjunctions is a purposeful exclusion, and with short, repetitive independent clauses, it is OK to use just commas in between rather than the more usual semicolon. Assonance (C) is a sound device (repetitive vowel sounds within words), making it an irrelevant response. Finally, polysyndeton (D)—the use of many conjunctions (poly) for stylistic effect—is the opposite of asyndeton and therefore incorrect.

7. (C)

Lines 45–47 say that "My metaphor will remind some of you of the famous picture in which Retzsch has depicted Satan playing at chess with man for his soul." A close reading of this section will show you that the only possible response to this question is that Retzsch was an artist.

8. (C)

The definitive paragraph that expresses the fundamental idea of this passage is in the middle, paragraph 5. Here, the author says "Education is learning the rules of this mighty game. In other words, education is the instruction of the intellect in the laws of Nature, under which name I include not merely things and their forces, but men and their ways; and the fashioning of the affections and of the will into an earnest and loving desire to move in harmony with those laws" (lines 52–59). This is the essential message of this passage.

9. (E)

"This standard" (line 62) refers to education. This paragraph talks about education and how it is "the instruction of the intellect and the fashioning of the affections and of the will into an earnest and loving desire to move in harmony with those laws" (of nature) (lines 54–59). According to the author, "education means neither more nor less than this" (lines 59–60).

10. (E)

Paragraph 6 contains many stylistic devices. Lines 68–72 set up a hypothetical situation (A). Lines 73–74 contains a series with a deliberate omission of conjunctions for stylistic effect, asyndeton (B). Nature is given human characteristics—personification (C)—and several series provide parallel structure (D). Nowhere in the paragraph is there an example of oxymoron (E), a figure of speech that combines two apparently contradictory elements, such as a riot for peace.

11. (E)

According to this passage, there is no end to education. Take a look at lines 100–104: "Nor should I speak of this process of education as past for any one, be he as old as he may. For every man the world is as fresh as it was at the first day, and as full of untold novelties for him who has the eyes to see them." This statement negates the truth of choice (E), thereby making it the correct response. Remember, in a question such as this, you are actually looking for the wrong piece of information as the correct answer.

12. (B)

When you read the final paragraph carefully, you will see that the poll refers to the minimally educated, those "who pick up just enough to get through without much discredit" (lines 112–113), and the pluck (used as both verb and noun) are "those who won't learn at all" (lines 113–114). Therefore, (B) is the correct response to this question.

13. (D)

Remember that when responses have two parts (such as two adjectives or an adverb and an adjective), BOTH parts must be correct. Based on the descriptors offered as choices, the best pair would have to be metaphorical and erudite (D). No other response describes the tone as well.

Questions 14–26

14. (A)

Much of the syntax of this passage is quite complex. In the first paragraph, however, you will not find a complex sentence that is introduced by a subordinate clause. All the other choices are present. The first sentence (lines 1–3) is compound-complex in structure (B), with the subordinate noun clause as the object of the preposition. The second sentence (lines 3–14) is a compound-complex sentence (D). Infinitives (C) are present in lines 15–16. Finally, in lines 14–17 you'll find an example of a simple sentence (E).

15. (C)

If you track the possessive pronoun/adjective back through the sentence, you will see that it refers to lines 4–5, clever and daring men who might propose a cause for the pestilence.

16. (B)

These lines refer to the fact that the pestilence was more or less a silent killer, a "languid" enemy whose victims least expected that they were doomed. When the situation takes a turn different than expected, it is a case of situational irony.

17. (B)

If you look at the second paragraph carefully, it is rife with prepositional phrases that complicate rather than simple sentence structures.

18. (D)

In the context of the sentence (lines 30–38), the disease was not evident to those who may have contracted it. In fact, it was so subtle that the infected were unaware of their contagion until it was too late.

19. (E)

This sentence says that caregivers were pitied, not because they were more susceptible, but because their very actions were to be admired. Theirs was a thankless and tiring task.

20. (D)

The "for when" and "and when" structure is known as *anaphora*, the regular repetition of the same word or phrase at the beginning of successive phrases or clauses.

21. (D)

If you read lines 55–66 carefully, you will see that those suffering from the plague either experienced a deep coma or a violent delirium. Those under the coma forgot all who were familiar to them and seemed to be constantly sleeping. Those in delirium suffered from insomnia and were victims of distorted imaginations.

22. (E)

The reality of the plague is that there was no means to combat it known to man. In fact, even today scientists wonder if faced with a similar pestilence would modern medicine would be much more successful in combating the pestilence than people were during the Middle Ages.

23. (A)

The author of this passage is as objective as can be expected, and he is careful to include analysis and detail wherever possible, making choice (A) the only reasonable description of the tone of the piece.

24. (D)

Due to the objective nature of this passage as well as the specific detail, clinical is the best term with which to describe the language of the piece. Although it does contain many exact details, it is not truly technical (C), and the language is accessible (A, B) without being too informal (E).

25. (A)

The BEST description of the author's attitude is one of regret and resignation to the inevitability of the pestilence and the tragedies that it caused.

26. (B)

Although the author does employ description (E) throughout the piece to give us a better idea of the horrors of the pestilence, and some comparison and contrast (C) is also present, the primary mode of discourse of this passage is that of *explication* (B)—a complete and thorough explanation of what happened using details and specifics to enhance the readers' understanding.

Questions 27–39

27. (C)

Lines 20–21 mention that Othello is more poetic than Hamlet (A). His background, as recounted in 5–16, sounds mysterious and otherworldly (B). Lines 12–15 tell us about his experiences in battle (E) and his being sold into slavery (D). Lines 18–19, however, state "He has not, indeed, the meditative or speculative imagination of Hamlet," making (C) the correct choice for this question.

28. (A)

Asyndeton (A) is a series of phrases or clauses wherein conjunctions have been omitted. Anadiplosis (B) repeats the last word of one clause at the beginning of the following clause; anaphora (C) repeats the same word or groups of words at the beginnings of successive clauses. Anachronism (D) uses historically inaccurate details in a text. Finally, antithesis (E) juxtaposes contrasting ideas.

29. (E)

"He has watched with a poet's eye the Arabian trees dropping their med'cinable gum, and the Indian throwing away his chance-found pearl; and has gazed in a fascinated dream at the Pontic sea rushing, never to return, to the Propontic and the Hellespont." These lines (22–28) use both personification—giving human characteristics to inanimate things—and allusion, referring to Arabia, the Pontic Sea, and the Indian who throws a fateful pearl away.

30. (C)

Despite the lengthy and often convoluted sentences within the rest of this passage, paragraph 4 is comprised of several simple sentences, and the compound clauses are short and rather uncomplicated in their structure.

31. (E)

In this paragraph, there is no evidence of synecdoche (E)—wherein a more inclusive term is used for a less inclusive one. Anadiplosis (A) repeats the last word of one clause at the beginning of the next clause. Isocolon (B) is a scheme of parallel structure which occurs when the parallel elements are similar not only in grammatical structure but also in length (number of words or even number of syllables). Assonance (C) repeats similar vowel sounds, preceded and followed by different consonants. Hyperbole (D) is exaggeration used for rhetorical or literary effect.

32. (B)

Nowhere are we told that he has royal ancestors (B). One might easily jump to that conclusion, but that information is not offered. But let's run through the rest of the choices to be sure. Paragraph 3 tells us that Othello is mature; lines 59–61 explain his inexperience in the romance department (A). Lines 18–19 state that "He has not, indeed, the meditative or speculative imagination of Hamlet" (C). Lines 17–18 tells us that "he is not a merely romantic figure; his own nature is romantic" (D). And paragraph 3 tells us that he is "grave, self-controlled" and "fully conscious of his worth," etc. (E).

33. (B)

Paragraph 6 is rife with "if" clauses, which indicate conditional or hypothetical statements. Thus, (B) is the BEST response to this question.

34. (D)

Paragraph 6 tells us that Othello is absolutely trusting when he trusts (A). Lines 76–77 tell us "If such a passion as jealousy seizes him . . . ," affirming that he can be moved in such a manner (B). Line 72 assures us that he "decides and acts instantaneously" (C). Othello the character could never be considered unflappable and easygoing, making (D) the correct response. But let's make sure by checking choice (E), and lines 71–72 affirms that Othello "is extremely self-reliant."

35. (C)

Paragraph 7 focuses upon the nobility of the character of Othello. As the author says, "his sufferings are so heart-rending, that he stirs . . . in most readers a passion of mingled love and pity which they feel for no other hero in Shakespeare." The only logical response to this question is answer (C). None of the other choices is as correct in assessing the character Othello.

36. (D)

Remember, when an answer offers two descriptors, BOTH must be accurate for the response to be correct. In that case, (D) is the best response. He is both romantic and self-assured. Othello is confident, but not shallow (A); he is vain, but not insecure (B); he displays a naiveté—at least where it concerns women—but there's no evidence of insolence (C); and, like his naiveté, he can be called gullible, but not regretful (E). One might argue the last response, because at the end of the play Othello is regretful of his actions, but *based on this passage*, we do not know that.

37. (A)

Overall, the nature of this passage is a critic's analysis of a Shakespeare character, Othello. With painstaking details and satisfactory examples, the writer analyzes this Shakespearean hero.

38. (A)

The author of this passage (Shakespearean critic A.C Bradley) is not haughty, contemptuous, cynical, or disgusted. Instead, in his analysis he shows a great empathy for the character Othello. He is generous with his praise, but he does not hesitate to mention Othello's shortcomings. The best description of this writer's analysis is that he is critical yet empathetic (A) when discussing Shakespeare's hero, Othello.

39. (B)

Without a doubt, this writer is enamored with the character of Othello. Of all Shakespeare's heroes, he tells us that Othello is the most noble, the most romantic, the most poetic, the most self-possessed, a Renaissance man in the true sense of its meaning. Not without flaws, Othello, according to A.C. Bradley, is truly "the most notable of Shakespeare's heroes."

Questions 40–50

40. (E)

Paragraph 1, only two sentences long, is strictly an introductory statement that actually sounds a bit mysterious or unfinished as it is. The second paragraph then explains just what is going on: after years of struggle, India is about to become a sovereign nation. Without the second paragraph's explication, the first two sentences would be a very weak and unclear opening to this speech.

41. (C)

Usually the word "tryst" is used in connection with a romantic liaison of some sort. Often such a meeting is clandestine in nature. Within the context of this speech, however, "tryst" is a reference to an agreement—with fate, providence, or destiny. The speaker here is saying that the time has come to fulfill intentions from long ago. The BEST response to this question would then be (C), contract with providence.

42. (B)

Lines 29–32 state, "Before the birth of freedom we have endured all the pains of labour and our hearts are heavy with the memory of this sorrow. Some of those pains continue even now." In other words, India's struggle to gain her freedom is being compared to the labor pains of a woman giving birth. This is clearly an analogy, the comparison of two things that are alike in some respect. Both simile and metaphor are a type of analogy.

43. (E)

Paragraph 3 of Nehru's speech contains many devices of rhetoric. Lines 23–26 contain a rhetorical question (A), which is asking a question not for the purpose of eliciting an answer but for the purpose of asserting or denying something obliquely. Anadiplosis (B), the repetition of the last word of one clause at the beginning of the following clause, is present in lines 26–27. Personification (C), attaching human characteristics to that which is not human, is evident in lines 30–31 with the mention of "our hearts are heavy." Metaphor (D), of course, is present within the labor and birth analogy. No example of litote (E)—understatement used for stylistic effect—is present within this paragraph.

44. (B)

Lines 33–34 say "the past is over and it is the future that beckons to us now." Then the paragraph goes on to say that the future will not be easy; it will be one of "incessant striving so that we might fulfill the pledges we have so often taken . . . ." When asked about a word reference in a paragraph as "busy" as this one, it is important to slow down your reading in order to trace back to the exact word that is being used as reference.

45. (C)

Lines 45–47 present a challenging syntactical structure. A zeugma (A) is an interesting syntactical structure in which a word is used to modify or govern two or more words, often so that its use is grammatically or logically correct with only one (e.g.: "He rose to crack the window as well as his knuckles"). Isocolon (B) is a scheme of parallel structure which occurs when the parallel elements are similar not only in grammatical structure but also in length. Chiasmus (C), the correct answer, is the reversal of grammatical structures in successive phrases or clauses. Reread the lines question: "so we have to labour and to work. And work hard . . . " Let's review the remaining two choices to be sure. Polysyndeton (D) is the deliberate use of many conjunctions, usually within a series of words, phrases, or clauses. Finally, alliteration (E) is the repetition of initial consonant sounds.

46. (E)

Paragraph 4 contains many rhetorical devices. However, understatement (E) is not one of them. Antithesis (A) is apparent in the "resting/striving" juxtaposition in line 35. The repetition of initial consonant sounds—alliteration (B)—can be heard (albeit not overwhelmingly) in "often taken and the one . . . take today." Repetition (C) is obvious in lines 42–43: "every tear from every eye." Chiasmus (D), the reversal of grammatical structure, is found in lines 45–46 ("so we have to labour and to work. And work hard").

47. (B)

"Peace has been said to be indivisible, so is freedom, so is prosperity now, and so also is disaster . . . " shows several instances of missing conjunctions within a series, or asyndeton. None of the other answer choices is appropriate for the first sentence of the final paragraph (lines 51–54).

48. (C)

The concluding reference to India as a noble mansion wherein all her children may dwell is an analogy, or a comparison of two things that are alike in some respect. Both India and a mansion are liable to hold people. Hyperbole (B) is not correct, because this text is not an exaggeration used for stylistic effect. Nor is this an apostrophe (D), wherein a person, thing, or abstract quality is addressed as if present.

49. (B)

More than anything, the final paragraph of this speech is an appeal to listeners and all the people of India to put all differences aside and unite in this new opportunity of freedom, for now India has obtained what it has long strived for, and without union, it cannot grow and flourish.

50. (A)

When Nehru gave this speech in honor of India's complete independence from Great Britain, he expressed many emotions. Most of all, he was hopeful. He looked forward to a positive future for his country. He was no Pollyanna, however. He knew that great struggles faced his country, and without the cooperation and efforts of all, India would be unable to fulfill the promise of her forefathers. Optimistic caution truly shades the tenor of his words.

SECTION II: FREE-RESPONSE QUESTIONS

Question One: Clinton's Inaugural Address

Analysis of Question One

This prompt first urges students to summarize the passage. Although this is not a common mission of many AP Language prompts, it enables AP readers to better judge what they are reading. If the AP reader notices that a student has misunderstood the passage as evidenced by the summary, he or she can know what to look for in terms of the analysis.

Then students are urged to consider how rhetorical devices have aided Clinton in presenting his argument. Basically, Clinton is saying that while ambition for a better life has become the credo of American living, we resist making change our friend. It is upon this dichotomy that Clinton dwells.

Clinton goes on to tell us that "we have drifted, and that drifting has eroded our resources, fractured our economy, and shaken our confidence." Instead of embracing the spirit of our forefathers and forging forward with our ideas and meeting new challenges with confidence and security, we have "drifted," with unfortunate results.

This is an open forum for AP English Language and Composition students. This passage yields itself to many contemporary interpretations, and the caveat task of summarizing what the student reads is helpful as well. This selection from President Clinton's 1993 inaugural address lends itself well to being an AP English Language and Composition passage.

Scoring Guide for Question One

9 Points: Essays earning a score of 9 meet all the criteria for papers that earn 8 points and, in addition, are particularly perceptive and demonstrate impressive stylistic control.

8 Points: The essay responds directly and thoroughly to the prompt. The student concisely summarizes the passage, writes a detailed analysis of how Clinton presents his argument, and refers to the text to illustrate how he uses tone, organization, and rhetorical appeals and devices. Overall, the essay presents a thorough, convincing analysis. It is well written, though it may contain flaws

7 Points: Essays earning a score of 7 fit the descriptions of essays that receive 6 points but are distinguished by fuller or more purposeful analysis or stronger prose style.

6 Points: The essay provides an analysis of how Clinton makes his argument, but it is not as thorough and convincing. It refers to the text to illustrate points about tone, organization, and rhetorical appeals and devices, but not in as detailed and effective a manner. The essay is well-written, but may show sentence-level weaknesses.

5 Points: Essays earning a score of 5 understand the tasks of the prompt, and they analyze rhetorical strategies used by Clinton to convey his views in this inaugural address. Their development of strategies may be limited, superficial, or inconsistent. A few lapses in diction or syntax may be present, but usually the prose in these essays conveys their writers' ideas.

4 Points: The essay fails to summarize the passage or effectively show how Clinton makes his argument. The student refers to the text, but may not substantiate his or her analysis with appropriate and convincing references. The student may understand tone, organization, and rhetorical appeals and devices, but fails to apply understanding in a detailed, analytical way to this passage. The essay may have sentence-level weaknesses, but it should be written clearly.

3 Points: Essays earning a score of 3 meet the criteria for essays that earn 4 points, but are less perceptive about the ways in which Clinton's speech utilizes rhetorical strategies. They are less consistent in their control of elements of good writing.

2 Points: The essay may lack a summary or a clear argument, or may fail to substantiate its argument with detailed references to the text. The essay may have sentence-level weaknesses.

1 Point: Essays earning a score of 1 meet the criteria for those that score 2, but in addition are especially simplistic in their ideas or weak in their control of language.

Sample Student Response to Question One

I wish now, nearly 10 years later, that I had paid attention when Bill Clinton took over as President of the United States. But I was just a kid, with kid things to do, and I would never have imagined that I would later be faced with a speech I might possibly have heard once when I was less than 8 years old.

Clinton is very clear about the focus of this inaugural address. He tells his audience that this is the time of change, and we must become very comfortable with change in order to survive best in America. He urges us not to drift, but to stay focused, to embrace the changes that are moving us forward.

Of course, in 1993, Clinton could not have imagined 9/11 and all the changes that would bring to the United States. He seems to think that in 1993 people were not doing very well with change. Well, in the last year we have experienced changes that even our worse nightmares might not have told us about. America did not drift, however; we have held together strong, and we are growing, and hopefully learning from the changes that have been made.

There are several stylistic devices evident in this section of Clinton's speech. The one that seems to be the most evident is the incredible rhythm of his words. He likes repetition: "investment is mobile, technology is magic, and ambition is universal." That series has a very nice ring to it. He also likes to repeat sentence styles. In paragraph two he keeps using "when" clauses: "<u>when</u> most people are working; <u>when</u> others cannot work; <u>when</u> the cost of health care; <u>when</u> millions of poor children," etc. By setting up a rhythm like this, I am sure Clinton quickly engaged his listening audience, suckering them to listen to him, whether they liked him or not.

The strength of the passage (from this excerpt, at least) is in the third paragraph. He calls upon all of us to join him in this challenge to move ahead. He reminds us of our common ground by mentioning the Revolution, the Civil War, the Great Depression, and the Civil Rights movement. What American could ignore such a call to action? Then in a final blow, Clinton hits us with reference to a favorite forefather, Thomas Jefferson. If Jefferson could see ahead to need for dramatic change, how can we not do the same. We who are so much more fortunate to live now and not then.

Commentary on Sample Student Response to Question One

Wow, who could not be moved by such an appeal? Certainly this student understands President Clinton's call to action. Although this essay response does not separate a summary of the inaugural address from a response to the tasks of the prompt, nevertheless, both missions have been accomplished by this AP English student.

This composition clearly shows that the student understands Clinton's message. The summary is actually woven within the entire answer. Some of you may then ask, is this good? Shouldn't this student have first summarized and then analyzed? The answer is probably yes. The chance of forgetting to include summary when it is enmeshed within the answer is great. This particular student has been successful in not offering a separate paragraph or two of summary, yet he still includes a summary. Not everyone is so clever, however, and it might be wiser, when asked to summarize a passage, to do that first and then get on with the task of responding to the rest of the prompt.

Not all avenues of rhetorical analysis are covered in this student response. Remember, however, the prompt says "and other such devices." That is the key phrase here. When a prompt uses terms like "such as," or "other such," it means that the prompt is only that—prompting you with suggestions. It is suggestive, not prescriptive. You must cover some of the rhetorical devices, but you are not expected to encompass all of them.

This student response is particularly taken with the rhythm and sound of Clinton's speech; repetition and structure have captured this student's attention. Also, there is an intrinsic discussion of tone as well. This student response would probably earn a 6–7 from the scoring guide. Not only does the essay provide an adequate analysis, it seems to have a strength and control that would move this essay into the 7 rather than the 6 range for a score.

Question Two: Jekyll's Cry for Help

Analysis of Question Two

Many novels written during the 18th and 19th century were prefaced with a passage that vouched for the "authenticity" of the story within. For instance, Daniel Defoe's *Moll Flanders* and *Robinson Crusoe* are both preceded by validating material. The "Preface" to *Dr. Jekyll and Mr. Hyde* includes a letter to and read by the narrator, Dr. Lanyon. This letter is followed by a short narrative by Lanyon, which then segues into the introduction of the main character, Henry Jekyll. AP students are challenged by the prompt to read this letter and explain how its rhetorical devices, such as word choice, imagery, and tone, blend to create the overwhelming sense of urgency projected by the letter's author. Although the true author of the letter is in fact the author of the book, Robert Louis Stevenson, for our purposes, we will refer to the letter as being authored by Jekyll, in case there are students who are unaware of the true source of this passage.

Most passages on the AP English Language and Composition exam are excerpts from nonfiction works. However, fiction is occasionally used. In a case such as this question, students are asked to investigate the rhetorical nature of the passage—no literary analysis is

KAPLAN

called for. Prefaces from some of the classic (English) novels are particularly rich in style. Such is the case in this letter to Dr. Lanyon, which comprises about one-half of the total preface to Stevenson's short, powerful novel. Lanyon later "tells" us that when he first received Jekyll's missive he was particularly surprised since he had recently dined with Hyde, and he could not imagine what was so important to necessitate such a formal summons.

As the story goes, Lanyon, upon completing the letter, is quite convinced that the man is insane. Nevertheless, he does as Jekyll asks him and retrieves the designated items from Henry Jekyll's quarters. After returning to his own quarters, Lanyon is still mystified by the letter, the drawer he has secured, and its contents. Soon a stranger comes to Lanyon's door, a horrible creature who fascinates and frightens him, but deepens his curiosity nonetheless. It is not until this strange visitor goes to the drawer, mixes some of the potions contained within, and drinks the mixture that the truth is revealed. From there the "Strange Tale" begins.

Scoring Guide for Question Two

9 Points: Essays earning a score of 9 meet the criteria for 8 papers and, in addition, are especially full or apt in their analysis or demonstrate particularly impressive control of language.

8 Points: Essays earning a score of 8 successfully analyze the rhetorical strategies that Henry Jekyll uses to establish the letter's powerful sense of urgency. They refer to the passage effectively and demonstrate a wide range of the elements of effective writing, but are not flawless.

7 Points: Essays earning a score of 7 fit the description of 6 essays but provide a more complete analysis of the rhetorical strategies and their effect on the mood of the letter, or demonstrate more mature prose style.

6 Points: Essays earning a score of 6 adequately analyze the rhetorical strategies that Jekyll uses in his letter to project his sense of urgency. They refer to the passage explicitly or implicitly, but their explanation of specific strategies is more limited. The writing may contain lapses in diction or syntax, but generally the prose is quite clear.

5 Points: Essays earning a score of 5 analyze Jekyll's strategies, but they may provide uneven or inconsistent explanations of how these strategies work to establish the letter's strong tone of urgency. While the writing may contain lapses in diction or syntax, it usually conveys ideas adequately.

4 Points: Essays earning a score of 4 respond to the prompt inadequately. They may misrepresent Jekyll's tone, analyze his strategies inaccurately, or offer little discussion of specific strategies. The prose generally conveys the writer's ideas but may suggest immature or undeveloped control of writing.

3 Points: Essays earning a score of 3 meet the criteria for the score of 4 but are less perceptive about Jekyll's strategies or less consistent in controlling the elements of writing.

2 Points: Essays earning a score of 2 demonstrate little success in analyzing Jekyll's strategies. These essays may offer vague generalizations, substitute simpler tasks such as summarizing the passage, or simply list techniques. The prose often demonstrates consistent weaknesses in writing.

1 Point: Essays earning a score of 1 meet the criteria for the score of 2 but are undeveloped, especially simplistic in their discussion or in essential mechanics, or are weak in their control of language.

Sample Student Response to Question Two

How many people today can boast of a friend so old in our affection that we could stake the existence of our "life, honour, reason" upon him? Not too many people, I don't imagine. Yet that is exactly what we have before us, the existence of such a friendship. Perhaps when this letter was written (for its style seems old and probably British because of the unusual spelling) such complete friendships might have existed, but rarely in today's world. Regardless, this letter urges Dr. Lanyon to help him (the writer of the letter, Henry Jekyll). He begs Lanyon not to let him down. His words, phrases, and even the structure of the letter all increase the incredible sense of urgency the letter manifests. The writer of this letter sounds like he is in utter desperation for Lanyon to respond to his plea.

The first paragraph pleads with Lanyon by reminding him of the closeness between them. He mentions that they are "oldest friends" and they've never suffered a "break in their affection." An opening such as this is sure to get the attention of the receiver of such a letter. The introductory paragraph even suggests that there may be something dishonorable going on, but Lanyon must be the judge of that. Who could ignore such a plea? Anyone's curiosity would be aroused, and a best friend would surely react positively to such an anxious plea.

The letter uses extreme exaggeration to extend its urgent mood to the reader. Even if Dr. Lanyon were "summoned to the bedside of an emperor." he should ignore such a summons and do what the letter says. A lot must be riding on Lanyon carrying this off. The letter even says Lanyon is to break down the door to the house if he cannot gain entry to carry out his mission. The letter's writer begs Lanyon to do all this.

The urgency of the letter is compounded by the feeling of mystery that surrounds everything. A servant will meet Lanyon; a locksmith will help dismantle any interfering locks; Lanyon is then to return home alone. Not even his own (Lanyon's) servants are to remain. Is this a sign of impending danger? And all of this must be done before midnight. I'm surprised he didn't mention the "witching hour." Whenever anything takes place at midnight, an anxious mood is common.

Henry Jekyll really lays it on thick with some of his word choices. He talks about "fear" and begs Lanyon to "be alone in your consulting-room" ready to admit "with his own hand" a stranger in from the dark. The stage is set here; who would not be caught up in the strange uncertainty of all these directions? The resounding last sentence of the second paragraph really brings the sense of anxiety to a fever pitch when Jekyll tells Lanyon "fantastic as they must appear you might have charged your conscience with my death or the shipwreck of my reason." By contrasting these rather regular chores (go to the house, get inside, retrieve drawer, and return home) with these exaggerated consequences if Lanyon fails, the tone of the letter becomes entirely anxious, spooky, and urgent. How could Lanyon not read the rest? How can I not continue reading? I can't.

In the final paragraph there is a slight lessening of tension. Henry Jekyll reminds Lanyon that he has confidence in him, and that this letter will be taken seriously. However, this is a brief, quiet sentence, for soon Jekyll uses the image of his own trembling hand to remind Lanyon how seriously important all of this is to the writer of the letter. He doesn't simply tell Lanyon he is stressed, he emphasizes his condition by saying he is "labouring under a blackness of distress." I would call this urgency to the max.

Just when Lanyon thinks he has read enough, H.J. hits him again with his worry in the P.S. Here he mentions being struck by a "fresh terror." What more urgency can the writer squeeze out of this? H.J. is afraid the letter may not get to Lanyon in time. (Maybe their mail is as unpredictable as ours.) Whatever the case, he says they might try again. This seems to take some pressure off, until H.J. says that "It may then already be too late."

I'm not sure who this Jekyll person is. Whoever he is, though, he sure knows how to get things going. He would certainly light a fire under me if I had received such a letter, and I'm not even the man's "oldest friend." From the start the letter establishes a dark and terrible sense of urgency. I sure hope that Lanyon was able to do what he was asked and help out this old friend of his.

Commentary on Sample Student Response to Question Two

This AP English student has certainly captured the essence of the mood of Jekyll's letter to his friend, Dr. Lanyon. Although it is clear that this student is not familiar with Stevenson's book, *The Strange Case of Dr. Jekyll and Mr. Hyde*, this response very successfully explains how various rhetorical devices such as tone, word choice, imagery, and syntax create the letter's overwhelming sense of urgency.

Just like the letter itself, this essay appeals to its audience's emotions, quickly involving the reader in the focus of the response through the clever use of the rhetorical question. Rhetorical questions can be very effective in involving and focusing the reader; however, a writer who chooses to utilize rhetorical questions must be careful not to leave any question unanswered or seemingly irrelevant. Used correctly, as this student has, the rhetorical question can be a highly effective writing technique.

This essay response focuses upon the word choice of the original letter. She points out Jekyll's clever appeals to friendship in this strange and haunting missive. The essay comments on Jekyll's crafty ability to pique Lanyon's (and thus our) curiosity early in his letter.

She also pinpoints how Jekyll compounds the urgent appeal to friendship within a shroud of mystery. This is bound to interest anyone—Lanyon or the general reader—enough to pursue the favors being asked. Mentioning the "witching hour of midnight" is also a nice touch in helping to explain the atmosphere of this entire letter and its missive.

This essay response spends some time discussing Jekyll's word choice, and how this word choice has enhanced the overall tone of urgency. The essay does not just mention word choice, but supports the claim with well-chosen examples from the letter. This student speaks of the "fantastic" and how it is the very tone of the letter that most likely urged Lanyon to perform the tasks Jekyll begs of him.

This student has also noted the pace of the letter. She comments on how Jekyll lures Lanyon into the action, then builds the tension, relieves it briefly, and finally, mentions his (Jekyll's) "blackness of distress." In addition, the student makes a point of Jekyll's final manipulation through the use of the postscript.

Overall, this student has done a fine job fulfilling the tasks of this particular prompt. Some may say that the student should have known who Jekyll was and how all of this fit into Stevenson's story. But that is the beauty of AP English: There are no required reading lists, no "must haves" that students need prior to the exam. The exam expects students to have gained a certain level of analytical and composition finesse; what students have read and studied to develop these skills is not really important. What is important is that an AP English student can respond successfully to a prompt, even after she has forgotten all of the things that she might have read while developing these skills. Most readers would be pleased to award a response such as this one with an 8 from the scoring guide for this particular question.

Question Three: Thatcher's Gender Politics

Analysis of Question Three

Margaret Thatcher's quotation presents an outstanding writing opportunity for AP English students. Whether they defend, challenge, or qualify her statement, most will have something to say. Hopefully, students will avoid responding with trite examples, such as stating that women do the work while men watch TV, or complaining about boyfriends or girlfriends.

Thatcher's comment lends itself to a multitude of approaches. Students can look to literature (Lady Macbeth, Medea, Nora), historical figures (Joan of Arc, Elizabeth I, Hillary Rodham Clinton), or their own experiences and observations for support to develop their essays. A plethora of examples are there for student choosing.

Students often wonder if it is better to defend, challenge, or qualify in such a situation. Which approach will bring them the better score? The answer is that it does not matter. The important thing for students to remember is that they need to develop their focus thoroughly, using appropriate examples where necessary. If in doubt, or seriously pressed for time, a defense or challenge may be a more direct and speedy approach than a qualification. If a student chooses to qualify, he or she is still required to remain focused and develop points thoroughly and concisely, so as not to appear to be hemming and hawing without purpose or direction.

Scoring Guide for Question Three

9 Points: Essays earning a score of 9 meet all the criteria for papers that earn 8 points and, in addition, are particularly persuasive or carefully reasoned, or demonstrate impressive stylistic and argumentative composition skills.

8 Points: Essays that earn a score of 8 persuasively defend, challenge, or qualify Thatcher's

KAPLAN

assertion about the tendency for men to be talkers and women to be doers. They present cohesive and carefully reasoned arguments using appropriate evidence from their reading, knowledge, or observations. The prose of these essays demonstrates the students' ability to control a wide range of the elements of effective writing, but they are not flawless.

7 Points: Essays earning a score of 7 fit the descriptions of essays that receive 6 points but are distinguished by a fuller or more purposeful argument, or stronger prose style.

6 Points: Essays earning a score of 6 adequately defend, challenge, or qualify Thatcher's assertions about men as talkers and women as doers by presenting arguments that are generally sound and that use appropriate evidence from students' reading, experience, or observations. A few lapses in diction or syntax may be present, but for the most part the purpose of these essays conveys the writers' ideas clearly.

5 Points: Essays earning a score of 5 understand the task and make assertions that defend, challenge, or qualify Thatcher's ideas. Their arguments are generally clear, but they may use superficial or limited evidence, or exhibit uneven or inconsistent development. Some lapses in diction or syntax may be evident, but for the most part the prose of these essays conveys the writers' ideas clearly.

4 Points: These essays inadequately respond to the tasks of the prompt. They may misunderstand, misrepresent, or oversimplify Thatcher's argument, or use evidence inappropriate or insufficient to make their own case. The prose of these essays usually conveys the writers' ideas, but may suggest inconsistent control over such elements of writing as organization, diction, and syntax.

3 Points: Essays receiving 3 points are described by the criteria for the score of 4, but are less persuasive in their attempts to state and defend a position, or are less consistent in their ability to control the elements of writing.

2 Points: Essays that earn a score of 2 demonstrate little or no success in defending, challenging, or qualifying Thatcher's views about men and women and their tendency to speak or to take action. They may seriously misread Thatcher or substitute a simpler task, such as merely summarizing Thatcher's position or writing responses only remotely related to the question. The prose of these essays often reveals consistent weaknesses in their control of elements of writing, such as organization, grammar, or diction.

1 Point: Essays earning a score of 1 are less qualified than those fulfilling the criteria for a score of 2, but are particularly simplistic in their response to Thatcher or particularly weak in their control of language.

Sample Student Response to Question Three

I think that Margaret Thatcher, former Prime Minister of England, must have had Queen Elizabeth I in mind when she said, "In politics, if you want anything said, ask a man; if you want anything done, ask a woman." Never has a woman in politics been more of a mover and shaker than Elizabeth I of England.

Elizabeth was the daughter of Henry VIII and Anne Boleyn, the second of Henry's wives. She grew up in a turbulent time, and she quickly learned that if she didn't fend for herself, no one else could be trusted to fend for her.

Elizabeth found herself queen after some hassle over Henry's succession. His first wife had no children, and his one son died before he could be king. There was a cousin of this young man who was queen, or something, but she soon found herself without a head. Nevertheless, Elizabeth found herself in charge of a very powerful country at a time when everyone (male) was interested in the power she held. She was determined, however, to wield that power alone. She was a mover and shaker, and not a woman easily cowed by any man who tried to talk her out of her rightful position.

Elizabeth was called the "Virgin Queen." Although there is some question as to the validity of that statement, she did maintain the single state her entire life. In fact, I understand it is just that—her being single—that enabled her to manipulate so many other powerful European men. I do know, for instance, that someone in Spain was really interested in marrying her. He promised her the moon and the stars, but all she did is suggest that he <u>might</u> have a chance at her. It is this type of manipulation that kept men like this prince (king?) of Spain dangling and eating out of her hand like he did.

Another of result of her "action attitude" came later, again having to do with Spain. Sir Francis Drake, really no more than a pirate, was putty in her hand and went off without a thought to the near impossibility of his task and proceeded to defeat Spain in 1588. Actually, historians tell us that he was full of bluster, and if it had not been his good fortune to attack Spain during a bad storm which worked in his favor and against Spain's, I would probably be writing this in Espanola right now instead of English.

I am sure that there are many men whose actions have truly changed the course of history. Also, I imagine many women have played lip service to things they never followed through on. Nevertheless, Elizabeth I of England, daughter of Henry VIII (talk about bluster!) and Anne Boleyn, is a good example of just who Margaret Thatcher may have had in mind when she made the statement found in this AP prompt.

Commentary on Sample Student Response to Question Three

Perhaps this student has read a lot of historical fiction about the Tudors. Maybe he did a research paper on Elizabeth I, or his teacher had a passion for the Tudor era. Whatever the case, this student has used his knowledge in defense of the provocative quotation from former Prime Minister Margaret Thatcher.

At first glance, one might think that the background information on Elizabeth is irrelevant to the tasks of the prompt. But it does offer a reason why Elizabeth was the type of person and leader she was. She had learned through some very traumatic experiences that most men (or women for that matter) were not to be trusted. Words were only that—words. If she wanted to survive she must rely only upon herself to act on her own behalf.

This argument is enhanced by two specific examples from Elizabeth's life that exemplify the validity of Thatcher's quotation. Granted, the specifics of the Spanish monarch's designs on Elizabeth are vague, but they are, surprising, generally accurate. In addition, the mention of Drake's final defeat of Spain at a later date creates a nice balance to the first example.

True, the final paragraph lacks the polish and style that readers look for in the very top-scoring responses, though it does bring closure to this essay response. Most would agree that this response to the Thatcher prompt is certainly more than adequate but less than wildly successful. Few would argue with giving this essay a deserved 7 points according to the scoring rubric.

The First Step to a Higher Score on Your Next AP* Exam!

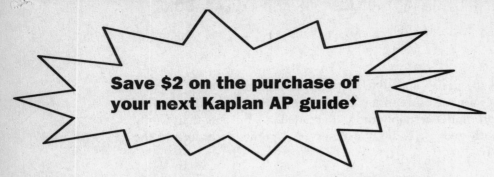

Save $2 on the purchase of your next Kaplan AP guide◆

When you purchase one of the following titles:

Kaplan AP Biology
Kaplan AP Calculus AB: An Apex Learning Guide
Kaplan AP Chemistry: An Apex Learning Guide
Kaplan AP English Literature and Composition
Kaplan AP Macroeconomics/Microeconomics
Kaplan AP Physics: An Apex Learning Guide
Kaplan AP Statistics: An Apex Learning Guide
Kaplan AP U.S. Government & Politics: An Apex Learning Guide
Kaplan AP U.S. History: An Apex Learning Guide

Publisher's Mail-In Rebate

Simply complete the **publisher mail-in coupon below**, attach it to the **receipt from your new Kaplan AP guide** (please see eligible titles above) as proof of purchase, mail it to Simon & Schuster Customer Service, and we'll send you $2.

Note: The rebate offer is not valid for this book you have already purchased; it applies to the purchase of a *second* Kaplan AP guide.

- -

Please Send Me My $2 Kaplan AP Publisher's Rebate!

I am enclosing:

1. this completed mail-in publisher's coupon from my *Kaplan AP* English Language & Composition* book.
2. the sales receipt of my **new** Kaplan AP guide as proof of purchase

Name (to whom check should be made payable): _____

Address: _____

City/State/Zip: _____

Telephone: _____   Email address: _____

Mail this coupon to:
Simon & Schuster Customer Service
100 Front Street
Riverside, NJ 08075–1197

Offer valid from September 1, 2002 through February 28, 2005. Mail your claim within thirty days of purchase. No reproductions of cash register receipt or mail-in certificate accepted. Offer good in U.S. except where prohibited, taxed, or restricted by law. Not valid with any other offer. Limit one per household. Requests from groups, post office boxes, or organizations will not be honored. Manufacturer reserves the right to reject incomplete submissions or submissions otherwise in violation of these terms without notification. Manufacturer not responsible for late, lost, or misdirected mail. Please allow 6-8 weeks for delivery.

*AP is a registered trademark of the College Entrance Examination Board, which neither sponsors nor endorses this book or offer.